FANTASY AND MYTH
IN THE ANTHROPOCENE

FANTASY AND MYTH
IN THE ANTHROPOCENE

IMAGINING FUTURES AND DREAMING HOPE
IN LITERATURE AND MEDIA

Edited by Marek Oziewicz, Brian Attebery and Tereza Dědinová

BLOOMSBURY ACADEMIC
LONDON • NEW YORK • OXFORD • NEW DELHI • SYDNEY

BLOOMSBURY ACADEMIC
Bloomsbury Publishing Plc
50 Bedford Square, London, WC1B 3DP, UK
1385 Broadway, New York, NY 10018, USA
29 Earlsfort Terrace, Dublin 2, Ireland

BLOOMSBURY, BLOOMSBURY ACADEMIC and the Diana logo
are trademarks of Bloomsbury Publishing Plc

First published in Great Britain 2022

Cover design and illustration by Rebecca Heselton
Moon texture © Daniel Fung / Shutterstock

A catalogue record for this book is available from the British Library.

Library of Congress Cataloging-in-Publication Data
Names: Oziewicz, Marek, editor. | Attebery, Brian, 1951- editor. |Dědinová, Tereza, 1982- editor.
Title: Fantasy and myth in the Anthropocene : imagining futures and
dreaming hope in literature and media / edited by Marek Oziewicz,
Brian Attebery and Tereza Dedinová.
Description: London ; New York : Bloomsbury Academic, 2022. |
Includes bibliographical references and index.
Identifiers: LCCN 2021037301 (print) | LCCN 2021037302 (ebook) |
ISBN 9781350203341 (hardback) | ISBN 9781350204164 (paperback) |
ISBN 9781350203358 (ebook) | ISBN 9781350203365 (epub)
Subjects: LCSH: Fantasy fiction–History and criticism. | Future, The, in literature. |
Ecocriticism. | Myth in literature. | Human ecology in literature. |
Speculative fiction–History and criticism. |Young adult
literature–History and criticism.
Classification: LCC PN3435 .F4 2022 (print) | LCC PN3435 (ebook) | DDC 809.3/8766–dc23
LC record available at https://lccn.loc.gov/2021037301
LC ebook record available at https://lccn.loc.gov/2021037302

ISBN: HB: 978-1-3502-0334-1
        PB: 978-1-3502-0416-4
        ePDF: 978-1-3502-0335-8
        eBook: 978-1-3502-0336-5

Typeset by Integra Software Services Pvt. Ltd.
Printed and bound in India

To find out more about our authors and books visit www.bloomsbury.com
and sign up for our newsletters.

To our beautiful planet and human capacity for loving care—the power that can make all the difference.

CONTENTS

Contents

PLATES

FIGURES

ACKNOWLEDGMENTS

The editors gratefully acknowledge the Andrews Family and the support from the Grace I. Andrews Endowment for Children's Literature at the University of Minnesota that made it possible to include color inserts in this book.

PERMISSIONS

ACADEMIC CONTRIBUTORS

Prema Arasu is a PhD candidate in Creative Writing at the University of Western Australia. Their research interests include gender in alternate fantasy worlds, queer theory, and monstrous ontologies. They have published both academic and creative work across these fields.

Brian Attebery is Professor of English at Idaho State University and editor of the *Journal of the Fantastic in the Arts*. He has written or edited several books on fantasy and science fiction, including *Decoding Gender in Science Fiction* and *Stories about Stories: Fantasy and the Remaking of Myth*. In 2019 he was Leverhulme Visiting Professor of Fantasy at the University of Glasgow. Along with Dimitra Fimi and Matthew Sangster, he is one of the series editors for *Perspectives on Fantasy*, a new monograph series from Bloomsbury.

Aneesh Barai is University Teacher in Education, with a focus on Digital Literacies, at the University of Sheffield. His research focuses on cultural representations of diverse childhoods, in particular queer and racially diverse childhoods, and young people's political engagement. He has recently published on queer and postcolonial childhoods in 1930s children's literature, on queer and pacifist youths in the Japanese animated films of Studio Ghibli, as well as on ecological readings of *The Little Prince* and its film adaptations.

Jacob Burg is Lecturer in the College of Arts & Sciences Writing Program at Boston University. His research interests focus on American literature, genre studies, and composition theory. He has published on the role of race in weird Westerns (2020) and the need to reimagine writing pedagogy through an intersection of public humanities and community literacy practices (2020).

Lindsay Burton is a third-year doctoral student at the University of Cambridge in the Faculty of Education's Centre for Research in Children's Literature. Her research interests focus on the intersection of children's and young adult literature and media and deconstructionist, posthumanist, and new materialist theory, particularly theory that pertains to artificial intelligence and climate change. Her most recent publication considers Derridean deconstruction and age normativity in Carlo Collodi's *The Adventures of Pinocchio* (2019).

Tereza Dědinová is Assistant Professor at the Faculty of Arts of the Masaryk University in Brno, where she teaches theory and history of fantastic literature and Czech literature. She has written a monograph (2015) and edited three titles focusing on various aspects of fantastic literature. She has published articles devoted to the fantastic from the cognitive perspective, the representation of the actual world in fantasy, and the Czech fantastika. Her most recent project is a co-edited volume entitled *Images of the Anthropocene in Speculative Fiction: Narrating the Future* (in press).

Melanie Duckworth is Associate Professor of English Literature at Østfold University College, Norway, where she teaches British and Postcolonial Literature. Her research interests include children's literature, Australian literature, contemporary poetry, and ecocriticism, and she is currently co-editing a book entitled *Plants in Children's and Young Adult Literature*. She has published on Australian fiction and poetry, the Scottish eco-poet Kathleen Jamie, and historical fiction for children, most recently "Genre, History and the Stolen Generations: Three Australian Stories" (2020).

Christopher D. Foley is Assistant Professor of English in the School of Humanities at the University of Southern Mississippi. His research interests include the intersections of environmental and public health concerns in English Renaissance drama, the environmental imagination in contemporary children's literature and film, and the role of service-learning pedagogies in place-based environmental education. His recent publications include peer-reviewed essays in *Early Modern Literary Studies*, *Studies in Philology*, and the *Ben Jonson Journal*. His current book project is entitled *Environmental Theatre and Its Embodied Reception in Shakespeare's London*.

Dr. Kim Hendrickx is Research Associate of the Fund for Scientific Research (FNRS) at the University of Liège in Belgium, and visiting scholar to the Science & Justice Research Centre at the University of California, Santa Cruz. He is an anthropologist interested in relations between the life sciences, society and speculative thinking. Working across the social sciences, humanities and life sciences, he has published in journals of different fields, such as *Configurations, Frontiers in Genetics, Science as Culture, Health* and *Social Anthropology*.

Markus Laukkanen is Doctoral Researcher at Tampere University, Finland, in the Faculty of Social Sciences Doctoral Programme in Literary Studies. His research interests include genre theory, interactive online-based communities as readers, depictions of climate change in contemporary speculative fiction, and poetics of post-postmodernism. He is currently working on his thesis *Building Speculative Communities—Interactive Communication in Internet Age Fantasy Fiction*.

Caryn Lesuma is Assistant Professor at Brigham Young University–Hawai'i in the English program, where she also serves as the Composition Coordinator. Her research interests focus on young adult literature, literatures of the Pacific, and place-based pedagogy and rhetoric. She has published on contemporary adaptations of Pacific folklore and place-based composition pedagogy.

Marek Oziewicz is Professor of Literacy Education at the University of Minnesota, Twin Cities and holds the Sidney and Marguerite Henry Chair in Children's and Young Adult Literature at the College of Education and Human Development. He teaches courses on how literature empowers young people to develop a multicultural mindset, environmental awareness, and justice literacy. His *Justice in Young Adult Speculative Fiction* (2015) examines how non-factual narratives help young people develop an understanding of real-life justice issues in the modern world. Dr. Oziewicz's current research is on representations of climate change in children's literature and anticipatory imagination in speculative fiction.

Alexander Popov is Assistant Professor at Sofia University "St. Kliment Ohridski" in the Department of English and American Studies; he is also a researcher at the Bulgarian Academy of Sciences in the Department of Artificial Intelligence and Language Technology. His research interests range over utopian and science fiction studies, posthumanism, ecocriticism, artificial intelligence, and cognitive science. He has recently published journal articles on climate fiction, and on possible worlds semantics as applied to fictional narrative. He is currently working on an interdisciplinary research project focused on artificial intelligence in the context of the humanities and social sciences.

John Rieder is Professor Emeritus of English at the University of Hawai'i at Mānoa. He is the author of *Colonialism and the Emergence of Science Fiction* (2008) and *Science Fiction and the Mass Cultural Genre System* (2017).

Derek J. Thiess is Assistant Professor at the University of North Georgia in the Department of English. His current research focuses on mythic violence in folk tales and their fantastic retellings across media. He has published on history, religion, and embodiment in the fantastic genres. He is the author of *Embodying Gender and Age in Speculative Fiction* (2015) and *Sport and Monstrosity in Science Fiction* (2019).

Drew Thornton is a research pre-candidate in the school of Media, Creative Arts and Social Inquiry at Curtin University, Western Australia. His research explores storytelling and creative worlding practices in the fields of animalities and environmental humanities. His Masters project—a cooperative arcade game for humans and house flies—exhibited in 2019 at The Nostalgia Box, Perth.

Stephanie J. Weaver is Professor of Liberal-Arts English at the Savannah College of Art and Design. Her research interests focus on children's and young adult literature of the twentieth and twenty-first centuries, fantasy literature, and ecocriticism. She has published on the ecological consciousness of J. K. Rowling and J. R. R. Tolkien. She is currently authoring a book on the ecological consciousness of world-building in fantasy literature scheduled for release in 2021.

ARTISTS

Hatem Aly is an Egyptian-born Canadian illustrator whose work has been featured on television and in multiple publications worldwide. His work ranges from editorial illustration to children's books, storyboards, and comics. *The Inquisitor's Tale*, written by Adam Gidwitz and illustrated by Aly, was a 2017 Newbery Honor and winner of the Sydney Taylor Book Award.

Katherine Applegate is an American young adult and children's fiction writer, best known as the author of the *Animorphs, Remnants, Everworld,* and other book series. She won the 2013 Newbery Medal for her 2012 children's novel *The One and Only Ivan* (2012). Applegate's most popular books are science fiction, fantasy, and adventure novels. She won the Best New Children's Book Series Award in 1997 in *Publishers Weekly*.

David Bowles is a Mexican American author from south Texas, where he teaches at the University of Texas Río Grande Valley. He has written several novels, most notably *The Smoking Mirror* (2015) and *They Call Me Güero* (2018). His work has also been published in multiple anthologies, plus venues such as *Asymptote, Strange Horizons, Apex Magazine, Metamorphoses, Rattle, Translation Review,* and *The Journal of Children's Literature*.

Joseph Bruchac is a Nulhegan Abenaki writer of books relating to the Indigenous peoples of the Americas, with a focus on northeastern Native American and Anglo-American lives and folklore. He is best known for his work as a Native writer and storyteller, with more than 120 books and numerous awards to his credit. In 1999, he received the Lifetime Achievement Award from the Native Writers' Circle of the Americas.

Molly B. Burnham is an American author of children's books, best known for her *Teddy Mars* (2015–17) chapter books series. She earned an MFA in children's writing from Hamline University.

Pavel Čech is a Czech painter, comic book author, and illustrator. He is an author of fairy tale picturebooks and short stories, which he illustrates himself. As a comic book author, he has been collaborating with *Aargh* magazine since 2002. He has published over thirty books featuring visual stories told through his innovative illustrations.

Grace L. Dillon is Anishinaabe Professor in the Indigenous Nations Studies Program at Portland State University in Portland, Oregon, where she teaches undergraduate and graduate courses on a range of interests including Native American and Indigenous studies, science fiction, Indigenous cinema, popular culture, race, and social justice. She is the editor of *Walking the Clouds: An Anthology of Indigenous Science Fiction* (2012) and *Hive of Dreams: Contemporary Science Fiction from the Pacific Northwest* (2003). She is well known for coining the term "Indigenous Futurism," which is a movement consisting of art, literature, and other forms of media which express Indigenous perspectives of the past, present, and future in the context of science fiction and related sub-genres.

Adam Gidwitz is an American author of the best-selling children's books *A Tale Dark and Grimm* (2010), *In a Glass Grimmly* (2012), and *The Grimm Conclusion* (2013) he received a 2017 Newbery Honor for *The Inquisitor's Tale: Or, The Three Magical Children and Their Holy Dog* (2016).

Barbara Henderson is the author of Scottish historical fiction and ecofiction for children. Her novels *Fir for Luck* (Highland Clearances, 2016), *Punch* (Victorian Scotland, 2017), and *Wilderness Wars* (eco-thriller, 2018) are already widely used in Scottish schools, and a smuggling novella featuring a real-life incident in the life of Robert Burns was published in October 2019.

Elin Kelsey is an educator, researcher, thesis supervisor, and award-winning author. Over the past decade, she has been a spokesperson for hope, resilience, and the environment. Kelsey conducts research into emotional responses to the culture of "doom and gloom" that permeates environmental issues. Her picturebook, *You Are Stardust* (2011), was lauded by the influential blog *Brain Pickings,* and won the 2013 Canadian Library Association and 2012 YABC Choice Awards. Her most recent book is *Hope Matters: Why Changing the Way We Think Is Critical to Solving the Environmental Crisis (2020).*

Donna Jo Napoli is an American writer of children's and young adult fiction, as well as a prominent linguist. Currently, she is Professor of Linguistics and Social Justice at Swarthmore College. Many of her children's books are retellings of fairy tales. She has won numerous awards for her work, including the Golden Kite Award, the Sydney Taylor Award, and the Parents' Choice Gold Award.

Craig Russell is a Canadian science fiction and fantasy author. In 2011, his young adult novel, *Black Bottle Man* (2010) won the Moonbeam Gold Medal for YA fantasy and was a finalist for the Prix Aurora Award for Best English SF/F Novel. His 2016 climate-crisis novel, *Fragment* is on the Yale University Climate Connections climate-fiction reading list.

Kate Samworth is an American artist, author, and illustrator whose *book Aviary Wonders Inc.: Spring Catalog and Instruction Manual* won the Kirkus Prize for Young Readers in 2014. Her illustrations frequently involve the natural world and human interaction with it. She gathers ideas from around the world and has found unusual ways to travel: touring Europe with her band in the 1980s, translating for a hiking guide in Brazil, and volunteering on organic farms in Spain and Turkey. She is currently working on a new series about a revolution led by bears.

Jon Scieszka is an American children's writer, best known for picturebooks created with the illustrator Lane Smith. He is also a nationally recognized reading advocate, and the founder of Guys Read—a web-based literacy program for boys. Jon was the first US National Ambassador for Young People's Literature, appointed by the Librarian of Congress for calendar years 2008 and 2009.

Nisi Shawl is an African American writer, editor, and journalist best known as an author of science fiction and fantasy short stories. She writes about how fantastic fiction reflects real-world diversity of gender, sexual orientation, race, colonialism, physical ability, age, and other sociocultural factors. She is the co-author of *Writing the Other: Bridging Cultural Differences for Successful Fiction* (2005), a creative-writing handbook derived from the authors' workshop of the same name, in which participants explore techniques to help them write credible characters outside their own cultural experience.

Eliot Schrefer is an American author of adult and young adult fiction, and a two-time finalist for the National Book Award in Young People's Literature. He is most known for his young adult novels *Endangered* (2012) and *Threatened* (2014), which are survival stories featuring young people and great apes. He is currently on the faculty of the Creative Writing MFA Program at Fairleigh Dickinson University.

Shaun Tan is an Australian artist, writer, and film maker. He won an Academy Award for *The Lost Thing*, a 2011 animated film adaptation of a 2000 picturebooks he wrote and illustrated. Other books he has written and illustrated include *The Red Tree* (2001) and *The Arrival* (2006). He received the prestigious Astrid Lindgren Memorial Award in 2011, honoring his contribution to international children's literature.

Jane Yolen is an American writer of fantasy, science fiction, and children's books. She is the author or editor of more than 350 books, of which the best known is *The Devil's Arithmetic* (1988), a Holocaust novella. Her other works include *Owl Moon* (1987), *The Emperor and the Kite* (1967), the Commander Toad series, and *How Do Dinosaurs Say Goodnight* (2000).

Steven Weinberg is an American author and illustrator of *Fred and the Lumberjack* (2017), *You Must Be This Tall* (2016), *Rex Finds an Egg! Egg! Egg!* (2015), and the illustrator of *Beard Boy* (2016).

David Wiesner is an American illustrator and author of children's books, known best for picturebooks including some that tell stories without words. As an illustrator he has won three Caldecott Medals recognizing the year's "most distinguished American picture book for children." In 2008 David was one of five finalists in the biennial, international Hans Christian Andersen Award, the highest recognition available for creators of children's books.

INTRODUCTION: THE CHOICE WE HAVE IN THE STORIES WE TELL …

Marek Oziewicz

The greatest challenge facing humanity in the twenty-first century is how to transition to an ecological civilization. For centuries we*—a white, Western, self-entitled "we" posing as "humanity"—have taken Earth to be, literally, "dirt cheap": a playground for endless human expansion. Now it appears that there is a hefty price tag. In less than a century we created a carbon-intense global civilization whose operations are tearing apart the planet's web of life. We became the primary driver behind the largest and accelerating mass extinction of animals and plants since the Cretaceous–Paleogene extinction event sixty-five million years ago (UN IBPES 2019, n.p.). And we heated up the world to a level unseen since the Miocene, sixteen million years ago (CO_2 Earth 2020; Jones 2017). We did all that with little understanding of the planet as a life-supporting system and little sense of our collective impact on that system. But no more. Scientific evidence accumulated over the past three decades is incontrovertible. We know more than enough to take action. We know what action needs to be taken. We even know how. The contrast between how much we know and how little we have acted on this knowledge may be the greatest puzzle of our time. Or the most obvious elephant in the room. Since all neoliberal trade agreements to date have failed to limit greenhouse gas emissions (Temple 2018; Tortell 2020), there is a growing sense that the market system is incapable of solving the problems of climate change on its own (Klein 2014, 2019; Kolbert 2015; Moore 2015; Scranton 2015). The many visions of dystopian futures that have emerged in literature and film since the 1990s are extrapolations from this realization. But the impotence of our political and economic institutions has also generated a growing grassroots resistance. Citizen organizations such as Extinction Rebellion, teenage activists such as Xiuhtezcatl Martinez and Greta Thunberg, educators, authors, scientists, parents, and millions of us—ordinary placental mammals—are finding creative ways to stand up for the planet. If there was ever "our" fight, this is it.

This collection is part of the resistance to what Amitav Ghosh has dubbed "the Great Derangement." It builds on the emerging knowledge that the urgencies of the Anthropocene—pollution, global warming, biodiversity loss, climate change, and expansion of human populations paralleled by rising racism, exclusion, violence, and xenophobia—are primarily challenges to our story systems. The stories we have been telling ourselves about human exceptionalism (we're the image of God), human entitlement (we're masters of this planet), and human identity (we're separate from and above "nature") channeled our creativity into projects that transformed the planet—in our eyes—into a purely human domain. This is how we arrived at the Anthropocene. The thing is, these stories are not true. They legitimized but did not prepare us for the reality of a world ruled by a single species.

The shock of recognition is our present moment. It is being met with denial or resignation, fury, or triumph. It has narrative analogues too. One of the most eerily prescient is Karel

Čapek's *The War with the Newts* (1936). In this science fantasy, the Czech author imagined what might happen if humanity discovered a source of cheap energy to fuel eternal progress. That energy is water-dwelling salamanders called the newts. Decades pass before it occurs to anyone that the slave-laboring newts are cheap only because the real price of their service is kicked into the future. As the world's industrial production soars, humanity glows with pride:

> Never in the history of mankind had so much been manufactured, constructed and earned as in this great age. With the newts came enormous progress and the ideal known as Quantity. The phrase, "We, people of the Newt Age," became widely used, and used with justified pride; ... The self-aware people of the Newt Age declared that the whole future of the world would consist in constantly rising production and consumption. ... Only now could man's ingenuity work at full effectiveness, because it was working on a huge scale with extremely high manufacturing capacity and a record financial turnover; in short this was a great age ... the Utopia we all longed for, where all these technical triumphs and magnificent possibilities would be harvested, where human happiness would combine with newts' industry to open new horizons further and further to beyond what anyone could imagine.
>
> (Čapek 1936, 144–5)

This "great age" of humanity devolves into a terrible shock. Despite international agreements on how to manage the newt workforce, the newts have their own agenda. When their population reaches twenty billion, the newts begin demolishing continents to create more bays in which they can live. And since the entire economy is dependent on newt production, humanity is forced to work for the newts. "You will be free to migrate inland," the Chief Salamander announces, "[but] you will collaborate with us in the demolition of your world" (231). The novel ends with the collapse of civilization as we know it. Small human bands survive in isolation and slavery to the newts in high-elevation remnants of former continents. Such is the victory achieved through one species' dominance.

The Anthropocene is our own Newt Age. Like newt-dependent humanity in Čapek's novel, we are waking up to the nightmare of our utter dependency on a particularly destructive form of energy. We assumed a world of endless abundance promised by fossil fuels. We created a culture of progress-as-consumption predicated on infinite growth on a finite planet. And we are beginning to realize that our industrial, market-driven civilization is utterly unsustainable. What should we do now? How do we transition to a culture of stewardship without losing everything we've worked for? Or losing just what *must* be lost? These questions will not go away. We live in a world made by fossil fuels. Our individual lifestyles, habits, professions, and identities are all shaped by the affordances of fossil fuels. On the collective level too, our societies' cultural values, economic practices, and art forms are imbricated with energy systems and modes of production based on fossil fuels. But even as our ordinary lives are destroying the biosphere, we intuit that there has to be another way. That we have been trapped by our success.

It is telling that we should name the trap and the success by the same term: the Anthropocene. That we need a new name, a new conceptual tool for grappling with the many unprecedented challenges of our times is clear. Just what that term should be is less so. The mainstream case for the Anthropocene is a seemingly neutral acknowledgment of humanity's global impact on the planet. According to the Anthropocene Working Group of the Subcommission on Quaternary Stratigraphy, phenomena associated with "marked and abrupt anthropogenic perturbations" (2009, n.p.)—another euphemism for human-caused devastation of the biosphere—have already been recorded in Earth's stratigraphic layers and will be readable to geologists millions of years into the future. While this might be true, the critics respond, to conceptualize humanity as a geological force is far from neutral. Masked as a statement of a geological fact is a delusion of grandeur, a belief that Earth is destined to be controlled by humanity and that there is no other way of our being with the planet. It is in this sense of a mistaken worldview, as Eileen Crist has shown, that the Anthropocene has come to function as a discourse. Rather than helping us tackle anthropogenic destruction, this discourse organizes our perceptions around assumptions that naturalize "the anthropocentric actionable worldview that generated 'the Anthropocene'—with all its looming emergencies—in the first place" (2016, 14). A number of alternative terms have thus been proposed: the Capitalocene (Jason Moore), the Ecozoic (Brian Berry), the Great Derangement (Amitav Ghosh), the Symbiocene (Glenn Albrecht), the Chthulocene (Donna Haraway), the Necrocene (Justin McBrien), the Age of Asymmetry (Timothy Morton), etc. What links them all is a recognition of language as a crucial site of intervention against anthropocentric myopia that drives the annihilation of life on Earth.

Finding the right label is no trifling matter. The terms we use represent or disguise our ideologies, spotlighting or sidelining their implications. To call trees timber, coasts beachfronts, and animals livestock are discursive operations that give narrative shape to our assumptions, structure relations, and legitimize action. Terms that become conceptual signposts for large human collectives accrue existential consequences. Consider this. In 1926 a disgruntled German veteran-turned-ideologue wrote a book called *Mein Kampf*. One of the key ideas of this conspiracy theory classic was the concept of *Lebensraum* or living space. Alongside a handful of other terms such as *race*, *Lebensraum* was framed as a biological-evolutionary given, necessary for the survival of the German people. Following the rise of Hitler to Chancellor, *Lebensraum* became the cornerstone of Nazi foreign policy and unleashed a war that cost 75 million human lives. One concern of those who oppose the term "Anthropocene" is that—as *Lebensraum* did for Nazi expansionism at the cost of "inferior races"—it appears to normalize human expansionism by making the biosphere expendable. This is a valid objection. Still, while nothing can be said in defense of *Mein Kampf*, the Anthropocene remains useful as shorthand for an ideological position. This is why it is used even by those who criticize it (Moore 2015; Trexler 2015; Alaimo 2016; Panagiotarakou 2020).

In this book we invoke the Anthropocene at once as a synecdoche of human supremacist worldview and as a humbling recognition that the planet has been irrevocably altered by human activities. One such crossover point occurred in 2020: for the first time in history the total weight of human-made stuff surpassed the weight of global living biomass, including human, animal, and plant bodies (Elhacham et al. 2020). We now live in a world where "on average, for each person on the globe, anthropogenic mass equal to more than his or her bodyweight is produced every week" (442), a world in which the total weight of plastic is twice that of all animals (444). Of course, not all humans have contributed to the Anthropocenic acceleration in the same way. At least since Rob Nixon's *Slow Violence and the Environmentalism of the Poor* (2011), the question of who really is responsible for "our" collective destruction of the biosphere has remained central to Anthropocene scholarship. By 2020 the consensus has moved beyond generalizations about the blame of the Global North vs the pain of the Global

South to identifying the main culprit as socioeconomic inequality (Piketty 2020). Studies show that anthropogenic climate change is largely driven by overconsumption of a wealthy minority, 1–5 percent of the global population (Picketty 2014; Joseph 2017; Lent 2017; Beuret 2019; Shiva 2020; Gore 2020). According to the UN *Emissions Gap Report 2020*, for example, the global rich must rapidly reduce their carbon footprint by 97 percent (United Nations Environmental Programme 2020; Ivanova 2020)—a feat that is hard to imagine in the current economic system designed to extract, monetize, and accumulate all resources in the hands of the few. When Native American scholar Robin Wall Kimmerer talks about global capitalism as a "Windigo" or demonic economy—a system which "artificially creates scarcity" and results in "famine for some and diseases of excess for others" (376)—she offers a Native perspective on the core operational principle of Western capitalism. Jason Moore dubs it "Cheap Nature" and defines as an accelerating appropriation of land and labor (2016, 114). Indeed, the postcolonial distribution of power in our world remains "one of the greatest obstacles to mitigatory action [on climate change], and all the more so because it remains largely unacknowledged" (Ghosh 2016, 146). These perceptions have been painfully confirmed by the events of 2020–21. The Covid-19 pandemic, "a dress rehearsal for climate change" (Spratt and Armistead 2020, 16), as well as social unrest following the murder of George Floyd in Minneapolis made it clear that overcoming the climate emergency will require dismantling the interlocking systems of racial, postcolonial, and anthropocentric exploitation on which global business-as-usual is based (Frankel 2020; Shiva 2020). The achievement of climate justice is inextricably linked to the goals of environmental, racial, and social justice movements (Holthaus 2020).

It is not our objective in this book to offer a comprehensive summary of what may be called the Anthropocene literary studies. Or engage with a massive body of scholarship in environmental humanities, posthumanism, and ecocriticism that takes up questions of meaning-making through stories. A number of existing studies have already covered this ground well enough (Nixon 2011; Cohen and Duckert 2015; Trexler 2015; Alaimo 2016; Emmett and Nye 2017; Menely and Taylor 2017; Weinstein and Colebrook 2017; Szeman and Boyer 2017; Quigley and Slovic 2018; Tarr and White 2018; Clark 2019). There is a gap though. None of the major works to date have considered fantasy and myth as productive spaces for anticipatory imagination to engage with the questions of the Anthropocene. In his 2015 *Anthropocene Fictions*, Adam Trexler rightly argues that climate fiction explodes generic conventions, yet the works he examines are limited to "literary" fiction and science fiction (7). Adeline Johns-Putra's *Climate Change and the Contemporary Novel* (2019) builds on a similar taxonomy, distinguishing between two strands of the climate change novel: one "indebted to the generic conventions of science fiction" (37), the other, "increasingly more prevalent," being the realist narrative set in a recognizable present (38). One of the most recent studies, Andrew Milner and J. R. Burgmann's *Science Fiction and Climate Change: A Sociological Approach* (2020), explicitly discounts fantasy as being "of little use in responding to real-world climate changes" (48). Of course, not all ecocritics have failed to appreciate the affordances of fantasy. For example, in a larger meditation *The Value of Ecocriticism* (2019), Timothy Clark notes that the Anthropocene's deeply counterintuitive action at a distance, coupled with its bizarre breakdown of distinctions between near and far, trivial and dangerous, perceived and unseen, "may find its analogue in modes of the fantastic" or even require "a turn away from realism" (2019, 99). Such exceptions notwithstanding, inattention to fantasy and myth has been remarkable. With this book we take the first step to fill this gap.

The other feature that sets this book apart is the focus on anticipatory imagination of sustainable futures rather than on critique of the ecocidal status quo. Most accounts of the Anthropocene start with the latter, listing the current damage and demonstrating connections between the operations of Capital and the ongoing ecocide. The problem with structuring a call to action this way is that the dominant "facts & rage" formula is antithetical to creating thought-spaces necessary for a radical transformation of how we imagine ourselves in relation to the biosphere. This has been the unintended failure of dystopias. Although meant as warnings, they have helped reinforce the belief in ecocide as unavoidable. When articulated in stories—recall the vision of future Earth in *Wall-E*—the ecocidal script of dystopias operates as a self-reinforcing prophecy. Even worse, given how modern capitalism reproduces itself through "feed[ing] on and learn[ing] from resistance and critique" (Haiven 2014, 9), an argument can be made that dystopia has been conscripted as a commodity to reproduce the system it supposedly challenges. If so, dystopia represents a de facto capitulation to the rhetoric of global capitalism which sees no alternative to the current carbon economy and no alternative to its peculiar idea of growth based on accelerating monetization, subjugation, and exploitation of the biosphere. For example, a recent empirical study shows that over 80 percent of cli-fi narratives employ the "disaster frame" (Schneider-Mayerson 2018, 490); instead of mobilizing action, this frame elicits despair, helplessness, and anger that lead to "ignoring or avoiding the topic" (490). Environmental themes in many books for young audiences have likewise been well-meant but misleading. As demonstrated by Clare Echterling, a surprising number of children's picturebooks misrepresent environmental action as a personal choice rather than a systemic issue. They also frame environmental emergency "as having clear temporal boundaries and straightforward solutions" (2016, 18).

Too long have we focused on projections of the futures we dread instead of the futures we want. We can do better. And we must. A growing body of scholarship and fiction suggests that we need to jump-start our imaginations to envision an ecological civilization. The challenge we face, hope scholar Elin Kelsey insists, is to replace the dominant narrative of gloom and doom with "an evidence-based argument for hope that improves our capacity to engage with the real and overwhelming issues we face" (2020, 11). In the words of Donna Haraway, "These are the times we must think. These are the times of urgencies that need stories" (2016, 40). This powerful notion informs a spate of recent works focused on the transformative power of words: Glenn A. Albrecht's *Earth Emotions: New Word for a New World* (2019), Matthew Schneider-Mayerson and Brent Ryan Bellamy's *An Ecotopian Lexicon* (2019), and Ayana Elizabeth Johnson and Katharine K. Wilkinson's *All We Can Save: Truth, Courage, and Solutions for the Climate Crisis* (2020). At present, we find ourselves at an impossible place where, as Shaun Tan pictures it in one of his tales, we put baby orca in the sky and "we don't know how to get it down" (Tan 2018, 157). Yet that is exactly—and metaphorically—what we must do. The first step is to reimagine ourselves and our place on a multispecies, biodiverse planet. The space for that reimagining is story. But not just any story. As Ursula K. Le Guin commented in her 2014 National Book Awards Acceptance Speech: "I think hard times are coming when we will be wanting the voices of writers who can see alternatives to how we live now, and can see through our fear-stricken society and its obsessive technologies to other ways of being, and *even imagine some real grounds for hope*" (n.p., italics added). Indeed: if "the environmental crisis is also a crisis of hope," any productive response to the Anthropocene requires that we "actively choose hope" (Kelsey 2020, 7). These are the stories we need.

Fantasy and myth are among the key spaces where the work of collective dreaming unfolds. It is in these intersubjective spaces that we generate patterns of possibilities to "stay with the trouble" of our time (Haraway 2016, 34). Following Brian Attebery's definition, in this collection we take *myth* to denote "any collective story that encapsulates a world view and authorizes belief" (2014, 2). This lens enables a reflection on older historical formations like Christian or Native American myths, but also helps expose the mythological core of such ideological formations as the Anthropocene, Capitalism, Human Speciesism, or White Supremacy. Equally important, we acknowledge the activity of mythtelling as humanity's primary form of dialogue with nature. As Sean Kane has shown, over millennia human cultures developed their mythtelling traditions based on different kinds of earth-relatedness. Nomadic (Paleolithic) peoples told different stories than settled (Mesolithic) hunter-gatherers; hunter-gatherers, in turn, developed different stories and beliefs than settled (Neolithic) agriculturalists. What linked these traditions was the perception of myth as "the ideas and emotions of the Earth ... expressed through stories" (1995, 15). These stories were articulated as "an affectionate counterpoint to the earth's voices, with no ambition to direct them or force them to give up their meanings" (14).

Our industrial, increasingly urban civilization developed a contrarian body of stories. It denied the earth's voices and asserted a proprietary relationship to the environment. These were the myths of the conquest of Nature by Culture. Having evolved in competition rather than sympathy with nature, these stories enabled colonialism, imperialism, racism, objectification, commodification, and other facets of the exploitative mindset that has brought us to the present moment. Ecocidal myths projected humanity as separate and superior to the rest of the biosphere, a detached bystander like the protagonist in Caspar David Friedrich's painting *Wanderer above the Sea of Fog* (1818). Climate change, biodiversity loss, and other urgencies of the Anthropocene are forcing us to reflect on our biospheric situatedness yet again. A more apt selfie, we are beginning to grasp, is one suggested by Timothy Morton: Wile E. Coyote in midair, realizing he is about to fall and there is nothing to stop it (2013, 160).

Fortunately, the ecocidal mythologies of techno-modernity are not the only tools in our think-box. Nor have they gone unchallenged. A strong revivalist mythtelling tradition geared to rediscover practices of living with the earth on the earth's terms is on the rise. In all its forms, it is heavily indebted to Native futurisms, solarpunk, and Indigenous mythtelling traditions that survived the settler-colonial onslaught. These traditions model what Native American scholar Grace Dillon dubs *biskaabiiyang*: an Anishinaabemowin word for "the process of returning to ourselves," which involves knowledges helpful to adapt to life on a damaged planet (2012, 10). Contemporary revivalist mythtelling is not merely a return to old mythtelling ways, to formations that dialogued with nature *before* the Anthropocene damage occurred. Rather, it is a search for new myths that decenter and contain the human *going forward*, as we begin to imagine a sustainable future on a damaged planet. We need new myths to replace Capitalocene's monologue about eternal progress with a dialogue that affirms cultural and biological diversity. Indigenous mythtelling traditions are central to this enterprise for these stories have a proven record of success in multispecies relations. It is no coincidence that Native peoples, a mere 4 percent of the world population, protect 80 percent of the world's biodiversity (LaDuke 2019).

The primary forge for articulating new myths aligned with planetary well-being has been fantasy and other genres of speculative fiction. Defining fantasy has been notoriously problematic. A robust tradition of critical reflection testifies to how each definition opens up different insights on an extremely diversified field of ever-new fantasy narratives (Attebery

1992; Mathews 2002; Mendlesohn 2008; Oziewicz 2008; Thomas 2019). In this book, we take *fantasy* to be a type of story that presents the magical, the supernatural, and the wondrous as a fact in the world of the narrative—whether or not it makes any ontological claims about the world of the reader's direct experience (Oziewicz 2008). In a broader sense—what John Clute dubs "fantastika"—fantasy also refers to stories through which we tell ourselves what is possible or impossible. This broader umbrella encompasses the fantasies of techno-modernity as well as narratives that imagine alternatives to these, such as Kim Stanley Robinson's *New York 2140* (2017): a work of cli-fi that explores the fantasy of a political revolution against an ecocidal system. A particle accelerator for ideas of radical change, including our relationship to the biosphere, fantasy and its transformative potential have received some critical attention— notably in Don D. Elgin's *The Comedy of the Fantastic* (1985), Marek Oziewicz's *One Earth, One People* (2008), and Brian Attebery's *Stories about Stories* (2014). Increasingly, fantasy has been used as a vehicle for "birthing visionary stories" in confrontation with the Anthropocene (Imarisha 2015, 3). Ambelin Kwaymullina's *The Interrogation of Ashala Wolf* (2012) imagines a dis-anthropocentric world of the future; Jewel Parker Rhodes's *Bayou Magic* (2016) enlists mermaids and magic of the sea to contain an oil spill; A. S. King's *Me and Marvin Gardens* (2017) introduces a plastic-eating creature that mobilizes a local community to stand up for the planet; Adam Gidwitz's the Unicorn Rescue Society series (2018–ongoing) stokes young children's fascination with the wonder of the nonhuman world, transforming it into lifelong activist commitments; Eliot Schrefer's *The Lost Rainforest: Mez's Magic* (2018) affirms the agency of nonhuman characters fighting to save their endangered homes; Shaun Tan's *Tales from the Inner City* (2018) explodes our arrogance about this world as merely a human domain; Katherine Applegate's *Endling, the Last* (2019) confronts the reality of species extinction. In these and many other narratives, fantasy "performs" myth when it helps us articulate dreams of alternative ways of being with the biosphere—dreams that may be unspeakable in "real" life or in other genres. According to Attebery, fantasy's main claim to cultural importance resides in "[its] capacity for mythopoiesis: the making of narratives that reshape the world" (2014, 4). We have never needed such narratives more than we do today.

In this book we have asked contributors to reflect on the new challenges and opportunities for fantasy and myth that arose out of debates over climate change, pollution, vanishing habitats, extinctions, mass pauperization, migrations, and other urgencies of the Anthropocene. Fantasy and myth have been used to explore the notions of heroism, identity, and power; to raise questions about the meaning of life; to express social criticism and speculate about the unseen. What do these questions mean at a time when human activity has altered the planet in game-changing ways? How can fantasy and myth challenge dystopian acquiescence of planetary death and mobilize resistance against petrochemical Ragnarok? How can they serve as vehicles for anticipatory imagination that articulates alternatives to the Capitalocene? How can they point a way to restoring the connection with the natural rather than the supernatural? Ultimately, how can fantasy and myth help us reimagine ourselves as a biocentric, ecological civilization?

The chapters are organized in four parts. "Trouble in the Air" offers a broad reflection on the modal and structural affordances of fantasy and myth in the Anthropocene. "Dreaming the Earth" zooms in on the biocentric turn in selected works of the fantasy canon. "Visions in the Water" examines retellings of myths that frame our relationship with the world's oceans. "Playing with Fire" brings together fantasy and myth that revision nonhuman agency and imagine our interaction with larger planetary forces. Inasmuch as the urgencies of the Anthropocene are more than an academic issue, we invited award-winning authors and illustrators of young people's literature to contribute personal reflections on how fantastic imagination equips us to confront the Anthropocene. The response has been overwhelming. With the artistic contributions, we were able to interlace the sixteen academic chapters with fifteen creative reflections and include eight illustrations grouped together in two color inserts following parts One and Three. Together, these visual and narrative reflections serve as reminders that our most advanced technology for imagining the future is storytelling, not analysis. Also, since we consider this project to be public service in the push for an ecological civilization, all royalties accruing from this book will be donated to a fund that supports the preservation of biodiversity. Our choice has been The Ocean Cleanup, a nonprofit organization that has developed and deployed ingenious floating systems to clean up the world's oceans of plastic pollution. By the time this book lands in your hands, The Ocean Cleanup will hopefully be getting close to a full-scale system roll-out, a project that is expected to clean up half of the Great Pacific Garbage Patch within an eyeblink of five years. As much as is possible in a book that engages with theories of the Anthropocene, we have minimized academic jargon and discussions of dystopia. We have prioritized instead narratives that offer what China Miéville calls "hope with teeth" (2016, 24), Indigenous, and minority literatures. Our focus on anticipatory futures explains why most fiction and film examined in this volume are works addressed to young audiences. Young people have more stake in the future than anyone else and more reasons to believe that a just, sustainable world is possible.

Our world is transitioning to an ecological civilization. We know that the crucial aspects of this ecological civilization are already being imagined in stories that challenge the banality and defeatism of our Newt Age. This is a fight for our planet's future and we can't settle for incremental remedies to an unsustainable system. What we need is counternarratives that mobilize resistance, offer visions of equitable futures, and jumpstart conversations about translating visions into lived realities. Here's where fantasy and myth come into play. As specialized story systems, they are uniquely positioned to articulate the change we want to see. We welcome you—reading these words—to the resistance. Together, word by word, we can enact a transition to an ecocentric future.

References

Alaimo, Stacy. 2016. *Exposed: Environmental Politics and Pleasures in Posthuman Times*. Minneapolis: University of Minnesota Press.

Albrecht, Glenn A. 2019. *Earth Emotions: New Word for a New World*. Ithaca, NY and London: Cornell University Press.

Anthropocene Working Group. 2009. "Definitions." Subcommission on Quaternary Stratigraphy. 2019. http://quaternary.stratigraphy.org/working-groups/anthropocene/.

Attebery, Brian. 1992. *Strategies of Fantasy*. Bloomington: Indiana University Press.

Attebery, Brian. 2014. *Stories about Stories: Fantasy and the Remaking of Myth*. New York: Oxford University Press.

Baratta, Chris, ed. 2012. *Environmentalism in the Realm of Science Fiction and Fantasy Literature*. Newcastle upon Tyne: Cambridge Scholars Publishing.

Beuret, Nicholas. 2019. "Emissions Inequality—A Gulf between Global Rich and Poor." *Social Europe*, April 10, 2019. https://www.socialeurope.eu/emissions-inequality.

Čapek, Karel. (1936) 2012. *The War with the Newts*. Translated by David Wyllie. Calgary: Theophania Publishing.

Clark, Timothy. 2019. *The Value of Ecocriticism*. New York: Cambridge University Press.

CO$_2$ Earth. 2020. Citizen-led Initiative of ProOxygen. https://www.co2.earth/daily-co2.

Cohen, Jeffrey Jerome, and Lowell Duckert. eds. 2015. *Elemental Ecocriticism: Thinking with Earth, Air, Water and Fire*. Minneapolis: University of Minnesota Press.

Crist, Eileen. 2016. "On the Poverty of Our Nomenclature." In *Anthropocene or Capitalocene: Nature, History, and the Crisis of Capitalism*, edited by Jason W. Moore, 14–33. Oakland, CA: PM Press.

Dillon, Grace. 2012. "Imagining Indigenous Futurisms." In *Walking the Clouds: An Anthology of Indigenous Science Fiction*, edited by Grace Dillon, 1–12. Tucson: University of Arizona Press.

Echterling, Clare. 2016. "How to Save the World and Other Lessons from Children's Environmental Literature." *Children's Literature in Education*, vol. 47: 283–99.

Elhacham, Emily, Liad Ben-Uri, Jonathan Grozovski, Yinon M. Bar-On, and Ron Milo. 2020. "Global Human-Made Mass Exceeds All Living Biomass." *Nature*, vol. 588: 442–4.

Emmett, Robert S., and David E. Nye. eds. 2017. *The Environmental Humanities: A Critical Introduction*. Cambridge, MA: The MIT Press.

Frankel, Jeffrey. 2020. "Covid-19 and the Climate Crisis Are Part of the Same Battle." *The Guardian*, October 2, 2020. https://www.theguardian.com/business/2020/oct/02/covid-19-and-the-climate-crisis-are-part-of-the-same-battle#comments.

Ghosh, Amitav. 2016. *The Great Derangement: Climate Change and the Unthinkable*. Chicago, IL: University of Chicago Press.

Gore, Tim. 2020. "Confronting Carbon Inequality." *Oxfam International*. September 21, 2020. https://www.oxfam.org/en/research/confronting-carbon-inequality.

Haiven, Max. 2014. *Crises of Imagination, Crises of Power: Capitalism, Creativity, and the Commons*. Halifax: Fernwood Publishing.

Haraway, Donna. 2016. "Staying with the Trouble: Anthropocene, Capitalocene, Chthulocene." In *Anthropocene or Capitalocene: Nature, History, and the Crisis of Capitalism*, edited by Jason W. Moore, 34–76. Oakland, CA: PM Press.

Holthaus, Eric. 2020. *The Future Earth: A Radical Vision for What's Possible in the Age of Warming*. New York: Harper One.

Imarisha, Walidah. 2015. "Introduction." In *Octavia's Brood: Science Fiction Stories from Social Justice Movements*, edited by Walidah Imarisha and Adrienne Maree Brown, 3–5. Chico, CA: AK Press.

Ivanova, Irina. 2020. "Global Rich Must Cut Their Carbon Footprint 97% to Stave off Climate Change, UN Says." *CBS News*. December 16, 2020. https://www.cbsnews.com/news/carbon-footprint-wealthy-people-97-percent-cut-un/.

Johnson, Ayàna Elizabeth, and Katharine K. Wilkinson. 2020. *All We Can Save: Truth, Courage, and Solutions for the Climate Crisis*. New York: One World.

Johns-Putra, Adeline. 2019. *Climate Change and the Contemporary Novel*. New York: Cambridge University Press.

Jones, Nicola. 2017. "How the World Passed a Carbon Threshold and Why It Matters." *Yale Environment*, vol. 360. January 26, 2017. https://e360.yale.edu/features/how-the-world-passed-a-carbon-threshold-400ppm-and-why-it-matters.

Joseph, Peter. 2017. *The New Human Rights Movement: Reinventing the Economy to End Oppression*. Dallas, TX: BenBella Books.

Kane, Sean. 1995. *Wisdom of the Mythtellers*. Peterborough: Broadview Press.

Kelsey, Elin. 2020. *Hope Matters: Why Changing the Way We Think Is Critical to Solving the Environmental Crisis*. David Suzuki Institute. Vancouver, BC: Greystone Books.

Kimmerer, Robin Wall. 2013. *Braiding Sweetgrass: Indigenous Wisdom, Scientific Knowledge, and the Teaching of Plants*. Minneapolis, MN: Milkweed Editions.

Klein, Naomi. 2014. *This Changes Everything: Capitalism vs. the Climate*. New York: Simon and Schuster.

Klein, Naomi. 2019. *The (Burning) Case for a Green New Deal*. New York: Simon and Schuster.

Kolbert, Elizabeth. 2015. *Field Notes from a Catastrophe: Man, Nature, and Climate Change*. Rev. ed. New York and London: Bloomsbury.

LaDuke, Winona. 2019. "Honor the Earth Newsletter." October 18, 2019. Received by email.

Le Guin, Ursula K. 2014. "National Book Awards Acceptance Speech." November 19, 2014. YouTube. https://www.youtube.com/watch?v=Et9Nf-rsALk

Lent, Jeremy. 2017. *The Patterning Instinct: A Cultural History of Humanity's Search for Meaning*. New York: Prometheus Books.

Mathews, Richard. 2002. *Fantasy: The Liberation of Imagination*. New York: Routledge.

Mendlesohn, Farah. 2008. *Rhetorics of Fantasy*. Middletown, CT: Wesleyan University Press.

Menely, Tobias and Jesse Oak Taylor. eds. 2017. *Anthropocene Reading: Literary History in Geologic Times*. University Park: Penn State University Press.

Miéville, China. 2016. "The Limits of Utopia: Introduction." *Utopia*. Thomas More, with Supplement by Ursula K. Le Guin and Introduction by China Miéville, 11–27. London: Verso.

Milner, Andrew, and J. R. Burgmann. 2020. *Science Fiction and Climate Change: A Sociological Approach*. Liverpool: Liverpool University Press.

Moore, Jason. 2015. *Capitalism in the Web of Life*. London: Verso.

Moore, Jason. 2016. "The Rise of Cheap Nature." In *Anthropocene or Capitalocene: Nature, History, and the Crisis of Capitalism*, edited by Jason W. Moore, 78–115. Oakland, CA: PM Press.

Morton, Timothy. 2013. *Hyperobjects: Philosophy and Ecology after the End of the World*. Minneapolis: The University of Minnesota Press.

Nixon, Rob. 2011. *Slow Violence and the Environmentalism and of the Poor*. Cambridge, MA: Harvard University Press.

Oziewicz, Marek. 2008. *One Earth, One People: The Mythopoeic Fantasy Series of Ursula K. Le Guin, Lloyd Alexander, Madeleine L'Engle and Orson Scott Card*. Jefferson, NC: McFarland.

Panagiotarakou, Eleni. 2020. "Who Loves Rats? A Renewed Plea for the Managed Relocations of Endangered Species." *Ethics & the Environment*, vol. 25, no. 1: 51–68.

Piketty, Thomas. 2014. *Capital in the Twenty-First Century*. Cambridge, MA: Harvard University Press.

Piketty, Thomas. 2020. *Capital and Ideology*. Cambridge, MA: Harvard University Press.

Quigley, Peter and Scott Slovic, eds. 2018. *Ecocritical Aesthetics: Language, Beauty, and the Environment*. Bloomington: Indiana University Press.

Schneider-Mayerson, Matthew. 2018. "The Influence of Climate Fiction: An Empirical Survey of Readers." *Environmental Humanities*, vol. 10, no. 2, November: 473–500.

Scranton, Roy. 2015. *Learning to Die in the Anthropocene: Reflections on the End of a Civilization*. San Francisco, CA: City Lights Books.

Shiva, Vandana (with Kartikey Shiva). 2020. *Oneness vs. the 1%: Shattering Illusions, Seeding Freedom*. London: Chelsea Green Publishing.

Spratt, David and Alia Armistead. 2020. "Covid-19 Climate Lessons." Breakthrough—National Centre for Climate Restoration. Melbourne, Australia. May 2020. https://52a87f3e-7945-4bb1-abbf-9aa66cd4e93e.filesusr.com/ugd/148cb0_44afa5f748604b71a6527b670b0a2cc2.pdf.

Szeman, Imre and Dominic Boyer, eds. 2017. *Energy Humanities: An Anthology*. Baltimore, MD: Johns Hopkins University Press.

Tan, Shaun. 2018. *Tales from the Inner City*. New York: Arthur A. Levine Books.

Tarr, Anita and Donna J. White, eds. 2018. *Posthumanism in Young Adult Fiction: Finding Humanity in a Posthuman World*. Jackson: University Press of Mississippi.

Temple, James. 2018. "The Year Climate Change Began to Spin Out of Control." *MIT Technology Review*. January 4, 2018. https://www.technologyreview.com/2018/01/04/3591/the-year-climate-change-began-to-spin-out-of-control/.

Thomas, Ebony Elizabeth. 2019. *The Dark Fantastic: Race and the Imagination from Harry Potter to the Hunger Games*. New York: New York University Press.

Tortell, Philippe D. 2020. "Earth 2020: Science, Society, and Sustainability in the Anthropocene." *PNAS*, vol. 117, no. 16, April 21, 2020: 8683–91. www.pnas.org/cgi/doi/10.1073/pnas.2001919117

Trexler, Adam. 2015. *Anthropocene Fictions: The Novel in a Time of Climate Change*. Charlottesville: University of Virginia Press.

Tsing, Anna, Heather Swanson, Elaine Gan, and Nils Bubandt, eds. 2017. *Arts of Living on a Damaged Planet. Monsters of the Anthropocene.* Minneapolis: University of Minnesota Press.

United Nations IPBES Biodiversity Report. 2019. United Nations. May 6, 2019. https://www.un.org/sustainabledevelopment/blog/2019/05/nature-decline-unprecedented-report/

United Nations Environmental Programme. 2020. *Emissions Gap Report 2020.* December 9, 2020. https://www.unep.org/emissions-gap-report–2020

Weinstein, Jami and Claire Colebrook, eds. 2017. *Posthumous Life: Theorizing beyond the Posthuman.* New York: Columbia University Press.

PART I
TROUBLE IN THE AIR

CHAPTER 1
ANTHROPOS AND THE AIR
Brian Attebery

A leafy branch came out of nowhere and hit Anthropos in the side of the head. "Who threw that?" said Anthropos, whose everyday name was Child of Man. But no one answered. Child of Man looked up at the sky and saw only light and a few distant birds. And Child grew angry. It was Air that had hit Child, Air that aimed the branch.

To get back at Air, Child built a great fire and when it was roaring, covered it with more leaves. Smoke billowed out; Air turned black. Child started coughing and before long Child had to run away from the dark cloud. But the cloud followed.

Pretty soon it began to get hot under the cloud. Child had the idea of driving Air away. Air was so big it would take a big force to make it move, so Child went to a nearby mountain and started cutting down trees. Child cut a whole forest and lashed the timbers together with vines to make a tower. Child placed a fan made out of branches at the top of the tower and harnessed a river to make it move. Behind the tower was a glacier: the fan would draw cold from the ice to make Child more comfortable.

It all worked: the running river turned the fan, the fan brought a stream of cool from the ice, and the cloud was pushed away to someone else's country. But the forest was gone and that made the river dry up. The ice had already started to melt because of the smoky cloud, and now the fan evaporated the melt-water. Child thought Air had gone away, but Air was still there, invisible without its load of smoke. "I have beaten Air," said Child. "Air is nothing."

Far from the tower, Air was gathering strength. And when Child was looking the other way, Air brought a great wind to the mountainside. The tower swayed and fell, the fan smashed to pieces, and with a great gust Air knocked Child face-down on the ground.

CHAPTER 2
FROM THE THIRD AGE TO THE FIFTH SEASON: CONFRONTING THE ANTHROPOCENE THROUGH FANTASY

Brian Attebery

The term "Anthropocene" summarizes the idea that the earth has been irrevocably altered, for the worse, by human activity. We live amid human-caused climate change, desertification, mountains of trash, and mass extinctions, and so it seems like the height of folly to go on telling stories about ambitions, love affairs, and financial scandals as if those purely social concerns were unaffected by, and had no effect on, the natural world. As Ursula K. Le Guin (1989a) said many years ago, realism can't do the job any more: it is "the least adequate means of understanding or portraying the incredible realities of our existence" (53). Yet what kind of literature can really encompass the sense that the world community includes more than just our species, and that we have done and are doing this community great injustice? Some poetry perhaps, and the kind of nature writing that bridges the gap between science and art. Political rhetoric, when it rises to rare greatness. An obvious answer is science fiction, which employs extrapolation and utopian critique to wake us to the devastation in which we are complicit and encourages us to imagine other ways to live and organize ourselves. But fantasy? Isn't that just escapist nostalgia and game-playing nonsense? How can a bunch of imaginary quests and wish-fulfillments tell us anything about the real environment or the economic and social systems that threaten it?

One way to address this question is to go back to the beginning. No one seems to agree on exactly when we entered the Anthropocene era, but I suggest a starting point that also coincides with the birth of written literature, the moment when oral storytelling, which is as old as humanity itself, gave birth to its less perishable twin and rival. The epic of Gilgamesh is often called the oldest story in the world, but really it is just the oldest long story committed to writing, with partial versions dating back more than 4,000 years. It is full of elements that seem fantastic to us—monsters, gods, transformations—and that were probably always seen as outside of everyday, secular reality. It's a mistake to extend the realism/fantasy divide back too far in time, but that distinction—between the everyday and the extraordinary—usually works. One of the story's key episodes concerns the hero Gilgamesh and his companion Enkidu entering a great forest of cedars to challenge its guardian, the monster Humbaba. Why? Because with its defender dead, the cedar forest can be invaded and exploited. The greatest of its trees is cut down to make a gate for Gilgamesh's city. The story treats this as a triumph, the moment when Gilgamesh, who begins as a tyrant, truly becomes a leader.

It is also a moment that sets the pattern for much fantasy, which traces the paternal side of its ancestry (on the distaff side are fairy tale and ballad) to epics like Gilgamesh's. A hero requires a quest, and the ur-quest is a journey into the wilderness to confront a primordial, chthonic monster like Humbaba. In other words, the hero narrative is about imposing oneself on the landscape, turning a complex environment into mere backdrop for a larger-than-life human figure. By becoming a hero Gilgamesh makes everyone around him into antagonists or helpers, spear-carriers or love-objects: only one hero to a story.

Gilgamesh's story is the story of civilization, quite literally: of the ascent of the *civitas*, or city-state, at the expense of the wild world outside the city walls. The city redefines wilderness as enemy, just as the Hero remakes the defender of the wilderness into a monster. As Le Guin (1989b) points out in another essay:

> Civilized Man says: I am Self, I am Master, all the rest is Other—outside, below, underneath, subservient. I own, I use, I explore, I exploit, I control. What I do is what matters. What I want is what matter is for. I am that I am, and the rest is women and the wilderness, to be used as I see fit.

> (161)

However, in Le Guin's own fiction, including her fantasy as well as her science fiction, woman answers, "Hold on! Not so fast." There are other stories—have always been other stories. There is no monomyth, Joseph Campbell notwithstanding, as Alan Dundes (2005) and others have pointed out.

One reason there are multiple stories is that we don't all live in the same world, or the same epoch of the world. For some, like Gilgamesh's people, the Anthropocene began (or began to begin) thousands of years ago. For others, such as the Barasana people of the Amazon, it has not yet happened: they still live in a world dominated by nature or God. For them, people are locked in a struggle for survival against powerful inhuman forces like hunger and disease and predators that walk on four legs instead of two. In such a world, only divine will can prevail against hostile nature. Actual wilderness is rare these days, but a lot of folk still see the world in such terms even if they themselves never tremble at the howling of wolves or the growling of tigers.

The Anthropocene, like any term for a period of history, covers not the entirety of experience at that time but whatever the majority perceives about it. Raymond Williams (1977) has a good way of sorting this out. There are at least three ways of living in any given historical moment.[1] The most evident is whatever is culturally dominant; the generalized spirit of the age; the mainstream. But if we are talking mainstreams, the same river has eddies and backwaters and cascades. Some groups will always hold onto beliefs, customs, entertainments from an earlier era. Williams identifies this as the *residual* part of culture. Others will rush ahead, riding the faster water at the outside of the river bend. They are already moving into the next era. Williams terms that kind of culture *emergent*. Residual and emergent cultures, says Williams, "are significant both in themselves and in what they reveal of the characteristics of the 'dominant'" (122). Of course, at any given time, it is impossible to tell whether a particular cultural phenomenon is going to prove itself to be emergent or merely eccentric: "Oh that crazy Gilgamesh and his wild ideas about subduing the earth. That'll never catch on!"

The cluster of beliefs, practices, and attitudes that constitutes the Anthropocene is now dominant worldwide, but it is unclear how long that has been the case. As mentioned before, starting dates for the epoch vary wildly, with common guesses ranging from the beginning of the Industrial Revolution to, essentially, yesterday. Other designations for our moment imply other starting points; for instance, if we term this not the Anthropocene but the Plasticene

(Ross 2018), we can date it from the time plastics began to form a significant portion of sediment that will eventually show up in layers of rock. But the exact date doesn't matter: we're here now, whether we want to be or not, and we need stories to tell us how we got here, where we are going, and how to live in the human-created world.

Many fantasies represent a shift from one configuration of the cosmos to a fundamentally different one. Gilgamesh is an example: by the end the gods have withdrawn, immortality has been grasped and then lost, and the king has learned to be responsible to his people. In the realm of modern fantasy, *The Lord of the Rings* depicts one of those great cosmic precessions, a realignment of heaven and earth. In the novel's third volume, *The Return of the King* (1965), J. R. R. Tolkien identifies the shift as the end of the Third Age: "The Days of the Rings were passed, and an end was come of the story and song of those times. With them went many Elves of the High Kindred who would no longer stay in Middle-earth" (309). The reconfiguration involves losses both epic and personal:

> To Sam the evening deepened to darkness as he stood at the Haven; and as he looked at the grey sea he saw only a shadow on the waters that was soon lost in the West. There still he stood far into the night, hearing only the sigh and murmur of the waves on the shores of Middle-earth, and the sound of them sank deep into his heart.
>
> (311)

The Appendixes at the end of *The Return of the King* make it explicit: the Fourth Age of Middle-earth belongs to men and their smaller kin, Hobbits. Leaders will be human, and so will their adversaries: in place of dragons and balrogs, people of good will must confront human tyrants and petty grifters like Sharkey, the former wizard Saruman. In the same volume, the chapter called "The Scouring of the Shire" can be read as a depiction of the coming Fourth Age—in miniature, as the Shire is a scale model of the world and Hobbits are humans seen through the wrong end of a telescope. Villainy in the Fourth Age is going to be accomplished through deception and demolition, rather than through enchantment. Heroism will likewise be stripped of magic and achieved without semi-divine mentors like Galadriel and Gandalf. Implied in the chapter is that a single scouring is not enough: other scoundrels will replace Sharkey and his crew, and other ordinary Hobbits will have to stand up to them as Merry and Pippin and Sam have done.

The Fourth Age is the Anthropocene, with all its ills forecast in the scene that greets the returning heroes in the Shire:

> The Old Grange on the west side had been knocked down, and its place taken by rows of tarred sheds. All the chestnuts were gone. The banks and hedgerows were broken. Great waggons were standing in disorder in a field beaten bare of grass. Bagshot Row was a yawning sand and gravel quarry. Bag End up beyond could not be seen for a clutter of large huts.
>
> (Tolkien 1965, 296)

We know this world. We live in it. We made it.

Much subsequent fantasy follows Tolkien's lead in showing the end of magic and the implementation of a strictly human, which is to say Anthropocene, order of things. The trajectory of these stories is summed up in the title of a story by Larry Niven: "The Magic Goes Away" (1976). Other examples of the pattern from around the same time include Lloyd Alexander's Chronicles of Prydain (1964–8) and Susan Cooper's Dark Is Rising series (1965–77), but the trope was already familiar from such earlier works as Lord Dunsany's *The Charwoman's Shadow* (1926) and Rudyard Kipling's *Puck of Pook's Hill* (1906). These fantasies share the bittersweet quality of Tolkien's ending, though few are as explicit about reconfiguring power and responsibility from a divine order to a purely human and perhaps self-dooming arrangement. These fantasies depict the structure of change into an Anthropocene order: humans take on power and responsibility but lose nonhuman guidance and grace. The world grows more uniform and thus less resilient. Mystery evaporates. We inscribe ourselves upon the land.

But to return to Williams's ideas of the residual and emergent, other fantasies in the same period invoke world-models based not on an Anthropocene configuration but on states of the world either prior to or following upon it. C. S. Lewis's Narnia books (1950–6) have an overall arc that runs counter to that of *The Lord of the Rings* even though they were written concurrently, by a close friend. Though the first couple of volumes bring humans to Narnia and give them increasing dominion over it, by the end the creator figure Aslan repossesses his creation and essentially smashes it to start over in a more perfect reboot, one that people can't mess up. Lewis offers a similar model of history in the third volume of his Space Trilogy, *That Hideous Strength* (1946), which ends with the planetary intelligences, the oyarses, descending to earth to reinstate an angelic order. The ascent of humankind has been halted; a residual viewpoint is represented structurally and thus validated.

But fantasy does not always speak for a residual, or even a dominant worldview. At the same time Lewis was publishing his Narnia books and Tolkien was polishing *The Lord of the Rings*, an American writer named Jack Vance began issuing a series of stories about the Dying Earth. The premise is that in an unimaginably far future, as the sun is burning out and the earth lies covered in rubble and ruins, magic has returned in the form of half-forgotten technology. A remnant population of humans must deal with magical hazards and bizarre creatures, some of which are our mutated cousins (Vance 1950).

This fictional set-up might seem more residual than emergent. Vance drew on earlier writers' creations to invent the Dying Earth trope: it harkens back to tales by Lord Dunsany and William Hope Hodgson, with imagery courtesy of Edgar Allan Poe, Mary and Percy Shelley, and H. G. Wells. In its influence on others, however, Vance's creation soon began to seem less nostalgic than prescient, especially when the Dying Earth concept was taken up by authors such as Roger Zelazny, Gene Wolfe, and Elizabeth Hand. As each of these writers in turn reinvented the end-of-the-world scenario, it became more explicitly an account of the end of human domination: what comes *after* the end of the world?

A recent version of the Dying Earth scenario is N. K. Jemisin's multiple-award-winning Broken Earth trilogy. Jemisin's work resonates strongly because it shows us where we might be headed, toward our own self-induced downfall. The world of the series, called the Stillness, is a geologic chaos and an ecological catastrophe. Near the beginning of the first volume, *The Fifth Season* (2015), this disastrous state is explained as the result of "Father Earth's tireless efforts" (8). Father Earth seems at first to be a myth, a fictional Someone to blame for the periodic catastrophes that bring down every civilization humans try to establish. It seems a little odd to have a masculine earth deity, but Jemisin knows what she is doing. This is a world that has no nurturing Mother Gaia; in her place is a vengeful, Old Testament-style father god.

Only much later do we discover that Father Earth is an actual, sentient being: the emergent consciousness of the planet's magical potential. And it was human activity that woke Father Earth to angry awareness. As we read through the trilogy, we discover more and more about the history behind the Stillness and its catastrophes. It is, in a sense, our history. Anthropologists Cymene Howe and Anand Pandian (2016) describe a shift in thinking that comes with awareness of the Anthropocene's history and its possible outcome:

> What happens … when the destruction of forests for mineral resources is conceived from the standpoint of enduring indigenous relationships with the land, or the ecopolitics of those who insist on collaborating with the forest as a sentient being? How would our sense of human power shift if we acknowledged the animals and other living beings we borrow our capacities from, or the photosynthesis that imbues the planet with so much of its available energy? Lodged in such terms are stories that can help us to imagine the fearsome domain of human agency in unexpected ways.
>
> ("Lexicon")

This passage comes from an essay in which Howe and Pandian propose a "Lexicon for an Anthropocene Yet Unseen," part of a developing interactive site focusing on culture and environmental change. They don't end the discussion by dwelling on devastation caused by the "fearsome domain of human agency," nor does Jemisin in her trilogy. Instead, both the novels and the essay try to imagine ways of coming to terms with a post-Anthropocene way of living.

The post-Anthropocene resembles the pre- in many ways. In both, human activity is restricted and human agency puny against powerful natural forces. Both concepts are attempts to make those forces comprehensible by telling stories about them, and that usually means anthropomorphizing them. Human-faced gods have always been a powerful device for thinking about the structure of the cosmos. However, in the fantasy scenario of the magical Dying Earth, the Gods After differ from the Gods Before. Jemisin's Father Earth is Mother Gaia minus any feminine-coded nurturing. The remainder is bitterness, hunger, and desire for revenge, and thus Father Earth is a sort of zombie version of the Mother Goddess.

A zombie is both a reminder and a parody of a living being. It's what is left when a person's life, soul, and intelligence are removed and something more sinister comes to inhabit the empty husk. Zombies, like other forms of undeath, move us toward the dark end of the fantasy spectrum, from wonder to horror. This move can stand structurally for the transition from the Anthropocene to what Donna Haraway (2016) has termed the Chthulucene.[2] Her coinage points toward two etymologies, and thus two readings of the coming age. First, most of us will hear in it a reference to Cthulhu and the other Elder Gods of H. P. Lovecraft's horrific mythos. Lovecraft calls those gods Elder; it's even more horrifying to think they might be Younger. Perhaps they are not remnants of an earlier, rawer creation, but harbingers of a coming self-creation: a cosmos we are bringing about by our acts. The Chthulucene, in this reading, is not just the ending of the Anthropocene but its inevitable outcome.

But Haraway pulls back from this reading, as does Jemisin by the end of the trilogy. The Chthulucene is not just a time-marking "cene" tacked onto Lovecraft's ultimate evil Cthulhu. In *Staying with the Trouble*, Haraway introduces a kind of spider, *Pimoa cthulhu*, whose species name points toward the Greek word for subterranean, earth-born, chthonic (Haraway 2016, 31). Lovecraft probably used the same etymology for his invention, although the spider's name is spelled slightly differently from the Elder God's. Haraway finds hope in the very lowliness of the cthulhu spider: in its creepy, hidden endurance. The Anthropocene has been especially hard on large, prominent beasts like cheetahs and rhinoceroses. Smaller, uncuddly tentacled or many-legged creatures survive or even thrive beneath our feet. The Chthulucene is not waiting to come into being: it is already here but hidden. And it may be the greatest hope for the living earth, for a non-zombie Gaia.

One possible take-away from Haraway's fable is the idea that geologic eras, like moments in human history, are always multiple. They represent overlays of different historical configurations, even mutually contradictory ones. The residual never really went away. The emergent is already here, although perhaps we don't see it because it is under our feet. One way to visualize this tripartite version of time is by translating it into spatial terms. A traditional cosmology divides the universe into three stacked-up zones: heaven, earth, and the underworld. Mapping Williams's historical model onto this cosmological one, the residual would be the world above: the sky, where so many traditional gods had their dwelling. The dominant is the earth's surface, which contains everything we are likely to encounter in the ordinary course of events. And the emergent is deep underground, the place to which we relegate everything we can't face in the world or in ourselves. Northrop Frye explores this three-layer world in his study of myth and romance called *The Secular Scripture* (1976). Humans, he says, inhabit the middle level, with a heaven above and underneath "a mysterious place of birth and death from whence animals and plants proceed, and to which they return" (Frye 1976, 97). His description rather pretties up the lower world, which can be rank and feculent—Frye's romance universe looks to the spiritual rather than the biological.

Focusing on the bottom layer, we can return to the word *chthonic*. In many myth systems, including not only Gilgamesh's Babylonian cosmos but also early Greek stories, Mother Earth was a dangerous entity—not the terrifyingly emptied out version that is Jemisin's Father Earth, but still no pushover. The poet Hesiod, in *Theogony*, outlines a succession of reigning celestial orders, starting with Gaia and her sky consort Ouranos, who were replaced by the Titans, who in turn were supplanted by the Olympian gods. Gaia was not happy about this, and so she produced an array of chthonic monsters to attack the gods. These included dragon-headed Typhoeus, serpentine Echidna, and their offspring. Similar battles between gods—or god-kings like Gilgamesh—and archaic monsters show up in many creation stories. From there, they flow into a lot of fantasy, including Lovecraft's and Tolkien's. If we are living in the Anthropocene, we, or our ancestors, have had to kill a lot of spiny or scaly or shapeless beings to establish ourselves as the dominant life form.

Or maybe we just drove them underground. They might just emerge from the depths to save us from ourselves. That is the direction Jemisin's trilogy takes: a race of stony beings who move through the earth's crust and another race with power over earthquakes are the despised but essential allies to ordinary humanity. Both races represent the chthonic, cthulhian beings that clean up after catastrophe. It is particularly telling that no one in the Broken Earth looks up. They have been conditioned not to think about the sky, the stars, the moon that once ruled the sky but was driven away by humanity's overreaching. They have lost the past but they might have a future.

Once, in myth at least, the gods ruled in heavens and all was orderly. That historical configuration corresponds to Williams's residual. Then humans pulled down the gods and claimed power, and along came civilization but also conflict and environmental devastation: our current dominant. Finally, lower beings will spill out of the ground to take over, as in the Norse Ragnarök, when the goddess Hel will lead an army of the dead to conquer Middle Earth. That is emergence, figuratively and literally.

The second and third of these ages, or the middle and bottom layers of the cosmic map, are the Anthropocene and the Chthulucene. We need a name for the top. Like the Anthropocene, it can be named in various ways, according to the aspects one wishes to emphasize. I considered calling it the Chrysocene, the Age of Gold, or the Theocene, Time of the Gods, but ultimately chose to think spatially and call it the Uranocene. That name points up toward the sky but also back to the time of Gaia's deposed and mutilated consort Ouranos. Fantasies that invoke the turnover from Uranocene to Anthropocene and thence to Chthulucene are stories of descent from a Golden Age to a Bronze and an Iron, or from an upper world to a middle and then a lower. Each act of the story is darker and grimier than the one before it. The bottom layer can be imagined as the horrific end of a Lovecraft novel. Or, worse, the end of everything, the Necrocene, Age of Death.

Yet the three-act sequence or three-layer universe can be interpreted a little more optimistically, provided we in the Anthropocene haven't completely alienated the Dwellers of the Deep who might replace us. Because all three layers are still present, or already here, to move between the Anthropocene and the Chthulucene only requires a shift in vision. An outstanding example of fantasy that represents such a shift in vision is John Crowley's novel *Ka* (2017).

Ka is an amazingly rich text, full of allusions to myth and literature and history, but it's also a simple story, a set of conversations between two beings. One is the nameless human narrator. The other is a crow, Dar Oakley. The reason they can converse is that Dar Oakley is no ordinary crow. He is immortal—but not deathless. He dies a lot. But he returns, and each time he returns, he gradually regains knowledge from his past selves, including human speech. The "how" of this immortality is an important part of the novel, but so is the pattern of communication between crow and human that enables the series of stories that form Dar Oakley's real, undying self.

The result of this set-up is that we get an account of human civilization, from its tribal origins to its sad decline, from an outsider's perspective. It is human history seen from above—as the crow flies, so to speak. As the narrator talks with Dar Oakley, what he gets is not a straightforward story because: "Crow talk, Crow jokes, Crow histories have the brevity of koans, or Confucian analects; their richness is in the speaking, like sign language in sounds. Translating from one human language to another is no comparison" (Crowley 2017, 7).

Human stories, says the narrator, are like paths along the ground, while "Crows live in a wide, trackless space of three dimensions" (8). We may live in the same world, but we inhabit different imaginative spaces, what the story calls "realms."

Dar Oakley's name for the human realm is *Ymr*. The crow realm is, naturally enough, *Ka*. It takes Dar Oakley a long time to understand the concept of realms, as well as a lot of interactions with humans. We only need the concept of realm when there is more than one; it is a product of what Mary Louise Pratt, speaking of merely human difference, calls a Contact Zone (Pratt 1991, 36). Just as the narrator has to try to understand Crows' three-dimensional space, Dar Oakley has to observe human movement and translate it into his own terms. Here's how we look to a crow: "Seen from above, it's as though their feet proceed from their hairy heads and then from their backs in turn. So many of them, each one seeming to go his own way, all scattering to engage the others one to one, but the Crows, no, all together above, single of purpose" (Crowley 2017, 77).

When you add to these differences of movement and ways of inhabiting space all the other differences between human concerns and crow life, crow community, crow desire, crow death—in sum, Ka and Ymr may overlap and interpenetrate, but they might as well be different planets.

Dar Oakley's human friends also try to understand how realms function. One finally tries out this deceptively simple formulation: "It's where you are when you are what you are" (76). Ymr is where humans are most human; Ka is where crows are nothing but Crow. An unstated corollary is that when Dar Oakley enters Ymr and the narrator enters Ka, they are no longer fully crow nor human but something less and more than either. The "less" part has to do with no longer quite fitting in. Dar Oakley becomes a stranger among crows. The narrator is estranged from Ymr, the human realm, which is dying. On the other hand, the "more" part of being suspended between realms is that new possibilities open up: new ways of seeing and being and expressing oneself. The narrator says, "We can only think about those things we can name, and his thought is Crow thought and is not mine; but if he can think about me, and my kind, maybe I can think as he does, and as he did then. If he can be in Ymr, I can be in Ka" (190).

To be fully human, to live entirely in the Anthropocene, is to face extinction when Ymr comes to ruin. The name Ymr probably refers to the figure of Ymir in Norse myth: the first giant, killed by Odin and his brothers, who dismember his body to make the earth, sky, and sea. Ymir is another of those chthonic beings, like Gilgamesh's Humbaba, that have to be defeated by the hero gods. His is a perfect name for an entirely human-centric worldview.

But in Ka, humans are neither gods nor heroes. Instead, we are food, at least when dead and broken up a bit by larger predators. Crows are carrion eaters. They are not sentimental about the dead, not their own and certainly not dead people. In the realm of Ka, we are not merely food for crows but also, with our habits of aggression and territoriality, particularly bountiful providers of such food. The more heroic—which is to say, the more violent—we are, the better providers we make.

Ymr and Ka coexist in time and space, like the residual, dominant, and emergent. Ka is above us, so it is at least partly the heavenly realm, the Uranocene. Ymr is the Anthropocene. But where is the third realm, the world below that emerges with the eclipse of the Anthropocene? I think it might also be Ka. Crows' eating habits group them with worms and beetles and bacteria: all the lowly, unlovely organisms who turn death into new life. As we enter the realm of Ka, we start to see death and decay as less abject than project: the start of something rather than the ruin. The book opens with the narrator contemplating mountains of trash, from which a few people are trying to salvage usable items, including food. That is a very Ka-ish activity. It seems grim at first; maybe by the end, not so much.

If the world below is also the world above, there is hope that the story of descent is part of a circle, which again fits Northrop Frye's theories of narrative structure. From Ka we fell; to Ka we may hope to return—if the universe follows the laws of narrative. In Crowley's novel, Ka and Ymr are not the only realms, or modes of perception. Storytelling itself is a kind of realm. Nature is a realm, as is its contrary, civilization. And life and death continually reappear as contrasting but interdependent realms. Dar Oakley accompanies his friend Fox Cap into an underworld filled with hosts of human dead. In that underworld—which they enter, says the narrator, through storytelling—they undertake the quest that underlies all quests, for an end to death. They are looking for the Most Precious Thing, the secret of immortality.

As in any good quest myth, they meet a series of guides, none of whom can entirely be trusted. The last of these is the Most Precious Thing itself, which speaks to Dar Oakley:

> I was not always as I am now, said the Most Precious Thing. Once I was an herb growing at the bottom of the sea. All was peaceful there for eternities. But then there came down through the waters a thing I had never seen before: white as a fish's belly, with a squinty eye, limbs going all which way. The next thing I knew I had been plucked up out of the eternal mud by the creature's ugly hand!
>
> (Crowley 2017, 139)

Dar Oakley doesn't recognize this incident, but we should. It is another part of the tale of Gilgamesh, the final quest he undertakes after killing the forest spirit and clashing with the mother goddess Ishtar. Because his actions have led to the death of his brother/lover Enkidu, it is up to him to try to undo that death. Eventually he does find the herb of immortality at the bottom of the sea, as in the story the Most Precious Thing tells to Dar Oakley.

But that story, whether it's about Gilgamesh or Baldur or Orpheus, always has the same ending: deathlessness is almost grasped and then lost. Gilgamesh loses the herb to a snake. Dar Oakley hides the Most Precious Thing under a tree root … and then misplaces the tree. As is typical of such quests, immortality doesn't end up in a high place—even a hero can never return to the lost past—but under the ground. The paradox of the Chthulucene is that we keep looking up to the sky for what may be under our feet. As Dar Oakley and Fox Cap quest for the Most Precious Thing, they are told by one of their guides that it is hidden "in a vast land down under" (131). This land turns out to be contained within a nest high in the tallest tree in the realm of death: "a tiny land high up" (134), but that too is a lie. Like Alice in Looking-Glass land, they have to face in the opposite direction of the thing they seek. We too must look down to go up; climb to reach the bottom of things; die to become immortal; embrace decay to find renewal. Above all, we have to leave our own realm to find it, whether Crow or human, Ka or Ymr.

This, then, is a way fantasy can conceive of the end of the Anthropocene, which might also be a beginning. Crowley's novel is a complex, braided narrative, and appropriately so: we do not live in a simple universe. Stories that make it seem so are lying to us, as the Most Precious Thing lies to Dar Oakley. Hero stories lie; Trickster tales tell the truth. Fantasy reminds us that the human perspective has never been the only valid one. If the Anthropocene has any chance of continuing, we who dwell within it must also learn to visit other realms to learn the languages of spiders and crows and earth-guardians like Humbaba. Fantasies of the end remind us that to go past the end, we need to embrace the engines of decay and to learn chthonic wisdom and ways of seeing.

Notes

1   In *Marxism and Literature* (1977) literary theorist Raymond Williams identified a threefold division in cultural productions. At any historical moment, there will be a dominant strain, a pattern of beliefs and forms of expression that represent whichever groups and institutions are in charge. The

novel, for instance, became a dominant genre as the business classes took over from the aristocracy. The dominant dominates by making its ways of doing things seem natural and inevitable, exercising what Marxists such as Williams call hegemony. However, as Williams points out, prior cultural patterns do not disappear despite their loss of hegemonic force; instead, they continue as residual culture, no longer the mainstream but still favored by a minority. At the same time, newer forms of expression are continually being invented, and if the social strata they represent gain influence, they may eventually become the new dominant. Williams terms this cultural strand the emergent.

2   The Chthulucene is science historian and philosopher Donna Haraway's alternative coinage for the contemporary era called variously the Capitalocene (coined by Jason Moore in 2016), the Plasticene (probably multiple coinages, recorded by Curt Stager in 2011), and most commonly the Anthropocene (popularized by Paul Crutzen in 2000). Haraway's term, introduced in *Staying with the Trouble* (2016), riffs on the work of horror writer H. P. Lovecraft, whose evil pantheon was headed by the cephalopodic god Cthulhu. She combines it with the species name of the spider *Pimoa cthulhu*—both stemming from the Greek root *khthon-*, of or from the earth. Haraway has chosen her term to emphasize the endurance of the nonhuman even in a time of world-shaping (or world-wrecking) human activity.

References

Crowley, John. 2017. *Ka: Dar Oakley in the Ruin of Ymir*. New York: Saga Press.

Dundes, Alan. 2005. "Folkloristics in the Twenty-First Century (AFS Invited Presidential Plenary Address, 2004)." *Journal of American Folklore*, vol. 118, no. 470 (Fall): 385–408. https://doi.org/10.1353/jaf.2005.0044.

Frye, Northrop. 1976. *The Secular Scripture: A Study of the Structure of Romance*. Cambridge, MA and London: Harvard University Press.

Haraway, Donna. 2016. *Staying with the Trouble: Making Kin in the Chthulucene*. Durham, NC and London: Duke University Press.

Howe, Cymene, and Anand Pandion. 2016. "Lexicon for an Anthropocene Yet Unseen." Theorizing the Contemporary, *Fieldsights*. January 21, 2016. https://culanth.org/fieldsights/series/lexicon-for-an-anthropocene-yet-unseen.

Jemisin, N. K. 2016. *The Fifth Season: The Broken Earth, Book I*. New York: Orbit.

Lakoff, George, and Mark Johnson. 1980. *Metaphors We Live By*. Chicago, IL: University of Chicago Press.

Le Guin, Ursula K. 1989a. "National Book Award Acceptance Speech." In *The Language of the Night*, edited by Susan Wood. Revised Edition, 52–3. New York: HarperCollins.

Le Guin, Ursula K. 1989b. "Woman, Wilderness." In *Dancing at the Edge of the World: Thoughts on Words, Women, Places*, 161–3. New York: Grove Press.

Lewis, C. S. 1946. *That Hideous Strength: A Modern Fairy-Tale for Grown-Ups*. Paperback edition. New York: MacMillan, 1965.

Pratt, Mary Louise. 1991. "Arts of the Contact Zone." *Profession*. Accessed September 12, 2020. https://www.jstor.org/stable/25595469.

Ross, Nancy L. 2018. "The 'Plasticene' Epoch?." *Elements*, vol. 14, no. 5: 291. October 01, 2018. Doi: https://doi.org/10.2138/gselements.14.5.291

Tolkien, J. R. R. 1965. *The Return of the King*. Part 3 of *The Lord of the Rings*. Second edition. Boston, MA: Houghton Mifflin.

Vance, Jack. 1950. *The Dying Earth*. New York: Hillman.

Williams, Raymond. 1977. *Marxism and Literature*. Oxford and New York: Oxford University Press.

CHAPTER 3
WHO KNOWS WHERE THE TIME GOES?
Nisi Shawl

When I announced this anthology's topic to my co-writing group, we laughed long and hard at the idea of going up against Exxon and the like armed with no more powerful weapon than literature. "Four or five novels ought to do it," one woman snarked.

But operating on the assumption that it really *is* possible to write what Octavia Butler called "change-the-world fiction," the next thing to figure out is how we're supposed to do that.

Per a beautifully succinct essay by Steven Barnes, the Three Questions the science fictional variety of fantastic storytelling asks are "What if?" "If only …," and "If this goes on—". Of course, only the first of these is actually a question; it would be more accurate to talk about "The Three Speculations." Also, unlike the king in Leo Tolstoy's short story also named "The Three Questions," we readers believe ourselves fortunate in receiving a multitude of answers. None of them cancel any of the others out. All are meaningful. All are valid.

When it comes to adopting approaches for preventing human-driven climate change, authors can easily opt for spreading the dystopic warnings that come from wondering what happens "If this goes on." Bleak scenarios extrapolated from current trends are foundational to much of science fiction. Think of all those tales about extraterrestrial colony missions mandated by the pollution/resource exhaustion of Earth. And in fact we continue to read and write warning stories—post-apocalypses, totalitarian societies intolerant of nature, "new normal" backdrops filled with drowned coastlines and mass extinctions. The problem with portraying dystopias, as was recently pointed out to me by another author, is that they're sometimes used as blueprints.

Stories based on the "If only … " line of thought are almost always alternate history, and "If only … " "eco-spec" focuses on climate change turning points. I've written my share of that sort of thing. Set in the same milieu as my novel *Everfair*, "Sun River" is about the attempted sabotage of a solar collector modeled on one actually built in Cairo at the turn of the twentieth century; "The Colors of Money" is about the choice between drilling for oil under the ocean and farming it on an island.

"Colors" appeared in an anthology called *Sunvault: Stories of Solarpunk and Eco-Speculation*. It seems a bit out of place in that book, honestly, because a lot of the fiction and poetry included there addresses the first and broadest of the Three Questions, the one that simply asks, "What if?" What if we used augmented reality to support our climate change protests? What if we had a time machine and could thwart ecological catastrophes before they occur?

But here's an issue I've been wrestling with: What do you call alternate history that takes place in the future? As I say, I write a fair share of "If only … " fiction. And there are certain stories of mine which follow the evolution of an imaginary activist movement, The Five Petals of Thought, that I've set ten years from now. Also, though the *Everfair* sequel I'm working on now (a novel titled *Kinning*) only covers the first half of the 1920s, I've already published *its* sequel, "Slippernet," and that's set after the next US presidential election. So how to label this category? Alternate future? Timeslip? Conditional fiction? Call it what you will, it's what I love.

It's what I really, really love to do, and it's what I plan to keep on doing. Despite the attraction of appearing sage-like in the wake of writing a particularly prescient "If this goes on—" sort of story; despite the freewheeling giddiness of giving myself permission to imagine any "What if?" in the multiverse; I'm happiest swimming in the uncertain currents, the deep waters of "If only … " And if those waters tug me in directions contrary to the ways most people think time flows, I'm still giving in to them. I'm going wherever and whenever they take me.

Who really knows where the time goes? Who knows where it's been? Philadelphia-based artist and author Rasheedah Phillips has declared that time is a lie. It's at the very least a dream, or perhaps it's a shared delusion—however potentially useful that dream or delusion can be. If I write an alternate history, or alternate future, or any sort of rumination building on "The Three Speculations"—say one in which greenhouse gas emissions never reach crisis levels—and you like my version of reality better? Then make it so.

CHAPTER 4
PLAYING WITH THE TROUBLE: CHILDREN AND THE ANTHROPOCENE IN NNEDI OKORAFOR'S AKATA WITCH SERIES

Lindsay Burton

Fantasy literature grounds itself in what Ursula K. Le Guin refers to as "green country" (2007, 86), a space in which animals, nature, and the unknown Other enjoy a power equal to or greater than that of humans. Tolkien's Middle Earth, Le Guin notes, "is not just pre-industrial. It is also pre-human and non-human" and her own fantasy world of Earthsea suggests that "modern humanity is in exile, shut out from a community, an intimacy, it once knew" (2007). These features suggest fantasy worlds as vehicles for making sense of the Anthropocene, an era in which nature, as a "separate and wild province" (McKibben 2003, 48), has been driven to extinction by humanity's overabundant industrialism. Yet green country's presence alone does not teach us how to address the challenges posed by the Anthropocene. Indeed, at the end of the *Lord of the Rings* trilogy, the nature-oriented elves and wizards remove themselves from Middle Earth, despite Frodo's victory over the evil, industrial Sauron. Middle Earth's magic has departed, leaving behind a world in which the only magic left, a small box of magic dust, has been pastoralized, gardened into submission by Samwise Gamgee. If the Anthropocene presents the separation between humanity and nature as problematic, then the distance between Middle Earth or Earthsea's humans and their local green country only amplifies that problem. The question that persists is whether or not fantasy literature, imbued as it is with green country, can bridge that problematic separation and thus appropriately make sense of the challenges presented by an Anthropocenic future—and if it can, how it might go about doing so.

The challenge to conceptualize and address with literature the problems posed by the Anthropocene is not limited to the fantasy genre. As Adam Trexler and Adeline Johns-Putra describe, "Climate change is as culturally as it is scientifically complex. It possesses an immensity of scale both spatially (as a global event) and temporally (as an unprecedented crisis in human history). ... Its solutions require network and negotiation, not magic bullets nor heroes" (2011, 2). Of course, many modern narratives rely on heroic protagonists to generate plot and conflict. Even fantastic narratives that seem focused on the consequences of climate change—one thinks of the globe-spanning superstorms featured in the film *The Day after Tomorrow* (Emmerich 2004)—cannot seem to capture the "slow violence" (Nixon 2011, 2) of climate change. Rob Nixon frames the problem as a question: "In an age when the media venerate the spectacular ... how can we convert into image and narrative the disasters that are slow-moving and long in the making, disasters that are anonymous and that star nobody ... to the sensation-driven technologies of our image-world?" (3).

In this chapter, I respond to Nixon's question by considering how Donna Haraway's theory of "staying with the trouble" (1) as an approach to the Anthropocene transforms into a livelier "playing" with the trouble when applied to fantasy literature for young people, in particular *Akata Witch* (2011) and *Akata Warrior* (2017) by Nigerian-American author Nnedi Okorafor. Haraway makes a case for confronting problems such as climate change, mass species extinction, and human overpopulation by staying with the trouble, which "requires learning to be truly present, not as a vanishing pivot between awful or edenic pasts and apocalyptic or salvific futures, but as mortal critters entwined in myriad unfinished configurations of places, times, matters, meanings" (2017). Yet I find the staidness of the word "stay" troublesome when considering the utility of literature as a tool to address Anthropocenic concerns. I argue that Okorafor's reimagining of conflict, nature, and humanity's role as residents of planet Earth through the adventures of protagonist Sunny and her friends provides readers with a useful template not only to *stay* with the trouble of the Anthropocene, but to *play* with that trouble. Playing with the trouble, an act expressed by Okorafor's group of young protagonists, involves engaging with the trouble and pain presented by the Anthropocene without disengaging from temporality and change. Through my analysis, I propose that the young characters in *Akata Witch* and *Akata Warrior* transform Haraway's concept of "staying with the trouble" into a vibrant magical game of playing with the trouble—that is, of acting in interfering ways within the context of the Anthropocene that mitigate its damage and make it more livable. By focusing my analysis on novels that center young people, both in narration and in intended audience, I also push back against Haraway's slogan for remaining active against Anthropocenic pressures: "Make Kin, Not Babies!" (102). I aim to demonstrate that the process of growth and maturation central to YA narratives like Okorafor's can provide a more engaging and relatable understanding of how we might be able to grow and change within an Anthropocenic context. I argue that just as Haraway reinterprets the human-centered term "Anthropocene" as the critter-oriented Chthulucene, so too do I use *Akata Witch* and *Akata Warrior* to reinterpret Haraway's call to "Make Kin, Not Babies" in a way that does not harmfully exclude the child—a being often defined temporally (e.g., Nikolajeva 2000; Beauvais 2015)—from conversations about the future. The irony, of course, is that today's and tomorrow's children will face the difficult realities of climate change and the Anthropocene at an ever-increasing rate. If anyone's literature should be taken into account with respect to the slow violence of climate change, it is surely theirs.

Learning from Troublesome Teens: The Utility of YA Literature

YA literature—as opposed to fantasy literature for younger children, or even for adults—possesses a particular utility when it comes to dealing with the Anthropocene, arising from the liminality of its intended audience's age. The phrases "teenager" and "adolescent" demarcate a physically, psychologically, and socially volatile time in the human lifespan, represented in publishing by the phrase "young adult." Hilton and Nikolajeva argue that regardless of the development of real teenagers, authors use the construction of adolescence in YA fiction as "a focus for adult anxiety" (2012, 1)—not only adult anxiety about teenagers themselves, whose newfound capacity for choice and independence poses a threat to adult supremacy, but also adult anxiety about "different forms of cultural alienation … the legacy of colonialism, political injustice, environmental desecration, sexual stereotyping, consumerism, madness, and death" (2012). The range of these anxieties, combined with the relative closeness of teens to adulthood, makes YA fiction a better platform for the difficult and mature themes than fiction for younger children, including the significant threat of human extinction heralded by the Anthropocene. Yet, unlike much adult literature, YA literature maintains some of the hopeful optimism commonly associated with children's literature. In the tumultuousness of adolescence, I argue, we find a potent literary representation of authentic hope in the face of equally authentic destruction that has much to teach us about Anthropocentric presents and futures.

YA fantasy, along with the rest of the fantasy genre, has not always been considered first or best at providing representations of Anthropocenic disaster or humanity's response to it. Trexler and Johns-Putra acknowledge that producing better representations of the Anthropocene "may require a shift in emphasis from literary fiction to genre fiction" (2011, 1), but they limit their evaluation of that shift to science fiction. However, there's evidence, including this very volume, that fantasy is on the border of entering into discussions of the Anthropocene. YA fantasy's liminality also extends to real YA fantasy audiences. Between 2014 and 2017, juvenile fantasy fiction sales outpaced adult fantasy and science-fiction sales four to one: on the order of fifty-two million units sold, compared to adult fantasy and science fiction's twelve million (Wilkins 2019, 1). This effect is one instance of what Henry Jenkins terms *convergence culture*, the "migratory behavior of media audiences who will go almost anywhere in search of the kinds of entertainment experiences they want" (2006, 2), which in this case includes a genre traditionally intended for young people. YA fantasy's vast and varied readership holds the possibility of significant social awareness and tangible financial impact, if and when the right story comes along.

Despite these unique, age-defying features, YA fantasy remains literature produced for individuals defined as "children," at least in several material and discursive ways. As Roberta Trites describes, "Books for adolescents are subversive—but sometimes only superficially so. In fact, they are often quite didactic; the denouements of many Young Adult novels contain a direct message about what the narrator has learned" (2000, x). It is common in YA studies to debate the merits of YA fiction's special mixture of subversiveness and didacticism. Here, however, I want to sidestep that argument and acknowledge that in the face of the Anthropocene we must all learn to subvert the systemic ways of being and thinking that have led us to our current predicament.

"This world is bigger than you": Playing with Troublesome Magic

At first glance, the Akata Witch duology presents a standard heroic narrative arc of the sort described by Trexler and Johns-Putra as unhelpful in the face of the Anthropocene. Our protagonist is Sunny, an albino Nigerian-American girl, who discovers that she is a "free agent Leopard Person" (2011, 52), i.e., a magic user from a non-magical family. All Leopard people possess unique magical skills rooted in their physiology; as an albino, Sunny is precognitive, and the first novel opens with Sunny seeing a vision of global destruction in the light of a candle: "I'd seen the end of the world in its flame. Raging fires, boiling oceans, toppled skyscrapers, ruptured land, dead and dying people. It was horrible. And it was coming" (2). After being initiated into Leopard Society, Sunny is tasked with defeating Ekwensu, a powerful Igbo spirit who manifests through a masquerade. Ekwensu plans on bringing Sunny's vision of destruction into the real one from the spiritual, other-worldly "wilderness" (116) she normally inhabits. Ekwensu, with an "oily, greasy smell, like car exhaust" (Okorafor 2017, 214), calls to mind the ecological devastation caused by global reliance on oil consumption. Like human-triggered climate change, Ekwensu, who is ushered into the real world by a powerful Leopard person named Black Hat Otokoto, "would turn the world into the apocalyptic place Sunny had seen in the candle's flame" (432). These references, scattered across both novels, underpin a standard plot in which the heroic Sunny defeats Ekwensu, an avatar of Anthropocenic destruction, to save the world and avert the apocalypse. However, several elements of the Akata Witch series serve to decentralize Ekwensu and her environmental apocalypse in the larger narrative. An examination of Okorafor's world-building of the Leopard People and their society, of the existence of Sunny's *oha* coven, and of the continuation of Sunny's narrative arc beyond her defeat of Ekwensu, demonstrates the significant Anthropocenic trouble that will remain central to Sunny's world—and ours—after Ekwensu is eliminated. This examination will also illuminate the tools Okorafor offers her readers to stay, and play, with that trouble.

Despite the Leopard people's own liminality between the real world and the wilderness, Leopard society views individuals who exist in liminal spaces as troublesome figures. In particular, Sunny's role as a free agent comes with the baggage of stereotypes; the "annoyingly prejudiced" (Okorafor 2017, 89) guidebook *Fast Facts for Free Agents*, which features as a paratextual device throughout *Akata Witch*, consistently implies that free agents are needy, unintelligent, and unskilled at magic. This manual functions as a consistent paratextual reminder of Sunny's general frustration at her sudden immersion into unfamiliar Leopard societal norms, a situation in which she feels like and is sometimes treated as an interloper. Yet, *Fast Facts for Free Agents* is itself treated ambiguously by Sunny's teacher, Anatov, who describes how the book's author, Isong Abong Effiong Isong, learned her attitude toward free agents while studying in Europe and the Americas:

> "While there, she developed the idea that free agents like you, Sunny, are the scourge of the Earth. She believed them ignorant and misguided. … " He paused. "Prejudice begets prejudice, you see. Knowledge does not always evolve into wisdom." … "What a bitch," Chichi said.
> "But useful," Anatov emphasized.
>
> (Okorafor 2011, 113)

Anatov's attitude toward *Fast Facts* encapsulates the tension in Sunny's narrative between two central yet conflicting truths: "Fact Facts" is prejudiced and imperfect but also useful and therefore worth Sunny's time. The flawed manual also outlines the many interferences of the Lamb, or non-magical world with the Leopard one. Despite Leopard society holding a low opinion of Lambs—indicated in no small part by their respective names—and despite prescribing severe punishment for any Leopard person caught doing overt magic in front of Lambs, Leopard society remains ensconced in non-magical geopolitical tensions. Anatov's aphoristic observation underscores the seriousness of the trouble caused by prejudiced attitudes; his reminder that utility must regardless be derived even from flawed sources forces Sunny not only to *stay* with these imperfections but to *play* with them. She must learn to bend the rules predicated on those imperfections in order to further her own goals and those of the *oha* coven.

The motif of using play to glean the value from a troublesome situation not only becomes a constant theme of Sunny's development but also emerges as the bedrock of Leopard society. She and her three friends—Efik Chichi, Igbo Orlu, and African-American Sasha—comprise an *oha* coven, "a group of mystical combination, set up to defend against something bad" (Okorafor 2011, 84). All four children have a penchant for creating trouble: sometimes, as with Sunny being a free agent, through their ignorance of Leopard society norms; sometimes, as with Chichi's and Sasha's rule breaking, through their ambitious intentions; and sometimes through their juju, or magical, abilities, as with Orlu who can take apart any juju with his hands. Even though the *oha* coven are Ekwensu's main combatants, their lives are so devalued by Leopard adults—and their mistakes met with such strict punishment—that their status as "heroes" is relegated to the background. Anatov summarizes their relative unimportance at the start of their first lesson, a mission inside the dangerous Night Runner Forest, with an admonishment: "Fear? Get used to it. There will be danger; some of you may not live to complete your lessons. It's a risk you take. This world is bigger than you and it will go on, regardless" (118–19). Sunny's silent follow-up question, "What kind of thing is that to tell your students?" (119), highlights her discomfort with the disposability of her life for Leopard adults. Yet, she must stay with this discomfort throughout both narratives, and play through it in order to remain a part of Leopard society. In doing so, Sunny and the *oha* coven recuperate the figure of the child into Haraway's conceptualization of "playing games of string figures," in which "multispecies players, who are enmeshed … redo ways of living and dying" (2016, 10). Their own enmeshment, with each other and with other species, relegates the classic hero's story to one drama out of many, because the world—and the Anthropocene—is bigger than any individual hero.

Spirit Faces and Doubling: The Trouble of Dual Identities

Liminality implies duality; a border cannot exist without something on either side of it. Correspondingly, Leopard society is full of dualities: between the real world and wilderness, between the magical Leopard world and the non-magic world of Lambs, and most crucially, between a Leopard person's self and their spirit face. A Leopard person's spirit-face is one of the primary sources of their magic. When a Leopard person's spirit-face is visible, they "cannot lie or hide anything. Lies are a thing of the physical world. They can't exist in the spirit world" (Okorafor 2011, 65). The physical, mortal self that is capable of lying and the magical, truth-bound, immortal self are shown to cohabit a single body, making ontological duality the Leopard people's default mode of existence. This duality is often hard to handle but pushes Sunny and the *oha* coven to learn to play with the troubles complexity presents.

Sunny lives between two worlds even before she enters into Leopardom: she is Black and albino, American and Nigerian, and a girl who loves to play soccer. Her relationship with Anyanwu extends that duality in ways that both benefit and challenge her. Physically, the duality between Sunny and Anyanwu is far less pronounced. Anyanwu, whose name means "eye of the sun" in the Igbo language, is an avatar of "the sun, all shiny gold and slowing with pointy rays" (93), all of which markers correlate with Sunny's name and albinism that gives her "light yellow hair [and] skin the color of 'sour milk' (or so stupid people like to tell me)" (3). As an albino, Sunny is unable to stand in direct sunlight without an umbrella, but once she becomes aware of Anyanwu's presence, she develops immunity to ultraviolet radiation. Sunny benefits tremendously from this protection, not only for medical reasons but also because she was previously limited to playing soccer at night. Sunny's relationship with Anyanwu also gives Sunny a greater ability to "play" the games of Leopard society: without Anyanwu, Sunny cannot even enter magically guarded locations such as Leopard Knocks or the Obi Library. Anyanwu provides Sunny with increased confidence, particularly when Anyanwu's face is brought forth: "[Sunny's] voice was deep and throaty, like some sultry, glamorous woman … When she got up, her movements felt effortless, amazing, full of poise and grace" (Okorafor 2011, 50). If Sunny's Lamb existence was marked by hiding in the shade, her spirit-face persona allows her to exude power. It holds the promise of personal, social, and magical mastery.

Beyond the physical aspect, however, the Sunny-Anyanwu's duality is troublesome. Sunny must fight to understand the irreconcilable paradox of Sunny-Anyanwu's existence: "All through the night, she battled herself. Or battled to know herself. She fell apart and then put herself back together and then she fell apart again and put herself back together, over and over" (93). Even though Sunny makes it through that first difficult night, her battle against herself and to know herself persists throughout both novels. The stress of balancing dual identities reaches a crescendo when Ekwensu strikes her with a magical bead in a moment of weakness that separates Sunny from Anyanwu. This act is "called doubling. It sounds like a misnomer because you have lost a part of yourself, but your spirit face is just not here. So in a sense, you've been doubled. Ekwensu did it to you" (Okorafor 2017, 225). The timing of Sunny's doubling is no coincidence, either; it takes place just as Ekwensu emerges from the wilderness into the real world, creating the oil spill that Sunny watches on television. Sunny's doubled state initially prevents her from accessing her magic. Nor can it be reversed. As Sunny's old mentor Sugar Cream tells her: "To be doubled is very sad … Death is always close by, but for you, he will always stand behind you" (467). In a sense, Sunny's doubling is the most Anthropocenic of the many dualities she faces as a Leopard person: its tragedy stems from a force of environmental destruction, and like the oil spill in the Niger Delta, it cannot be undone. The fact of her doubling will always interfere with the sense of confidence and poise Anyanwu brought to Sunny; as with humanity's relationship with climate change, neither self-confidence nor an optimistic attitude cannot overcome the damage that has been done. Sunny must live with the reality of her doubling for the rest of her life, knowing that it has brought death closer to her than it otherwise would be.

Despite the dire prognosis of her situation, Sunny chooses to play with liminality to transform her doubling from a weakness into a strength. Sunny learns that her natural ability to walk in the wilderness—an ability derived from her albinism, not from Anyanwu—has saved her life, as doubling normally kills those afflicted. Sunny is also given advice on how to coax Anyanwu back to her, even though they cannot be fully joined again: "Sunny, you need Anyanwu. That old one is like an *ogbanje*. Tempt her back to you with love" (2017, 235). An *ogbanje* is an Igbo version of a changeling, a child spirit that comes and goes, leaving sadness in its wake; this description is the key to Sunny's ability to coax Anyanwu back, as it indicates Anyanwu's own duality of being a very old spirit but also a childlike one. Sunny's approach to calling Anyanwu to her demonstrates the power of childhood love over that of old, experienced magic: Sunny engages in all of her favorite hobbies, including cooking with her mother, reading a graphic novel, listening to Mozart, and imagining her favorite ballerina dancing, and finally, playing soccer.

This last activity, which makes "her heart leap with a familiar joy" (232) finally calls Anyanwu back, but not before Sunny experiences the power of play first-hand:

> All alone under the churning sunless sky, she enjoyed her own footwork, imagining that she was playing a one-on-one game against herself. … She did a bump and run, shoving herself out of the way and then taking off with the ball across the field. She laughed, because it had almost felt like she'd shoved someone. She'd shot the ball directly at the goal when she realized it. And her realization was immediately verified when the ball didn't go in. Instead, it was deflected by a seemingly invisible force.
>
> Then the force became visible, and Sunny thought for a moment lightning had struck the field. (2017, 239)

The "churning sunless sky" reflects Sunny's own doubled and troubled state without Anyanwu, but instead of being concerned by it, she "enjoyed her own footwork" instead. Her "one-on-one game against herself" is a far cry from the crisis she experienced upon discovering Anyanwu, during which she spent an entire night falling apart and putting herself back together again, physically, emotionally, and mentally. When she plays with her trouble, she transforms a lethal crisis a moment of self-discovery. The lightning strike of Anyanwu appearing in front of her is akin to the sensation of deep insight. Sunny realizes that while she must stay with her troubles, she does not *only* have to stay with them. In fact, her troubles are more bearable when she *plays* with them instead. There can be no resolution to Sunny-Anyanwu's doubling, just as there can be no resolution to the many paradoxes and dualities present in the Anthropocene. Haraway's approach to staying with these troubles is "not interested in reconciliation or restoration, but [is] deeply committed to the more modest possibilities of partial recuperation and getting on together" (2016, 10). However, Sunny's engagement suggests that playing with these troubles—facing them with self-care, bravery, and perhaps even some competitiveness— productively blurs the line between "getting on together" and "reconciliation." It improves our approach to "the trouble" beyond merely modest possibilities.

Spiders and Webs: Playing with Storytelling Juju

In Leopard society the particular duality of truth and lies is perhaps best expressed in the realm of storytelling. Through storytelling, an earlier cousin of reading-based knowledge-acquisition, Sunny cements the value of playing with the trouble. We have already seen one example of a troublesome book that acts as a key source of information for Sunny in *Fast Facts for Free Agents*. A closer look at Leopard society's interwoven system of reading, learning, and storytelling demonstrates that even the tools used to stay and play with the trouble are themselves sources of trouble, as stories provide the best way forward into the troublesome Anthropocenic era.

Sunny's path to becoming a storyteller is a tangled web of interlocked circumstances. Along with *Fast Facts*, Sunny purchases a book written in the magical Nsibidi language. Nsibidi writing is peculiar: when reading Nsibidi, the story's sights, sounds, smells, and physical sensations become a lived reality for the reader. As a result, reading Nsibidi exacts a stiff physical toll on the reader, draining them of their energy and, in extreme cases, their life. Yet Nsibidi becomes a crucial component not only of Sunny's quest to defeat Ekwensu, but also of her own difficult journey of self-discovery. Sunny's Leopard grandmother, who died before Sunny was born, left a Nsibidi letter for Sunny that assists her in finding the magical city of Osisi, where her final battle against Ekwensu takes place. Like *Fast Facts*, things written in Nsibidi present a troublesome challenge that, when faced and embraced, can result in significant gains for the reader.

Being able to read Nsibidi is rare, and the book's author, Sugar Cream, takes on Sunny as a student because of Sunny's affinity for Nsibidi. Sugar Cream's tutelage is even rarer than fluency in Nsibidi; Sunny would be "one and only student" Sugar Cream would ever mentor (Okorafor 2011, 190). Yet, Sunny meets with Sugar Cream for the first time not to discuss Nsibidi but to receive punishment for showing her spirit-face to a Lamb, an act which is forbidden by Leopard Society laws. Rare and full of trouble, Sunny's mentorship with Sugar Cream feels fated to end in disaster, as Sunny's liminal transgressions constantly disappoint her mentor. Even after Sunny and the *oha* coven have defeated Ekwensu, Sugar Cream and the rest of the Leopard Council, the ruling authority of the Leopard people, bring the children in for questioning and for punishment over the accidental involvement of Sunny's Lamb brother, Chukwu, in their magical activities. To defend their actions and save their magical animal companion Grashcoatah from execution, Sunny launches into a long story of their journey and the choices they made while on it, including their choice to involve Chukwu: "She was shaking, but it wasn't from fear; she felt she would burst if she didn't say what she desperately wanted to say. She told them everything, from the beginning to the current moment. ... Not long after that, the four of them were told that they could go" (Okorafor 2017, 466–7). Sunny's ability to tell the story of their journey is the only thing, throughout both novels, that is shown to prevent the Leopard Council's life-threatening punishments, which makes it matter more to her status as a Leopard person, to the *oha* coven, and to Grashcoatah's life than anything, even their defeat of Ekwensu.

Sugar Cream is not Sunny's only, or even best, storytelling mentor; Sunny learns as much or more about storytelling from Udide, the Igbo trickster spider deity (Okorafor 2018), and her descendants, many of whom live in Sugar Cream's office as poisonous red spiders. The spiders are another source of fear and anxiety for Sunny. Their constant presence represents a punishment ready to be doled out as soon as Sunny steps out of line. Yet during the worst of her awaited paybacks, while she is locked in the dangerous Obi Library basement as punishment for showing her magical abilities to a Lamb student, Sunny gains the trust of these red spiders, whose mother is named Ogwu. I note here that animals can also be Leopard people, as in the case of Grashcoatah, Ogwu and her children, and all cats. Ogwu has also been condemned to languish in the basement for a magical mistake that she made:

"You were on the plane," Sunny said. "The Enola Gay. I know. You were on the bomb, and you tried to weave the storytelling juju your people are most known for. You wove a thick thread that was supposed to cause the bomb not to work when they dropped it on Hiroshima. But when you attached it, you misspoke one of the binding words, and it snapped when the bomb was released. You failed and no one has seen you since. So, this basement is where you came with all your descendants to hide from the world."

(Okorafor 2017, 168–9)

Although Ogwu initially wishes to harm Sunny, Sunny uses her own "storytelling juju" to convince Ogwu to help her survive the dangerous basement by telling her the story of her quest to defeat Ekwensu. By saving Sunny, Ogwu is "[given a] chance to finally act, to *play a role*" (174, emphasis mine), for which she is saved by Udide and freed from the basement. Playing means acting, and this playful engagement with storytelling becomes a direct conduit to life-saving action, action which works to continue and resolve different threads of the story: Sunny resolve's Ogwu's story, and Ogwu continues Sunny's story, in a web-like configuration of cause and effect.

Storytelling's ability to play with trouble emerges again in Sunny's interactions with Udide herself. Udide, even more so than Ogwu and Sugar Cream, is a fearsome force that can only be quelled by storytelling; indeed, Udide surpasses all of Sunny's other sources of trouble, due to her power and her literal and figurative control over Sunny's narrative: "Udide is the ultimate artist, the Great Hairy Spider, brimming with venom, stories, and ideas. Sometimes she is a he and sometimes he is a she; it depends on Udide's mood" (Okorafor 2011, 144). A version of the classic trickster god from Igbo folklore, symbolizing duality, ambiguity, and storytelling, Udide provides assistance necessary in the *oha* coven's quest to defeat Ekwensu. Sunny's final battle against Ekwensu takes place in the magical city of Osisi, which can only be reached with a flying grasscutter, a magical creature that only Udide can make. For this purpose, Sunny and the coven visit Udide in her underground lair in Lagos. Because Udide treats the coven's mission as a game—one whose rules the children must learn as they play—Sunny learns that only by playing can existential trouble be tackled. As her game "move," Sunny chooses to tell Udide a brand-new story of a being called *akata*—a Nigerian term for "bush animal" but "used to refer to black Americans or foreign-born blacks. A very, very rude word" (11). In another web of cause and effect, Sunny's risky move wins the game for the *oha* coven, leads to Udide's creation of Grashcoatah, and leads to Sunny later having to tell another story to the Council in order to save Grashcoatah's life. The entire episode illustrates what Haraway calls "tentacular thinking" in which "tentacular ones [are those who] make attachments and detachments; [who] make a difference; [who] weave paths and consequences but not determinisms" (2016, 49–50). The *oha* coven's stories and paths position them as tentacular ones, entangled in the production of "the patterning of possible worlds and possible times … gone, here, and yet to come" (2016), which is precisely what humans must learn to do within the context of the Anthropocene.

Udide's game also exists outside the narrative, appearing in the margins of Sunny's story through *Udide's Book of Shadows*, which Sasha finds on the same shopping trip during which Sunny finds *Fast Facts* and her Nsibidi book. Only a few copies of the *Book of Shadows* exist, and Udide chooses who will find it through mysterious, unseen means. Once purchased, the book (and Udide) infringes on the reader's senses like Nsibidi does, although Udide's version of this infiltration occurs while the reader is asleep: "[Sunny] must not have put the book far enough away because her dreams were full of scuttling and cartwheeling spiders" (Okorafor 2017, 317). Udide's marginal presence becomes physically embodied when Udide's spider children sting Sunny and Chichi during their meeting in Lagos. Udide warns them as they part that "The venom of my people is in both of you now. It will never leave you. It has decoded and bonded to your DNA. I can find you anywhere. I will know where you are at all times" (354). Udide's move here has ambiguous results; after Sunny and the coven defeat Ekwensu, Sunny and Chichi are approached by Udide and instructed to embark on a different kind of quest, the details of which remain vague and likely to be addressed in a future sequel. This narrative turn indicates Udide's—and storytelling's—deep control over Sunny's path. At the same time, this molecular bond between Sunny and Udide can be seen to account for Sunny's increase in storytelling prowess, as she is ultimately able to convince the Council of the coven's innocence. Whether it stems from Udide or not, Sunny's "tentacular thinking"—her fluency in Nsibidi, her commitment to self-narrative, and her bravery in the face of competing stories of her demise—represent her primary set of moves in the game of being a Leopard person. She enacts these moves to pattern a world, to tell a story, of survival and thriving for herself and her coven in the face of possible extinction. Sunny's stories—the ones she tells to others, the one she tells to us—are also stories for how to thrive in the perpetually troublesome Anthropocene.

Conclusion: Youth as Valuable Kin

When Sunny and the *oha* coven play with the trouble—through storytelling, ambiguous figuring, and at times, literal play—they demonstrate the short-sightedness of Donna Haraway's plea that we "Make Kin Not Babies!" (2016, 102). Initially, Haraway's reconceptualization of the Anthropocene as the Chthulucene seems supportive of Sunny's story, since it draws on Udide herself, on "the diverse earthwide tentacular powers and forces and collected things with names like … Spider Woman" (101). Where the word "Anthropocene" centers man, "Chthulucene" centers networked webs of "people and other critters" (3). Yet when its motto is "Make Kin, Not Babies!," Haraway's Chthulucene subtly excludes young people as critters, relegating them as a problematic and integral part of the "Great Acceleration of human numbers" (6). While not explicitly rejecting children as kin, Haraway's commitment to a future with far fewer humans implies a future with far fewer children. I'm cautious about throwing the bathwater out with the baby, so to speak; if human numbers must decrease, we must correspondingly work to preserve the learning, growth, and change associated with youth and youth literature, as demonstrated here in Okorafor's novels. Sunny and the *oha* coven show us that a learner's approach can elevate the practice of staying with the trouble from an exercise in meditating under a metaphorical waterfall—or, as Sunny experienced it, falling apart and putting ourselves back together again under the pressure of the Anthropocene—to the more intimate, achievable, and dare I say *enjoyable* activity of playing with the trouble.

Playing with the trouble involves telling stories about it, stories that remain, as Okorafor puts it, "part of a long story of humanity" (2017, 342) even as they're being told to spider gods to create magical critters with whom to co-exist. Although Haraway insists that "it matters which stories tell stories" (2016, 101), she forgets that amongst humans, stories told by children and for children are not the same as stories told by and for adults. Sometimes, stories told by children are required to make kin and to *save* kin, as in the case of Grashcoatah, whose creation is paid for by Sunny's *akata* story and whose life is saved by the *oha* coven. Playing with the trouble involves small, daily actions in the face of permanent liminality. Sunny must continue to learn about magic and improve herself as a Leopard person despite the constant dual worlds she must negotiate. Most subversively, playing with the trouble involves literal play, at which children excel more than any other human. As Sunny demonstrates, merely staying with the trouble is insufficient in the long run. Staying with the trouble for more than a moment requires looking that trouble in the eye and bumping yourself out of the way in a fierce game of self-on-self soccer. Haraway says that we must make kin, not babies, but Sunny teaches us that young people *are* kin. As such, they can offer insight and improvement to the staid narrative norms of adulthood through their own approaches to the trouble. If the advent of the Chthulucene requires human Terrans to become citizens of our own local green country, we may well benefit from the examples of magical young kin like Sunny and the *oha* coven as we embark on that collective journey.

References

Badmington, Neil, ed. 2000. *Posthumanism*. Readers in Cultural Criticism. Houndmills, Basingstoke, Hampshire and New York: Palgrave.

Beauvais, Clémentine. 2015. *The Mighty Child: Time and Power in Children's Literature*. Amsterdam and Philadelphia, PA: John Benjamins Publishing Company.

Emmerich, Roland, dir. 2004. *The Day after Tomorrow*. Twentieth Century Fox, Centropolis Entertainment, Lions Gate Films.

Ford, Jennifer. 2016. "Taboo Teens and Ancient Adults: Overpopulation Motifs in Fictional Literature for Children and Young People." *Oxford Literary Review*, vol. 38, no. 1: 27–46.

Haraway, Donna. 1997. *Modest-Witness@Second-Millennium.FemaleMan-Meets-OncoMouse: Feminism and Technoscience*. New York: Routledge.

Haraway, Donna. 2004a. "A Manifesto for Cyborgs: Science, Technology, and Socialist Feminism in the 1980s." In *The Haraway Reader*, 7–45. New York: Routledge.

Haraway, Donna. 2004b. "The Promises of Monsters: A Regenerative Politics for Inappropriate/d Others." In *The Haraway Reader*, edited by Donna Haraway, 63–124. New York: Routledge.

Haraway, Donna. 2016. *Staying with the Trouble: Making Kin in the Chthulucene*. Durham, NC: Duke University Press.

Hilton, Mary, and Maria Nikolajeva, eds. 2012. *Contemporary Adolescent Literature and Culture: The Emergent Adult*. Ashgate Studies in Childhood, 1700 to the Present. Farnham: Ashgate.

Jaques, Zoe. 2015. *Children's Literature and the Posthuman: Animal, Environment, Cyborg*. New York: Routledge.

Jenkins, Henry. 2006. *Convergence Culture: Where Old and New Media Collide. Fulcrum.Org*. New York: New York University Press.

Le Guin, Ursula K. 2007. "The Critics, the Monsters, and the Fantasists." *The Wordsworth Circle*, vol. 38, no. 1/2: 83–7.

McKibben, Bill. 2003. *The End of Nature*. 2nd Revised edition. London: Bloomsbury Publishing.

Nikolajeva, Maria. 2000. *From Mythic to Linear: Time in Children's Literature*. Lanham, MD: Children's Literature Association: Scarecrow Press.

Nixon, Rob. 2011. *Slow Violence and the Environmentalism of the Poor*. Cambridge, MA: Harvard University Press.

Okorafor, Nnedi. 2011. *Akata Witch*. New York: Viking Children's Books.

Okorafor, Nnedi. 2017. *Akata Warrior*. New York: Penguin Random House USA.

Okorafor, Nnedi. 2018. "Nnedi Okorafor, PhD on Twitter: @raganwald @MissTariN I Don't Write about Anansi. I Wrote about the Igbo Spider Deity Udide. Yup, Anansi Isn't the Only African Trickster Spider." June 29, 2018, 6:47 p.m. https://twitter.com/nnedi/status/1012739365389438976.

Trexler, Adam, and Adeline Johns-Putra. 2011. "Climate Change in Literature and Literary Criticism." *Wiley Interdisciplinary Reviews: Climate Change*, vol. 2, no. 2: 185–200.

Trites, Roberta Seelinger. 2000. *Disturbing the Universe: Power and Repression in Adolescent Literature*. Iowa City: University of Iowa Press.

Wilkins, Kim. 2019. *Young Adult Fantasy Fiction: Conventions, Originality, Reproducibility*. 1st ed. Cambridge: Cambridge University Press.

CHAPTER 5
REWRITE
Katherine Applegate

As once again
a plague descends—
our punishment,
our reprieve—
we bang our kettles
in the evening breeze,
busy with fear,
deafened by loss.
Six feet apart.
Six feet under.
This is not a time for
nuance.

Sly earth, meanwhile,
has other plans.

Coyotes
stroll the freeway.
Geese cruise
the Strip,
confident goslings
trailing.

Fish stripe
Venice canals
while jellyfish,
impossibly,
balloon.

The sky unmasks,
fresh slate
chalked with clouds,
proud with hawks and
endless.

We are lost,
say the pundits.

Fantasy and Myth in the Anthropocene

We are dying,
say the papers.
But if every story has been told
then each can be retold,
tweaked, erased,
savaged or
soothed.

It's only a draft,
rough and wrong,
I tell our children.
Tell it again,
this time truly.
This time let it
weep and breathe
and sing.
This time
be gracious.

Here is the only thing to know:
writing is rewriting,
humbling, solitary.
Stories are sighs
and pencil dust,
but they are supple, too,
and sometimes even
merciful.

Take the gift of these hard days,
seek our redemption,
retell the tale
like the bold coyotes,
the righteous geese,
the unruly sky,
staking claim to what was theirs
and what could be theirs again.

CHAPTER 6

STAYING WITH THE SINGULARITY: NONHUMAN NARRATORS AND MORE-THAN-HUMAN MYTHOLOGIES

Alexander Popov

Lifeboats out of stories

The environmental humanities of the twenty-first century have vigorously popularized the "Anthropocene" label beyond its original use within geological science. Yet, much about it remains unfixed, slippery. The name itself has been the subject of much debate, with various alternatives being put forward to draw the focus away from the "Anthropos": Capitalocene, Plantationocene, Chthulucene (Haraway 2015), Thanatocene, Phagocene (Bonneuil and Fressoz 2016). This prolonged collective meditation on the cause, effects, and imperatives of the epoch is testament to the enormity of the situation. The Anthropocene is a challenge to the survival of our world, but also to our ability to represent both—the era and the world. The analytical apparatus of the humanities and social sciences falls apart when it comes in contact with the Anthropocene: binaries like subject–object, inside–outside, human–nonhuman, nature–culture, elide crucial details. Collapsing these dualisms into monisms, however, as some posthumanist theories have done, flattens out differences (Morton 2009, 14–21, 141–3) and falls into the trap of logocentrism (Kohn 2013, 41–2, 91–2).

Fully inhabiting this state of indeterminacy might be just what is needed. One philosophical handle on it is the notion of *singularity*: a critical threshold between two states of being, a moment of ontological instability, whose unfolding in the encounter between things cannot be known in advance (Deleuze 2015). Singularity can only be recognized in motion; it is "a point of perceptual recommencement and of variation," at which one can learn to notice things (Conley 2010, 255–6). If the Anthropocene can be thought of as a singular moment of tension— on timescales beyond the human—what agencies are made noticeable at the inflection point must become the central question of the present. In other words: What kind of singularity are we steering toward? Do we want to build an ark or an escape pod?

Such radical uncertainty cannot but infiltrate cultural artifacts. In this chapter I argue that certain forms of modern fantasy are already processing these issues by shifting nonhuman perspectivization and focalization from the supernatural to the natural. In these works, point of view is recast as a tool for understanding differently the material world, instead of being subservient to secondary world creation or allegory. The fantastic becomes a necessary medium, through which human semiotic systems can encounter what Timothy Morton calls the strange stranger of ecological thought (Morton 2010, 38–52). This ongoing attunement of the genre to anthropogenic effects on the planet has produced a spate of stories told from, or in conjunction with, nonhuman perspectives: animal, sylvan, cyborgian, nonliving. In John Crowley's *Ka: Dar Oakley in the Ruin of Ymr* (2017), a crow learns to use symbols, while teaching a human his own language, Ka, woven out of iconic and indexical signs. In Brooke Bolander's *The Only Harmless Great Thing* (2018), an elephant and a young girl, both damaged and doomed by the military-industrial complex, establish a line of cross-species communication, grounded in pain and solidarity, which echoes through history. And in Richard Powers's *The Overstory* (2018), trees guide the human characters and engage in their own form of speculative science.

The fantasy texts examined in this chapter share a preoccupation with mythological narrative, which is mutually constitutive with their nonhuman characters and narrators. I will argue, henceforth, that this entanglement into "more-than-human mythologies" is key to reading contemporary fantasy in the context of the Anthropocene. Brian Attebery writes that fantasy's primary cultural work is to recontextualize myth and furnish it with new meanings. Because fantasy claims no authority to truth and engages in sustained play with symbols, the reader of fantasy is encouraged "to see meaning as something unstable and elusive, rather than single and self-evident" (Attebery 2014, 2). Myth, on the other hand, provides coherent worldviews with generational authority (6).[1] As Gow (2001) has observed, myths congeal history, serving as "instruments for the obliteration of time" (quoted in Kohn 2013, 240). Fantasy, therefore, is in a position to rework the deep myths about humans' place in the world and to uncouple the flow of time from universalizing frameworks. Mythological fantasy can be postmodern metafiction, but it can also be a *contact zone*, where worldviews are engaged in communication and change (Pratt 1991; Attebery 2014, 169–85); it can even be both.

But if it is so difficult to establish what counts as a subject in the first place, how does a community even begin to codify meaning into useful stories? Fantasy tackles this problem by embracing it fully. A growing number of contemporary texts turn this question into their central conceit: What if nonhumans were subjects? What if they were capable of narrating their own stories? These nonhuman characters and narrators do not bear typical trappings from earlier fantasy: anthropomorphism, supernatural origins, allegory. Their stories work hard to convince the reader that such nonhuman subjectivity is possible, and indeed plausible. They borrow strategies from other modes or representation, like science, science fiction, and even the realist novel. An all-important paradox defines this approach: in order to make nonhuman narrators plausible, their narration must be *diffracted* through human points of view. Anything else would suggest that nonhumans can only represent the world in terms of human language: a fall back into representationalism, nonhumans as merely lesser humans.

The notion of *diffraction* has been proposed by Donna Haraway (1992) and further developed by Karen Barad (2003). Barad's work challenges the assumption that descriptions of reality mirror it. She moves "away from the representationalist trap of geometrical optics … to physical optics, to questions of diffraction rather than reflection" (Barad 2003, 803). Whereas *reflection* as a tool lays claim to being able to represent reality mimetically, i.e., to produce "displaced" copies of it, "[a] diffraction pattern does not map where differences appear, but rather maps where the effects of differences appear" (Haraway 1992, 300). Diffraction as a critical tool is used to trace interference patterns between differential agencies which "take measure" of one another. Just as different configurations of scientific apparatuses—e.g., the double slit experiment for demonstrating the wave/particle duality—measure differently, different discourses constrain subjectivity in specific ways.

Diffracting the narrative capabilities of a human with a nonhuman perspective stabilizes both the human and the nonhuman in a manner specific to that particular system. Barad calls such assemblages "phenomena" and analyzes them as the primary elements of her ontology of *agential realism*: objects are meaningful units only within phenomena (Barad 2003, 818). Phenomena are performances, or enactments, of the universe. They depend on open-ended practices—apparatuses—for stabilizing and dissolving boundaries. The more explicit the diffraction pattern, the more convincingly is the conceit carried by a text. The more playfully it suggests its own construction, the more serious its treatment of alterity. Making diffraction patterns visible also makes visible—and thinkable—the mechanisms which make diffraction possible. As Eduardo Kohn writes in his ethnography of the Runa people in the Ecuadorian Amazon, "It is through our partially shared semiotic propensities that multispecies relations are possible, and also analytically comprehensible" (Kohn 2013, 9).

Kohn's "anthropology beyond the human" is rooted in the semiotics of Charles Sanders Peirce and its hierarchy of sign types: icons, which refer to things via perceived similarities, e.g., onomatopoeic words or a scarecrow as a stand-in for humans; indices, which "point" to absent things, like smoke as a sign of fire; and symbols, which pair arbitrarily a perceptual mark with something in the world—the way the word "tree" bears no intrinsic relation to actual trees. Kohn shows that symbols—the distinctively human semiotic modality—and their mutual systemic relations that imbue them with meaning are woven out of iconic and indexical relations (51–6).

Iconic relations depend on ignoring differences between things. Just as a human learns to ignore the differences between an emoticon and a human face, a monkey witnesses the collapse of a tree and connects it to similar events in memory. In the same way it learns to equate situations of danger. According to Kohn's interpretation of Peirce's thought, through witnessing the recurrent succession of "tree-crashing-down" and "danger," the monkey then learns an indexical relation: falling trees signal impending danger (52). This associative projection, a prediction of what will be perceived in the future, arises out of iconic relations. Analogously, symbols are built on top of indexicals. Humans learn the meaning of words by memorizing what the sign vehicle "points to" in the world, but mastering a language involves learning the relations of words among one another, as mapped to the relations between things (55–6). We learn the meaning of "tree" by learning its relations to "forest," "leaves," "chop," "maple," and by mapping these linguistic relations to inter-objective relations in the world. This too is accomplished by suspending the differences between sign and object relations and seeing them as similar in the web of signification. At bottom, a symbol is made out of iconic relations between things.

This complex interrelation between different sign types has significant implications for the affordances of fantasy as it establishes continuity between the sign systems employed by all living beings. Multispecies communication need not be mediated via the supernatural, since all communicative systems within an ecology rely on the same principles of semiosis. Human language grows out of a semiotic web stretching as far as there are organisms acting as *interpretants*, which must project possible futures—i.e., worlds—to arrive at useful interpretations. Selves emerge as "waypoints in the lives of signs" (Kohn 2013, 90); they are in this way radically "of the world" (60) and constitutive of "open wholes" (66) which lose their meaning if cut off from the semiotic web. "In important ways, then," Kohn argues, "life and thought are one and the same: life thinks; thoughts are alive" (16). This analytical framework gives us tools to trace diffraction patterns between human and nonhuman narration that are radically of the world—i.e., rooted in it—but also radically other—i.e., rooted differently.

Northrop Frye writes that in the mythic mode the hero is superior in *kind* to other men and their environment. Heroes are *outside* of the world, their passage through it tells a universal truth, guaranteed by the entity's immutable relation to reality. As the characters' superiority to men and environment shades into inferiority, fictional modes slide with it: through romance, high/low mimesis, and finally to irony. This is a vertical, anthropocentric scale of access to reality representation, at the top of which is myth (Frye 2000, 33–43). More-than-human myth shifts collective wisdom sideways, since in it the world is accessed through other, nonhuman perspectives. Environment and humanity are no longer static reference points measured by static conceptual apparatuses; rather, they themselves become apparatuses, "dynamic (re) configurations of the world" (Barad 2003, 816). More-than-human myth needs to shift between different modes of storytelling, in order not to become yet another congealed history.

This kind of mythological fiction seems closer to indigenous mythology and to what Attebery calls *situated myth* (Attebery 2014, 192). It echoes Le Guin's *carrier bag theory of fiction*, according to which the bag—and metaphorically also the house(hold), or a boat— is a more fitting shape for fiction that seeks to hold worlds than other organizing narrative frameworks, like conflict, hunting, or the hero's journey. A bag contains and preserves things, putting them in social relations with one another (Le Guin 1989). Barad's agential realism does something similar by giving ontological primacy to phenomena. Objects gain meaning only within those phenomenological containers, which, like a bag, are made of human and nonhuman labor. Being permeable, breakable, reusable, retailored, and patched up, these story-bags are about boundaries and their crossing. It comes as no surprise that such situated, carrier-bag mythological fiction is frequented by tricksters and that metamorphosis is its operative principle.

What things do these stories hold together, to make visible and transform? Donna Haraway writes about "staying inside shared semiotic materiality" (Haraway 2008, 72), where beings exist together in "subject-changing ways" (57), where selves are made (64) and where "the capacity to respond" grows (71). Such change happens in what Haraway calls "the contact zone," after Mary Louise Pratt's work in linguistics: "A 'contact' perspective emphasizes how subjects are constituted in and by their relations to each other" (Pratt 1992, 6–7). Entities in the contact zone engage in risky play; space and time are diffracted in unexpected ways.[2] The risk is grave, but the reward of coherence is bigger: "An achieved actual entity is outside time; it exceeds time in … the sheer joy of that coming together of different bodies in coshaping motion, that 'getting it,' which makes each partner more than one but less than two" (Haraway 2008, 244). Entities meet in the contact zone on unequal terms but are always capable of surprising one another.

This harks back to Kohn's Peircian framework in which the semiotic capacities of selves might differ but are always connected via bodily mediated signification. More-than-human myths in fantasy focus our attention on such contact zones and invite us to learn how to see nonhumans as *their own* selves. This kind of learning becomes possible only when we can grasp—rationally and/or intuitively—the material-semiotic structure of living ecologies, i.e., their economy of signs.[3] Icons organize meaning through spatial congruities, indices use temporal ones. Symbols are made of both, diffracting space *and* time. We can now bring together the theories of Kohn, Haraway, Le Guin, and Barad, with a quote from Barad: "This ongoing flow of agency through which 'part' of the world makes itself differentially intelligible to another 'part' of the world and through which local causal structures, boundaries, and properties are stabilized and destabilized does not take place in space and time but in the making of spacetime itself" (Barad 2003, 817).

This is Kohn's *open whole*, which comes to know itself through the selves that (re)make it in the contact zone. Epistemology and ontology are melded into *onto-epistem-ology* (Barad 2003, 829). This is what more-than-human myths set out to accomplish by weaving bags of world-holding capacity: the remaking of space-time through subjectivity. I now turn to a number of narrative singularities where such metamorphoses can be observed—if one cares to look with a useful set of eyes.[4]

From the Birth of Stories to the End of the World

John Crowley's *Ka: Dar Oakley in the Ruin of Ymr* (*Ka*) tells of the end of the world, and how crows discovered stories. Its protagonist, Dar Oakley of the crows, learns to communicate with Fox Cap, a human girl from a prehistoric European tribe, subsequently a shamanic priestess. It is a mutual learning, which brings closer their worlds: Ymr, the world of human symbols and stories, and Ka, the world of the crows. Later on Dar Oakley travels with Fox Cap to a place outside of the material world—the realm of the dead, Heaven, Hell, or something else entirely. From there he steals "the Most Precious Thing" and thus gets to live many following lives. He journeys again and again to "that placeless place" (Crowley 2017, 412), as companion, go-between, or psychopomp for various humans: a medieval monk, an Emily Dickinson-like spirit talker, and the narrator himself.

The crow's story is framed by that of the unnamed human who finds the dying bird in an unspecified, almost-apocalyptic future. While Dar Oakley convalesces, they establish a mutual language and the crow tells his savior of his many lives. The narrator signals repeatedly that his words are a translation rather than a straightforward rendering, a diffraction through human knowledge and sensibilities (106, 190, 216). Like the narrator, we often realize that Dar Oakley's stories are the product of semiotic negotiation between crow and others. Say, when he and the monk reconstruct what Hell is like out of their meager memories and inadequate language (208); or when Dar Oakley listens to Native Americans telling children's stories about himself and is unable to decide "where the story ceased and began, whether he heard it in Ka or acted it in Ymr" (259). The human narrator, too, feels that he is writing the account for some unseen reader (429).[5] As a result, the general flow of diffractive narration employed in Crowley's novel looks as in Figure 6.1 below.[6]

This foregrounding of metafictionality and the diffractive nature of the novel is consonant with its central motif: the very possibility of inhabiting shared semiotic worlds. Despite having to reverse-engineer the narrator's translations, it is possible to reconstruct a plausible path for Dar Oakley's learning of human language. Crows typically dwell in iconic webs of signification. The new is juxtaposed with the familiar: people are like bears, horses are like deer, carts are like

(Implied reader — Human narrator — Crow narrator) ⟶ World

Figure 6.1 Schematization of the narrative hermeneutics of *Ka: Dar Oakley in the Ruin of Ymr*. The reader grasps the fictional world through affordances which arise from the diffraction of several narrative functions, most notably those of the human and crow narrators.

deer "caught in a deadfall," and so on (19–20, 30). Crows are also proficient users of indexicals, which brings them in close contact with humans—this is how "their own history began" (48). Crows learn the signs of impending battle and are the first scavengers to descend to the fields of dead bodies (77). By attuning to human rhythms, crows learn that people live outside of themselves, always trying to see ahead: "Stories were the way People lived. Like paths, they could be traveled in any direction, yet always ran from beginning to end" (124). Stories are the ultimate condensation of world into symbols, the fabric of Ymr. When Dar Oakley and Fox Cap venture into the world beyond, they find nothing but symbols: "In a land where signs are the only things, you needed only one of each, one castle, king, lover, rival, child, animal, fish, bird, tooth, eye, cup, bed" (131–2).

Ymr is "the realm where what People think is true *is* true" (275)—*realm* being a special word in the novel, akin to Uexküll's *Umwelt*: that part of reality which an organism is able to perceive and act upon. The more Dar Oakley learns about humans, the more he becomes of their realm. Throughout history, he brings many new things from Ymr to Ka, like names and the concept of "future": a kind of new land of plenty that comes to replace the old; time emerging out of space (331). It is Dar Oakley's most radical entwining of human and nonhuman worlds that enables him to invent "the Future"—namely, the discovery of the land where the dead crows go, akin to humans. He is taken there on an Orphic journey to meet a former love of his. As with the humans venturing to the land beyond, Dar Oakley is left profoundly uncertain whether any part of the trip has been real. If not, he wonders whether having the "unreal" storyspace is not a good thing after all—as a way to preserve what is gone.

Death as a container for relations becomes an organizing myth. Everything that Dar Oakley tells the narrator is held in that space and by the end of his narrative the crow wants to die, or at least to stop remembering. Humanity is dying, too, because it has given up on maintaining that otherworldly space; the same way the dead are left to rot, no longer contained by graves, Ymr's stories—human stories—are growing "vast but thin" (409). Toward the end, Dar Oakley meets a coyote, that old master of border crossing. The coyote tells the crow his own myth-like story: how he locked one of the two doors separating the living from the dead, dooming humans to always seek reunion with the spirits of the departed (424–5). The integration of timelines happens off-world: in Heaven, Hell, or simply in a grove filled with everybody you have ever known in your life. It happens in stories. Ultimately, the world is ending because it is devoid of meaning. Landscapes have changed and species have died out, stories have untangled and realms have crumbled.

The human narrator is denied entry into the world of the dead because the dead are no longer there—our semiotic ties to them have been dissolved. Humans have nowhere else to retreat but to our own, living home, which we must become-with once again. The most powerful moment of such becoming-with does not even involve humans: other worlds will persist after us. When Dar Oakley attempts to cross the Atlantic and is about to die of exhaustion, a flock of terns carries him to land. Their kin have told them of the crow who learned their language and might one day need help:

> It was the only time in all his existence that beings not of his own kind and close kin had given help to him with no advantage to themselves, anyway no advantage that he could imagine, and it would never happen again. … Dar Oakley thought a thought no Crow

has likely ever thought before or since: that if only he could, he would become a being of another species; that there was a species better than his own to wish to be.

(236–8)

Becoming an entity of another species is an irresponsible notion when contemplated by humans, as is escape into death. But becoming-with companion species in a way that maximizes our capacity to respond and tell more-than-human stories might be just what is needed for the construction of a non-anthropocentric Ymr. For Dar Oakley and the coyote, staying with the singularity is ultimately tragic, as they become trapped in an endless cycle of remembering and death. Their tragedy, however, is mythical—it spans history and the world, and as such diffracts the inevitability of death with storytelling. For the human characters, staying with the singularity—ultimately staying with everyday trouble and bringing new, expanded life to stories (Haraway 2016)—is the only workable way to regaining a world. *Ka* shows us how beings of different species can come into contact and even gain a desire to become more than themselves. It is a decidedly utopian moment in a novel preoccupied with ruin and death.

Suffering-with and Making Peace

Containing the dead within storyspace is explicitly tied to the survival of life in Brooke Bolander's *The Only Harmless Great Thing* (*TOHGT*). On an alternate Earth, science and history have progressed along slightly different paths: nuclear power has been exploited even more aggressively and humans have established contact with another sentient species: elephants. The novella entangles these divergences with several narratives. One brings together two separate events from the beginning of the twentieth century: the contraction of radiation poisoning by "the Radium Girls," from painting dials with self-luminous paint; and the electrical execution of the elephant Topsy. In our world Topsy killed a circus spectator,[7] but in *TOHGT* elephants labor as replacements for the Radium Girls. Topsy kills Slattery, a floor supervisor at the factory, in a fit of long-held rage at his cruel treatment of both her and Regan, a radium girl spending her last days as her instructor. Another narrative, roughly parallel with our present, involves the negotiation between Kat, a scientist, and an elephant matriarch. Kat wants to persuade the elephant community to become guardians of nuclear waste materials buried beneath a US mountain; they would be given the surrounding land, and in exchange their bodies would be genetically engineered to produce bioluminescence in proximity to radioactive materials. This warning system is considered in the first place because of Topsy's story and its status in popular culture due to a widely viewed Disney retelling. Still another narrative tells the mythical story of Furmother, who tricked a bull elephant and set free all the stories hoarded by him, making possible the coming together of the elephant species into a hive-like mind: the Many Mothers, stretching to the beginning of time, and into the future.

Whereas *Ka* creates the illusion that narrative flows only forward, *TOHGT* diffracts subjectivities in a circular shape, perhaps even bag-like in the way it seeks to contain all of time and bind it in nonlinear topologies (see Figure 6.2[8]). The Many Mothers is the super-mind making it possible to tell the story of Furmother while referring to the future in which elephants glow; it is connected to all narrative agencies in the text, containing their stories and

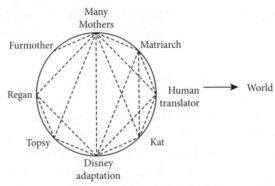

Figure 6.2 The narrative hermeneutics of *The Only Harmless Great Thing*. The various agencies that provide access to the world mutually constitute each other, coalescing into a multiplex and many-voiced narrative apparatus which is most prominently figured in the Many Mothers entity.

making some of them possible—including Topsy's access to collective memory through the semiotic materiality of song. In the future, when the "pink squeakers," or humans, are no more, the bargain is seen by the Many Mothers as "a truce with the Dead"; the Mothers themselves are "nothing more and nothing less than the memories of the Dead, the sum total of every story ever told them" (Bolander 2018, 9). They hold together the structure by providing linkages of solidarity between otherwise isolated points.

Each agent in this mesh-like containing device carries out their own important labor in the ecology of selves. Regan does not have access to the hive mind, even though her story is imprinted in it through Topsy's mind. She is bonded to Topsy by shared suffering and their mutual recognition—which would be impossible if signs did not share roots. The circumstances of this recognition align with human material-semiotic mega-constructs: capitalism and paternalism. One could even speculate that Proboscidian, the human–elephant sign language, has been invented in order to better exploit the nonhumans, as suggested by Topsy's situation. Both Regan and Topsy have been exposed to radium; they are both victims of a system stretching across gender, species, and class. Suffering—the most immediate and basic relation to space (Morton 2009, 182)—connects them iconically. Without this semiotic relation, there would be no Disney movie, without which in turn, however flawed, there would be no negotiation, in which the human translator also plays a significant role, occasionally taking the side of the elephants. The fashioning of the index, of *bioluminescent elephants = danger*, is the final product of a complex web of iconic, indexical, and symbolic mappings.

All these narrative nodes—tying together past and future in the nexus that is the Many Mothers—are entangled through acts of (feminine) struggle against oppressive (male) systems. The bull in the story of the Furmother is a hoarder and war-monger. When Furmother finds the stolen stories at the bottom of the lake—in which she "sank like a Story" (Bolander 2018, 31), making herself part of discourse—her struggle has only just begun: "Furmother did not stop until all were grasped and gulped. Her belly bulged with endless Story, all the tales that were and all the tales that would ever be. Even yours, O best beloved mooncalf. Even mine. The reason we glow—that, too, was there" (41–2).

Furmother becomes a hyperobject containing past, present, and future, never fully comprehensible from a single point of view (Morton 2013). Those stories in her "were shattered into pieces, like The Great Mother who had scattered them, and no one tale held to the ear by itself could ever be fully understood. To make them whole required many voices entwined" (Bolander 2018, 45). Making the story whole amounts not so much to helping the humans, but to staying with the trouble and "guarding the truth" (46).

TOHGT foregrounds more-than-human myth as a tool for establishing links of solidarity across ways of being-in-the-world: physical modalities, labor, suffering, emancipation, and mere survival. Its diffractive narrative sensitizes us to the possibility of other subjectivities and to our own entanglement with material-semiotic structures extending far beyond human bodies. A nonhuman myth and an animated movie can thus not only have profound impact on more-than-human history, but also become integral parts of our expanded subjectivity. The novella reinterprets the work of translation as much more than simple transfer—it is rather an act of noticing agencies and allowing them to coexist in those moments of singular tension that shape history (Latour 2005, 108).

Another Kind of Singularity

Richard Powers's *The Overstory* is an epic reinvention of myth that attempts to change the conceptual and experiential landscape of the Anthropocene, not so much through argument but through "a good story" (Powers 2018, 336). Its attack on anthropocentricity mobilizes both metafictionality and contact zones. Both these strategies depend on its main conceit: trees, and more so forests, are animate subjects capable of their own kind of thought and agency. The text focuses on actual scientific findings that destabilize previous ontological assumptions. Trees communicate with individuals within and outside of their own species—utilizing thousands of chemical compounds they breathe out (123); they can signal threats, fend off insects, and summon allied predators; through sprawling underground networks of fungi, called by some a "wood wide web," they take care of each other—sending information, and if need be, food (Wohlleben 2015).[9]

Powers's dramatization of such findings challenges Western intuitions and sometimes achieves affective tone typically associated with fairy tales and fantasy. Certain descriptions can leave the reader, as they do the human characters, "stupid and speechless" (Powers 2018, 264): an aspen forest of a single male genotype, which "has been roving around the hills and gullies in a ten-millennium search for a female quaking giant to fertilize" (133); a single tree whose roots have grown over thousands of square acres (82); humans encountering pristine ecologies high up in the crown of a giant redwood (266–7). However, the text always grounds these seemingly fantastic images in reality. It does that through its human characters whose experience and expertise cover a wide range of entanglements with nature: biology, psychology, art, literature, theatre, law, engineering, and even actuarial science.[10]

The Overstory poises between fantasy, fairy tale, realism, postmodernism, and science fiction. Its narrators are difficult to pin down, oscillating between third person perspectives and limited omniscience. Gradually it becomes clear that there is perhaps a single, albeit multiplex, entity which is narrating: the trees themselves, connected in a brain-like network enveloping human space and historical time. Some clues are crude and could be taken for postmodern tricks, such as inserting nonhuman narration in-between sections. Others are more subtle, like using an already referenced scientific mechanism for tree communication—

(Implied reader — Tree narrator(s)— Human characters) ⟶ World

Figure 6.3 The narrative hermeneutics of *The Overstory*. The schema is the reverse of that in *Ka*: it is the nonhuman narrator, itself a multiplex entity, who accesses the world through the human points of view.

"chemical semaphore"—to provide a perspective from inside a character's brain (254). Reading with an unpredictably omniscient and somewhat postmodern narrator presents difficulties to interpreting the novel's structure; *reading-with* a nonhuman narrator that is both single and multiplex allows the heterogeneity of content and generic forms to cohere. The meeting of forms becomes a contact zone, where readerly attention is maintained in a state of increased response capacity.

Perspectivization "flows" from nonhuman to human (Figure 6.3), with the other significant difference—vis-à-vis, say, *Ka*—that humans are not marked as narrators. The structure of the novel is itself a key: its first part is titled "Roots" and introduces the nine human protagonists through their own separate stories; the next, "Trunk," brings these protagonists together in a struggle to preserve the forests of the US Pacific coast; in "Crown," the protagonists once again take to their own narrative trajectories; and finally, "Seeds" intimates a possible version of the future of life. A surface reading would relegate the tree-like organization to a mere gimmick. But reading with the nonhuman narrator(s) identifies it as a diffraction pattern: the topology of forest minds, thinking and communicating at unimaginable spacetime-scales, and shaped in interaction with human agents.

Learning to notice diffraction patterns makes it easier to notice previously unheeded modes of being:

> A person has only to look, to see that dead logs are far more alive than living ones. But the senses never have much chance, against the power of doctrine. …
>
> What are you studying?
>
> "Fungi, anthropods, reptiles, amphibians, small mammals, frass, webs, denning, soil … Everything we can catch a dead log doing."
>
> (Powers 2018, 139)

The dead go on living through their entanglement with material-semiotic life. Agency, time, and space are analyzed differently. The redwood Mimas, whose crown hosts several of the characters, is called "keeper of half a million days and nights" (262). A recurrent theme is that "[a] good answer must be reinvented many times, from scratch" (3), and that "long answers need long time" (255). Reinventing time as a function of space and more-than-human subjectivity is as good an answer as any for which such narration could be harnessed:

> But people have no idea what time is. They think it's a line, spinning out from three seconds behind them, then vanishing just as fast into the three seconds of fog just ahead. They can't see that time is one spreading ring wrapped around another, outward and outward until the thinnest skin of Now depends for its being on the enormous mass of everything that has already died.
>
> (358)

Life contains past life, and conditions the future. The entanglement between material and semiotic, organism and stories, is explored through multiple references to myth, especially to Ovid's *Metamorphoses*, whose first sentence reads thus: "Let me sing to you now, about how people turn into other things" (117). Trees are engaged in myriad semiotic activities: they are scientists "running a billion field tests" (454). Humans and trees share genetic material (132), as paired words like "oak-door" (67), "beech-book" (116), and "tree-truth" (501) share common ancestors. Ray Brinkman, a copyright lawyer, ponders granting legal standing to trees, akin to corporations (249–51). Dorothy reads to the paralyzed Ray hundreds of novels, meditating on the shapes of plots as contrasted with the shapes of nature (382–3). Most strikingly, a tree in South America has grown into the unmistakable shape of a woman, as if forests have learned to produce iconic representations of humans (393–5).

Patricia Westerfield, the tree scientist in the character ensemble, muses that her colleagues would relegate this finding to *pareidolia*, the tendency to incorrectly identify stimuli as familiar objects.[11] She also reasons that the probability of this coincidence is far greater than those attached to the emergence of life and multicellular organisms. Coincidence plays a fundamental role in the plot, as it does in the evolution of life. Seemingly random associations with trees are the catalysts for most of the "root" stories: Adam Appich grows up alongside his own maple tree; Ray and Dorothy spend their first hours together in an amateur production of *Macbeth*, in which Ray is disguised as a tree; Douglas Pavlicek's fall from a crashing plane is arrested by the branches of a banyan tree. These chance mappings forge symbolic interfaces between humans and trees. When semiosis is analyzed as pertaining to all life, with signs connecting disparate selves in the ecology of living thought, random combinations become the foundation for new signs used by the ecosystem to think about itself. This symbolic space makes sense within a holistic system of material-semiotic relations occurring at wholly different spacetime-scales— comprehensible only when diffracted through sylvan minds.

Neelay Mehta, a software engineer and creator of a civilization simulator game, takes inspiration from the branching algorithms of trees. His work is transmuted into a nascent distributed artificial intelligence that will perhaps establish contact with forests, as is finally hinted at (496). Through Neelay, the novel foregrounds the vision of the technological Singularity. Since childhood, he is fascinated by computers and science fiction. He has always tried to "turn his innermost hopes and dreams into active processes" (94) and to invent "self-learning, self-creating" living things (107). Even though it seems that Neelay's game *Mastery* is just a newer machine for turning space and time into profit (276), his endeavors ultimately equate code to the "instructions Vishnu managed to cram into something smaller than a boy's fingernail," i.e., to life (435). The game that Neelay has always dreamt of is finally realized in the world itself. His AI creations, capable of reading millions of words and images per second and of constantly growing connections of knowledge, are on the cusp of reinventing the good questions.

The novel gestures rhetorically that its implied readers are the AIs, that the humans are merely the conduit: life talking to itself, through itself. At its conclusion, Nicholas Hoel is roaming the country incognito and leaving giant messages in the open: first street graffiti, and finally a single word composed of downed wood and visible from space: "STILL" (502). The AIs read it via satellite eyes and follow the semiotic traces which will open up the overstory to them. This is another kind of singularity, countering the Promethean myth of progress: not a launch pad into the future, but a field of entangled life forces leading to many possible worlds.

Staying with this kind of singularity means staying in the contact zone and learning how selves transform in more-than-human ecologies. Whereas a technological Singularity is projected to accelerate the speed of communication and being—to transport our semiotic systems to a qualitatively different plane of interpretation (Kurzweil 2005)—more-than-human myth entangles us ever more surely with the present.

The Overstory deemphasizes human agency as a transcendental given and folds it in a complicated pattern of diffractions that operate across matter and information alike. It complements *Ka* and *TOHGT* in the sense that the balance between narration and narrative agency is shifted along the human–nonhuman spectrum in the three texts. Together these three embody some of the major possibilities for narrative assemblage in more-than-human storytelling. When read as a corpus, they can ultimately reframe the human–nonhuman binary—not by dissolving it, but by translating it into a complex web of interaction which is at least partially traversable through narrative means. Fantasy literature of this stripe catalyzes a desire for becoming-with other species and for an expanded capacity for noticing and responding.

Coda: Possible Worlds

This chapter has offered close readings from an emergent corpus of more-than-human texts that challenge anthropocentric narratives from a multinaturalist stance, including narratives of the technological singularity. It has tied their interpretation with a theory of how signs bind the whole of life into a complex semiotic web. Saying within the semiotic materiality of this world, then, requires different kinds of stories—much less linear and much more capable of holding humans and nonhumans together in the contact zone. Inhabiting the bag-like narratives of more-than-human fantasy often feels difficult and uncanny. To enter such stories is after all a form of collective dreaming, whereby humans allow themselves to be invaded by nonhuman subjectivity, however awkwardly translated. This dreaming is a process of re-enchantment in which our ability to imagine possible worlds is strengthened through entanglement with more-than-human perspectives.

Trees are likened to many things in *The Overstory*: spaceships, space elevators, scientists, philanthropists, bridges between earth and sky, cathedrals, welfare states, brains. Each of these mappings speaks to different sensitivities to semiosis and the projection of possible worlds. As one astute reading suggests, the novel might actually contain more than a single fictional world—if we interpret Olivia Vandergriff as the human avatar of the chestnut tree in Ray and Dorothy's backyard, which they imagine to be their grown-up daughter (Balee 2019). Crowley's *Ka* tells of how crows built their own possible worlds in overlap with humanity. Bolander's *TOHGT* shows that more-than-human worlds are possible when nonhumans are recognized as their own selves. Thinking with alternative worldings takes us to singularities where life meets itself, those "unruly edges" of totalizing systems where unexpected encounters and translations occur (Tsing 2015, 17–25). More-than-human mythological fantasy allows us to learn the arts of noticing by diffracting our perspectives through other bodies and stories. By choosing to stay with the singularity, we might gain the future *and* the past. Otherwise, we risk losing both.

Notes

1 Thomas Pavel differentiates mythological from fictional systems: in their proper historical context, the first are deemed as reality. Only after becoming weakened do they start leaking entities into fictional domains; Pavel calls the reverse process *mythification* (Pavel 1986, 41–2, 77).

2 Haraway writes that "time opens up" in play, as a result of "altered temporal sequences" of motor activity (Haraway 2008, 240). Implicitly, time flows from the spatial organization within the assemblage of organisms and environment. A similar view is offered by Von Uexküll: environment spaces (*Umwelten*) are organized in terms of the local signs produced by the interaction between body and world; time arises from the "moment signs" experienced by the subject (Von Uexküll 2013, 53–72). Shanahan (2010), a cognitivist treatment of the issue, identifies working memory as that which locates the subject in space, while episodic memory accomplishes it with regard to time.

3 "Economy" in its etymological sense of "household management" is much closer to Le Guin's container framework than to its present, implicit association with an ever-shifting horizon of growth.

4 I take inspiration for this observation partially from Le Guin's novelette *Buffalo Gals, Won't You Come Out Tonight* (1987). Its protagonist, the girl Myra, enters into a mythical world of talking animals and is gifted a new eye to replace her injured one. Learning to notice implies a change in subjectivity, a willingness to give up part of yourself in exchange for new affordances. As the chapter argues throughout, narrative points of view and the ability to keep track of their diffractions across the more-than-human spectrum constitute important tools for grappling with the Anthropocene.

5 On *the implied reader,* see Iser (1978).

6 I borrow this method of representation from Verbeek's discussion of material hermeneutics (Verbeek 2005, 122–8).

7 Topsy's execution is documented in the black-and-white movie of 1903, *Electrocuting an Elephant* (available online).

8 The implied reader position is omitted, as it is not explicitly signaled. The narrator does address a "mooncalf," but this does not significantly determine the structure of the text.

9 Wohlleben's book references a great deal of recent research in plant science to support its claims. However, partly due to it being a popular science book written to elicit a strong affective response, it often veers into strongly speculative and anthropomorphic statements. For an overview of the criticism leveled against it, see Kingsland (2018). Some of the communication channels described by Wohlleben and relevant to *The Overstory* are also investigated in Sheldrake (2020). The issue of "giving voice" to nonhumans is central to Powers's novel and to the present argument that this kind of program can be truly effective only when it is fully aware of its own diffraction patterns. This is another sense in which fantasy literature, because it doesn't assume authority to truth but rather plays with and challenges it, seems to be well suited to complement science in rethinking the Anthropocene.

10 For a discussion on the possibility and limitations of human experts giving trees "voice" in a legal context, see Bertenthal (2019).

11 A related concept is that of *magical environments* (Von Uexküll 2013, 119–26).

References:

Attebery, Brian. 2014. *Stories about Stories: Fantasy and the Remaking of Myth*. Oxford: Oxford University Press.

Balee, Susan. 2019. "Another Story in The Overstory: One of Richard Powers's Trees Has a Human Avatar." June 29, 2019. http://politicsslashletters.org/features/another-story-in-the-overstory-one-of-richard-powerss-trees-has-a-human-avatar/.

Barad, Karen. 2003. "Posthumanist Performativity: Toward an Understanding of How Matter Comes to Matter." *Signs: Journal of Women in Culture and Society*, vol. 28, no. 3: 801–31.

Bertenthal, Alyse. 2019. "Standing Up for Trees: Rethinking Representation in a Multispecies Context." *Law & Literature*: 1–19. September 10, 2019. https://doi.org/10.1080/1535685X.2019.1635355

Bolander, Brooke. 2018. *The Only Harmless Great Thing*. New York: Tor.com.

Bonneuil, Christophe, and Jean-Baptiste Fressoz. 2016. *The Shock of the Anthropocene: The Earth, History and Us*. New York: Verso Books.

Conley, Tom. 2010. "Singularity." In *Deleuze Dictionary: Revised Edition*, edited by Adrian Parr, 254–6. Edinburgh: Edinburgh University Press.

Crowley, John. 2017. *Ka: Dar Oakley in the Ruin of Ymr*. New York: Saga Press.

Deleuze, Gilles. 2015. *Logic of Sense*. London: Bloomsbury Publishing.

Frye, Northrop. 2000. *Anatomy of Criticism*. Princeton, NJ: Princeton University Press.

Gow, Peter. 2001. *An Amazonian Myth and Its History*. Oxford: Oxford University Press.

Haraway, Donna J. 1992. "The Promises of Monsters: A Regenerative Politics for Inappropriate/d Others." In *Cultural Studies*, edited by Lawrence Grossberg, Cory Nelson, and Paula Treichler, 295–337. New York: Routledge.

Haraway, Donna J. 2008. *When Species Meet*. Minneapolis: University of Minnesota Press.

Haraway, Donna J. 2015. "Anthropocene, Capitalocene, Plantationocene, Chthulucene: Making Kin." *Environmental Humanities*, vol. 6, no. 1: 159–65.

Haraway, Donna J. 2016. *Staying with the Trouble: Making Kin in the Chthulucene*. Durham, NC: Duke University Press.

Iser, Wolfgang. 1978. *The Act of Reading: A Theory of Aesthetic Response*. Baltimore, MD: Johns Hopkins University Press.

Kingsland, Sharon Elizabeth. 2018. "Facts or Fairy Tales? Peter Wohlleben and the Hidden Life of Trees." *Bulletin-Ecological Society of America*, vol. 99, no. 4. https://doi.org/10.1002/bes2.1443

Kohn, Eduardo. 2013. *How Forests Think: Toward an Anthropology beyond the Human*. Berkeley: University of California Press.

Kurzweil, Ray. 2005. *The Singularity Is Near: When Humans Transcend Biology*. London: Penguin.

Latour, Bruno. 2005. *Reassembling the Social: An Introduction to Actor-Network-Theory*. Oxford: Oxford University Press.

Le Guin, Ursula K. 1987. *Buffalo Gals and Other Animal Presences*. Santa Barbara, CA: Capra Press.

Le Guin, Ursula K. 1989. "The Carrier Bag Theory of Fiction." In *Dancing at the Edge of the World*, 165–70. New York: Grove Press.

Morton, Timothy. 2009. *Ecology without Nature: Rethinking Environmental Aesthetics*. Cambridge, MA: Harvard University Press.

Morton, Timothy. 2010. *The Ecological Thought*. Cambridge, MA: Harvard University Press.

Morton, Timothy. 2013. *Hyperobjects: Philosophy and Ecology after the End of the World*. Minneapolis: University of Minnesota Press.

Pavel, Thomas G. 1986. *Fictional Worlds*. Cambridge, MA: Harvard University Press.

Powers, Richard. 2018. *The Overstory*. New York: W. W. Norton & Company.

Pratt, Mary Louise. 1991. "Arts of the Contact Zone." *Profession*, vol. 91: 33–40.

Pratt, Mary Louise. 1992. *Imperial Eyes: Travel Writing and Transculturation*. London: Routledge.

Shanahan, Murray. 2010. *Embodiment and the Inner Life: Cognition and Consciousness in the Space of Possible Minds*. Oxford: Oxford University Press.

Sheldrake, Merlin. 2020. *Entangled Life: How Fungi Make Our Worlds, Change Our Minds & Shape Our Futures*. New York: Random House.

Tsing, Anna Lowenhaupt. 2015. *The Mushroom at the End of the World: On the Possibility of Life in Capitalist Ruins*. Princeton, NJ: Princeton University Press.

Verbeek, Peter-Paul. 2005. *What Things Do: Philosophical Reflections on Technology, Agency, and Design*. University Park: The Pennsylvania State University Press.

Von Uexküll, Jakob. 2013. *A Foray into the Worlds of Animals and Humans: With a Theory of Meaning*. Translated by Joseph D. O'Neil. Minneapolis: University of Minnesota Press.

Wohlleben, Peter. 2015. *The Hidden Life of Trees: What They Feel, How They Communicate—Discoveries from a Secret World*. Translated by Jane Billinghurst. Vancouver: Greystone Books.

CHAPTER 7
THE EYE OF THE STORY
Joseph Bruchac / Nokidahozid

1
See through the eye of Story
and not just the narrow vision
of human time on this earth.

See everything as a circle
and not a straight line.
Remember before,
remember beyond
the brief memories
or whatever nation
where you believe
you belong.

In our oldest tongues
there are no words
for fantasy,
no words for myth.

There is only Story
and Story
is alive.

2
The world
has ended more than once.
It is only Story
who has not forgotten
those times of fire,
those times of flood,
those time when foolish deeds
destroyed it all,
those times when life
returned again from lands
beyond the sky.

It is a simple thing,
Story reminds us
This Earth will go on
with us or without us.

I'm not sure when it was that I was first introduced to the concept that there were clear divisions between myth and legend, fantasy and reality. (Confession. I love reading fantasy. *The Magazine of Fantasy and Science Fiction* is one of my faves. I've even been published in it a couple of times. But I'm talking about seeing things more than one way. And seeing more than one way more than one way.) It was probably around the same time that I was being fed the idea that human beings are above, apart from, and different from everything else in creation. That Old Testament "dominion over" thing.

Even as a child, I had a hard time accepting those things. And, in the decades that followed, the more I listened to indigenous elders—not just on the "American" continent, but in other parts of the planet—the more I realized that such concepts as myth and legends and clear distinctions between fantasy and reality are deeply flawed and that accepting them as gospel could mean following a perilous road.

So now we are calling this the Anthropocene Era? I get it. A time when all life is shaped by human actions? I can see that to some degree. Plus it suits the need some feel to classify and divide up geological time. Like talking about the Pleistocene period now past. The Phanerozoic Eon divided into the Paleozoic, the Mesozoic, and the Cenozoic. All that jazz.

The idea of an Anthropocene Era can be a useful concept. But only if it reminds us of such things as responsibility and hubris. The need to hold ourselves in check before it's too late.

On a certain level there's some vanity connected to the term "Anthropocene," an implicit empowering of humanity's ability to change everything, even destroy everything. The final step in colonialism. Something those of us who connect to our indigenous roots understand all too well—and not as part of the past.

So, instead of myth and legend, fantasy versus reality, what I turn to is the truth of story.

Here, just off the top of my head, are a few examples.

Back in 1992—500 years after that Genoan navigator stumbled into our very old world—I had the opportunity to visit the Lacandon Mayan village of Naha in the Yucatán peninsula. There, the elder of the village Chan Kin, a deeply honored storyteller who was well over 100 years old at the time, told us stories. One of them had to do with a farmer who asked the gods of the forest to turn him into a jaguar so that he could drive away the useless animals that came to eat his crops. His wish was granted and from then on, in the shape of a jaguar, he chased away all the useless animals he saw and invited all the people who came to that farm to come and eat, while the people of his village stayed away from that farm where a jaguar chased away all the humans who approached and invited in all the animals.

Chan Kin also told us that whenever we cut the great trees, the gods of disease will come out of the forests. Now, of course, we know that not to be fantasy or legend. It is the truth. All of the various modern epidemics appear to have begun that way. When we destroy the wild, we set loose viruses formerly held in the trees or the animals.

In that same year of 1992 I spent time in Mali, West Africa, among the Dogon people in the village of Tireli. My 22-year-old son James and I learned many things from elders eager to teach us. Among those was that human villages are regarded traditionally as "black holes" which are constantly absorbing everything from the natural world around. The only ways to regain balance are to behave with care and respect and—now and then—invite into the village the spirits of nature. Those spirits were embodied in masks carved to represent animals and insects and the trees. One tree mask in particular was spectacular—more than 20 feet tall. When it was worn by one of the masked dancers, incredible acrobatics would be performed. We were told that after the masks were used in that ceremony, they no longer held the spirits within them. At that point, in the old days, the mask would just be placed in the forest and allowed to rot back into nature. Nowadays, though, those masks provided a source of revenue by being sold to tourists or used by Dogon dancers to perform for visiting Europeans.

A group of German or French tourists came to the village one day. They'd arranged for one of those dancers to perform for them. Our Dogon friends, Meninyu and Asama, invited us to come and watch. But as we sat there watching, suddenly the white man leading the tour stood up, walked over to the drummers and put his hands on the drums stopping them. Everyone, my son and I included, were shocked by that this kind of irreverence. Only the drummers should touch the drum, much less stop them. "Those two must go!" the tour group leader said, pointing at Jim and me. "We did not pay to see white people here." Our hosts were upset by it, but we left without protesting. As the drums started again, our friends led us back up the hill to the men's house. The men's house has a very low roof and you almost have to crawl to get into it. It reminds people to always be respectful and not try to elevate themselves above others. We had only been there for a few moments when the drums stopped. Then we heard the sound of people talking angrily as they came up the hill. It was the dancers carrying their drums and their masks. As soon as they had started to dance again the giant tree mask broke in half—something that never happened before. They stopped the dance and left the European tourists looking confused.

It was an example of European arrogance not just toward indigenous people but toward the natural world in general. Being in control. Getting what was paid for. A commercial relationship rather than a sacred one. They had no understanding of story.

The reason why indigenous people have traditions and stories such as these I've just mentioned is not that they are perfect or always live in absolute balance. It is because their ancestors made mistakes and learned from those mistakes. Those stories are lessons to help us stay connected. The Hopi people—who still regularly send messages to the rest of the world—talk of there being several worlds before this one. Each time one of those worlds was destroyed by foolish behavior and the surviving people had to climb up to a new world. We are now—by some native accounts—in either the fourth or the fifth world.

Another of the widespread so-called creation myths of the indigenous people of this continent speaks of life coming from the sky. It may have been, as the Lenape people explain, in the form of the root of a great tree dropping from the heavens. Or, in the Haudenosaunee story, it is in the shape of a woman who fell from the Skyland grasping in her hands the seeds of life. Rather than myths, those are deep lesson stories holding memories that may help us see something beyond our everyday comprehension.

We are not the owners or the true rulers of the planet. We are part of a great circle and the stuff of stars.

CHAPTER 8

FANTASY FOR THE ANTHROPOCENE: ON THE ECOCIDAL UNCONSCIOUS, PLANETARIANISM, AND IMAGINATION OF BIOCENTRIC FUTURES

Marek Oziewicz

In Susanna Clarke's *Jonathan Strange and Mr. Norrell* (2004) two characters find themselves under a spell. Each night they are whisked to an enchanted mansion to dance in fairy revels only to wake up in the real world the next morning. Although they remember the ball, whenever they try to reveal their predicament a stream of gibberish emerges from their mouths. When Stephen attempts to explain what is happening to him, he finds himself lecturing, at one time, about the cultivation of beans; at another, about Julius Caesar's dealings in Britain. Lady Pole's endeavors to communicate about her fate are, likewise, baffling: the spell makes her blather about a man who bought a carpet or about a hunter lost in the woods. "No, wait!" Lady Pole exclaims, dismayed. "That is not what I wished to say!" (Clarke 2004, 267). The impossible situation continues until the spell is broken, and just how this happens is a story for another time. Consider, however, how it would feel to be under such a spell. Or, if our entire society were spell-bound to engage in self-destructive activities but unable to talk about them. Imagine the anguish of knowing that what we do is crippling, yet being unable to articulate the alternative. Imagine this—but compounded by the awareness that what is at stake is nothing less than our collective survival.

This analogy may appear far-fetched but it illustrates the opening premise of this chapter, which is that our attempts to grapple with the challenges of climate change—particularly, to tell its stories in ways that lead to action—have been derailed by a spell. This spell, which I propose to call the ecocidal unconscious, was not cast by a fairy. It emerged from the ecocidal ontologies that have infiltrated our story systems to the point that even narratives envisioned to defend the biosphere tend to get twisted into narratives that reinforce the anthropocentric myopia which is destroying the biosphere in the first place. This spell can be broken though. Following a brief outline of the notion of the ecocidal unconscious, the chapter offers a reading of *Captain Planet and the Planeteers* (1991–2) and *Un Lun Dun* (2007). These are evoked to showcase some of the most common manifestations of the ecocidal unconscious in fantasy. The argument then shifts to consider how fantasy can help us imagine a way forward, toward a biocentric future. I introduce the concept of planetarianism as, at once, *a biocentric philosophical commitment to standing up for the planet* and *an applied hope articulated through stories*. Planetarianism, I suggest, offers us tools to expose the ecocidal unconscious; but it is planetarianist fantasy in particular—stories that articulate visions of hope for the biosphere—that can truly make the difference. The remaining part of the chapter develops a proposal about how *fantasy for the Anthropocene* can disrupt the *fantasy of the Anthropocene*—a mistaken belief that we are masters of the planet. Readings of Jon Scieszka and Steven Weinberg's *AstroNuts* (2019), Oliver Jeffers's *The Fate of Fausto* (2019), and Barbara Henderson's *Wilderness Wars* (2018) are offered as examples of hopeful moves for the planet's future gaining traction in recent fantasy. The goal is not to argue that these works form a new genre but rather to suggest that they each seek to articulate what may be called planetarianist imperatives. Each opens spaces for anticipatory, hope-oriented imagination; each empowers readers to imagine biocentric alternatives to the ecocidal status quo; and each articulates resistance to ecocide in ways that lead to action. The overall argument is that sustainable, equitable future for all forms of life on this planet must first be imagined in stories. And that fantasy has a key role to play in helping that future become reality.

One of the most valuable insights of twentieth-century critical theory is that we are other than what we imagine ourselves to be. This line of thinking owes much to Freud's critique of the liberal subject, especially his use of the notion of the unconscious. Like other psychoanalytical concepts, which Freud developed for clinical work with individuals and applied to collective processes only by analogy, the unconscious has been a contested ground, but in its classic Freudian formulation it refers to a knowing that has been repressed. The notion of the repressed content can be illuminating. Taken in a broadly metaphorical sense, it serves as "idealization"—a term Kwame Anthony Appiah uses for "sorta true" concepts (2018, 34) that provide a more productive way to think about certain subjects than the truth in all its complexity would (5). In *The Political Unconscious* (1981), for example, Marxist critic Fredric Jameson evoked the unconscious as an idealization that helps conceptualize both "the repressed and buried reality" of class struggle masked in literary texts (20) and the filter—or spell—of "interpretive codes" (9) which habituate us to read narratives in ways that miss how they function as symbolic acts in the collective "class discourses" (76). The unconscious-as-idealization has also been adapted to discussions of environmental degradation, especially the relationship between literary forms and the sources of energy that made them possible. Within a few years after Patricia Yaeger coined the term the "energy unconscious" (2011, 306), a whole new field of energy humanities arose around the challenge to "render fuels nameable, readable, and visible" (Szeman and Boyer 2017a, 6). As energy humanities scholars see it, the more we learn about our civilization's dependency on petroenergy, the more we repress the awareness that it is lethal and impossible to maintain. This repressed knowledge contributes to the formation of our energy unconscious. "Part of the critical work of energy humanities," Szeman and Boyer write, "is to sound the depths of this energy unconscious, probing the symptoms and effects of various modernities and their entanglements with fuel and electricity" (2017b, 27).

The ecocidal unconscious I invoke here is an idealization too. It serves the conceptual purpose of reflecting on our response to ecocide and refers to the tension between two contradictory knowledges: the awareness that our very existence is enabled by the rich complexity of life on this planet and the awareness that our everyday practices are destroying that complexity. Ecocide is a blanket term for human activities that contribute to a lethal degradation of the planet's biosphere—from habitat and species extinction to expansion of human populations, pollution, and global warming (Merz 2016, 17). The ecocidal unconscious denotes our refusal to acknowledge ourselves as agents of ecocide. This refusal is deeper than a mere denial of our responsibility for any contemporary environmental issue, say, biodiversity crash. It involves a refusal to let go of a more ancient notion: the dominant Western identity construct since the Neolithic revolution, which is a vision of humanity in "a state of contest with nature" (Kane 1995, 19). One name for this contest is "work," also known as Adam's curse, for it takes work to manipulate food into being and it is work that apparently separates humans from other creatures—although I am not sure bees would agree on this point. Another name of this contest is "transcendence"—with its secular flipside "progress"—an assumption that humanity is unique, distinct from other life forms, and constituted by a higher call to transcend the shackles of the natural order and regain its rightful place in a supernatural one. As a byproduct of the clash between our idea of ourselves as higher entities defined by transcendence and our experience of ourselves as biological beings constrained by our environments, the ecocidal unconscious predates the current environmental crisis.

To complicate the picture, the ecocidal unconscious is more than *repression*. It is also a form of *expression*, operating as a narrative structure and cultural convention. The ecocidal unconscious is thus, at once, a classic Freudian "dynamic unconscious" (Lumer 2019, 2), in which the uncomfortable implications of ecocide are repressed by unconscious motives such our unwillingness to confront the shame and guilt for the human assault on the biosphere, and part of the cognitive "new unconscious" (Uleman 2005, 6), in which the unconscious technical habits of our language-processing cognitive architecture perpetuate ecocide through our everyday thoughts and actions. In this latter, non-dynamic capacity, the ecocidal unconscious constitutes the cultural expression of what environmental sociologist Eileen Crist calls "the human-supremacist worldview" (2019, 3)—a worldview foundational to "the discourse of the Anthropocene" that Crist has so eloquently criticized elsewhere (2016, 130). On this level, the ecocidal unconscious frames articulations of our ontologies, habituated behaviors, cultural assumptions, and ways of reasoning that have accrued around the delusion of ourselves as masters of the biosphere. It is through these notions that the ecocidal unconscious has penetrated the narrative structure of the stories we tell.

Take the nature-loving Tolkien, for example. At one point in *The Hobbit* he introduces Bilbo's stone-throwing skills in the following sentence: "As a boy he used to practice throwing stones at things, until rabbits and squirrels, and even birds, got out of his way as quick as lightning if they saw him stoop" ([1937] 2003, 201). This aside is meant as praise. It codes that the value of nature is not intrinsic but based on human needs. It normalizes the anthropocentric bias, human supremacy, and expendability of small animals, which can be stoned on a whim. While Tolkien would likely be appalled by such meanings ascribed to his words, this is exactly how the ecocidal unconscious works. It replicates and perpetuates our habitual, unreflective ways of being in relation to the biosphere.

How and when did these notions infiltrate our story systems? And what have they to do with fantasy? In 1972 American ecologist and literary scholar Joseph W. Meeker published a study which argued that Western culture is unique on the planet in having developed the tragic view of life—predicated on defining humanity as separate, above, and in conflict with nature. According to Meeker, this view became a philosophical attitude enshrined in the most esteemed Western literary form called tragedy, a form that celebrates destruction as ennobling and has led to innumerable "cultural and biological disasters" ([1972] 1974, 24). For Meeker, the entire Western civilization is caught up in perpetuating tragedy as the only means of identity formation. Since continuing on this path poses an existential threat for humanity, Meeker considers "the rejection of the tragic view of life" as "an important precondition for the avoidance of ecological catastrophe" (59). In the framework of this chapter, it does not seem to be a stretch to say that Meeker's issue, at heart, is with the culturally sanctioned narrative expressions of the ecocidal unconscious. Certainly, when read today, his argument for non-ecocidal literary epistemologies—including those derived from non-Western, Indigenous or Native storytelling conventions—remains critical. Just as relevant is Meeker's call to retool our story systems from narratives that celebrate destruction to ones that celebrate life. Indeed, writing in 2016, Amitav Ghosh remarks that the challenges of thinking about climate change "derive ultimately from the grid of literary forms and conventions that have come to shape [our] narrative imagination" (7). To stop the ecocide, we must change how we tell stories.

A compelling argument has been made that the biocentric literary form we need is fantasy. In *The Comedy of the Fantastic* (1985), for example, Don D. Elgin applied Meeker's framework to the development of the literary fantastic, arguing that fantasy co-evolved with the idea of ecology and represents a major alternative to literary conventions wedded to the tragic. "It is the comic, ecological perspective," Elgin contends, "that principally distinguishes the fantasy novel from the tragic, formally realistic, and/or existential approaches of the traditional novel" (2). In nuanced readings of several key works, Elgin shows that fantasy offers models for reintegrating humanity in the physical universe, reflecting and creating attitudes about the relationship between humans and the nonhuman world that are fundamentally comic—that is, oriented toward "multiplicity and interdependence as the norm, adaptability and survival as the virtues, spiritual and emotional self-aggrandizement as the vices, and the pursuit of abstractions as the ultimate folly" (178).

This argument has merit and much has since been added to it. Ursula K. Le Guin's *Cheek by Jowl: Talks and Essays on How and Why Fantasy Matters* (2009), Brian Attebery's *Stories about Stories: Fantasy and the Remaking of Myth* (2014), and Daniel Heath Justice's *Why Indigenous Literatures Matter* (2018) are just some studies to suggest that of all Western literary modes fantasy is least guilty of instrumentalizing the environment. As fantasy scholars, we like to point out that fantasy is most open to subjectivity of nonhuman agents, from animals, plants, and natural elements, to animistic formations like rivers, continents, and planets. But this is only one side of the picture. The troubling other side is that fantasy has also been shaped by ecocidal literary epistemologies. A mental child of the coal and oil era—stained, too, by colonialist, imperialist, and racist inflections (see Thomas 2019)—much of early fantasy is informed by yearnings for a pastoral pre-industrial world, in which the value of the environment is aesthetic or otherwise determined by white man's needs. On a deeper level, even modern fantasy—too much of it, at least—has continued to enact the structures of what Ursula K. Le Guin has dubbed "the killer story" instead of "the life story" (1989, 168). Much of fantasy has remained heir to tragedy, a tradition of Western thought that has been the primary venue for the ecocidal unconscious.

Just how the tragic mode enables operations of the ecocidal unconscious can be appreciated in the example of Marvel Comics series Captain Planet and the Planeteers. Launched in 1991 as a spinoff of a popular cartoon series, the series was intended to mobilize comic readership to stand with the planet. Issue one, *A Hero for Earth*, introduces the conflict and the formula in which it will be resolved. The antagonist is Hoggish Greedly, "the greediest man who ever lived" (*Captain Planet* 1991a, 1), operating a giant land blaster which enables him to drill for oil anywhere and to any depth. The victim is Gaia, the spirit of Earth, woken up by spills from the drilling. The solution is the hero team that Gaia creates to stop the destruction of the planet. Called the Planeteers, the team is made up of five youths, each of whom receives a magic ring that allows them to channel one force of nature: Kwame from Africa controls earth, Gi from Asia—water, Wheeler from North America—fire, Linka from the Soviet Union—wind, and Ma-Ti from South America—the unifying power of heart. Thus equipped, the Planeteers are sent out to stop Hoggish. When they fail, the combined powers of the rings form "a being created from the very Earth itself": Captain Planet (17). The muscular blue-skinned superhero seals off the spill at the bottom of the ocean and destroys Hoggish's rig. The episode ends with Captain Planet dissolving back into the rings and the teens cleaning sea creatures contaminated by the spill. All issues that follow reiterate the same script: a singular "eco-emergency" arises, the Planeteers are sent into action but fail, Captain Planet's superhuman intervention eliminates the danger, the Planeteers help the local folks clean up the mess.

There are many problems with this story and its structure. Writing about the cartoon version of this series, for example, Susan Jaye Dauer has criticized the replication of gendered assumptions about the passive feminine Earth—"a weak creature, constantly in need of rescue" (2004, 258)—and challenged the story's questionable message about environmental destruction as being the children's responsibility to solve (261). Beyond these issues, however, the Captain Planet series is doubly crippled by the ecocidal unconscious. First, each eco-emergency always results from a one-time evil scheme of a supervillain—Hoggish Greedly who drills for oil, the evil scientist Dr. Blight, whose genetically modified dragon is responsible for air pollution, or a terrorist Argos Bleak, who threatens to release toxic waste on Washington, DC. Outside of these emergencies, humanity's business-as-usual relationship with Gaia is projected as harmonious, even consensual, which effectively denies the reality of the ongoing ecocide. Second, the heroic convention of pitting a supervillain against a superhero in a showdown that resolves the issue once and for all perpetuates the human-supremacist arrogance that causes ecocide in the first place. Not only are environmental threats presented as instances of personalized evil that can be eliminated by killing the villain; environmental action is framed as a form of warfare—even as absurd as when Ma-Ti engages terrorist Bleak in a "battle of wills," in which Bleak, overwhelmed by seeing his dark heart, passes out (Captain Planet 1991b, 21). Meeker claims that "as patterns of behavior, both tragedy and comedy are strategies for the resolution of conflicts" ([1972] 1974, 37) and the Planeteers illustrate what happens when the conflict—or problem—is misrepresented to fit the solution. In the tragic mode the only solution is warfare, "the basic metaphor of tragedy" (38). Indeed, while the series "giv[es] its violence a moral purpose" (Dauer 2004, 255), it is exactly the promise of violence as a solution that misrepresents the nature of the climate emergency. Put otherwise, the ecocidal unconscious operating in the Planeteers reinforces the tragic view of life—a view, in which the threat to the biosphere is reduced to an evil scheme and any serious consideration of ecocide, its systemic causes or nature, is actively blocked from view.

The Captain Planet series was discontinued only after twelve issues, but the legacy of tragedy in fantasy lives on. Too many fantasy narratives continue to project ecocide as an individual's moral errors, framing it as personal tragic experiences rather than systemic outcomes of how our society is organized. China Miéville's Un Lun Dun (2007) is one such example. The novel tells a story which casts personified smog as a supervillain bent on taking over the world. The Smog's advance is admittedly made possible by specific individuals: in London, its unwitting ally is Elizabeth Rowley, secretary of state for the environment. Driven by political ambitions, she creates a government-sanctioned plan to reroute carbon emissions from London to UnLondon. In the alternate universe, the Smog's instrument is the character of Brokkenbroll, the master of broken umbrellas, who employs the Smog in hopes of becoming UnLondon's sole ruler. Still, the rise of Smog is presented as the villain's own choice and no connection is made to the human energy systems that generate it. Driven by insatiable ambition, the Smog declares:

I want to grow, and grow, and know. … I will gather everyone. And fire will spread, and all UnLondoners and all their houses and their lovely books and all their lovely minds will float in smoke and come and be in me. And I'll know everything. And be everyone. No one will end. I will be all of you. Is that so bad?

(Miéville 2008, 433–4, italics in the original)

By establishing the Smog as anthropomorphized evil agency, Miéville's narrative sidesteps issues of human responsibility and offers yet another version of the Planeteers as saviors. Admittedly, as Anita Tarr has noted, the supervillain is defeated by an ordinary human—albeit wielding a superweapon—so one trope of "the typical hero's journey" is subverted (2018, 251). Still, the plot unfolds as a conflict between two clearly defined sides, culminates in a war in which outnumbered UnLondoners fight against the Smog's army, and concludes with a spectacular shoot-out, in which the protagonist kills the Smog using the bullets of nothingness. When Deeba fires the final shot, sucking the last of the Smog down the barrel of her magic gun, the Smog becomes sequestered. The UnGun is then buried in a concrete slab and Deeba returns to her own London, luxuriating in the awareness that *"It'll always be me got rid of the Smog"* (Miéville 2008, 467). The utter finality of this victory—coupled with the novel's silence on the systemic, human-driven causes for the rise of atmospheric pollution—is instructive about how the ecocidal unconscious, operating in a narrative's structure, is able to distort the story's environmental message. Unlike the Planeteers, *Un Lun Dun* succeeds in communicating that pollution is a negative externality of the global economy which often gets dumped on the poor elsewhere—in this case, into an alternative world. Still, the novel remains wedded to the tragic view of life through its root metaphor of warfare. It ends up glorifying a human hero triumphing over a force of nature and reinforces the tragic mode's core binary of nature versus culture. In this sense, the "irritatingly didactic" *Un Lun Dun* (Tarr 2018, 268) represents the limitations of trying to conceptualize the challenges of the Anthropocene as an epic conflict with clearly defined sides and an unambiguous victory.

It is not encouraging to realize that our literary conventions work against our survival. Yet, the recognition of the ecocidal unconscious is a necessary first step toward challenging the dominance of the tragic mode. The next steps include experimentation with plot structures, tropes, and themes to enable the imaginative processes required to productively engage with ecocide and other urgencies of the Anthropocene. Just how this feat can be accomplished has been a subject of a debate that stretches from Meeker, Elgin, Buell, Glotfelty, and other early ecocritics, to Szeman, Moore, Haraway, Morton, Crist, Heise, Trexler, Curry, and other contemporary scholars in the fields of environmental and energy humanities. What unites this extremely diverse tradition is the premise that the challenge of addressing climate change is not primarily scientific or technological, but one for the humanities and social sciences, "disciplines that have long attended to the intricacies of social processes, the nature and capacity of political change, and the circulation and organization of symbolic meaning through culture" (Szeman and Boyer 2017a, 3). Indeed, only the humanities—and especially our story systems—are capable of rewiring our affective and cognitive modes of being in relation to the ongoing ecocide: away from collusion and ignorance, toward active resistance and hopeful dreaming. "Hopeful dreaming" is Lloyd Alexander's ingenious term for fantasy (1968, 389) and I want to suggest that linking resistance with hope is a key factor for enabling articulations of emancipatory imagination through stories. When Miéville insists that we should "utopia as hard as we can" (2016, 25) and Le Guin challenges writers to "imagine … real grounds for hope" (2014, n.p.); when Patrick Curry celebrates "the Earthly origin and nature of enchantment" (2019, 26) and Adeline Johns-Putra highlights "the ecocentric possibilities of wonder" (2019, 140)—one idea emerging in these voices is that resistance to ecocide must start in imagination focused on hope. Fantasy, I contend, has a major role to play in this process.

The discourse of the Anthropocene has been described as a collective delusion, delivering "a Promethean self-portrait" of humanity "on a par with Nature's own tremendous force," or on the cusp of achieving full mastery over it (Crist 2016, 17). Another name for this mistaken belief is *the fantasy of the Anthropocene*. This fantasy is the exact opposite of what *fantasy for the Anthropocene* must be. To assist us in the transition to an ecological civilization, I suggest, fantasy in the age of Great Derangement must challenge the fantasy of the Anthropocene. It can no longer ignore the multiple evils of climate change but should help us imagine fantastic alternatives beyond ecocide. And what can be more fantastic today than visions of a biocentric sustainable civilization on a thriving, multispecies planet? What can be more fantastic than stories about how ecocide was reversed? The challenge for fantasy today is to dream about exactly that hope. To weave it from words into visions that inspire action.

Given that the Anthropocene is predicated on an assumption that the entire biosphere is doomed to be reshaped into a domesticated, purely human project, one way to resist the fantasy of the Anthropocene would be to adopt an epistemological orientation of not giving up on the planet. Suppose we call it planetarianism. A two-level phenomenon, planetarianism would then be, on the one hand, *a biocentric philosophical commitment to stand up for the planet*— thus, a counternarrative to the discourse of the Anthropocene that legitimizes ecocide and renders it inevitable. On the other hand, planetarianism would also be *applied hope articulated through stories*—a form of hope-as-resistance that enables us to design alternatives to ecocide through stories that imagine a non-ecocidal sociopolitical system, a disanthropocentrized planet, and a biocentric, multispecies future that is worth living for. On this level, in a very practical sense, planetarianism can be examined as a component of narrative fiction.

There is no single perfect model of what planetarianist fantasy can be. Indeed, there is no certainty about whether we will see the emergence of planetarianist fantasy as a distinct category, say within ecofiction or cli-fi. Still, a number of recent works appear to be engaged in exploring planetarianist moves through the fantasy format. One of them is Jon Scieszka and Steven Weinberg's early-grade chapter book *AstroNuts: Mission One: The Plant Planet* (2019). *AstroNuts* offers a good example of the affordances of the fantastic in defense of Earth's unique capacity to support a rich diversity of life. Narrated by Earth itself, the book recounts a reconnaissance mission of four mutant animal superheroes who travel to the distant Plant Planet to see if it is suitable for human habitation. What they find is a world dominated only by one form of life: plants. The plants' unbalanced ecosystem renders the entire planet vulnerable to a catastrophic extinction of life, even after such minor trigger as the AstroNut StinkBug's fart. When this indeed happens, Earth comments on Plant Planet's fate as having "showed the AstroNuts exactly what can happen when one species takes over the planet. Like what humans are doing on me" (194). The AstroNuts return to their secret base behind Thomas Jefferson's nose at Mount Rushmore and will continue exploring other planets in the sequels.

Silly as the plot appears to be, *AstroNuts* succeeds in its choice of strategies to engage with some of the key questions of the Anthropocene. Unlike the Planeteers, sent into action to stop a single drilling venture, the AstroNuts' mission begins when the level of CO_2 in Earth's atmosphere rises above 400 PPM. The systemic and planetary-wide nature of ecocide is made clear when Earth declares this to be "a deadly emergency, … caused by you humans" and goes on to explain that putting more carbon in the atmosphere is already resulting in "overheating my oceans, melting my ice caps, killing my plants and animals and even yourselves" (10). The concept of the Goldilock planet is introduced at the outset, highlighting the uniqueness of Earth through contrast with other planets which are unable to support complex multispecies ecosystems. The novel is interspersed with episodes of research, in which the AstroNuts study interactions among various systems within a biosphere. For example, when SmartHawk explores the ecosystem of Plant Planet, she notes that "without animals to keep the balance [between oxygen and carbon dioxide], the levels here are all messed up" (48)—a point further stressed by Earth's insistence that "the balance of a planet is key to its survival" (65). The choice of Earth as a framing narrator is significant too. Unlike the passive, swooning Gaia from the Planeteers, the gender-neutral Earth in *AstroNuts* is able to tell its own story, unapologetically drawing young humans into an awareness of how humanity must act to prevent its own demise. After it compares its current situation to having "a Humans-Burning-Fossil-Fuels Flu" (96), for example, Earth concludes: "If your species decides to temporarily wreck my finely balanced climate and ecosystems by ending all human existence—I'll be sad … but I will also … be just fine" (97).

The way *AstroNuts* radically decenters the human is another sharp contrast to the Planeteers. The only humans in the story are the implied audience. The leading voice is Earth, and the mission is accomplished solely by the nonhuman characters. Each of the four mutant animal heroes is constructed as a characteristically irreverent Scieszkian personage—exuberant, over the top, and feature-tagged to be decodable by pre-teen readers—but also represents a real-life species with their real-life special powers. AlphaWolf, a timber wolf, has superhuman smell and hearing; SmartHawk, a broad-winged hawk, boasts amazing "9,000x zoom vision" (25); LaserShark, a great white shark, can navigate by sensing the electromagnetic field; and StinkBug, a dung beetle, is unbeatable at high-altitude jumping and playing dead. This collection of characters at once breaks away from animal fantasy's preference for mammal characters and establishes a truly diverse nonhuman coalition to communicate how the survival of Earth as home matters to more than just humans. The hero team is foolish, ridiculous, and bumbling. Far from diminishing the seriousness of the challenge they face, this choice enables the book to articulate the key patterns of the comic mode: celebration of life, adaptation to the environment, and recognition of the destructive nature of abstractions—such as, say, AlphaWolf's ridiculous ideas of glory. As a result, and in a way that would likely delight Meeker and Elgin, *AstroNuts* is able to navigate past the traps of the tragic mode, including the ecocidal unconscious with its anthropocentrism and preference for violence as a solution. For instance, at the book's climax, when the plants seemingly attack the AstroNuts and the events are about to take a heroic turn, Earth unabashedly cuts in with its own story. "I'm so sorry to interrupt this fierce AstroNut vs. Plant battle," it says, but "if you don't do something [about your own planet], you are cooked" (92). This abrupt shift mocks the heroic conflict as a distraction, reestablishing the comic notion of survival as the narrative's central thrust. The book's affirmation of the comic mode is likewise communicated through Steven Weinberg's goofy illustrations: each of his collaged reworkings of artwork from the Dutch National Museum is a challenge to the notion of epic seriousness. Not surprisingly, the book does not end with any clear-cut victory that solves Earth's problems once and for all; it ends with a humble survival-for-now, without any guarantees of a happily ever after. This is a hopeful ending, but it raises more questions about our precarious present than any heroic triumph ever could.

AstroNuts illustrates a number of planetarianist moves with a pronounced hopeful potential for disrupting the ongoing ecocide. It decenters the human perspective in favor of a biospheric focus; it reveals systemic drivers of ecocide that must be addressed through collective action against the business-as-usual operations of our civilization; it rejects the tragic mode's heroism with its root metaphor of warfare; and it celebrates our planet's uniqueness, stressing that we can choose to stop ecocide and create a sustainable biocentric civilization. Each of these moves offers a different kind of hope for the planet. On a particularly beautiful morning, for example, one may well imagine that in a fully realized work of planetarianist fantasy, for certain readers at least, these multiple hopes would lead to a ratchet effect, in which the more hope the readers decode on any one level, the more they are able to absorb from other aspects of the story. This plural, actable-conceptual hope that ecocide can be stopped is a form of enchantment that fantasy for the Anthropocene can, indeed must offer. As Patrick Curry describes it, enchantment is an experience of wonder that emerges when we enter, even if for a moment, into a relationship with another and recognize that other being as a person. "Whether the other party is technically human or not, or even alive or not, is unimportant" (2019, 14); what matters is the sense of deep relationality with the other, accompanied by "fearless receptivity" in which we recognize the constitutive power of this relationship (16).

Fantasy, of course, has been conceived as a vehicle of enchantment. It succeeds only when it enchants. Today, however, the particular kind of enchantment many authors seem to aspire to is for the reader to recognize their personal relationship with the planet: not just with some particular place but with the planet and biosphere as such. This is an ambitious project requiring that we conceptualize the hyperobjects called the "planet" and "biosphere" as specific beings rather than abstractions. Curry notes that disenchantment—the notion of nature as "nothing but a blank canvas, an inert, featureless nothingness"—is the prime enabler of ecocide and "a fundamental prerequisite for the entire process" (2019, 91). If so, narrative renderings of the planet as having agency and subjectivity—as a being we can personally relate to and apprehend while being apprehended by it—emerge as forms of resistance to ecocide. Weaving that enchantment, fantasy as a literary mode seems to be especially well suited to engender a specific kind of hope, a very fantastic hope indeed, that the planet, or nonhuman life in general, would speak to us and become an active, if non-personalized agent to counteract human destructiveness. We may not necessarily want a nonhuman agent like a pandemic, although the Covid-19 emergency has certainly demonstrated that a nonhuman force, in the space of mere weeks, is able to cool down the human enterprise more effectively than twenty-five years of climate change negotiations and neoliberal free-trade agreements. The hope that ecocide can likewise be stopped by some nonhuman and nondystopian planetary intervention is a noticeable feature of recent fantasy too. Whether the flipside of anxiety that if left alone we would be unable to stop the destruction we have unleashed—as in Shaun Tan's story about how we put the orca in the sky but "don't know how to get it down" (2018, 157)—or an expression of our yearning for re-connecting with the nonhuman and planetary life, this hope has taken a variety of forms.

In Oliver Jeffers's picturebook *The Fate of Fausto: A Painted Fable* (2019), the planetary interlocutor is plural and does not challenge human destructiveness directly. Instead, the book offers a parable of the human-supremacist worldview, presented through a series of encounters that end with the demise of the human. "There was once a man who believed he owned everything," the story begins, "and set out to survey what was his" (n.p.). Starting with small things like flowers or sheep, the haughty Fausto goes on to claim a tree, a field, a forest, and a lake. When a mountain claims to belong to itself, Fausto throws a fit until the mountain acknowledges Fausto as being in charge. Not satisfied, Fausto embarks to claim the sea. "Now, admit you are mine," he demands, or "I will stomp my foot and make a fist." Curious, the sea invites him to do so. "In order to show his anger and importance," Fausto steps out of the boat and drowns. A warning about misconstruing humanity's place in the world, *The Fate of Fausto* extrapolates from the belief in human separateness from nature, showing that the consequences of the supremacist worldview will be disastrous primarily for humanity. "The sea was sad for him, but carried on being the sea. The mountain, too, went to its business"— everything "carried on as before" for the fate of Fausto "did not matter to them" (n.p.).

Another strategy for imagining the voice of the planet can be found in Barbara Henderson's *Wilderness Wars* (2018). The novel recounts a failed attempt to build a luxury resort on the uninhabited Outer Hebrides island of Skelsay—a project that Skelsay's entire nonhuman environment doggedly resists. Narrated by twelve-year-old Em, the daughter of the chief engineer, the novel begins on the ferry, where workers and their families are attacked by a frenzied flock of gulls. When they unload on the island, weird waves and wind gusts sink one of the containers. From then on, improbable disasters follow: when the workers are ready to pour foundations, the island freezes to prevent it; when they need building supplies, the island surrounds itself in fog so thick that the supply boat cannot get in; when people hunker down to wait it out, their food supplies are wrecked by voles, weasels, and other critters that invade the storehouse. The children realize it first: "We are destroying the habitats—the homes—of all these plants and animals … [N]ature, the wilderness, is fighting back. To get us all out of here, to get the island back" (139). Time and again adults refuse to recognize that the concatenation of coincidences reflects nature's agency and the conflict ends only when children begin to talk with and for the island. Em writes a story, recounting adult unwillingness to recognize the island's resistance, in which she imagines the fantastic solution of a weird earthquake and tsunami that forces the project to shut down. "It's pretty convincing. For fiction," she reflects. "I can only pray it makes a difference in real life" (146). Fantastically, the island picks up the idea. It thanks Em by giving her a dream, showing the warning signs of the disaster. When these happen a few days later, Em is able to lead the still-unbelieving community up the slopes of the mountain, saving them from a massive tidal wave that destroys the construction site. Although Henderson's novel stops short of giving nature a direct voice, it affirms that the world is alive and speaking to those who would listen. The book targets human expansionism, envisions Skelsay as a nonhuman personality or synecdoche of planetary wilderness, and attests to the need of human–nonhuman coalitions in defense of the biosphere. It offers a fantasy in which ecocide is averted and a biocentric future, based on respect for the nonhuman and planetary life, can be envisioned.

Like characters in *Jonathan Strange and Mr. Norrell*, we need to break the spell of the ecocidal unconscious. Learning to articulate our situation with clarity and courage will require challenging the centuries-worth of unreflexive mental habits through which we have asserted our separateness. When one character in Clarke's novel awakens to the world's aliveness, the experience feels "as if his mind had fallen down" (2004, 669). It is scary. But if our core assumptions are wrong, falling down from them can only be liberating. Accordingly, Clarke ends the book with Mr. Strange's assurance that "it is not so hard as we have supposed" (667). As animals immersed in ecosystems, we are of this planet. To betray it would be a callous act of self-destruction. Imagining the way forward, toward a biocentric future requires that we abandon the disenchanted "Cartesian fantasy" of nature as inert (Curry 2019, 91) and call into question the fantasy of the Anthropocene, a false belief that we are masters of the biosphere. The Anthropocene confronts us with the largest challenge humanity has ever faced and how we will meet it depends on how we will use our imaginations. Will we find the courage to imagine that the world is alive? Will we find the courage to imagine alternatives to ecocide? Fantasy has long been underrated as a tool for social and political change, but fantasy for the Anthropocene will succeed only when it spurs readers toward a biocentric commitment to the planet. Only by confronting the reality of ecocide can it offer hope that will become an investment in protecting the possibility of the Earth's survival. *AstroNuts*, *The Fate of Fausto*, and *Wilderness Wars* are some of the recent works which suggest that planetarianist moves are gaining traction in fantasy and that the search for a different relationship with the biosphere is well under way. Whatever the future holds, it must first be imagined in stories. Fantasy is the best tool we have to envision futures in which our current ecocidal practices have been replaced with relationality that sustains all life.

References

Alexander, Lloyd. 1968. "Wishful Thinking—Or Hopeful Dreaming?" *The Horn Book Magazine*, vol. 44: 383–90.

Appiah, Kwame Anthony. 2018. *As If: Idealization and Ideals*. Cambridge, MA: Harvard University Press.

Attebery, Brian. 2014. *Stories about Stories: Fantasy and the Remaking of Myth*. New York: Oxford University Press.

Captain Planet and the Planeteers. A Hero for Earth. 1991a. Marvel Comics, vol. 1, October 1991.

Captain Planet and the Planeteers. Heart Attack. 1991b. Marvel Comics, vol. 3, December 1991.

Clarke, Susanna. 2004. *Jonathan Strange and Mr. Norrell: A Novel*. New York: Bloomsbury.

Crist, Eileen. 2016. "On the Poverty of Our Nomenclature." In *Anthropocene or Capitalocene: Nature, History, and the Crisis of Capitalism*, edited by Jason W. Moore, 14–33. Oakland, CA: PM Press.

Crist, Eileen. 2019. *Abundant Earth: Toward an Ecological Civilization*. Chicago, IL: The University of Chicago Press.

Curry, Patrick. 2019. *Enchantment: Wonder in Modern Life*. Edinburgh: Floris Books.

Dauer, Susan Jaye. 2004. "Cartoons and Contamination: How the Multinational Kids Help Captain Planet Save Gaia." In *Wild Things: Children's Culture and Ecocriticism*, edited by Sidney I. Dobrin and Kenneth B. Kidd, 254–66. Detroit, MI: Wayne State University Press.

Elgin, Don D. 1985. *The Comedy of the Fantastic: Ecological Perspectives on the Fantasy Novel*. Westport, CT: Greenwood Press.

Ghosh, Amitav. 2016. *The Great Derangement: Climate Change and the Unthinkable*. Chicago, IL: University of Chicago Press.

Henderson, Barbara. 2018. *Wilderness Wars*. Blacksheep Croft: Pokey Hat.

Jameson, Fredric. 1981. *The Political Unconscious: Narrative as a Socially Symbolic Act*. Ithaca, NY: Cornell University Press.

Jeffers, Oliver. 2019. *The Fate of Fausto: A Painted Fable*. New York: Philomel Books.

Johns-Putra, Adeline. 2019. *Climate Change and the Contemporary Novel*. Cambridge: Cambridge University Press.

Kane, Sean. 1995. *Wisdom of the Mythtellers*. Peterborough: Broadview Press.

Le Guin, Ursula K. 1989. "The Carrier Bag Theory of Fiction." In *Dancing at the Edge of the World*. 165–70. New York: Grove Press.

Le Guin, Ursula K. 2014. "National Book Awards Acceptance Speech." YouTube video. 06: 08. November 19, 2014. YouTube. https://www.youtube.com/watch?v=Et9Nf-rsALk

Lumer, Christoph. 2019. "Unconscious Motives and Actions—Agency, Freedom and Responsibility." *Frontiers in Psychology*, vol. 9, no. 2777 (February): 1–16. Doi: 10.3389/fpsyg.2018.02777

Meeker, Joseph W. (1972) 1974. *The Comedy of Survival: Studies in Literary Ecology*. New York: Charles Scribner's Sons.

Merz, Prisca. 2016. "Ecocide." *Socialist Lawyer* (October): 16–19.

Miéville, China. 2008. *Un Lun Dun*. New York: Del Rey Books.

Miéville, China. 2016. "The Limits of Utopia: Introduction." In *Utopia*. Thomas More, with Supplement by Ursula K. Le Guin and Introduction by China Miéville, 11–27. London: Verso.

Scieszka, Jon, and Steven Weinberg. 2019. *AstroNuts, Mission One: The Plant Planet*. San Francisco, CA: Chronicle Books.

Szeman, Imre, and Dominick Boyer. 2017a. "Introduction: On Energy Humanities." In *Energy Humanities: An Anthology*, edited by Imre Szeman and Dominick Boyer, 1–14. Baltimore, MD: Johns Hopkins University Press.

Szeman, Imre, and Dominick Boyer. 2017b. "Energy and Modernity: Histories and Futures." In *Energy Humanities: An Anthology*, edited by Imre Szeman and Dominick Boyer, 27–31. Baltimore, MD: Johns Hopkins University Press.

Tan, Shaun. 2018. *Tales from the Inner City*. New York: Arthur A. Levine Books.

Tarr, Anita. 2018. "China Miéville's Young Adult Novels: Posthumanist Assemblages." In *Posthumanism in Young Adult Fiction: Finding Humanity in a Posthuman World*, edited by Anita Tarr and Donna R. White, 247–72. Jackson: University Press of Mississippi.

Thomas, Ebony Elizabeth. 2019. *The Dark Fantastic: Race and the Imagination from Harry Potter to the Hunger Games*. New York: New York University Press.

Tolkien, J. R. R. (1937) 2003. *The Annotated Hobbit*. Annotated by Douglas A. Anderson. Boston, MA: Houghton Mifflin.

Trexler, Adam. 2015. *Anthropocene Fictions: The Novel in a Time of Climate Change*. Charlottesville: University of Virginia Press.

Uleman, James S. 2005. "Introduction: Becoming Aware of the New Unconscious." In *The New Unconscious*, edited by Ran R. Hassin, James S. Uleman, and John A. Bargh, 3–15. New York: Oxford University Press.

Yaeger, Patricia, et al. 2011. "Editor's Column: Literature in the Ages of Wood, Tallow, Coal, Whale Oil, Gasoline, Atomic Power, and Other Energy Sources." *PMLA*, vol. 126, no. 2: 305–26.

CHAPTER 9
ASTRONUTS, THE ORIGIN STORY
Jon Scieszka

Enjoying a cold beer in a dark bar after an absolutely inspired Book Festival day of showing and telling stories to thousands of insanely excited kids, author-illustrator Steven Weinberg and I decided we needed to make a graphic novel series as fun, wild, and smart as our audience.

We both threw out a handful of ideas, and both quickly realized the single most compelling, necessary, and inescapable challenge facing our modern little humans was … the already happening global catastrophe of human-caused climate change.

We knew we had to show and tell the real science.

We knew we had to give kids a realistic hope to change.

We knew we had to somehow make our homo sapiens-driven ecocide personal … and funny.

And so the *AstroNuts*, a not-very-secret NNASA (Not NASA) project of superpowered SmartHawk, AlphaWolf, LaserShark, and StinkBug searching for a Goldilocks planet, was born.

At the heart of the *AstroNuts* series lies the idea that any species over-dominating a planet could mess it up. This goes against the glib arrogance of those who champion the human supremacy over the biosphere as a desirable goal. One of my favorite things about the series is that we pop this delusion of species grandeur called the Anthropocene. So *Book #1*, *The Plant Planet*, has plants destroying every other species and over-oxygenating their planet. *Book #2*, *The Water Planet* has a biosphere ruined by oil-drilling dominant species clams. And *Book #3*, *The Perfect Planet* features—Spoiler Alert!—Earth. One million years ago. Before an unlikely primate species discovers fire, starts burning fossil fuels, and throws their entire planet out of whack.

My other most favorite part of *AstroNuts* is Steven's artwork—a wild and gorgeous collaged mix of copyright-free museum masterpieces and Steven's own comic drawings and additions. The re-mixed art tells the AstroNut story in exactly the same way the text does—in a provocative funny mix of real and fantasy.

The other fun and deeply educational feature of Steven's AstroArt is a two-page spread at the end of every book, showing kids how Steven created the art, and giving them the links to our astronuts.space website, and the open source museum websites so they can build their own creations.

Though now that I think of it, my most favorite part of *AstroNuts* has to be Earth as our narrator.

Earth has been around for a long time.
Earth has seen a lot.
So it's probably best, as in every book, that Earth have the last word.

Plate 9.1 *AstroNuts*, museum feature, *Jon Scieszka*

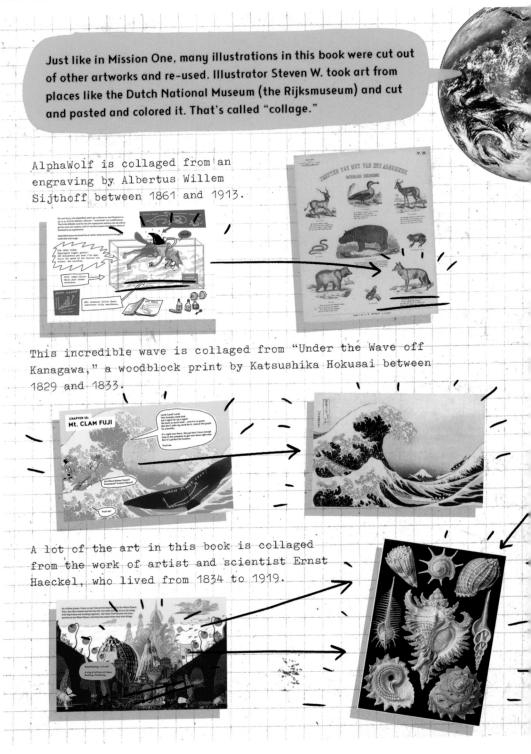

Just like in Mission One, many illustrations in this book were cut out of other artworks and re-used. Illustrator Steven W. took art from places like the Dutch National Museum (the Rijksmuseum) and cut and pasted and colored it. That's called "collage."

AlphaWolf is collaged from an engraving by Albertus Willem Sijthoff between 1861 and 1913.

This incredible wave is collaged from "Under the Wave off Kanagawa," a woodblock print by Katsushika Hokusai between 1829 and 1833.

A lot of the art in this book is collaged from the work of artist and scientist Ernst Haeckel, who lived from 1834 to 1919.

Now I know as Earth, I'm not supposed to play favorites, but this Haeckel guy was pretty special. He studied some of the smallest organisms on me, drawing and classifying them in his most famous book *Art Forms in Nature*. Haeckel provided early evidence for Darwin's Theory of Evolution, inspired Art Nouveau, and did just what the AstroNuts missions do: show science and art working side by side!

Ernst Haeckel

And don't forget! Make your own AstroNuts on the book series website: AstroNuts.Space. Download printouts and MORE!

COLLAGE YOUR OWN!!

Don't worry. Steven is not breaking any laws. The Rijksmuseum wants people to see and use their amazing collection of artwork. So they have put almost all of it online. For more information, go to: RIJKSMUSEUM.NL

Plate 9.2 *AstroNuts*, Earth, *Jon Scieszka and Steven Weinberg*

Plate 9.3 Collaging change, *Steven Weinberg*

Like this painting: "The Oxbow" by Thomas Cole. It's positively screaming to be remixed into a book about our climate crisis. (We use it in book 3!) The painting is about the climate devastation caused by the US industrialization in the 19th century. Why not enlist it in our contemporary conversation?

Ha! Yeah and we should be just as blunt as Cole was. How's that farmland in the floodprone oxbow gonna handle this storm? Humanity is in trouble.

We sure are. But as we try to figure out a solution to our giant mess, perhaps we can find some inspiration from the past. We need all the help we can get!

Special thanks to the Metropolitan Museum of Art for adding The Oxbow to the public domain!

Plate 9.4 Together we sail, *Hatem Aly*

One suggestion for the title of this piece was "Rising, Together" but I thought it was patronising. We humans have managed to raise a lot of things including sea levels and CO2 so I wanted to tone down the sense of conceitedness and go for something humble and hopeful. How do we create art that keeps the feeling of togetherness and emphasizes collective effort? Art that communicates a sense of working together for the planet and orients us, especially young people, to a better (not "the right" or "the best") direction? Humans are unflinching when they put something in their minds and the image shows a little of the impossible and the fantastic that we could bend to make better choices for the future. So I went with

Together We Sail

PART II
DREAMING THE EARTH

CHAPTER 10
ANTHROPOS AND THE EARTH
Brian Attebery

Child of Man didn't pay much attention to Earth for a long time. Earth provided plentiful food, lying among vines, hanging from low branches, and—Child wasn't particular—crawling under leaves. There was no need to bother Earth for anything more.

But one day, Child found a half-buried tuber—the kind that tasted like chestnuts after roasting—and picked up a stick to dig it out. Child began to play with the stick, poking it into holes in trees, turning over rocks, and dragging it across the ground. The stick made a mark on Earth that pleased Child. Child tried pushing the stick deeper and the mark was even more noticeable, for Earth in that place was red under a layer of grass and leaves. The scar in Earth, and the exposed roots on its sides, gave Child an idea. Child would like to have more tubers and didn't want to go searching for them. Maybe Child could find others over there and bring them back to plant here. So Child did just that.

The soil where Child was digging was rich and deep. The river flooded it every year, and Water brought new wealth to Earth. Child brought more favorite foods and planted them nearby. For a time, Child was happy with this new supply of roots and seeds and fruits. But it wasn't enough. Child got a bigger stick and dug more trenches to plant in. Child began to pull up the plants that Child couldn't eat; then to cut away trees and bushes that shaded the food plants. Child's new friend Fire could burn away whole fields and leave them ready for planting. Child worked on the stick to make it sharper and stronger. With Fire's help, Child made a new kind of stick out of metal, which Child fixed in a wooden frame to make it drag even deeper into Earth. Child talked the Ass and Bull into helping: they could pull the metal stick through even the toughest places.

Child grew excited watching the new invention cut through Earth and expose its hidden parts. It made Child think about other things: other furrows, other kinds of penetration. Child decided this was a new sacred thing: a marriage between Child and Earth, with Child playing the man part and Earth the woman.

But Earth had not consented to the marriage. Earth grew dry without its green cloak. Air blew Earth away in clouds of dust. Child had to block up the river to turn it onto the land, and Water stopped flooding Earth so Earth could no longer nourish the things Child planted. This wasn't fair. Child was doing Child's part in the sacred marriage: plowing and seeding. Why wasn't Earth doing its part?

The flood plain became an arid waste. The small folk who hid in the soil and kept it alive, many too small for Child to see, suffered when the plow exposed them to Air and sunlight. They began to die off. Soon there was no soil, only sand. Child was hungry and didn't like living in a desert. So Child moved on to a new place, bringing the plow, animal servants to pull it, and a basket of seeds. It was time for a new marriage with this new Earth. Now everything would be good again, as it was in the time that Child half-remembered and half-imagined, the time before the Anthropocene began.

CHAPTER 11
EMBODYING THE PERMACULTURE STORY:
TERRY PRATCHETT'S TIFFANY ACHING SERIES
Tereza Dědinová

The hat makes the witch. Not only is it a hallmark of witchcraft, it also represents the witch's personality. Tiffany Aching, a young girl who "had made herself the witch because [her land] needed one" (Pratchett 2010, chap. 1) throws away a pompous dwarf-made hat and politely refuses a much simpler one offered her in an unprecedented expression of respect by Granny Weatherwax, the unofficial yet undisputable leader of witches in the Ramtops. Although Tiffany appreciates the old witch's gesture, she instinctively understands that the "only hat worth wearing was the one you made for yourself ... Your own future, not someone else's" (2004, chap. 15). So, after defeating a hiver—an incorporeal, yet immensely dangerous creature that she let occupy her body in a single moment of vanity—Tiffany climbs a hill overlooking the Chalk, her homeland, makes a hat out of the sky and lets it fill up with stars.

Coming late in the second novel of Terry Pratchett's Tiffany Aching series (2003–2015), this act of defining herself in co-creation with nature represents an organic connection between an individual and her environment. From all possible means of obtaining her hat, Tiffany chooses to wear the sky, to transcend boundaries between herself and nature. She can do this not because she commands nature, but because she merges with it. In this chapter I propose this as a defining moment for the series. It crowns the evolution of its central character as a witch whose power stems from connection with her homeland. It also suggests something about fantasy as a cultivation of invisible connections that aligns the logic of fantasy with that of permaculture.

The sensation of belonging, happiness, and strength derived from the intimate relationship with a particular place can be very real yet hard to express in everyday language. Fantasy is an excellent means of conveying just such relationships with the nonhuman and has a long tradition of doing so (see, e.g., Elgin 1985; Le Guin 2007; Oziewicz 2008; Attebery 2014). Free to play with the so-called consensual reality and draw on characters and ideas from mythic narratives, fantasy enables readers to experience crucial concepts not as mere metaphors but analogues of truth. When reading, we slip past disbelief and get immersed in fictional reality, which allows us to react with greater empathy than in real life (Keen 2007, 27–35). After closing the book, we might look around with what Tolkien called a regained clear view (Tolkien 1947) or perhaps acknowledge the limitations of our habitual interpretation of the world. G. K. Chesterton characterized fantasy as a tool for showing the everyday world "from a different perspective, so that once again we see it for the first time and realize how marvelous it is" (Peschel 2006). A third fantasy master Ursula K. Le Guin famously claimed that fantasy does "include the nonhuman as essential" (Le Guin 2007, 87). The work of Terry Pratchett is a continuation of this tradition in the Tiffany Aching series, especially due to the entwining of human character and her environment. While Pratchett does not explicitly ask how fantasy can help us reinvent our role in the biosphere, he uses the affordances of fantasy to explore the meaning of one's connection to the land. In this endeavor, he arrives at the concept remarkably akin to principles of permaculture, which proposes practical methods for mutually nurturing culture–nature relationship. As a philosophy and design, permaculture empowers individuals to rethink their position vis-à-vis the nonhuman world and renders "alternative ways of organizing in response to the Anthropocene" (Roux-Rosier, Azambuja and Islam 2018). Permaculture is both a source of practical know-how and, as an applied philosophy, a wellspring of enthusiasm and hope (see Smith 2020).

Overcoming the imagined separation between humanity and nature is critical for enabling a biospheric civilization. Building on this notion, I read Terry Pratchett's Tiffany Aching series as a narrative exploration of how the modern perception of the self as distinct and detached from nature can be replaced with a concept of symbiotic coexistence of these two realms. In the series, witches stand as mediators between culture and nature and embody a hybridized essence of reality. After surveying the broader context of Pratchett's work, I outline the philosophy of permaculture and take a closer look at the parallels between permaculture ethics and Pratchett's subversion of the culture–nature divide. The intention is not to determine whether Pratchett was familiar with permaculture. While I do consider the author's real-world inspirations, my focus lies in how Pratchett's portrayal of a decentralized human organically embedded in her environment appears to communicate the realities and requirements of a permaculture lifestyle.

Terry Pratchett's Discworld series started in 1983 with *The Colour of Magic*. The final novel *The Shepherd's Crown* was published after the author's death in 2015. In over thirty years of developing this universe, Pratchett's fictional world came to reflect a broad range of social issues from xenophobia, nationalism, and religious fundamentalism, to sexism, environmentalism, politics, education, and culture. Presented in a comic mode that exposes the hypocrisy, silliness, and illusions of grandeur of the human psyche, the Discworld universe mirrors both failings and heroic endeavors taking place in our real world. The intertwining of comedy with serious questions makes the reading of Pratchett's books a unique pleasure and has undoubtedly contributed to their enormous popularity. As Marion Rana sums up the achievement, "Pratchett's writing is deep and insightful, but it is also accessible, imaginative and truly and deeply funny" (2018, 3).

The relationship between an individual and her environment, central to this chapter, is reflected in many of Pratchett's novels. Aside from books set in Ramtops mountains with witches as central characters, to which I will later refer, it forms a consistent thread in books that explore the intimate connection of Samuel Vimes or Carrot Ironfoundersson with the city of Ankh-Morpork.[1]

The Tiffany Aching series consists of five novels published between 2003 and 2015. Set in the rural downs of the Chalk—modeled on the chalklands of the Chiltern Hills, the region of Pratchett's childhood where he returned to live as an adult—the novels are some of the most place-based works of Pratchett's fiction that considers the meaning of the countryside. As Pratchett himself confirmed, the connection between the real and fictional Chalk is profound and mediated by Tiffany, who mirrors the author's childhood memories.

> And a lot of the things that Tiffany thinks and sees, in fact, I thought and saw when I was her age; a lot of the way Tiffany comprehends the landscape is based on my own

experiences. I don't come from a farming family, but I spent a lot of time among farmers and their families when I was a kid.

(qtd. in Peschel 2006)

The intimate connection with the land present in the series is thus based on the real-world relationship the author developed with the region where he grew up. As Marc Burrows sums up this relationship in Pratchett's biography, "Terry's land was in the bones of the Tiffany stories, just as Tiffany could feel the land in her bones" (2020, 267).

The novels follow the growing up of the central character from her ninth year to her late teens. They trace Tiffany's gradual mastery of magic as linked with her developing understanding of the witch's role in her community. In this process, Tiffany is helped by Nac Mac Feegles, a rowdy tribe of fairy folk always ready to drink, fight, and steal who, nevertheless, are firmly connected to the land and memory—mostly through their female leaders. Since Tiffany evolves from an inquisitive child into a powerful witch, most of the critical commentary addressing the series has focused on the process of growing up and learning her identity (e.g., Froggatt 2007, Croft 2009, Bradford 2019). Reinhardt and Haberkorn, for example, read Tiffany's training in magic as "a metaphor for the work of adolescence" (2011, 44) with emphasis on the importance of humanistic education. Clare Bradford follows Tiffany's growing appreciation of her predecessor Granny Aching's legacy: from Tiffany's memories of her early childhood to a realization that although she is deceased, Granny's heirloom and protective power remain in the Chalk. Bradford also notes the value of Tiffany's attachment to her family, the whole community, and the land and its features (2019). Alice Nuttall analyzes a relationship between womanhood and witchcraft (2018) and similar gender lenses have also been adopted by Lian Sinclair (2015) and Rebecca-Anne Do Rozario (2016). Nuttall emphasizes the witch's "paradoxical position" of being both in the center of the community—due to a witch's responsibility to care for it—and distanced from the same community because of a witch's connection to the supernatural (2018, 32). McGillis similarly interprets the witch as "the other" (2014, 21). This seems to be true even in *I Shall Wear Midnight*, in which novel, as Sinclair comments, Tiffany "has broken free of the loner archetype" and calls on others to join her rebellion against the overbearing Duchess (2015, 15). Many commentators have additionally reflected on the key themes of Pratchett's work in general—especially how stories and stereotypes frame our perceptions and people's lives (Webb 2006, Do Rozario 2016, Rana 2018, and others). Regarding this chapter's theme, the closest approaches are the analyses by Eileen Donaldson and Siddharth Pandey, both focused on Tiffany's relationship with the Chalk. Donaldson interprets the Chalk as one of Tiffany's uncanny doubles, "a continuing, valuable double-presence in her psyche" (2017, 7). Pandey draws on Ingold's concept of "taskscape"[2] to interpret the vivid reciprocal contact between Tiffany and her land maintained by daily tasks as the roots of witch's magic (2020). My goal in this chapter is to advance this argument even further and present Tiffany as a hybridized entity, connecting human being and the land.

To Be a Witch on Discworld

There is not much glamour for a Discworld witch. Her days are filled with endless work, going around houses in her steading—one or several villages and their surroundings—and taking care of people too old, too sick, or too stupid to look after themselves. Witchcraft merges the professions of midwife, doctor, marriage counselor, judge, and many others. However, there is a less mundane part of the business too. Witches guard the edges of the world, protecting both the land and its people from supernatural dangers. In the series, First Sight and Second Thoughts—respectively, an ability to see the world as it is rather than as you want it to be, and a capacity to observe and think about what you are thinking—are pronounced as fundamental to witchcraft. While witches ordinarily make do with applied psychology—which they call headology—and a bit of placebo, in a time of need they use serious magic. Such magic is then engaged to perform extraordinary deeds like moving an entire kingdom fifteen years forward (Pratchett 1988) or expelling elves from the land (Pratchett 2015). Due to their connection to local community and land, witches are able to grasp the whole reality of being. As Tiffany explains the nature of her thankless work to her father, "Sometimes you get a good day that makes up for all the bad days and, just for a moment, you hear the world turning" (Pratchett 2010, chap. 2).

Permaculture Ethics in the Tiffany Aching Series

The unwritten rules of witchcraft articulated in Pratchett's series bear a significant similarity to permaculture ethics. The core of these ethics can be expressed in three broad principles, with the second and third deriving from the first: Care for the Earth, Care for people, Set limits to consumption and reproduction, and redistribute surplus (Holmgren 2011, 1).

Permaculture is a set of design principles based on whole system thinking rooted in observation and employing or imitating natural patterns to create "sustainable human environments" (Mollison and Slay 1991, 1). The term was coined in 1975 by wildlife biologists Bill Mollison and his student David Holmgren at the University of Tasmania and initially referred only to permanent or regenerative agriculture. In time, to capture the widening range of its applicability to various social matters, the meaning was extended to permanent culture. The intrinsically grassroots movement spread from Australia to the world, evolving and adapting to diverse conditions. It continued to absorb both philosophical and practical local knowledge, the process embodying one of its fundamental postulates: to apply universal principles through according to place and situation varying methods (Holmgren 2011, xxv).

One result of this development is that today it is almost impossible to find a single agreed-upon definition of permaculture. For a working definition, that will also be adopted in this chapter, many refer to Mollison's summary inspired by Masanobu Fukuoka's natural farming philosophy:

> Permaculture is a philosophy of working with, rather than against nature; of protracted and thoughtful observation rather than protracted and thoughtless labor; and of looking at plants and animals in all their functions, rather than treating any area as a single product system.
>
> (Mollison and Slay 1997, 1)

While for many of its practitioners permaculture represents a means of sustainable organic gardening, its principles apply to a broad range of individual and collective human interactions with the nonhuman world—specifically, interactions aimed to create a sustainable future. The design and ethical principles of permaculture first focused on land and nature stewardship. Nowadays, they are being applied to other domains including the built environment, tools and technology, education and culture, health and spiritual well-being, finances and economics, land tenure, and community governance (Holmgren 2011, xix). Thus, for example, Laura M. Hartman frames permaculture as a voluntary practice of environmental modesty (2015), whereas Thomas W. Henfrey suggests permaculture principles as a means for strengthening community resilience (2018), Jamie Vishwam Heckert proposes permaculture ethics as a cooperative approach to challenges of the present (2014), whereas Jody Luna, Erica Dávila, and Alyssa Reynoso-Morris argue for permaculture principles as good starting points to reimagine education and ensure food justice (2018). These and other proposals establish permaculture as a flexible and complex framework that provides humanity with a means to rethink itself and its activities in the Anthropocene.

In their early writings, Holmgren and Mollison believed that permaculture principles could be derived from natural systems and practice of preindustrial sustainable societies and applied to the post-industrial development of the global community (1978, xxiv). They did not use the term the Anthropocene nor did they seem aware of the Great Acceleration: the explosion of the human population, technology, and a whole modern society resulting from massive tapping of fossil fuels. However, already in their influential *Permaculture One*, first published in 1978, Holmgren and Mollison considered the then-present reality to be unsustainable and destructive to the environment (3–4). Even at that early stage, permaculture emerged as a "positivistic response" to the inevitable crisis (Holmgren 2011, xv). Taking the necessity of radical change as a fact, this early articulation of permaculture focuses on practical, down to earth solutions starting from individuals and households as initiators of the low-energy sustainable culture (xxix). Today's permaculture ethics build on these general values and express them in more detail. What is the connection between that ethic and the world of witch's responsibilities as imagined in Pratchett's series?

Care for the Earth

While witches spend most of the time tending to people's immediate needs, a deep connection to their steading and the land itself is the essence of their power and purpose. A witch must know "where she is, who she is, and when she is" (Pratchett 2003, chap. 2). Tiffany is firmly situated in both place and time to the extent that the land she is intertwined with defines her personality: "She belonged to the Chalk. Every day she'd told the hills what they were. Every day they'd told her who she was" (2004, chap. 5).

Tiffany was born to Chalk, the region of green downlands built over eons by billions of seashells. As a child, she sometimes saw an "ancient fish" (2010, chap. 5), a reminder of the history of the Chalk. When walking the downlands, she felt "centuries under her feet" (2004, chap. 5). Her intrinsic connection to the Chalk and its history begins with Tiffany's name. In a fairy tongue of the Nac Mac Feegles, being Pratchett's Discworld version of Scottish Gaelic, Tir-far-thóinn means Land Under Wave. Care for the Earth runs in the tradition of Tiffany's family, folks who had run a farm there for hundreds of years and have "these hills in their bones" (2003, chap. 1). Tiffany also follows in the footsteps of her grandmother, Granny

Aching, who was highly renowned on the Chalk as a moral authority embodying unwritten but binding laws of the hills. While before Tiffany, officially, there were no witches on the Chalk, Granny Aching acted like one. Even when spending most of her time alone upon the hills, she "made [people] help one another … She made them help themselves" (2004, chap. 4). Her care extended beyond people to the animals and the land itself, when she used to "speak up for those who don't have voices" (2003, chap. 2). Like her granddaughter years later, Granny Aching was so deeply part of the Chalk that she "made the sky her hat" and "the wind her coat" (2004, chap. 14).

In permaculture ethics, care for the Earth is a facet of planetary stewardship, based on "our individual and collective responsibility in the care of particular natural resources about which we have some understanding and power" (Holmgren 2011, 5). Since permaculture is a grounded attitude to life, it emphasizes "bottom-up 'redesign' processes, starting with the individual and household" (xvi). One of the models permaculture advocates for is indigenous traditions imperative of caring for one's home, area, or using more modern terms, bioregion.[3] This model of care is presented as a necessary part of the solution to global issues.

Pratchett's witches are intrinsically connected to their environment. They devote their lives to attend to their steadings. When temporarily leaving the Chalk to learn witchcraft, Tiffany promises the land to come back as a better person and a witch. Indeed, she honors her word: "'I've come back!' she announced to the hills. 'Better than I went!'" (Pratchett 2004, chap. 15). The relationship with the Chalk is reciprocal, Tiffany never lets it fade from her mind, and the land makes her a witch: "Can I be a witch away from my hills? Of course I can. [Because] I never really leave you, Land Under Wave" (chap. 11).

An essential feature of the care-for-the-Earth approach is reverence for all living things, including the soil as a source of terrestrial life. The permaculture lens perceives every organism as "valid parts of the living earth with intrinsic value" (Holmgren 2011, 6) without regard to its potential usefulness. While many permaculture practitioners are vegetarian or vegan, the concept itself does not require refraining from killing animals for food. These choices are left to personal responsibility.[4]

In the series, the Aching family and many other Chalk inhabitants have been shepherds for generations. They use sheep wool, milk, and meat. Tiffany never questions this use. However, she would not ever agree to unrespectful treatment of animals, and Granny Aching was famous for her stern critique of any cruelty against those who have "no voices" (Pratchett 2003, chap. 8). The kindness and responsibility extend even toward tiny nonhuman beings. At one point, when Tiffany exposes a patch of soil to frost, she does not walk away without considering the effects of her action: "Feeling guilty about the worm, she breathed some warm air on the soil and then pushed the leaves back to cover it" (2006, chap. 9).

An approach close to veganism is represented by Geoffrey, a young man appearing in the last book of the series who refuses to accept any all-too-quick answers about the natural order of things. He decides to become a witch even when "everybody knows men can't be witches" (Pratchett 2015, chap. 1) and contests the limited perception of sex and gender: "I've never thought of myself as a man, Mistress Tiffany. I don't think I'm anything. I'm just me" (chap. 9). Similarly, Geoffrey resists to the so-called natural way of living based on eating meat. When Tiffany suggests that everybody needs to live on something, Geoffrey replies: "not at the expense of others" (chap. 10). Consistent with Pratchett's unsentimental approach, nature is not idealized in the series. Even Geoffrey is aware that "world can be cruel and merciless" (chap. 1) and accepts the need to protect farm animals from predators. However, he emphasizes, "We take so much and we give back nothing" (chap. 1). Significantly, Geoffrey appears in the last book of the series, coming from outside to challenge the little community's traditions and to teach even Tiffany to rethink old ways of dealing with the world. In my reading, the introduction of the character of Geoffrey is Pratchett's warning against complacency regarding how much we are already doing for the planet. It suggests that we can always do more, especially when it involves questioning or reexamining the established ways of being.

Care for People

Holmgren calls permaculture an "unashamedly human-centred environmental philosophy" (2011, 6). At the same time, he emphasizes the practicality of this approach: as a human people, we have competences to influence our circumstances. Anthropocentrism in permaculture philosophy is thus a means to stress personal responsibility for our lives and choices in regard to our relationship with the Earth. Blaming external forces for our own choices is against permaculture's imperative to seek productive opportunities even under extreme circumstances.

Care for people starts with responsibility for oneself. Like many philosophical and spiritual traditions, permaculture insists that for an individual to be able to care for others and the Earth, she must first manage to help herself. With oneself in the center, the circle of the care broadens to include the loved ones, neighbors, and communities, with the strongest impact close to the center where we have the greatest influence. Care for people, according to Granny Weatherwax, is "the root and heart and soul and center of witchcraft" (Pratchett 2004, chap. 9); as too is taking responsibility one's own actions. In *A Hat Full of Sky*, one advice Tiffany receives from an older witch captures these principles in a nutshell: "Even if it's not your fault, it's your responsibility" (chap. 2). Tiffany has already witnessed Granny Aching following the same rule and as an adolescent, she makes it a defining part of her personality. "I make it my business. I'm a witch. It's what we do. When it's nobody else's business, it's my business" (Pratchett 2010, chap. 2).

The immediate inspiration of permaculture is awareness of the fact "that our own comfort is based on the rape of planetary wealth, depriving other people (and future generations) of their own local resources" (Holmgren 2011, 7). With this knowledge, the emphasis on providing for one's own needs demands responsible action toward other communities and the Earth, thus implying practicing a modest way of life and aiming at nonmaterial well-being. Once again, permaculture takes inspiration from indigenous communities with their recognition of non-material values and draws on the growing awareness within rich countries that excessive consumption does not lead to happiness (8). For example, Oregon biologist and plant breeder Caroll Deppe devotes one whole chapter in her influential book *The Tao of Vegetable Gardening* (2015) to the topic of joy arising from the relationship with her environment, from paying attention to her surroundings, enjoying simple pleasures, and developing a very witch-like sense of her place and role. "I'm happy in this garden," Deppe writes, "tending this rich, generous fertile soil, nurturing these plants. This is who I am. This is who I am meant to be. This is what I am meant to do. This is where I belong" (234).

A similar sense of joy and belonging characterizes Pratchett's witches. They own next to nothing. The witch's cottage is a service apartment passing from one witch to another. Money and material wealth have no practical function for them. The witches' economic system is based on gift and barter. The self-imposed restraint and even contempt for material wealth—the last distinctly practiced by Granny Weatherwax—allows witches to focus on nonmaterial well-being stemming from their connection to the land and community. This sense of belonging provides Tiffany with inner strength, purpose, and happiness.

> And people drank a toast and there was more food, and more dancing and laughter and friendship and tiredness, and at midnight Tiffany Aching lay alone on her broomstick high above the chalk hills and looked up at the universe, and then down on the bit of it that belonged to her. ... The stick rose and fell gently as warm breezes took it and as tiredness and darkness took her, she stretched out her arms to the dark and, just for a moment, as the world turned, Tiffany Aching wore midnight.
>
> (Pratchett 2010, chap. 15)

Limits to Consumption and Reproduction, and Redistribution of Surplus

As already mentioned, permaculture ethics invite self-restraint and emphasize nonmaterial well-being. However, they also recognize the formative experience of abundance, since it "encourages us to distribute surplus beyond our circle of responsibility (to the Earth and people) in the faith that our needs are provided for" (Holmgren 2011, 8). The seeming contradiction in those two claims should inspire reflection on these aspects of nature and their relevance to an ethical response to life's challenges. Luxury has its function when remaining exceptional and not part of everyday reality—a moment, like a baby's utter dependence and comfort, rather than permanent state. But a sense of limits only grows from "a mature understanding of the way the world works" (8). Thus, arising from consideration of one's needs and wants on the one hand and from the capacity of the Earth and people to supply them on the other, permaculture highlights the voluntary recognition of limits. Living in abundance does not refer to fat bank accounts. It rather gestures at the luxury of clean air, a beautiful environment, regenerative leisure, and wholesome, healthy food.

Sharing the surplus also means deciding what and how to support with resources and time, when providing for those "beyond our immediate circle of power and responsibility" (9). Furthermore, the redistribution of wealth is applied not only to people but to the whole Earth and connects to the concept of the Earth stewardship. The tradition of planting forests to benefit both the land and future generations of human and nonhuman inhabitants is one example Holmgren brings to highlight permaculture's understanding of redistribution (10).

In the Tiffany Aching series, self-restraint, recycling, and the concept of redistributing are essentials in the unwritten witch's code. It also comes naturally for people in the Chalk used to live from the land and to buy new things only when necessary. For her constant care of people, a witch receives no payment. Then again, when villagers have a surplus of food, clothing, or other necessities, it is natural to share some of these with the local witch. As Tiffany's mentor responds to her doubts: "It evens out ... You do what you can. People give what they can, when they can" (Pratchett 2004, chap. 4). Keeping for herself only what she immediately needs, the witch redistributes most of the received goods to the needy. No one is excluded from this circle of care, even those who abuse the system. As Tiffany's mentor puts it, "You can't not help people just because they're stupid or forgetful or unpleasant. Everyone's poor around here. If I don't help them, who will?" (chap. 4).

Land as an Agent

The Chalk is presented as a whole organism with grass, sheep, people, and other animals as its living parts. The relationship between land and people is mutually nurturing. People live from the land, transforming it to meet their needs within limits; thus, cutting trees and making clearings in a forest is presented as opening new niches not only for people but for other living beings too (Pratchett 2004, chap. 8). Interacting with pristine areas, people are shown to create unique, though imperfect, nature-culture symbiosis.

For Tiffany, the Chalk is a magical place. The fact she sees it almost every day does not diminish her appreciation. Nevertheless, even as a witch, she glimpses its full reality only rarely, mostly in time of distress, when she needs all her strength to stand up for the Chalk and its inhabitants:

> She heard the grass growing, and the sound of worms below the turf. She could feel the thousands of little lives around her, smell all the scents on the breeze, and see all the shades of the night. The wheels of stars and years, of space and time, locked into place.
>
> (Pratchett 2003, chap. 13)

Such a state of wide-awake-all-life awareness is a powerful experience, unbearable for a longer period. As Tiffany admits, most people, including herself "sleepwalk through our lives, because how could we live if we were always this awake?" (chap. 13). Nevertheless, witches remember how it feels to open their eyes truly, and this knowledge shapes their everyday lives. They know the land is alive and time and people are part of it. Thanks to this perception, Tiffany recognizes footprints of history in the present. The Chalk is a land "made of life," full of memories of past times. Through the Chalk, the ancient sea, in a sense, still roars under Tiffany's feet (Pratchett 2015, chap. 17). Past experiences—her own and of humanity as a whole—are thus engraved into Tiffany's personality: "Everything we've ever been on the way to becoming us, we still are" (Pratchett 2004, chap. 11). Even death is not shown to break this circle connecting time, place, and living beings. When Granny Weatherwax dies in *The Shepherd's Crown*, she does not disappear from the land she had spent her life caring for. As Tiffany realizes, "She was indeed here. And there. She was, in fact, and always would be, everywhere" (Pratchett 2015, Epilogue).

In Pratchett's work, the land typically does not express itself openly. However, the land is endowed with a kind of collective consciousness and knows how to defend itself. Usually it acts through its witch, who stands as a mediator listening to both the land and people. The land "finds its witch" (2003, chap. 3) and it is the witch's job to listen to the land and act accordingly. For instance, Esmeralda Weatherwax considers the forest constituting most of her steading to be a different kind of life, slower than people, yet conscious: "In addition to being a collection of other things, the forest was a thing in itself. Alive, only not alive in the way that, say, a shrew was alive" (Pratchett 1988, 62). Granny Weatherwax treats the land accordingly and deems herself part of it. At the end of her stewardship to the land and its inhabitants, preparing for the encounter with Death, she bids farewell to plants and animals. Then the other witches bury her in the forest in a spot "where she wanted to be *planted*" (Pratchett 2015, chap. 4, emphasis mine). The kinship between the witch and the living land is mutual; after the burial, numerous animals come to her resting place to express reverence. "The whole forest now sang for Granny Weatherwax" (chap. 4).

At other times the land speaks directly. Already in the first book, Tiffany is drawn into the Chalk to experience its wholeness in time and place and her connection with it. The land provides her with the power to shield it against the elven queen. It lets Tiffany know she is one in a long line of its protectors: "There's always been someone watching the borders. They didn't decide to. It was decided for them. Someone has to care" (Pratchett 2003, chap. 13). Accordingly, when in each book Tiffany faces a different danger, she succeeds because she does not protect only herself. Caring as she does for the land and community, Tiffany can reach powers exceeding her own. In the first and last novels, for example, Thunder and Lightning, two shepherd dogs of her grandmother's, materialize from the chalk to help Tiffany in her mission. It remains unclear whether the dogs are actual animals rising from death in a time of need, or—which seems more likely—embodied manifestations of the Chalk itself helping its protectors. In *A Hat Full of Sky*, a horse figure carved into the chalk—the fictional representation Uffington White Horse—leaps out from the land and runs to Tiffany's aid. The last novel *The Shepherd's Crown* is named after an ancient seashell that symbolizes both the living past of the Chalk and its long tradition of mutual care between people and land. The little seashell functions as a token of this intimate connection: "Her fingers curled around the odd-shaped little stone, tracing its five ridges, and somehow she felt a strength flow into her, the hardness of the flint at its heart reminding her who she was" (2015, chap. 15). In the final battle with elves, the land itself talks to Tiffany through the seashell and guides her to comprehend the true meaning of the fact that the shepherd's crown came to her: "The voice came from nowhere, as though it was part of that ocean from Time: 'Tiffany Aching is the first among shepherds, for she puts others before herself'" (chap. 17).

Perhaps most telling is a passage in *A Hat Full of Sky*, when a hiver occupies Tiffany's body and her soul retreats to the innermost refuge in her mind. This last haven takes the form of the Chalk downlands, thus manifesting the permeable boundaries between Tiffany and her land. When fighting the hiver, grassy hills form themselves into the shape of Tiffany's body and throw the hiver out of her. A Feegle witnessing this asks whether it is the witch dreaming of being the hills or are the hills dreaming of being the witch (2004, chap. 8). The answer would be both. In their essence, the Chalk and Tiffany are one extended being: transformed into a hybrid land–human creature, they bridge the culture–nature divide. Tiffany, in this sense, transcends the boundaries between humans and the animate and inanimate nature. She literally carries the hills in her bones (chap. 3) and the soul of the land in her head (chap. 8). This is where the deepest magic roots. The land and the witch are intertwined and mutually dependent.

Permaculture grows from a down-to-earth philosophy based on careful observation and systems thinking; nevertheless, many of its branches include spirituality as an integral part. Inspired by the Gaia hypothesis and similar concepts, permaculturists often see Earth as a conscious being who communicates with humanity through local spirits and elements. While personification and anthropomorphism enhance "connectedness to and protectiveness toward nature" (Tam, Lee and Chao 2013, 514), they may complicate embracing permaculture as a framework open to "all people everywhere, regardless of their culture and preferred belief system" (Mackintosh 2011). On the other hand, the core of permaculture derives from indigenous traditions with pronounced spiritual beliefs. Holmgren, for instance, emphasizes the value of myths in comprehending complex and sometimes abstract concepts essential for the adoption of a permaculture lifestyle: "I believe many of the insights of systems thinking that are difficult to grasp as abstractions are truths that are embodied in the stories and myths of indigenous cultures" (2011, xxvi). As the actualization of myth, contemporary fantasy can perform many of the same functions. The Tiffany Aching series presents the Chalk as a conscious being comprised of a larger whole with both its human and inhuman inhabitants. Pratchett emphasizes the mutually nurturing relationship between people and land, in the process decentralizing people by making them a part of the whole rather than its center. However, Pratchett's is a realistic fantasy when it comes to humanity and its flaws. So even in a community of shepherds connected to nature, Tiffany and Granny Aching stand out as rare characters, different from others due to their holistic grasp of reality and their ability to communicate with the Chalk and protect it.

Reading the series through the permaculture lens underlines significant overlaps between permaculture and what Pratchett imagined as witches' ethics. It also brings out the points Pratchett seems to have overlooked. The most significant ones are a global view and communally shared responsibility. While permaculture is a grassroots movement, it understands itself as a means for global change. It requires many people to follow its ethics and principles in their daily and long-term decisions. By contrast, the series almost exclusively focuses on the local level, and witches usually do not concern themselves with matters of distant regions. Also, many inhabitants of the Chalk seem to be indifferent to the land and even to their community. While quite willing to help with little issues, they often tend to forget others and do not generally bother with a world outside their immediate locales. Only witches accept this larger responsibility and people take it for granted. In *A Hat Full of Sky*, Pratchett wrote that "there hadn't been much life in [ancient forests]" (2004, chap. 8), and "mostly it was just hot and silent" (chap. 8.) before people cut down trees and opened new niches in emergent clearings. While it may seem that Pratchett tends to side with people—even when bridging the nature–culture divide—in the context of the entire series, the boundary between people and the land fades. Due to the mutual dependency favoring one side means protecting the other.

The reading of the Tiffany Aching series offered here also invites the larger question about how fantasy as a mode aligns with the imperatives of permaculture—a question that calls for more extensive comparative study. Aspects of permaculture certainly seem to be ingrained in a wide range of fantasy and cli-fi stories. Kim Stanley Robinson's Mars trilogy (1992–6) applies many of permaculture principles to imagine a sustainable Martian community that is fair to both the people and the land. Phillip Pullman's *The Secret Commonwealth* (2019) indicates a whole hidden world where all stones and creeks are alive. In Nnedi Okafor's *Lagoon* (2014), aliens make contact not only with humans, but they first merge with and communicate with marine life. These and other stories convey the reality that people are part of the biosphere, not its rulers; they offer inspiration for transforming the human community into a plurispecies community.

Graham Bell, chair of Permaculture Scotland and a creator of a forest garden for a moderate climate, describes permaculture as "being in harmony with the world around us": a method for designing "how we can live lightly on the Earth, an Earth we respect and understand better every day" (n.d.). Drawing on the affordances of fantasy, the Tiffany Aching series voices values of environmental modesty, self-restraint, and voluntary responsibility. It captures the inherent magic of the land, its beauty and resilience. While not fully embodying permaculture or all of its requirements, the series offers an inspiring representation of the intimate relationship between the land and human. It allows readers to experience a compelling vision of the culture–nature connection—something we urgently need to navigate our way through the Anthropocene toward a biospheric future. Appreciation of the places we live in is a necessary first step. At the end of the series, Tiffany learns the carpenter's craft. She builds a little shepherd's house on a hill to live where Granny Aching was buried and where the connection to the Chalk is not disturbed by village life. When asked whether she used any magic, her answer is simple and telling: "I didn't have to ... The magic was already here" (Pratchett 2015, Epilogue).

The chapter is published with the support of the Faculty of Arts, Masaryk University.

Notes

1   However, there is a significant difference between rural environment like the Chalk and the city— with its central river Ankh "too stiff to drink, too runny to plough" (Pratchett 2007, 143), referring parodically to heavily polluted industrial cities of eighteenth and nineteenth centuries—where nature is subdued, and people dominate the environment.
2   A social anthropologist Tim Ingold coined the term to analyze a landscape's temporal and spatial dimensions in human life. For more details, see, e.g., Ingold: *The Temporality of the Landscape* (1993).
3   Bioregionalism, closely connected to permaculture and indigenous land ethic, claims humans and their activities "fundamental components of ecosystems" (Lockyer, Veteto, 6) and points out that geographic organizational boundaries need to reflect natural systems.
4   As Holmgren comments: "It is easy for most of us, living separated from nature, to agree that all life is sacred because we do not have to deal personally with the killing done consciously and unconsciously on our behalf" (6). However, any harm to a living thing must be done in a conscious way and with great respect, as is still practiced by many indigenous communities, and never without serious reason.

References

Attebery, Brian. 2014. *Stories about Stories: Fantasy and the Remaking of Myth*. Oxford: Oxford University Press.

Bell, Graham. n.d. "What Permaculture Is and Isn't." *grahambell.org.uk*. Accessed May 4, 2020. http://grahambell.org.uk/permaculture-2-2/what-permaculture-is-and-isnt

Bradford, Clare. 2019. "Where Girls Rule by Magic: Metaphors of Agency." In *Child Autonomy and Child Governance in Children's Literature*, edited by Christopher Kelen and Bjorn Sundmark, 107–19. London: Routledge.

Burrows, Marc. 2020. *The Magic of Terry Pratchett*. Pen & Sword History. Yorkshire, PA: White Owl.

Croft, Janet Brennan. 2009. "The Education of a Witch: Tiffany Aching, Hermione Granger, and Gendered Magic in Discworld and Potterworld." *Mythlore*, vol. 27, no. 3/4 (105/106): 129–42.

Deppe, Carol. 2015. *The Tao of Vegetable Gardening: Cultivating Tomatoes, Greens, Peas, Beans, Squash, Joy, and Serenity*. White River Junction: Chelsea Green Publishing.

Do Rozario, Rebecca-Anne. 2016. "The Charity of Witches: Watching the Edges in Terry Pratchett's Tiffany Aching Novels." *Papers: Explorations into Children's Literature*, vol. 24, no. 2: 74–95. http://www.paperschildlit.com/pdfs/DoRozario_Papers_24_2_2016_74-95.pdf

Donaldson, Eileen. 2017. "See Me: How the Uncanny Double Supports Maturing Girlhood in Terry Pratchett's Tiffany Aching Series." *Mousaion*, vol. 35, no. 2: 1–16.

Elgin, Don D. 1985. *The Comedy of the Fantastic: Ecological Perspectives on the Fantasy Novel*. Westport, CT: Greenwood Press.

Froggatt, Juliana. 2007. "Children in the Discworld Series." In *An Unofficial Companion to the Novels of Terry Pratchett*, edited by Andrew M. Butler, 64–7. Oxford: Greenwood World Publishing.

Haberkorn, Gideon, and Verena Reinhardt. 2011. "Magic, Adolescence and Education on Terry Pratchett's Discworld." In *Supernatural Youth: The Rise of the Teen Hero in Literature and Popular Culture*, edited by Jes Battis, 43–64. New York: Lexington Books.

Hartman, Laura M. 2015. "Environmental Modesty Reclaiming an Ancient Virtue." *Journal of Religious Ethics*, vol. 43, no. 3: 475–92.

Heckert, Jamie Vishwam. 2014. "Planning for Abundance: Permaculture and Radical Transformation." *Theory in Action*, vol. 7, no. 4: 97–106.

Henfrey, Thomas W. 2018. "Designing for Resilience: Permaculture as a Transdisciplinary Methodology in Applied Resilience Research." *Ecology and Society*, vol. 23, no. 2: 33–43.

Holmgren, David. 2011. *Permaculture: Principles & Pathways beyond Sustainability*. Hampshire: Permanent Publications.

Ingold, Tim. 1993. "The Temporality of the Landscape." *World Archaeology*, vol. 25, no. 2: 152–74.

Keen, Suzanne. 2007. *Empathy and the Novel*. Oxford: Oxford University Press.

Le Guin, Ursula K. 2007. "The Critics, the Monsters, and the Fantasists." *The Wordsworth Circle*, vol. 38, no. 1–2: 83–7.

Lockyer, Joshua, and James R. Veteto. 2013. "Environmental Anthropology Engaging Ecotopia. An Introduction." In *Environmental Anthropology Engaging Ecotopia: Bioregionalism, Permaculture and Ecovillages*, edited by Joshua Lockyer, and James R. Veteto, 1–31. New York: Berghahn Books.

Luna, Jody M., Erica R. Dávila, and Alyssa Reynoso-Morris. 2018. "Pedagogy of Permaculture and Food Justice." *Educational Foundations*, vol. 31, no. 1–2: 57–85.

Mackintosh, Craig. 2011. "Permaculture and Metaphysics." *The Permaculture Research Institute*, December 8, 2011. https://www.permaculturenews.org/2011/12/08/permaculture-and-metaphysics/

McGillis, Roderick. 2014. "The Wee Free Men: Politics and the Art of Noise". *Critical Explorations in Science Fiction and Fantasy*, vol. 45: 15–25.

Mollison, Bill, and David Holmgren. 1978. *Permaculture One: A Perennial Agriculture for Human Settlements*. Sister Creek: Talgari Publications.

Mollison, Bill, and Reriy Mia Slay. 1991. *Introduction to Permaculture*. Sister Creek: Talgari Publications.

Nuttall, Alice. 2018. "Be a Witch, Be a Woman: Gendered Characterisation of Terry Pratchett's Witches." In *Terry Pratchett's Narrative Worlds: From Giant Turtles to Small Gods*, edited by Marion Rana, 23–36. London: Palgrave Macmillan.

Oziewicz, Marek. 2008. *One Earth, One People: The Mythopoeic Fantasy Series of Ursula K. Le Guin, Lloyd Alexander, Madeleine L'Engle and Orson Scott Card*. Jefferson, NC and London: McFarland & Company.

Peschel, Bill. 2006. "Interview with Terry Pratchett." *www.planetpeschel.com*, September 14, 2006. https://planetpeschel.com/2006/09/interview-with-terry-pratchett/

Pratchett, Terry. 1988. *Wyrd Sisters*. London: Victor Gollancz Ltd.

Pratchett, Terry. 2003. *The Wee Free Men*. New York: Doubleday. EPUB.

Pratchett, Terry. 2004. *A Hat Full of Sky*. New York: Doubleday. EPUB.

Pratchett, Terry. 2006. *Wintersmith*. New York: Doubleday. EPUB.

Pratchett, Terry. 2007. *Equal Rites*. London: Harper Collins.

Pratchett, Terry. 2010. *I Shall Wear Midnight*. New York: Doubleday. EPUB.

Pratchett, Terry. 2015. *The Shepherd's Crown*. New York: Doubleday. EPUB.

Rana, Marion. 2018. "Shedding the 'Light Fantastic' on Terry Pratchett's Narrative Worlds: An Introduction." In *Terry Pratchett's Narrative Worlds: From Giant Turtles to Small Gods*, edited by Marion Rana, 1–20. London: Palgrave Macmillan.

Roux-Rosier, Anahid, Ricardo Azambuja, and Gazi Islam. 2018. "Alternative Visions: Permaculture as Imaginaries of the Anthropocene." *Organization*, vol. 25, no. 4: 550–72.

Sinclair, Lian. 2015. "Magical Genders: The Gender(s) of Witches in the Historical Imagination of Terry Pratchett's Discworld." *Mythlore*, vol. 33, no. 2 (126): 5–18.

Smith, C. J. 2000. *The Getting of Hope: Personal Empowerment through Learning Permaculture*. PhD thesis, The University of Melbourne, Accessed May 20, 2020. https://minerva-access.unimelb.edu.au/handle/11343/35351

Tam, Kim-Pong, Sau-Lai Venus Lee, and Melody Manchi Chao. 2013. "Saving Mr. Nature: Anthropomorphism Enhances Connectedness to and Protectiveness toward Nature." *Journal of Experimental Social Psychology*, vol. 49, no. 3: 514–21.

Tolkien, J. R. R. 1947. "On Fairy Stories." In *Essays Presented to Charles Williams*, edited by C.S. Lewis, 38–89. Grand Rapids: William B. Eerdmans Publishing Company.

Webb, Caroline. 2006. "'Change the Story, Change the World': Witches/Crones as Heroes in Novels by Terry Pratchett and Diana Wynne Jones." *Papers: Explorations into Children's Literature*, vol. 16, no. 2: 156–61.

CHAPTER 12
WHERE IS THE PLACE FOR SEAGRASS AND WEEVILS IN CHILDREN'S LITERATURE?
Eliot Schrefer

I've recently backed my way into the academy. After writing my ape quartet and *Lost Rainforest* series, which focused on furry and adorable monkeys and apes and panthers, I've entered the NYU Animal Studies program as a part-time master's student. Partly it's to give myself somewhere to be once a week, and partly it's to see if I can't find ways to broaden my writing to lifeforms other than charismatic megafauna. I guess the question guiding my studies is: Where is the place for seagrass and weevils in children's literature?

As a discipline, Animal Studies is very much focused on the implications of our Anthropocene epoch. I'm new to the science of it, trying to catch myself up on genetics and evolutionary mechanics. But the act of communicating urgency around our environment feels like a familiar glove.

Two things have jumped out to me during my new studies: First is that the most widely read pieces of non-fiction science writing tend to include some human element to them, whether through the author's characterizing the scientists doing environmental work, or establishing an ecological crisis's impact on human life. Second is that Western worldviews, in which human exceptionalism is most deeply rooted, came to be in places of the world without access to nonhuman primates, while Buddhism and Hinduism, which figure humans more as equals within a web of animal life, came to be around monkeys. Had nonhuman primates been around early in our Western cultural development, we might have decided early that we were different from the rest of nature in kind rather than in degree—and I'd assume we'd have a heightened feeling of ecological responsibility.

To me that's one of the most wonderful correctives of speculative children's fiction, though. A young reader, the majority of whose loyalties and affections are to other humans, will spend hours caring instead about an alien or a panther, a bonobo or a penguin. That reader will expand the radius of their empathy, even if for just a short time. And maybe, one day, they'll spare a feeling or two for the seagrass and the weevils.

CHAPTER 13

ARBOREAL MAGIC AND KINSHIP IN THE CHTHULUCENE: MARGARET MAHY'S TREES

Melanie Duckworth

The Earth needs trees. Humans and other species depend on trees, and yet humans continue to destroy them, regarding them as resources rather than as fellow living beings. Humans cut down an estimated 15 billion trees each year, and "the global number of trees has fallen by 46 percent since the start of human civilization" (Crowther et al. 2015, 201). Forests are endangered by logging, agriculture, and fires exacerbated by climate change. Since 1990, 420 million hectares of forest have been lost, yet "deforestation and forest degradation continue to take place at alarming rates" (FAO and UNEP 2020, xvi). Nearly half of the world's rainforests have already been lost and each year humans destroy another 8 million hectares: an area the size of South Carolina or the Czech Republic (Conservation International). Trees are necessary to store carbon, and primary forests provide rich ecosystems that cannot be easily replaced by plantations. Making up over 80 percent of the Earth's biomass (Bar-On et al. 2018), plants provide the conditions of our existence—the air we breathe and the food we eat. Yet, as Solvejg Nitzke points out, "No one profits from trees as humans do and the ensuing relationship, or, more precisely, exploitation, has prevented humans from seeing … how trees actually live for themselves" (2020). In contrast, trees have long been revered in myth, religion, and stories, and hold a special position in fantasy literature. J. R. R. Tolkien, the father of modern fantasy literature, who championed trees through his characters of the Ents, the tree-like shepherds of the forest, wrote: "I take up the part of the trees as against all their enemies" (Tolkien 1981, 419).[1] One of Tolkien's successors, Margaret Mahy (1936–2012), an award-winning New Zealand writer of over one hundred books for children and young adults, also defended trees, and frequently invoked them as emblematic of her approaches to literature, magic, and life. This chapter argues that the magic described in Mahy's novels is distinctly arboreal and encourages an understanding of trees as kin. It thus presents a vital alternative to the perilous position of trees in the Anthropocene.

Mahy's novels explore the juxtaposition of myth and magic with everyday life through the characters of magicians or witches who discover special powers of connecting with the natural world, in contrast to evil antagonists who try to consume it. The magic in Mahy's texts can operate as a metaphor for fiction itself—a powerful yet elusive mode of transforming minds and connecting with the more-than-human world. Drawing on Donna Haraway's notion of "making kin in the Chthulucene" (2016) and recent developments in critical plant studies, I argue that the literal and symbolic trees in Mahy's texts affirm her characters' intuitions that a magical connection between humans and plants is mutually healing. Her arboreal magic, myth, and fantasy do not offer a quick fix or an overarching solution to a world transformed by human greed and overdevelopment. However, they do model ways of, as Haraway says, "staying with the trouble" (2016)—of becoming present to the lives of more-than-human others. Mahy's work suggests that answers may lie in opening ourselves to other ways of being.

Mahy's Magic and the Chthulucene

Haraway's concept of the "Chthulucene" provides a useful frame with which to approach Mahy's everyday, fractured worlds. The Anthropocene denotes the geological era in which humans have irreversibly affected the ecosphere. For Haraway, however, the term is filled with hubris—by emphasizing the irreparable damage to the earth by humans, the term "Anthropocene" both sidelines the presence of the "more than human" and encourages despair. She proposes "Chthulucene" as at once more hopeful and more accurate.

> *Chthulucene* is a simple word. It is a compound of two Greek roots (*khthôn* and *kainos*) that together name a kind of timeplace for learning to stay with the trouble of living and dying in response-ability on a damaged earth. Kainos means now, a time for beginnings, a time for ongoing, for freshness … Chthonic ones are beings of the earth.
>
> (2016, 2)

Thus the term combines an openness to the present moment with a focus on the earth, and earth-beings, both of which can be found in Mahy's novels. Admittedly, Mahy's descriptions of trees sometimes draw on celestial imagery, a strain of imagery of which Haraway is wary, but Mahy's trees are ultimately rooted in the ground. While Mahy's YA novels foreground the self-realization of her human adolescent protagonists, and are not, at first glance, explicitly environmentalist texts, her characters' magical connections with trees are situated in depictions of contemporary New Zealand landscapes altered by development. As Ruth P. Feingold has shown, Mahy engages with postcolonial "ghosts" of settlement, including colonial aspects of tree planting and gardening (2015, 227–9), ultimately celebrating the landscape formed when "two landscapes [settler and Indigenous] ran into each other and created a new countryside altogether" (1988, 19). The care and connection she expresses here for a merged settler and Indigenous landscape accord with the kind of work necessary in the Chthulucene: accepting a rich and imperfect present rather than yearning for a lost, uncontaminated ideal.

Haraway proposes that the central task of the Chthulucene is to "make kin" beyond, or at least in addition to, biological kin. For Haraway, one way of "making kin" is through creative use of a multiply signifying "SF": "science fiction, speculative fabulation, string figures, speculative feminism, science fact, so far" (2016, 2). A number of these terms could be used to describe Mahy's fiction itself, but also the ways in which the magic of her protagonists apprehends the vegetal world. While it may seem counterintuitive to turn to fiction, let alone "magic," in the face of urgent ecological catastrophe, one of the reasons that catastrophe is occurring is because of a failure of the imagination. If fantasy fiction—if magic—can help humans encounter and "make kin" of trees, it has a role to play in cultivating an ethic of care.

Alison Waller describes Mahy's YA novels as "fantastic-realism," which differs from magic realism in that the fantastic elements appear wondrous to the characters of the novels, instead of commonplace (2004, 78). The magic of Mahy's novels is visible and astonishing, even as her magical characters come to realize that their powers are linked to their innermost beings.

As Elizabeth Knox points out, Mahy "had a curious, scientific mind, so her magic is always systematic and logical" (2018, x). Mahy's magic connects with natural flows of energy and can alter the physical world, but costs something to the witch or magician who produces it, leaving them at least temporarily depleted. The evil magicians in Mahy's worlds respond to such exhaustion by relentlessly consuming the magical powers of others, as well as any other forms of vitality they can find. In *Alchemy* (2002), Mahy suggests that the best use of this magic is not as power or spectacle but simply as wonder and communion, particularly directed toward trees.

The magic of Mahy's magicians is consistently associated with an affinity with the vegetal world. At the end of *The Haunting* (1982), when Troy reveals her magical powers to her family, "she held out her arms, became a flowering tree, a flying bird, a creature made of stars" (chap. 11). A botanical aspect to magic is by no means new, partly because one source of magic in fantasy literature is witchcraft, which has always been associated with the knowledge and uses of plants. Commenting on the role of plants in Ursula K. Le Guin's *A Wizard of Earthsea* (1968), Liam Heneghan points out that "this is generally a truth in fantasy literature: before dragons and gold, before strenuous heroism, comes botany. Hobbits farm the Shire, Harry Potter visits the greenhouses with Professor Sprout, and Ged walks the mountains of Gont with Ogion the Silent, learning the uses of plants" (2018, 180–1). Mahy's arboreal magic thus connects with an established tradition linking magic to plants, but it differs from these examples in that the *goal* of magic in many of her texts, especially the later ones, is to connect and commune with trees. Resonating again with Haraway's call to "make kin," Mahy is interested in encounters with plants, rather than uses for them.

Mahy's Trees and Critical Plant Studies

In recent years, there has been a rapid flourishing of critical plant studies, also called human plant studies. In addition to scientific and popular scientific works emphasizing the sentience and communicative strategies of plants, such as Peter Wohlleben's *The Hidden Life of Trees* (2017 [2015]), there have been significant philosophical works published by Michael Marder (2013a), Mathew Hall (2011), and Luce Irigaray and Michael Marder (2016).[2] Driven partly by scientific advances advocating plant sentience, communication, and intelligence, and at once building on and departing from ethical arguments in critical animal studies, scholars in the field question the tendency to regard plants as merely the background to human and animal drama. Rooted in the earth and largely silent, plants have long been relegated to the lower reaches of the Aristotelian chain of being, positioned between animals and stones. As Marder puts it, "If animals have suffered marginalization throughout the history of Western thought, then non-human, non-animal living beings, such as plants, have populated the margin of the margin, the zone of absolute obscurity undetectable on the radars of our conceptualities" (2013a, 2). Of course, as fantasy literature and the mythological caucus it draws upon both attest, despite plants' marginal status, people have engaged with them through myth, science, philosophy, art, and stories for thousands of years.

In *Plant-Thinking: A Philosophy of Vegetal Life*, Marder asks: "How is it possible for us to encounter plants? And how can we maintain and nurture, without fetishizing it, their otherness in the course of this encounter?" (2013a, 3). Scholars in critical plant studies have provided varied, and sometimes contradictory, responses to this question. In *Plants as Persons* (2011), Matthew Hall urges us to regard plants as persons and as kin, an approach Marder challenges as too anthropocentric (Marder 2013b). Defending his position, which draws on animist traditions of non-Western cultures, Hall argues, "In contrast to a human-centred monologue, recognising and relating to plants as persons opens up the possibility of a dialogue in which distinct 'voices' and presences are heard and amplified" (2019, 10). While Marder might regard Mahy's celebration of trees as a kind of fetishism, Mahy's magicians, in a process of listening to and amplifying the nonverbal voices of trees, relate to them as kin.

In their lyrical and perceptive book, *Radical Botany: Plants and Speculative Fiction* (2020), which traces radical engagements with plants from pre-Romantic French culture to the present, Natania Meeker and Antónia Szarabi argue that while plants are frequently anthropomorphized in Western thought, there is another more radical tradition that imagines "plants as both vibrantly alive and fully material—which is to say without a hidden or transcendent animating principle (e.g., anima, spirit, personality, will or desire)" (chap. 1). While in some ways Mahy's approach to trees fits into this tradition, and she certainly maintains a sense of the otherness of trees, Mahy does not shy away from the concept of "spirit." I regard Mahy's approach to plants as particularly interesting because she is interested in the spiritual AND the material: she describes the forests of fairy tales and myths, but also the tree beside the road, and the weed growing in the sidewalk. She is interested in explanations of both story and science, and especially in the overlap between the two. When explaining her relationship with the world, Mahy speaks of an outer landscape one can grow to love, an inner landscape of self and dreams, and of moments when the two collide. She points toward a tree to illustrate her point:

> And look [sighting an autumn poplar beside the road] there's the tree burning up from the ground like a flame in all its autumn colouring. It comes into my eye and into my mind through a complex system of nervous reactions which I can't attempt to describe, and I see, simultaneously almost, an autumn tree, a flame, a shower of bright arrows, somebody standing in a golden robe, a magician, an enchanter and an ancient spirit whirling in a spindle of gold. In a moment the boundaries between outer and inner landscapes are down, and they flood into one another and combine.
>
> (Duder 2012, chap. 3)

This radiant experience of inner and outer landscapes converging in a tree feeds into Mahy's portrayal of magic in her YA novels.

Each of the novels I discuss here explores aspects of this arboreal magic, which Mahy describes as "wonderful, pure insight into the structure of nature" (Duder 2012, chap. 5). There is, however, a clear progression from her novels published in the 1980s to those published in the 2000s: an increasing refocusing from a mythic connection with trees toward more specific encounters with material trees. In her fantastic realist novels of the 1980s, the magic of her protagonists, particularly in *The Changeover* (1984), is described in arboreal terms, drawing heavily on fairy tales and myth. In the novels of the 2000s, Mahy experiments further with fantasy-inflected genres in order to explore the scope of this magic. *Alchemy* (2002) is a fantastic realist novel along the lines of *The Changeover*, but *Maddigan's Fantasia* (2005) is a post-apocalyptic narrative drawing on both fantasy and science fiction, and *Heriot* (2009) is a more traditional, sprawling fantasy narrative. In these novels, Mahy does not abandon the mythic nature of the magic she describes, but she allows her magicians to focus it more precisely upon actual trees. The magic thus participates in the work of "making kin," allowing encounters with vegetable beings beyond the restrictive capacities of human subjectivity. In what follows, I will begin by outlining the arboreal magic of *The Changeover* before discussing its development in the later novels.

The Changeover

The Changeover tells the story of fourteen-year-old Laura Chant, who lives with her single mother and three-year-old brother in Gardendale, a new suburban development perched uneasily in space once occupied by farmland. As always in Mahy's work, names are significant, and Gardendale ironically invokes gardens and dales in a space where vegetal life has been razed to make way for houses and shops. Laura's own name invokes both enchantment and the laurel tree of Ovid's *Metamorphoses* (Martin 2004, 37). Her life is turned upside down when her little brother Jacko is invaded and possessed by a malignant incubus/demon, Carmody Braque, who threatens to consume and destroy him. Laura realizes this is no ordinary illness, and so seeks the help of Sorry Carlisle, a school prefect she inexplicably knows to be a witch, along with his mother Miryam and grandmother Winter, also witches. They assist Laura to make a "changeover" in order to become a witch herself, after which she is able to deceive and destroy Carmody Braque, rescue Jacko, and begin a romantic relationship with Sorry. As Knox points out, the story of braving great danger and defeating a monster for one you love draws on countless stories and myths, including "*The Snow Queen, Beauty and the Beast,* Christina Rossetti's *The Goblin Market,* with lineages running all the way back to Persephone and Demeter" (Knox 2018, ix). Several of these myths and stories have strong vegetal elements, and *The Changeover* also hinges on images of the vegetal world, particularly the forest of fairy tales.

Laura's attitude to Gardendale is ambivalent but not negative. While she knows it is considered crass in some quarters, and is rough and dangerous at night, she quite likes it, and is grateful that her single mother is able to own their home. The land, however, is haunted by the ghost of the farmland that came before it, as the farmland itself is presumably haunted by the wilder landscape that it displaced. This rich, layered present can usefully be thought of as the Chthulucene, which Haraway describes as "tentacular": "probing creepers, swelling roots, reaching and climbing tendrilled ones" (2016, 31). Tucked away in the subdivision is the original farm, Janua Caeli, the home of the Carlisle witches:

> However, at the heart of the subdivision, set among the new houses with their new gardens, their bareness, and the constant autumnal fluttering of red nursery labels on young trees, there stood a wood of silver birches and poplars showing above a tall hedge that had marked, in previous days, the division between the Carlisle farmhouse lawn and the orchard and the vegetable garden.

> (Mahy 2018, 57)

The European birches and poplars, as well as the thick hedge that flowers "with a fairytale tapestry of Tom Thumb roses in early summer," demarcate a fairy-tale temporality, and fairy-tale possibilities (2018, 57). The significance of forests to fairy tales has been discussed extensively (Zipes 2002; Maitland 2012), but, as Daniela Kato points out, the fairy-tale forest tends to be conceptualized as a place where things happen, rather than as a "multilayered biocultural landscape" (2020, 390), a term applicable to Mahy's forests. For Laura, the forest potentially conceals tigers and other frightening beasts, but the plants themselves turn out to be its most vital inhabitants.

Laura's changeover involves a perilous journey through an interior world, imagined in vegetal terms. She enters "the forest that was all forests," encompassing the forests of fairy tales and that of *Alice Through the Looking Glass* (Carroll 1871) overlaid upon the exterior forests of Janua Caeli and Gardendale: "Laura's own forest, the forest without trees, the subdivision, the city" (Mahy 2018, 145). This dreamlike forest is peopled with characters from fairy tales and Laura's own life. Most significant, however, are the agentic plants that are ultimately revealed to be aspects of Laura's own self:

> The trees cried out to her as she passed, some seductively, others in voices of pain … Briars crept over the road and she pushed through them, scratching herself so she dripped blood once more … [Laura's] sword slid easily through the woody stems, and the briar immediately reared up, then thrashed about in anguish, screaming with a voice Laura recognised dimly as her own.
>
> (147)

As Laura cuts away at the briars, she begins to bleed as though she were attacking herself. The bleeding, painful plants here recall the tortured souls of suicides in Dante's *Inferno* (Canto XIII), trapped in the bodies of trees that bleed when torn; bleeding, wounded trees in Ovid's *Metamorphoses* (Martin 2004, 65, 295); and the briars in "Sleeping Beauty" ("Briar Rose"), through which the prince must pass in order reach the princess (Olcott 1927, 179). In an inversion of the original tale, not only must sleeping Laura hack through the briars herself, but the briars *are* herself. Kato points out that there is a long tradition in horror films and literature of women merging with plants, including the thorns conjured by the witch Maleficent in Disney's 1959 and 2014 adaptations of Sleeping Beauty (2020, 406 note 2). For Zoe Jaques, arboreal metamorphosis in children's literature frequently limits or troubles a character's developing sexuality: "At a moment when the child is crossing a boundary into an essentially adult, eroticized world—a metamorphic movement itself—such fantastical botanicals conceptualize the experience of growing up, and offer comment on the contrastive models for sexual behaviour open to the human child in the real world" (2013, 165). Being transformed into a tree often restricts the sexuality of female characters, as in the case of Ovid's story of Daphne transformed into a laurel tree in order to escape the sexual advances of Apollo (Martin 2004, 37). In this case, unlike her laurel namesake, once she has cut through the briars, vegetal metaphors of growth and freshness signal Laura's sensual and magical awakening. Laura envisages the gaining of magic as a parched, seemingly dead forest within her suddenly coming into leaf (Mahy 2018, 150): "She saw plainly that she was remade, had brought to life some sleeping part of herself, extending the forest in her head" (153). Anna Smith points out that Laura's changeover suggests menarche, as Laura wakes up covered in blood (2005, 49), but the recurring metaphors insist also on a vegetal aspect of the magic she has acquired.

The intensely vegetal and specifically arboreal nature of Mahy's magic attests to a significant connection between magic and the forest environment. Laura uses her magic to defeat Carmody Braque—reducing him to a pile of dead leaves. Braque's insatiable desire for life itself, as he steals the vitality of humans and nonhuman beings in order to secure his own immortality, pits him against the values of the Chthulucene: "living and dying in response-ability on a damaged earth" (Haraway 2016, 2). By returning him to dead leaves—a potent symbol of natural cycles of death and renewal—Laura restores a necessary death, and safeguards the lives of others. The novel also hints that magic may have a role in attending to and "becoming with" the natural world. When Sorry Carlisle reflects on what to do with his life and magic, he proposes that he might be able to use his natural skills and his magical skills together in the service of conservation. "I'd like to work for: I don't know—the wild-life division, be a ranger or something. I could use what I've got in some tactful, useful way, helping damaged bush regenerate, helping threatened bird populations" (*Changeover* 2018, 119). This desire, couched as it is in the context of the fairy-tale forest of Janua Caeli, the raw, new forest of Gardendale, and the New Zealand landscapes surrounding them both, positions the magic of Mahy's protagonists as a force in a mutually life-giving relationship with the natural world.

Alchemy

While *The Changeover* employs trees as metaphors and symbols, drawing especially on their presence in fairy tales, *Alchemy*, published nearly twenty years later, focuses on the inner lives of real trees as sources of wonder. The novel explores adolescent Roland's awakening to his latent magical powers and his friendship with magician Jess Ferret. Roland is quite aware of Browning's poem about his namesake, "Childe Roland to the Dark Tower Came," and by the end of the novel, he enacts the knight's adventure, climbing the dark, enchanted stairs of Jess's house (Browning 2019, 781–7). Extending the vegetal motifs of *The Changeover*, the surname Ferret, for which Jess is teased at school, "actually comes from an old Italian word *fioretto* which was a certain sort of silk, and that word probably came from *fiore* which means flowers" (chap. 30). Jess, a loner at school, spends her lunchtimes reading beneath a linden tree. Once Roland understands her powers, he wonders if she is communing with the tree, instead of merely sitting beneath it: "If she was merely pretending to read and was really linking with that tree. The diagrams of last year's biology suddenly sprang into his mind … she might ride, he supposed, through the long cells that carried water from root to leaf. She might sit at the growing tips of the tree, feeling the explosion as cells divided" (chap. 26). Here Mahy uses scientific language to imagine her protagonist magically inhabiting the being of a tree. Once Roland awakes to his own magical powers, he finds that plants sing to him: "A weed growing through a crack in the sealing of the road spoke in a green voice. The fenced-in trees spaced out along the pavement, a piece of wastepaper, driven by a slight breeze to throw itself under the wheels of the bike, all sang to him in their different voices" (Mahy 2002, chap. 26). We do not discover exactly what the plants sing, but there is a sense here that plants are persons worth listening to, as Hall (2011) attests.

As in *The Changeover*, the protagonists of *Alchemy* are threatened by a powerful malignant being, in this case a magician/politician, Quando. Unlike Carmody Braque, who devours the life of his victims, Quando is only interested in his victims' magical powers. Using an explicitly sexual metaphor, he threatens to "ravish" the magic out of Jess and Roland, having already taken advantage of Jess's mother. He assures them they won't miss it after a couple of days, but Roland understands "that his new dimension had become part of what he was. There would be no recovery from that loss" (Mahy 2002, chap. 31). While Carmody Braque wanted only to lasciviously enjoy life at the expense of others, Quando craves power in both spiritual and material realms. He despises the young magicians for what he views as wasting their powers: "Jess, your mother never used her power for anything but play. And what do you ever do with yours? Listen in to plants and stones? Eavesdrop on worms?" (chap. 32). While Jess and Roland are saved by their own resilience and their families' cooperation, not directly by plants, the novel thus suggests that listening to plants is in fact a valuable activity, although one incomprehensible to those fixated on power.

Maddigan's Fantasia

In *Maddigan's Fantasia*, Mahy produced one of her most explicitly environmental texts. The novel was published at the same time as a TV series of the same name, for which Mahy wrote the screenplay (Duder 2012, chap. 5). The novel is set in a post-apocalyptic New Zealand landscape and draws on the genre of science fiction, in that three of the characters travel though time, from a distant future, in order to change the past. Mahy's familiar fantasy elements remain present in the character of Eden, one of the boys from the future, who possesses magical powers and has a deep kinship with trees. The focus, however, is on a group of traveling performers, Maddigan's Fantasia, who travel about between the "leftover places" raising the spirits of those in scattered communities and restoring the land as they go (Mahy 2014, 6). There has been a nuclear catastrophe, the "Destruction," followed by the "Chaos" and then the "Remaking," the present time of the story. The land is still reforming itself, "the damaged land that held still while you looked at it, but which seemed to spin and shift and tangle, turning tricks of its own once you looked away" (4). The journeys, songs, and stories of the Fantasia are actively involved in the land's restoration: "we're the ones who stitch the land together … we're the ones who carry the news … the ones who unravel the roads, who make people laugh and feel at ease with the world, even if it is only for a single evening" (21). Thus the novel affirms a significant role for tricks, laughter, and entertainment, operating as an apology for fiction itself.

Eden, whose name of course invokes a pristine garden, is consistently described as tree-like. Little is made of this connection in the narrative, apart from two incidents involving the main protagonist, Garland. When Garland shoots an arrow into a tree, Eden himself feels wounded: "'But it's only a tree,' said Garland. 'It's not a person.' 'It's not a person but it's a bit like a person,' said Eden, straightening, and looking, as he often did, like some sort of mysterious creature, half-tree himself. 'It has power flowing through it'" (50). Eden's kinship with trees, which is linked to his significant magical powers, grants him a deep sense of care and responsibility toward the environment. Later, when Garland is in peril, Eden saves her by hiding her inside a tree. Garland enters the tree's being so completely that the tree's subjectivity becomes more compelling than her own, and she loses the desire to leave: "She was becoming alive in a different way … a strange way … an ancient way. She had turned into something else … All that mattered was stretching up towards the sun and down into the ground. All that mattered was the flow upwards and outwards into her invisible leaves. She had become part of the tree" (73–4). Inside the tree, Garland experiences an altered temporality and mode of experiencing the world. The tree's alterity offers both refuge and danger to Garland, as Eden has difficulty extracting her. While this is an isolated incident within the novel, it is a clear development of Roland's desire to magically inhabit a tree, and in both cases Mahy suggests this experience is compelling, and hints that it may be significant. It is not until her sprawling fantasy novel *Heriot*, however, that Mahy imaginatively explores the full reach of her arboreal magic.

Heriot

In *Heriot*, Mahy turns to a traditional fantasy format in order explore the scope of magic in a way that was impossible in her narratives set in the everyday world. She actually began writing this in the 1980s, but was discouraged by her editors (Duder 2012, chap. 5). "This novel," she says, "has transposed all the supernatural elements of my other books to a more conventional supernatural setting, in that it's an imaginary world where it's possible to envisage [where] the sort of energy like Laura (in *The Changeover*) and Troy (in *The Haunting*) have, [is] able to go" (chap. 4). The novel is set in an unspecified, pre-industrial European-like landscape. Along with a couple of subplots, it follows the discovery and development of magical powers in a young magician, Heriot. It received mixed reviews, and lacks a little of the liveliness of Mahy's fantastic realist works. However, its deep exploration of Mahy's arboreal magic is compelling.

Partly against his will, Heriot is acquired as the court magician of the kingdom of Hoad, where his role is to assist the king by reading the minds of his enemies and impressing foreign ambassadors with magical displays. His magical powers are thus drawn into political intrigues. Heriot's use of these powers culminates at a huge feast at which the king's ally-turned-enemy the Hero of Hoad, also assisted by a magician, is attempting to sow discord and restart a brutal war. The Hero's magician, Izachel, composes a vision of a raging battlefield and the deaths of the soldiers, which stirs up hate and fury among those present. Heriot steps in, and for the first time gives himself over completely to the full extent of his magical powers. Everyone present comes under his spell and begins to dream his dream. Heriot transforms the bloodstained battlefield into a vision of a forest:

> Their stiffening grimaces relaxed, their expressions were dazed into gentleness, a slow vegetable vision reanimating their dead minds. Heriot's memory of connection with the inner life of apple trees, in winter, spring, and early summer became part of his spell. Slowly, slowly the dead men rose up again, arboreal men turning faces as mild as a green spring up to the sky.

(160)

Heriot uses his deep knowledge of and respect for individual trees in order to conjure an experience of vegetable being in the minds of his audience: "There were no words in the language of Hoad for the layers of cells or the busy, inner life of the tree, but he could make others feel, as he felt, that each tree was not only a changing object, but a process of spirit" (161). Surrounded by a primeval forest, the imaginations of people of Hoad are released from the poison of old treacheries and they become open to paths of reconciliation.

For the people of Hoad, surrender to a vegetal mode of being enables peace and forgiveness. We can read this development through Irigaray's argument that willful ignorance of our dependence on the vegetal world for the very air we breathe has contributed to conflict, alienation, and mistreatment of the earth: "Instead of uniting their breathing towards an increase and sharing of life, people are, without knowing it, fighting against one another in order to appropriate air and vital energy that they need so they would not die, and it is only in a vegetal environment that they, finally, look quiet and happy" (2017, chap. 6). For Irigaray, a vegetal environment naturally exudes peace, and Heriot's spell spectacularly achieves this.

This victory of the imagination, however, is not the final victory of the novel. In fact, Heriot must restrain his magical powers as his lover and companion Cayley challenges the hero to a fight to the death. At the end of the novel, Heriot retreats from the city and his role at court in order to take up the role of the true Magician: "To soak outwards into the vast spaces beyond the moon, to soak inwards, down and down, into huge spaces at the heart of wood and stone, the space within his own heart and head, spaces which were not simply emptiness, not simply the absence of anything else, but an essential part of the structure of the world" (350–1). Heriot muses that his act of comprehending trees and earth, stars and stone, may in some way enable the trees and stones to comprehend themselves: "Perhaps when the Magician springs to life in some tree, flowing with its sap, the tree understands in some peculiar way just what it means to be a tree, tied into the soil of the land" (347). On a first reading, it seemed to me that Mahy steps back from her contemplation of what magic can really achieve. In many ways, what Heriot does here is no different from what Eden does in *Maddigan's Fantasia* or Jess and Roland in *Alchemy*. The magician retreats into a chthonic interior vegetal world; we cannot quite follow. The notion that a human magician can grant consciousness to a tree or a stone is in some ways quite anthropocentric. On the other hand, Mahy's magic is never quite—or never only—human anyway. What Heriot describes here is a deep kinship and understanding with the vegetal world that is mutually transforming—he is shaped by it, but it also shapes the world. This is also Laura's experience in *The Changeover*, as she enters the forest and the forest enters her.

In Mahy's novels, magic is powerful and impressive, yet paradoxically it is linked to the quiet, sessile nature of the vegetal world—to flowering trees and water rising through woody cells. Wondering in, and standing with the trees, like Tolkien, Mahy's magicians prevail over those whose only wish is to exploit the world for their own gain. Quando mocks Roland and Jess for "listen[ing] in to plants and stones" (Mahy 2002, chap. 32) but *Heriot* argues that this practice is vital. These actions are practices of the Chthulucene, and they offer a quiet yet powerful alternative to the exploitations of the Anthropocene. As Haraway puts it, "Staying with the trouble requires making oddkin; that is, we require each other in unexpected combinations and collaborations … We become-with each other or not at all" (2016, 4). Mahy proposes that the odd kinships of magic—and fiction—open a space for this mutual becoming.

Notes

1   For further discussion of Tolkien and trees, see Ryan (2015).
2   There is a growing number of anthologies dealing with the relationships between plants and literature, and their interface with other disciplines, including *The Green Thread: Dialogues with the Vegetal World* (2015), *The Language of Plants: Science, Philosophy, Literature* (2017), *Plants in Science Fiction: Speculative Vegetation* (2020), and *Plants in Children's and Young Adult Literature* (2021).

References

Bar-On, Yinon M. et al. 2018. "The Biomass Distribution on Earth." *PNAS: Proceedings of the National Academy of Sciences USA*, vol. 115, no. 25: 6506–11. June 19, 2018. https://doi.org/10.1073/pnas.1711842115

Bishop, Katherine E., David Higgins, and Jerry Määttä, eds. 2020. *Plants in Science Fiction: Speculative Vegetation*. Cardiff: University of Wales Press.

Browning, Robert. 2019. "Childe Roland to the Dark Tower Came." In *The Norton Anthology of English Literature: The Major Authors*. 10th edition, volume 2. Edited by Stephen Greenblatt. New York: Norton.

Carroll, L. 2001 [1871]. "Through the Looking-Glass and What Alice Found There." In *The Annotated Alice*, edited by Martin Gardner, 137–288. London: Penguin.

Conservation International. n.d. "Deforestation: 11 Facts You Need to Know." Accessed November 30, 2020. https://www.conservation.org/stories/11-deforestation-facts-you-need-to-know

Crowther, T., H. Glick, K. Covey *et al.* 2015. "Mapping Tree Density at a Global Scale." *Nature*: 201–5. https://doi.org/10.1038/nature14967

Dante, Alighieri. 2001. *The Inferno*. Translated by John Ciardi. New York: Signet Classics.

Duckworth, Melanie, and Lykke H. Guanio-Uluru, eds. 2022. *Plants in Children's and Young Adult Literature*. New York: Routledge.

Duder, Tessa. 2012. *Margaret Mahy: A Writer's Life. A Literary Portrait of New Zealand's Best Loved Children's Author*. Auckland: Harper Collins (New Zealand). Kindle.

FAO and UNEP. 2020. "The State of the World's Forests 2020. Forests, Biodiversity and People." Rome. https://doi.org/10.4060/ca8642e

Feingold, Ruth P. 2005. "Gardening in Eden: Margaret Mahy's Postcolonial Ghosts and the New Zealand Landscape." In *Marvellous Codes: The Fiction of Margaret Mahy*, edited by Elizabeth Hale, and Sarah Fiona Winters, 210–33. Wellington: Victoria University Press.

Gagliano, Monica, Patrícia Vieira, and John C. Ryan, eds. 2017. *The Language of Plants: Science, Philosophy, Literature*. Minneapolis: University of Minnesota Press.

Hall, Matthew. 2011. *Plants as Persons: A Philosophical Botany*. Albany: State University of New York Press.

Hall, Matthew. 2019. *The Imagination of Plants: A Book of Botanical Mythology*. Albany: State University of New York Press.

Hall, Matthew. 2019. "In Defence of Plant Personhood." *Religions*, vol. 10, no. 5. https://doi.org/10.3390/rel10050317

Haraway, Donna. 2016. *Staying with the Trouble: Making Kin in the Chthulucene*. Durham, NC and London: Duke University Press.

Irigaray, Luce. 2017. "What the Vegetal World Says to Us." In *The Language of Plants: Science, Philosophy, Literature*, edited by Monica Gagliano, John Charles Ryan, and Patrícia Vieira. Minneapolis: University of Minnesota Press. Kindle.

Irigaray, Luce, and Michael Marder. 2016. *Through Vegetal Being: Two Philosophical Perspectives*. New York: Columbia University Press.

Jaques, Zoe. 2013. "Arboreal Myths: Dryadic Transformations, Children's Literature and Fantastic Trees." In *Transformative Change in Western Thought: A History of Metamorphosis from Homer to Hollywood*, edited by Ingo Gildenhard, and Andrew Zissos, 163–82. Oxford: Legenda.

Kato, Daniela. 2020. "The Plantation, the Garden and the Forest: Biocultural Borderlands in Angela Carter's 'Penetrating to the Heart of the Forest.'" In *Re-Orienting the Fairy Tale: Contemporary Adaptations across Cultures*, edited by Mayako Murai, and Luciana Cardi, 383–410. Detroit, MI: Wayne State University Press.

Knox, Elizabeth. 2018. "Introduction." In *The Changeover*, by Margaret Mahy, vii–x. London: Orion Children's Books.

Mahy, Margaret. 2018 [1982]. *The Haunting*. London: Orion Children's Books. Kindle.

Mahy, Margaret. 2018 [1984]. *The Changeover*. London: Orion Children's Books.

Mahy, Margaret. 1988. *The Tricksters*. London: Penguin Books.

Mahy, Margaret. 2002. *Alchemy*. London: Harper Collins. Kindle.

Mahy, Margaret. 2014 [2005]. *Maddigan's Fantasia*. London: Faber and Faber. Kindle.

Mahy, Margaret. 2010 [2009]. *Heriot*. London: Faber and Faber. Kindle.

Maitland, Sara. 2012. *Gossip from the Forest: The Tangled Roots of Our Forests and Fairy Tales*. London: Granta.

Marder, Michael. 2013. *Plant-Thinking: A Philosophy of Vegetal Life*. New York: Columbia University Press. EBSCOhost.

Marder, Michael. 2013. "Is It Ethical to Eat Plants?" *Parallax* 19: 27–37.

Martin, Charles, trans. 2004. *Ovid: Metamorphoses*. New York: Norton.

Meeker, Daniela, and Antónia Szabari. 2020. *Radical Botany: Plants and Speculative Fiction*. New York: Fordham University Press.

Nitzke, Solvejg. 2020. "Listening to What Trees Have to Say." *Edge Effects*. Last modified October 27, 2020. https://edgeeffects.net/tree-story/

Olcott, Frances Jenkins, ed. 1927. *Grimm's Fairy Tales*. Philadelphia, PA: The Penn Publishing Company.

Ryan, John Charles. 2015. "Tolkien's Sonic Trees and Perfumed Herbs: Plant Intelligence in Middle Earth." In *The Green Thread: Dialogues with the Vegetal World*, edited by Patrícia Vieira, Monica Gagliano, and John Ryan, 37–58. Lanham, MD: Lexington.

Smith, Anna. 2005. "Contagious Knowledge: Margaret Mahy and the Adolescent Novel." In *Marvellous Codes: The Fiction of Margaret Mahy*, edited by Elizabeth Hale, and Sarah Fiona Winters, 44–61. Wellington: Victoria University Press.

Tolkien, J.R.R. 1981. *Letters of J.R.R. Tolkien*, edited by Humphrey Carpenter and Christopher Tolkien. London: Allen & Unwin.

Vieira, Patrícia, Monica Gagliano, and John Ryan eds. 2015. *The Green Thread: Dialogues with the Vegetal World*. Lanham, MD: Lexington.

Waller, Alison. 2004. "'Solid All the Way Through': Margaret Mahy's Ordinary Witches". *Children's Literature in Education*, vol. 35, no. 1: 77–86.

Wohlleben, Peter. 2017 [2015]. *The Hidden Life of Trees: What They Feel, How They Communicate: Discoveries from a Secret World*. Translated by Jane Billinghurst. London: William Collins.

Zipes, Jack. 2002. *The Brothers Grimm: From Enchanted Forests to the Modern World*. 2nd edition. Basingstoke: Palgrave Macmillan.

CHAPTER 14
JUST IMAGINE
Barbara Henderson

Some time ago I wrote a book in which a developer tries to convert a wild island into a luxury resort for the super-rich. When nature begins to fight back, the only ones to recognize the danger of this assault on the wilderness are the children. Looking at the artist's impression of the project, the protagonist struggles to articulate a response to what she sees:

> Beneath the swirly title, "Skelsay Skies Resort", the sun is shining on the turquoise sea. Dolphins leap against the sunset, and the gleaming buildings are filled with happy and contented people, none of whom are old or overweight—or children, for that matter. The small group of golfers on the immaculately groomed green are raising their hands in celebration, at a particularly good shot, I imagine. It feels so unreal, so mad, to think that this wild island could soon look like this.

> *(Wilderness Wars*, 22–3)

Why do we have such an insatiable compulsion to control?

We strive to control our own feelings. We strive to control the behavior of others. Worst of all, we assume the right to control the world around us, too.

It is an age-old problem, of course. The Victorians were particularly obsessed with what they called "improvements." Theirs was an era characterized by natural optimism, a faith in science and engineering, and yes, a belief in the creative supremacy of man. A handmade product, lovingly crafted? Make more, make them quicker, make them cheaper! A journey on horseback? Move faster, move further, waste no time! Wild creatures roaming an empty landscape? Hunt them, shoot them, mount them, eat them. And what about the wilderness—majestic, unkempt, windswept and free? Tame it. Groom it. Level it. Build on it. Our arrogance is breath-taking. Hey human, I've got news for you: You may not always know best.

And yet there is hope. The counterweight to our conceit is our capacity to imagine. Think about it: stories and books are no more than little black marks on white paper, but they have the power to set a reel in motion in the minds of readers. The potent human imagination is our most eloquent ally in the argument for a better world.

As storytellers, our gift to the globe lies in the *what ifs*. With every alternative vision, every alternative worldview and every character whose choices and motivations differ from our own, we pose a *what if* question which will play out in young readers' minds. *What if* humanity chose a path of less consumption and more creativity? *What if* we chose a path of less interference and more imagination? Not a backward step, but a dancing leap toward living in the world rather than dominating it? Imagine wild spaces, green spaces, blue spaces, wide spaces. Imagine room to breathe.

Just imagine …

CHAPTER 15
FROM PORTABLE LANDSCAPES TO THEMED THRILL RIDES: ROWLING'S HETEROTOPIC HOPESCAPES

Stephanie J. Weaver

In the spirit of examining landscapes in fantasy literature as well as responding to the sense of urgency for contributions to critical studies on the Anthropocene, the purpose of this project lies in placing both J. K. Rowling's and Warner Brothers' Wizarding World within the ecological conversation. The term "Wizarding World," though used as the title of a well-trafficked webpage, refers more generally to the established fantastic world first built by J. K. Rowling with the publication of her Harry Potter series. It now includes the narratives of her collaborations with Warner Brothers as well as playwright Jack Thorne, and will be used throughout this exploration to refer to the established world that includes Harry Potter and other narratives. Although subtle in its initial commentary on the Anthropocene, the Wizarding World's most recent attention to the current state of the climate crisis both problematizes and proposes potential visions for solutions to combat climate crisis, placing Rowling alongside Speculative Fiction writers like China Miéville, Lev Grossman, and Travis Beacham. Through an analysis of how Rowling constructs ecologically resilient spaces, the chapter suggests that the Wizarding World's notions of resiliency, restoration, and heterotopic ecology as a response to climate chaos run far deeper than the simplistic notions of a posthuman dystopian "solution" or a mere "return to nature." Instead of constructing a world that adheres to other popular notions of world-building that predicate on either the utopian or dystopian extremes, Rowling's world-building techniques shift to a synthesis of human sustainability and nonhuman resiliency. From Newt Scamander's suitcase and London flat to the Parisian carnival coach and Hagrid's motorbike tour, Rowling reinvents urban and what I call "portable" landscapes—self-contained landscapes that are not rooted in one location—as spaces for sustainable multi-species collaboration and coexistence. These ecologically resilient spaces offer visions of hope that are markedly different from other "explorations" of the Anthropocene found in climate fiction and fantasy: embracing the posthuman, the notion that nature survives and flourishes in the age without human interference, or returning to Edenic innocence that Karl Kroeber and Carolyn Merchant called green Romanticism (Kroeber 1994, 1–21; Merchant 2004 3–8; 39–46). Instead, Rowling uses world-building to construct a hopescape: a landscape that provides audiences with a view of the possibilities of a world that is neither devoid of humanity nor fully returned to Eden.

World-Building in the Anthropocene: Heterotopias, Mindscapes, and Rowling's Hopescapes

This chapter uses the Foucauldian term "heterotopia" to describe the landscapes that balance the juxtaposing forces of human progress and advancement with attention to nonhuman entities and their preservation, especially in a rural context. Besides defining heterotopia as a "real place" deviating from the term for a perfected place "utopia," Foucault elaborates that heterotopias are either "of crisis" or "of deviation," meaning that these "places" emerge as a result of cultures in crisis or cultures experiencing deviation in societal constructs; they are simultaneously transforming and problematizing the real world (Foucault 1984, 24–5). Throughout this chapter, I propose to apply the concept of a heterotopia to the ecological crisis rather than political or cultural crises in Foucault's original formulation. By looking at landscapes in Rowling as a synthesis of forces resulting from juxtaposing human and nonhuman entities, I propose that fantasy literature may envision a future apart from the Romantic and posthuman landscapes. Unlike other genres, fantasy holds the potential to create hopescapes, or imagined landscapes that focus on the potential for a future where humans and nonhumans survive and coexist together. Besides exploring the landscapes created in narrative fiction, the chapter also looks at landscapes created for the Universal Studio's Wizarding World's adventures, suggesting how, increasingly, each installment envisages a landscape that withstands crisis.

Previous ecocritical criticism of the Harry Potter series has focused on the exploration of mythic and mystical plants or nonhuman fauna within the novels, as well as on significant objects in the Wizarding World. For example, Melanie Dawson's (2011) look at deep ecology in the series revealed that many objects in the Harry Potter world are given "consciousness" which, she argues, blurs the line between human and nonhuman (83). Zoe Jaques (2015) applied the plant studies lens, arguing that Rowling's "imagined" sentient tree and plant life protests human maltreatment and manipulation while also focusing on how wizards in the novels manipulate fantastic "botanicals" for human purpose (134–5). This reflection set a precedent for exploring the relationship between Harry Potter and plant studies; Jaques's attention to trees and various magical botanicals in Harry Potter built on already-established criticism from Noel Chevalier (2005) on the Whomping Willow, while also concentrating on representations of the posthuman in children's literature and Harry Potter (Chevalier 2005, 397–415; Jaques 2015, 131–40). Keridiana W. Chez (2016) examined the use of Mandrakes in *Harry Potter and the Chamber of Secrets*, arguing for the liminal status of a plant that "lives like a human, and dies like a plant" (72–3). Other scholars, including Peter Dendle (2009), looked at the relationship between humans and nonhuman mythical fauna, as well as at the constructs of human stewardship of animals (163–76).

Building upon, yet going beyond these conversations, this chapter explores how urban and portable landscapes within the Wizarding World articulate hopeful-fantastic responses to the urgencies of the Anthropocene. By imagining the potential of humans to adopt heterotopic and ecologically restorative practices that mitigate the destructiveness of the Anthropocene, the most recent film releases and themed adventures in the Wizarding World of Rowling and Warner Brothers offer visions or imagined solutions in which humans remain part of the biosphere, even integral to it, rather than being eliminated for the sake of planetary health.

Before continuing, I wish to provide some context for Rowling's world-building techniques as a method of critical cultural commentary by drawing on Poul Anderson's definition of mindscape (Anderson 1989, 3). For Anderson, a "mindscape" refers to "geographies of the mind as used in fiction" in which audiences can enter imaginary spaces to critically consider alternative ideas (3–4). A mindscape is therefore the product of the world-building of the author. Rowling's intended construction of the Wizarding World to include landscapes focused on ecological sustainability provides a critical opportunity for conversation around how we need fantasy to imagine possibilities of existence where humans and nonhumans interact symbiotically, stewarding rather than destroying or manipulating nonhuman forms of life. With the mindscape arguably at the center of world-building, Rowling, in collaboration with Warner Brothers, eventually develops her world further to construct a hopescape, or a vision of a reimagined world through which audiences can gain knowledge that is applicable to their own cultural moment.

Early explorations of landscape in literature, in what Lawrence Buell and Ken Hiltner have dubbed the first wave of ecocritical discourse (Buell 2005, 1–21; Hiltner 2015, 1–3), were driven by a "return to nature" imperative, in which humans search for an ecological paradise. According to Carolyn Merchant, such search is designed to fail; even when perceived to be successful it leads to a re-creation and further manipulation of landscape (2004, 1–5). Many early fantasy novels took this pastoral, Edenic space as their ideal. From Katherine Patterson's sweeping vistas, through Frances Hodgson Burnett's garden, and on to Tolkien's Shire, the return to pre-industrial landscapes has been a consistent motif in fantasy, even if this ecological paradise is imagined differently across different genres. For example, Edenic mindscape in urban fantasy functions as a landscape that synthesizes "folkloric topoi" with the technological innovations of the metropolis: a setting found in the works of China Miéville or Jeff VanderMeer (Irvine 2012, 200–7). Another approach, evident in much cli-fi, has been to imagine post-destruction future landscapes in which humanity exists as posthumanity, and where technocultural forces both frame and undermine what it means to be human (Clark 2011, 63–6).

Such worlds are to be found, for example, in Nancy Farmer's *The House of the Scorpion* (2002), Julie Bertanga's the Exodus Trilogy (2002–7), and Cherrie Dimaline's *The Marrow Thieves* (2018). Despite being a newer installment of the ecocritical conversation, posthuman mindscapes have long been a feature in science fiction and steampunk narratives like Phillip Pullman's His Dark Materials Trilogy (1995–2000), and in some ways going back even to Shelley's *Frankenstein* (1818). For Rowling, the audience and readers do not need to travel to Cameron's Pandora, Grossman's Fillory, or one of Pullman's world in Cittagazze for an alternative to a world in environmental crisis. Instead Rowling constructs a world within our own to provide a landscape of hope in a place that is already home. This pathway of world-building lends to an accessible reimagining of our world, but also holds limitations, which are two perspectives that I will explore through her creation of portable landscapes in her world.

The Wizarding World does not subscribe to either Edenic or posthuman imaginations of future landscapes. It does not create a "return to nature" where technology and human advancement are eliminated, or a new world where humans do not play an integral role. On the contrary, the forms of Wizarding Commerce, the use of flying technologies, and the invention of marketable products throughout the Harry Potter series all suggest that technology is an essential feature of human civilization. Nor can the world-building of Wizarding World be described as an exploration of the posthuman, in which, say, the Forbidden Forest takes over Hogwarts. The familiar–unfamiliar landscapes are not destroyed, and humans, be they wand-carriers or Muggles, are not eliminated from the planet. Instead, Rowling's world-building of the Wizarding World, also in collaboration with Warner Brothers, can be better thought of as providing a heterotopic landscape—something akin to what Raymond Williams advocated in *The Country and the City* (1973). When describing our society's construction of binaries between country and city and between urban and rural, Williams claims that landscape functions as a facet of civilization, redefining the nature of "development" and "human achievement" commenced by agrarian reproduction (1973, 1–2). Instead of a simplistic return to nature, Williams calls for a new approach which recognizes the need for a possible "New Eden," but only as a synthesis of both country and urban landscapes, where nature is "transformed" and country life is not merely an aesthetic escape from society (Williams 1973, 129–31). Rowling's world-building illustrates Williams's logic. It imagines the Wizarding World's mindscapes as an alternative to pastoral Romanticism on the one hand and dystopian posthumanism on the other.

Rowling's Portable Mindscapes as Hopescapes in the Anthropocene

Rowling's Wizarding World consistently points to mindscapes where humans steward rather than manipulate their environments, further exploring the idea of a hopescape where there is collaboration between human and nonhuman entities. Early hints of this trend can be found within the Harry Potter series (1997–2007), for example, through the Weasley's home as a place where garden gnomes find comfort due to Mr. Weasley's maintenance of the garden (Rowling 1998, 37–8). After the completion of the Potter series, Rowling refined her activist response to environmental crisis by creating portable and urban landscapes in the world of Newt Scamander (2016, 2018, ongoing), the subject of her first two forays into screenwriting. In the first two cinematic installments of her Fantastic Beasts series (2016, 2018, ongoing), Rowling constructs a series of ecosystems that succeed in maintaining a heterotopic environment where human and nonhuman entities coexist. Her world-building highlights the success of landscapes that focus on sustainable and restorative practices, specifically in places like The Burrow and Hogwarts, while also stressing that similar magically portable and urban landscapes must maintain a commitment to multi-species cohabitation and preservation. The most notable example of such a mindscape is a small case introduced in Rowling's screenplay and eventual film production of *Fantastic Beasts and Where to Find Them*. The protagonist is young Newt Scamander, later known as the most notable magizoologist and protector of magical creatures in the Wizarding World. Although the 1926 setting predates the general awareness of biodiversity loss by approximately half of a century, Rowling builds Newt's character around protecting animals that have been mistreated or commodified. She then uses Newt's adventures to provide education to others—characters and readers alike—about the value of biodiversity including these nonhuman creatures. It seems only fitting that Scamander's heterotopic ideas are also manifest in a heterotopic ecological place, very different from any other hybrid ecological landscape found in fantasy literature. The space exists within a brown leather suitcase which contains a self-contained ecosystem that houses hundreds of animals that need protection and space to live. Rowling describes: "The perimeter of the leather case is dimly visible, but the place has swollen to the size of a small aircraft hangar. It contains what appears to be a safari park in miniature. Each of Newt's creatures has its own perfect, magically realized habitat" (Rowling 2016, 100).

Upon first encountering this description, the reader feels a sense of ambivalence concerning the true value and role of the case. The language of Rowling's description, which strikingly uses postcolonial and Anthropocentric references to tourist culture, again lends support to racial and cultural otherness. When she notes that the case becomes a miniature "safari park," she alludes to a notion that Ralf Buckley further explores in his article concerning tourism and wildlife safari parks in former colonial territories (Buckley 2013, 16). By initially using this language Rowling calls attention to a problematic legacy of imagining the nature of Africa and Asian landscapes as the property of West, only to go on to describe the portable landscape as more akin to a rehabilitation center, rather than a spectacular zoo where audiences can escape to. This role becomes clear when the audience witnesses the case becoming an array of habitats where Newt can provide homes and protection for the creatures that he not only studies but considers his friends and equals, and whom he intends to restore to their rightful ecosystems. In this sense this portable landscape becomes an environment where the nonhuman can be cared for and eventually brought back to the habitats where they can thrive.

Newt's case protects its inhabitants, but it is also a hopescape for audiences to witness the power humans have to protect and preserve the nonhuman. Despite being tested by both Jacob and Grindelwald in disguise, the case remains safe for the creatures that call it their home. Within the case, Newt provides the creatures with a slice of their own habitat of origin, until they are able to return home. He shows Jacob, his Muggle accomplice, the value of caring for the creatures and the importance of environmental education as opposed to manipulation of resources and nonhuman entities. This type of instruction is better than a zoo system in part because Newt releases the animals back to their habitats once he provides them with the care they need. The portable landscape, in fulfilling this conservationist function, provides a hopescape that focuses on the potential of preserving endangered species and a way to eventually restore those creatures to a preserved habitat. As mentioned, the critical attribute of the case is its durability; it can withstand crisis. The implications of this detail in Rowling's depiction of the case show how vital nonhuman species are to her world and the planet at large; the case suggests that with collaboration our world can withstand the current climate crisis, even though it does not ensure a foolproof solution. The durability of the case directly correlates with the conscious effort of humans to care for their nonhuman counterparts.

Through the creation of places that exhibit aspects of both the urban and rural binary—or even the human and nonhuman binary—Rowling provides a clear representation of the ecological crisis that results from human domination. She gestures at a path forward through restoring resilient landscapes and ecological spaces where wildlife can exist. In this sense, her forming of a heterotopic landscape may even be seen as a development of the ideas that Williams contemplated in his explorations of the county and the city (1973, 1–10). Newt's case itself, a product of industry and a factory system, becomes, through magic, a protective tool for nonhuman species even within the confines of New York City. The case serves as one of Rowling's comprehensive examples of the process of a restoration ecology. It is a landscape that results from "intentional activity that initiates or accelerates the recovery of an ecosystem with respect to its health, integrity, and sustainability" (Zeunert 2013, 238–9). In creating these landscapes as tools, Rowling's world-building focuses on providing a space for humans to act as preservers of nature and protectors of natural entities while maintaining their vision of a future where advanced technologies exist.

The repurposed, urban-centered, and often portable landscapes serving as centers of ecological sustainability in an anthropocentric reality are further developed in the latest cinematic installment to the Wizarding World. Newt Scamander's Victorian house in London, yet another representation of durability, provides another foray into fantastic world-building techniques as an opportunity to assert the possibility of heterotopic spaces existing even in the center of urban landscapes. The identification of the house as Victorian may be intended to cue audiences to recall the relationship between the Victorian Era's Industrial Revolution and the destruction of nature (Rowling 2016, 51). This parallels the relationship between Newt's house and the industrial mentalities of the urban world outside it. That said, Newt's basement, like his portable suitcase, becomes yet another opportunity for Rowling to provide audiences with a landscape that serves a different purpose than manipulation and spectacle. Although the screenplay uses the designation of "menagerie," which—as Buckley notes—evokes a construct of tourism and being merely observers as well as associations with an imperialist form of exploitation (Buckley 2013,1–6), in the next sentence the term is replaced by the more specific denotation of "hospital" for the creatures (Rowling 2016, 54). This phrasing seems more accurate. The film and screenplay alike provide images of Newt's basement as a landscape that maintains the constructed form of the urban house while showcasing its function as a refuge of sorts: a Kelpie, for instance, inhabits an underground pool that mirrors a loch ecosystem which the creature calls home (2001, 43–4). Although the reader of the screenplay and audience of the film are only in Newt's basement for a few moments, the constructed haven for flora and fauna within the London home clearly represents an urban landscape that is a product both of human industry and ingenuity operating within a metropolis and of nonhuman forces that construct landscapes which meet the needs of specific and diverse creatures. In this sense, there is an acknowledgement of techno-industry, but alongside a reimagining of the wizards' role in relation to that industry, so that both industrial mentalities like suitcases and tenement-style homes can exist but are repurposed to advocate for all species.

The Wizarding World, as a mindscape, also involves a series of spaces that combine human advancement and creation with natural elements that are not always sustainable or durable in the wake of crisis. Not all of Rowling's portable landscapes provide hopescapes for the future of human and nonhuman collaboration in the Anthropocene, even if they hold heterotopic qualities. In order for there to be the potential for a tangible vision, humans must play an active role in creating that heterotopic hopescape. There are instances, for example, where Rowling's mindscape shows that good intentions fail to consistently act as spaces of preservation in crisis. Instead, some landscapes within Rowling's world pose as the point of crisis—crises directly correlated to a community's response to preserving or respecting the integrity of these habitats. An example of this failure comes in the form of a portable Parisian form of entertainment. This portable landscape fails and is eventually destroyed due to its unsustainable role as an ecosystem manipulated by wizards for human gain and power, rather than one which preserves its the flora and fauna. The creatures within this portable landscape are not cared for, but rather imprisoned, with no hope of ever being returned to their initial habitat. Taking the form first as a circus with its rhetoric of mistreatment at the center of the descriptions, and later as a Parisian entertainment cart that again mirrors Buckley's (2013, 16–17) analysis, the landscape of the Circus Arcanus provides audiences with an image of a prison. Designed for entertainment and spectacle, the creatures and humans in the circus are treated as property (Rowling 2018, 82–9). The ornaments in the circus have been severely manipulated, mistreated, and abused. Not long after the audience views the mistreatment of the creatures, the portable "heterotopic" landscape catches fire when captive firedrakes release a series of flames, incinerating the Circus's big top (88–91). The juxtaposition of the circus's portable landscape with that of Newt's case and hospital in the basement of his Victorian townhouse provides a stark contrast with respect to the role that humans must play in the restoration efforts while also showing how heterotopic spaces problematize the potential for a solution to crisis in an anthropocentric world. Rowling also provides a vision of warning: when there is exploitation of flora and fauna, the result is fire, be that through magical or natural means. Once the Circus Arcanus is reduced to rubble, its owner packs the rest of his wares and leaves. He takes no responsibility for the destruction, nor for the creatures that have escaped. This attitude is contrasted with Newt's quest to find and nurse the abused creatures back to health, which he eventually does. The world-building provided in the early scenes of the film shows the effects of manipulation of nonhuman creatures, landscapes, and plants. But this introduction is used only to highlight the responsibility of everyone to maintain, protect, and, when needed, heal destroyed landscapes. In other words, Rowling provides the audience with a mindscape of crisis in the urbanscape alongside a mindscape of resolution. This model of choice in the present—especially in the face of past destruction—suggests that our future need not be dystopian. It does not need to end in our demise.

Through the seven novels, companion texts, films, and forms of themed entertainment, the Wizarding World explores place and landscape as an evolving critical component to Rowling's narratives. It uses interactions between characters and their environment to provide commentary on the need to respect and protect natural space. Through these portable and often-repurposed spaces, in which human intervention and natural processes are equally present, the constructed fantastic world communicates that the fate of humanity in the Anthropocene is determined by human approaches to the nonhuman. It depends on the fine line between successful heterotopic ecologies and their failures. Some damaged spaces show a potential for rebuilding, where the landscape can be fully restored. Others become tools for ecological literacy in their state as ruins, a notion that the themed entertainment industry uses when exploring the narratives around their rides.

Thrill Rides as Heterotopic Hopescapes in the Midst of the Culture Industry

It almost seems contradictory to discuss themed entertainment in the context of ecological literacy, considering that themed entertainment such as theme parks, resorts, and merchandise represents what Adorno and Horkheimer's "Culture Industry" condemns as a destructive force to human advancement and cultural durability (2002, 94–100). Themed entertainment, its history, and its place in culture represent a legacy of consumer capitalism that has led to the overconsumption which correlates with the environmental crisis. The endless rides that end in gift shops, the plethora of plastic and disposable waste in the parks, and even the bulldozing of habitats to create these resorts designed for escape, all seem to contradict the core philosophy of ecological literacy in the Anthropocene. Yet, even in this place predicated on cash flow and overconsumption, there is a sense of hope. Because of the desire to physically escape the world outside the theme park's walls while still maintaining meaningful experiences, themed entertainment designers are seizing the opportunity to create narratives that convey messages of human responsibility for the natural world. Universal's themed entertainment thrill rides at the Wizarding World of Harry Potter in both Orlando and Los Angeles have thus used world-building to contemplate the dangers of the Anthropocene and establish dialogue with Rowling's hopescapes from the films. These thrill rides—three in Orlando and two in Los Angeles—are designed for a wide range of audiences. Each tells a story rooted in the ecological consciousness of Rowling's Wizarding World. Even in the midst of a corporate and consumer-focused theme park environment, where every ride ends up in a gift shop, Warner Brothers creative teams seek to maintain Rowling's construction of a mindscape where there is attention to the significance of preserving environments for the sake of protecting nonhuman species. The narratives that are included in each thrill ride explore different stories, from that of the Muggle riders helping to save Hogwarts to a lesson on stewardship of the flora and fauna of Hogwarts with Hagrid as the audience's teacher and guide. The rides allow the audience to immerse themselves in the world of Harry Potter through a mix of computer-generated effects and intricately constructed production design. With each ride, a participant is physically inserted into the narrative through the use of sensory interactive queue lines, captivating computer imaging, production design, interactive cars themed for the ride, and even 3D experience to fully immerse the audience into the story the ride is designed to tell. Every ride also allows the audience to be a protagonist in a story alongside their favorite characters as they embark on an adventure that eventually focuses on preserving facets of the Wizarding World and all of its inhabitants. By transforming narratives that explore ecological ideas and provide opportunities for ecological literacy into experiences of direct engagement and immersive entertainment, the theme parks draw the audience in even further than a film, because now the audience has the opportunity to play an active role. The audience is cast as characters and each rider holds a stake in the narrative. Even in the construct of a "mindscape," the audience still becomes invested when they are included as characters. This form of entertainment offers a unique opportunity to educate participants on their role within the Anthropocene and also begins to witness the reimagining of potential visions for solutions. In this sense, the themed entertainment installments, the rides, the constructed villages filled with endless troves of consumerist products, show that although hopescapes do not annul consumer capitalist mentalities, there is still opportunity to think about heterotopic mindscapes within the Wizarding World. The following section provides an analysis of my experience in Universal Orlando in the winter of 2020.

In each of the respective narratives of the three thrill-themed entertainment rides constructed in Orlando's Universal Studios before 2018, there lies an underlying sub-narrative of the dangers of anthropocentric mentalities and the effect that those mentalities pose for the wizarding population, including the rider. "Harry Potter and the Forbidden Journey" begins as a tour for Muggles to follow Harry through the grounds of Hogwarts. It leads into a portion of the ride where "the forest" is not safe for humans and ends with a scene where the inhabitants of the castle and the forest are safe once again (Universal Studios Orlando "Harry Potter and Forbidden Journey" 2020). "Harry Potter and the Escape from Gringotts," another digital thrill ride, also engages in narratives that involve environmental literacy. In this ride, human manipulation of rock and stone, while riders travel in a nineteenth-century-styled mine-cart, shows how the Wizarding World is implicated with extractive industries and thus engages with specific dangers of the Anthropocene. The broad underlying concept in the narratives surrounding the rides seems to be inviting the participant to establish a balance between human-centered advancement and production, and nonhuman preservation and resiliency (Universal Studios Orlando "Harry Potter and the Escape from Gringotts" 2020). For example, in "Harry Potter and The Escape from Gringotts," the initial entrance way is designed to dazzle readers with its attention to detail from the ornamental chandelier in the entry way to the use of early-twentieth-century design in the form of bankers lamps. This is then followed by an interactive ride that focuses on the natural placement of stone and the creatures that are found under the vaults at Gringotts. The natural stone and creatures are manipulated by the wizards in power, which leads to destruction initially, but then is resolved through the hero's work within the narrative of the ride. This focus is especially clear in Universal's latest themed entertainment installment, which provides riders with a chance to develop ecological literacy in the form of a lesson in Care of Magical Creatures.

"Hagrid's Magical Creature's Motorbike Adventure" is yet another example of how anthropocentric and industrial mentalities can be placed alongside resilient and heterotopic landscapes. Beginning with the queue line and culminating in the audience's inclusion in the entertainment, "Hagrid's Magical Creatures Motorbike Adventure" is an innovative "story coaster" (Fitch 2019) whose ecological consciousness illustrates the shifting focus of the Wizarding World-themed entertainment design. The narrative surrounding the ride begins on the queue line. The riders are brought through a mazed structure that first exists on the outside and eventually enters into an underground location. The ride from the outside appears to be grounded in the ruins just beyond Hogwarts. The ruins and stones are covered by lichen, a plant known to grow in areas affected by extreme temperatures and changes in the environment. As audiences look at the structures surrounding the ride, the design provides a synthesis of nonhuman resiliency and human construction. For example, the ruined castle structure offers a habitat for wild vegetation to grow in. Even the materials used are a mixture of natural wildlife and human-constructed simulacra of wildlife. Once the riders enter into the structure of the ride, the designed queue focuses on Hagrid as an educator on magical creatures, exploring ways of stewarding and nurturing of the nonhuman creatures. While in the queue, audiences are moved to explore the walls of the ride, especially introductions to the lessons about the creatures the "students" will encounter during the experience. Just before the participants mount their respective motorbikes, the narrative turns to focus on Hagrid's "office," that is his motorbike, which does not run on Muggle fuel. Instead, the bike is propelled by magical renewable energy and the article around the queue charts movement toward renewable energy in our Muggle world too. In this way, the ride blends ideas of sustainability, promoting a synthesis between human ingenuity and the preservation of natural systems. During the high-intensity speed ride, the narrative follows Hagrid's lesson plan, in which the audience learns about various creatures and maintaining their environments. Halfway through the three-minute ride, there is a moment where the motorbike needs to be "recharged" which leads to a backwards free-fall that "recharges" the motorbike to continue the coaster. At the end, Hagrid provides a review of the "lessons" from the "field experience" and delivers "students" back into their world through a moss-laden stone arch. Built into the thrill of a ride is the intention to leave audiences with a moment of recognition of their responsibility for both human and nonhuman aspects of their environment. Offering heterotopic imaginings of technology and landscape, the rides suggest to the audience that there is a vision for the future in the seemingly hopeless Anthropocene.

Hopescapes and a Vision for the Future in the Twenty-First Century

From its early developments through its recent iterations in books, films, games, and immersive experiences, fantasy continues to imagine worlds and build landscapes where nature and humanity can coexist without significant environmental harm. Rowling's and Warner Brothers' latest installments of the Wizarding World in the form of screenplays, films, and themed attractions provide a series of models for how world-building can propose and reimagine solutions to anthropocentric crisis. Even in the Anthropocene there are opportunities to hope for a sustainable and resilient coexistence of human and nonhuman beings. One only has to look to the news coverage of the positive changes to the environment due to the Covid-19 quarantine. Despite overconsumption of things like disposable personal protective equipment, this current cultural moment opens up spaces for hope. From the lions of South Africa's Kruger National Park returning to claim a space that is now covered in asphalt, to the change in air quality on a global scale and quieting industry even in small ways leads, we are reminded that the biosphere is resilient and can rebound if given a chance. Sowry's photograph of the South African lions was designed to show how there is a potential for human and nonhuman animals to share space (Sowry 2020). Even on a local level, more animals are emerging in suburban areas because of the quieting of the bustle of urban and industrial lifestyles. Perhaps there is a silver lining in the time of Social Distancing. In the midst of the pandemic, audiences seem to be more open to new ideas than ever before, even to the idea that the nonhuman world needs its own space, where the nonhuman may breathe, talk, and live alongside the human. Fantasy literature has the potential to educate audiences on our role in the Anthropocene while mobilizing us to take a more active stand toward the preservation of the nonhuman. Providing narratives that reimagine landscapes on Earth while also noting the potential to restore such landscapes through human action remains a key element in fantasy literature, even beyond the grounds of Hogwarts. As Rowling's Wizarding World continues to evolve, so has a sense of ecological consciousness within each of the collaborative projects that have followed the world of the Harry Potter series. Through Rowling's collaborative construction of ecologically heterotopic spaces, or spaces that detail a vision of multi-species cohabitation, Wizarding World provides readers with greater literacy regarding sustainable solutions where there is both ecological preservation and human advancement.

References

Anderson, Poul. 1989. "Natures: Laws and Surprises." In *Mindscapes: The Geographies of Imagined Worlds*, edited by George E. Slusser and Eric S. Rabkin, 3–15. Edwardsville: Southern Illinois University Press.

Buckley, Ralf. 2013. "Material Culture and Postcolonial Wildlife Tourism." *Griffith University Research Online*, Griffith University, 2013, research-repository.griffith.edu.au/bitstream/handle/10072/52531/85447_1.pdf%3Bsequence=1

Buell, Lawrence. 2005. *The Future of Environmental Ecocriticism: Environmental Crisis and Literary Imagination*. Malden, MA: Blackwell Publishing Ltd.

Chevalier, Noel. 2005. "The Liberty Three and the Whomping Willow: Political Justice, Magical Science, and *Harry Potter*." *The Lion and the Unicorn*, vol. 29, no. 3: 397–415.

Chez, Keridiana W. 2016. "The Mandrake's Lethal Cry: Homuncular Plants in J. K. Rowling's *Harry Potter and the Chamber of Secrets*." In *Plant Horror: Approaches to the Monstrous Vegetal in Fiction and Film*, edited by Dawn Keetley and Angela Tenga, 72–88. London: Palgrave Macmillan.

Clark, Timothy. 2011. *The Cambridge Introduction to Literature and the Environment*. Cambridge: Cambridge University Press.

Dawson, Melanie. 2011. "Sugared Violets and Conscious Wands: Deep Ecology in the *Harry Potter* Series." In *Environmentalism in the Realm of Science Fiction and Fantasy*, edited by Christopher Baratta, 70–89. New York: Cambridge Scholars Publishing.

Dendle, Peter. 2009. "Monsters, Creatures, and Pets at Hogwarts: Animal Stewardship in the World of Harry Potter." In *Critical Perspectives on Harry Potter* Second Edition, edited by Elizabeth E. Heilman, 163–76. New York: Routledge.

Fitch, Hailey. 2019. "7 Thrilling Details about Hagrid's Magical Creatures Motorbike Adventure." *Discover Universal Blog.* May 20, 2019. https://blog.universalorlando.com/destination/7-thrilling-details-about-hagrids/?_ga=2.229493407.2048888264.1589650124-1659096480.1589650124

Foucault, Michel. 1984. "Of Other Spaces: Utopias and Heterotopias." In *Architecture /Mouvement/ Continuité*, Translated by Jay Miskowiec, October 1984. PDF. https://post.at.moma.org/sources/17/publications/210

Hiltner, Ken. 2015. "First Wave Introduction." In *Ecocriticism: The Essential Reader*, edited by Ken Hiltner, 1–3. New York: Routledge.

Horkheimer, Max, and Theodor W. Adorno. 2002. "The Culture Industry: Enlightenment as Mass Deception." In *Dialectic of Enlightenment: Philosophical Fragments*. edited by Gunzelin Schmid Noerr. Translated by Edmund Jephcott, 94–137. Stanford, CA: Stanford University Press.

Irvine, Alexander C. 2012. "Urban Fantasy." In *The Cambridge Companion to Fantasy Literature*, edited by Edward James, and Farah Mendlesohn, 200–14. New York: Cambridge University Press.

Jaques, Zoe. 2015. *Children's Literature and the Posthuman: Animal Environment, Cyborg.* London: Routledge.

Kroeber, Karl. 1994. *Ecological Literary Criticism: Romantic Imagining and the Biology of the Mind.* New York: Columbia University Press.

Merchant, Carolyn. 2004. *Reinventing Eden: The Fate of Nature in Western Culture.* New York: Routledge.

Rowling, J. K. 1998. *Harry Potter and the Chamber of Secrets.* New York: Scholastic Inc.

Rowling, J. K. 2001. *Fantastic Beasts and Where to Find Them by Newt Scamander.* New York: Arthur A Levine Books.

Rowling, J. K. 2016. *Fantastic Beasts and Where to Find Them: The Original Screenplay.* New York: Arthur A Levine Books.

Rowling, J. K. 2018. *Fantastic Beasts: The Crimes of Grindelwald: The Original Screenplay.* New York: Arthur A. Levine Books.

Sowry, Richard. "Coronavirus: Lions Nap on Road during South African Lockdown." *British Broadcasting Corporation.* April 16, 2020. https://www.bbc.com/news/world-africa-52314282

Universal Studios Orlando. 2020. "Harry Potter and the Escape from Gringotts." Accessed May 15, 2020. https://www.universalorlando.com/web/en/us/things-to-do/rides-attractions/harry-potter-and-the-escape-from-gringotts

Universal Studios Orlando, 2020. "Harry Potter and the Forbidden Journey." Accessed 15 May, 2020. https://www.universalorlando.com/web/en/us/things-to-do/rides-attractions/harry-potter-and-the-forbidden-journey

Williams, Raymond. 1973. *The Country and the City.* Oxford: Oxford University Press.

Zeunert, Joshua. 2013. "Challenging Assumptions in Urban Restoration Ecology." *Landscape Journal,* vol. 32, no. 2: 231–42. Project MUSE [Johns Hopkins University Press].

CHAPTER 16
DOES FANTASY LITERATURE HAVE A PLACE IN THE CLIMATE CHANGE CRISIS?

Craig Russell

Many people still live in a world where climate change itself is a fantasy. They believe that the CO_2 crisis has been manufactured by mysterious "others" to deprive them of their freedom to burn fossil fuels without consequence.

So, for authors like me who describe futures where the dramatic consequences of climate change fall hard upon humanity and the planet, there's a concern. Are we helping the cause? Are we doing something of value? Or are we giving aid and comfort to those who might twist our dramatic, fictional depictions of climate change into props for their strawman arguments? This is a worry that isn't faced in most fiction.

To explain: although my cli-fi novel *Fragment* depicts many scientifically proven facts about the physics of melting ice, wave formation, and so on, I did also allow myself the artistic license to depict events as dramatically as I could imagine they *might* happen. Is it likely that a large section of Antarctica's thousand-foot thick Ross Ice Sheet could survive months at sea, as an intact mega-iceberg many scores of miles in diameter, despite the mechanical and thermal impacts of its journey from the Antarctic Ocean to the Caribbean Sea? I honestly don't know.

Certainly, much-smaller icebergs make their way hundreds of miles from Greenland to the North Atlantic shipping lanes each year. And so, I permitted myself license to imagine the most dramatic possibility—that the Fragment could reach the American Gulf Coast, and in a fitting twist of fate, visit immense damage to one of the nations most responsible for its release upon the world.

My publisher, my editor, and I agreed that in the social contract between disaster-story novelist and their reader, the reader's expectation for a "pay off" **must** be met. As with Chekhov's gun, one cannot show the makings of a massive environmental catastrophe in the first act, and not visit it upon the larger world by the story's end. It is wrong for a writer to make narrative promises that they don't keep. But is it wrong to apply the rules of fiction to the serious, real-world time-bomb that is global warming?

There is a dark side to cli-fi. For example, Michael Crichton's bizarre 2004 techno-thriller *State of Fear* imagines a plot by a "radical eco-terrorist" group to publicize the danger of global warming—by manufacturing their own man-made disasters! And although, according to climate scientists and science journalists, *State of Fear* is filled with errors and distortions, it does—in a fashion—follow the rules of fiction. So, perhaps it *can* be wrong to fictionalize serious matters.

But I take some hope from past problems and past fictions.

Slavery was a hideous, real-world tragedy for the United States. And then Harriet Beecher Stowe offered a fictionalized account of the lives of enslaved African Americans. *Uncle Tom's Cabin* reached millions and there is little question that it energized anti-slavery sentiments throughout the country.

Beecher Stowe hoped that *Uncle Tom's Cabin* would create empathy for the people that slavery sought to dehumanize. And similarly, I hope that my depiction of Ring and his fellow blue whales in *Fragment* may help some readers imagine that nonhuman creatures might be persons too.

If we fail to meet the challenges of the climate crisis it will be a failure of the imagination.

For much of my life I worked as a lawyer for the government, managing the land titles system; enforcing and protecting the rights of private landowners. As I look back, I can see that for most of Western history, ownership granted the right to take from the land, never demanding that owners take responsibility to husband it and care for its creatures.

I hope that we can imagine a time in the near future where our long-unchallenged assertion that we are the unfettered owners of land and masters of resources is justly balanced by the rights of other species to have their own place in the universe. A time when we'll truly embrace our responsibility to care for and nurture the lives of our fellow creatures.

CHAPTER 17

"THE EARTH IS MY HOME TOO, CAN'T I HELP PROTECT IT?": PLANETARY THINKING, QUEER IDENTITIES, AND ENVIRONMENTALISM IN *THE LEGEND OF KORRA, SHE-RA,* AND *STEVEN UNIVERSE*

Aneesh Barai

Introduction

A number of recent fantasy television shows for children are marked by pronounced environmental focus. Shows like *Avatar: The Last Airbender* (created by Michael Dante DiMartino, Bryan Konietzko and Aaron Ehasz 2005–8), *Gravity Falls* (created by Alex Hirsch 2012–16), *Hilda* (created by Luke Pearson 2018), and several others emphasize the magic of nature, while a strategy of other shows is to represent climate crisis and environmental destruction as embodied in the character of enemy "other" that needs to be stopped. Out of many recent shows, three stand out in their choice of queer ecology as a tool to challenge heterosexist and cisgender norms in conjunction with fighting against colonialist and environmentally destructive societies. These shows are *The Legend of Korra* (created by Michael Dante DiMartino and Bryan Konietzko 2012–14), *She-Ra and the Princesses of Power* (developed by Noelle Stevenson 2018–20), and *Steven Universe* (created by Rebecca Sugar 2013–20). This chapter offers a reading of *Korra, She-Ra,* and *Steven Universe* as climate-conscious narratives grounded in anti-capitalist, anti-colonialist and queer ecologies, in which the response to climate crisis is achieved not through destruction but through a loving engagement with an enemy Other. The choice of love as a strategy to solve the problem of environmental devastation depends heavily on how the fictional world is imagined and, in the latter part of this chapter, I take a closer look at the complex world-building in *Steven Universe*. The show's sustained reflections on planetary destruction and fantastical engagement with mineral life forms such as sentient gems, I argue, are crucial to how it imagines embracing nonhuman life with love and care. Where, in his seminal ecocritical work of the 1970s, Roderick Nash raises the question "Do Rocks Have Rights?," *Steven Universe* unequivocally answers "Yes." Like other queer animated shows, *Steven Universe* highlights our moral responsibility to the nonhuman world.

    Steven Universe centers around the boy Steven, who begins the series aged thirteen, living with three Crystal Gems—Garnet, Amethyst, and Pearl—in Beach City, a fictional town on the east coast of the United States. Crystal Gems are sentient mineral lifeforms who create bodies of light around their gems in the figure of female humans. Steven himself is half-gem and half-human: his father is a human called Greg Universe, and his mother was one of the four leaders of the Gem empire, Pink Diamond, who later rebelled, hid her identity, and lived as the leader of the Crystal Gem rebellion under the name Rose. Steven is initially unaware of his own past and the roots of the Crystal Gems, but through encounters with other Gems throughout the series, comes to learn of his background. Having encountered the remaining three Diamonds, he ultimately convinces the Gem leader White Diamond to abandon their military activities and rescind their authority over the planets they had colonized.

Korra focuses on the life of the reincarnated Avatar, following the series *Avatar: The Last Airbender*. Korra learns to fulfil the role of the Avatar, whose purpose is to create balance between the elemental powers of their world and to act as a bridge between the human and spirit worlds. Aang, the previous incarnation of the Avatar, fought against the colonial power of the Fire Nation, as the last living Airbender, i.e., having control over magical air powers. Following on in the next generation, Korra faces challenges in a postcolonial world of warring political ideals and complex power relations of neocolonialism centering on Republic City. She initially finds friends and allies in two brothers—Mako and Bolin—and later in their new friend Asami. Korra enters into a relationship with Mako, but after suffering serious injuries in her fights and retreating from society to recover, she breaks up with him and, at the very end of the series, starts to date Asami. This has been heralded by many (see Sindu 2014) as a "groundbreaking" moment for queer representation on mainstream children's television.

She-Ra follows on from the classic 1980s *She-Ra* series, focusing on the life of Mara's successor as the wielder of She-Ra's superpowers: Adora. Adora grows up under the military training of the violent colonizing power the Horde, along with a catgirl called Catra. She learns of the evil activities of the Horde and leaves them to join the Princess Alliance, a resistance group. The Princesses have magical powers and several of them have connections to power crystals around the planet Eternia, such as Adora's close friends the Princesses Glimmer, Perfuma, and Mermista. The military force of the Horde on Eternia is only a small branch of an intergalactic power, against which Adora and her friends face off. For the first few seasons of the show, Catra works with the Horde and against the Princesses. In the final season though, she joins Adora in the fight, ultimately confessing her love to Adora, and becomes her partner in the final episode. As this chapter proposes, the queer romances of these three series are not just central to their plots but closely interwoven with the attitudes toward protecting the environment. They each model queer ecologies for their young viewers to learn from.

Fantasy and the Other: Imagining and Working toward Better Futures

Fantasy often sets up a racial, cultural, or alien "other" (Thomas 2019) in order for the characters to group together against it, though not always successfully. The concept of the Other originates in continental philosophy. Hegel's account in *The Phenomenology of Spirit* (1807) posits the need for a constitutive Other to define the self. This line of argument was developed by Husserl and Sartre who considered individual identity and relations of self and other. George Herbert Mead (1934) expanded on this approach in proposing the category of the "generalized other," an imagined construct that figures social norms, to enable an individual to situate themselves in relation to society. Over time, the Other has come to represent those who are marginalized in relation to the dominant group and social norms, such as whiteness, maleness, heterosexuality, and cisgender identity. These arguments have been developed in works by critical thinkers such as Simone de Beauvoir on gender (1945), Edward Said on race (1978) and Judith Butler on sexuality (1990). Some recent fantasy works embody climate crisis itself in the form of the Other, which entails engaging with that Other and thus encountering the destabilizing effect of otherness itself. As with gender or race, encountering the Other can be an opportunity to question and interrogate the subject's experience of the status quo.

For a recent example, the *Game of Thrones* television series sets up White Walkers as the dangerous Other, who many have read as a metaphor for climate crisis (see DiPaolo 2018). In an interview about the series, George R. R. Martin notes the parallels between the infighting of the Westerosi leaders, distracting them from the fact that "Winter is coming," and the squabbles of politicians in our world: "We're fighting over issues, important issues, mind you—foreign policy, domestic policy, civil rights, social responsibility, social justice. ... But none of them are important if, like, we're dead and our cities are under the ocean" (Sims 2018). Marc DiPaolo usefully links the television adaptation of Martin's series to Naomi Klein's key environmentalist work *This Changes Everything* (2014) to highlight Martin's message on confronting climate crisis. The animated series discussed in this chapter take a different approach, however, and my argument will focus on why it is problematic to embody climate crisis as the terrifying Other that needs to be destroyed by force—an old narrative template also discussed in Marek Oziewicz's chapter in this volume. These recent fantasy shows often focus on the challenges of imminent climate crisis. Yet, in contrast to the aggressive military approach of *Game of Thrones*, they present a more nuanced and complex ecological response. In these shows, climate justice is explored more intersectionally.

In identifying the ways that these shows encourage us to care for the Other, and particularly in *Steven Universe*'s search for nonviolent resolutions to crises, this chapter works in dialogue with Judith Butler's recent work, *The Force of Nonviolence* (2020). In it, Butler speaks against the hegemony of neoliberal and "anthropocentric individualism" (40). They assert we need to reconceptualize our connections to others, for the sake of both society and the planet itself:

> The idea of global obligations that serve all inhabitants of the world, human and animal, is about as far from the neoliberal consecration of individualism as it could be, and yet it is regularly dismissed as naive. So I am summoning my courage to expose my naiveté, my fantasy—my counter-fantasy, if you will.
>
> (27)

My argument is that the children's fantasy television shows discussed in this chapter engage in precisely such a counter-fantasy, imagining the desire to care for whole worlds and universes. Sharing responsibility through our connections to others operates as a force that counters the individualizing and oppressive structures of capitalism, heterosexism, and colonialism. These shows recognize that these structures of oppression are interconnected. In "The Coloniality of Gender," Maria Lugones (2016) sets out numerous examples of how the gender binary, and even the biological concept of sexual dimorphism, were not "natural" to many cultures but were imposed through colonialism. One can thus interpret colonialism as triply damaging: to racial Others, to the environment—i.e. exploiting natural resources often to the point of permanently damaging the land—and to queer identities. My intention is to demonstrate how *Korra*, *She-Ra*, and *Steven Universe* challenge this cluster of colonial effects.

To understand how these shows engage children in issues of climate crisis, one needs to develop a sense of what possibilities young people have to actively fight against the ongoing ecocide. Civil disobedience campaigns, such as school strikes to protest inaction on climate change ignited by teen climate activist Greta Thunberg, have been powerful means of raising international awareness about climate crisis and challenging world leaders. In one of her speeches, published in *No One Is Too Small to Make a Difference* (2019), Thunberg explains:

> We children are not sacrificing our education and our childhood for you to tell us what you consider is politically possible in the society that you have created … We children are doing this to wake adults up. We children are doing this for you to put your differences aside and start acting as you would in a crisis. We children are doing this because we want our hopes and dreams back.

(67–8)

Other forms of civil disobedience and awareness-raising direct action have been advocated by other youth activists, especially BIPOC (Black, Indigenous and People of Color) youths, such as Isra Hirsi, Jamie Margolin, or Xiuhtezcatl Martinez. One key aspect of youth protest against climate crisis is the effort to shift the narrative away from individual responsibility and onto to the need for radical shift in social, political, and economic systems. Neoliberal economies thrive on individualizing issues, thus allowing corporations to continue in exploitative and destructive practices with impunity (Timperley 2020). Political leadership often feeds this narrative, while rolling back legal protections of natural habitats and reducing regulations on air and water pollution at the request of oil and gas companies (Milman 2017). Thunberg has had the opportunity to directly challenge world leaders, including President Obama, on their failures to appropriately respond to climate crisis. In 2016, a youth collective formed to sue the US government for failing to protect their future (Holthaus 2016). The shows discussed in this chapter emphasize the political agency that young people can have in speaking back to power through both individual and collective action. They communicate that young people are able to change the narrative around states of crisis, disrupt damaging systems that have been normalized, and demand a better future.

Fantasy as a genre may be particularly suited to imagining such potential positive futures and challenging existing norms. Indeed, Rosemary Jackson has famously argued that fantasy is a powerfully subversive genre, and Mark Bould and Sherry Vint open their discussion of fantasy with the proclamation that "all fantasy is political" (2012, 102). In discussing colonial fantasy, Brian Attebery asserts that fantasy can be a "borderland, a meeting place where cultures struggle and change" (2014, 122), and later calls fantasy a "contact zone" (184). Fantasy, of course, often overlaps and merges with adjacent genres, such as science fiction, superhero stories, animal fables, and horror, and this is evident in "science fantasy" shows such as *Steven Universe*, *Gravity Falls*, and *She-Ra*. Many of these shows draw heavily from horror tropes as well, such as early episodes of *Steven Universe*, *Gravity Falls* (see Carter 2016 and Piatti-Farnell 2014), and *Hilda*. At the same time, existing research suggests that children's science fiction television shows often reinforce normativity even in their representations of futurity or supposed Otherness (Neighbors and Rankin 2011). Such is the case, for example, with representations of patriarchy in the *Jetsons* (Cowlishaw 2011, 191) and with ideas of Britishness in "classic" (1963–89) *Doctor Who* (Brown 2011, 174–5). In contrast to this, and also in line, perhaps, with more recent children's science fiction—such as the more progressive messages of storylines for the Thirteenth Doctor (since 2018)—the science fantasy children's shows such as *Korra*, *She-Ra*, and *Steven Universe* strongly and explicitly challenge social norms and institutional power.

Specifically for science fantasy, Attebery contends that "one of the most important functions of science fantasy ... is to show us our own preconceptions and offer ways to bypass them" (2014, 185). Indeed, one of the common threads linking *Korra*, *She-Ra*, and *Steven Universe* is how they challenge preconceptions about the environment, race, gender, and sexuality. Against the dominant paradigm, identified by Dafna Lemish, in which female representation in children's media is either missing or offers unrealistic and sexualized female body shapes (2010, 2–3), shows like *She-Ra* and *Steven Universe* stand out as subversive by presenting their predominantly female casts of various shapes and sizes. Attebery (2002) has analyzed the range of expressions of gender identities in science fiction, particularly the ways that "Androgyny was not only transgressive, but trendy as well" (129) in the 1960s and 1970s. Continuing in this vein, I contend that transgressive queer and non-binary identities have become trendy in recent children's media and culture.

The three shows examined here connect with what have been described as "enviro-toons" (Pike 2012). Deidre Pike draws on ideas from Jaime Weinman's blog (2004) and later interviews to define "enviro-toons" as "animation that, in its form and content, offers balance through often-comedic portrayals of complex environmental discourse" (Pike 2012, 13). Pike's work opens with a useful categorization of media as either "monologic" or "dialogic" in how it engages the viewer with ideas about nature (16). In contrast to the often-explicit interest in environmental issues in the media Pike discusses, I suggest that *Korra*, *She-Ra*, and *Steven Universe* are primarily nonverbal, imagistic, and figurative in the ways that they engage with ecological destruction. Ideas of "saving the planet" are not uncommon in fantasy. In these shows, however, protecting the planet from destruction is central to the plot, such as can be gleaned from the repeated image in *She-Ra* and *Steven Universe* of a giant drill draining life from the land around it. That is, environmental destruction is the assumed context through which the viewer understands evil, rather than an issue that is raised or debated separately. It is perhaps for this reason—despite the existence of some published research, numerous magazine reviews of *Steven Universe*, *Korra*, and *She-Ra* (discussed below), and active fandom discussions of all of these shows—that these shows have not yet been discussed as environmentally conscious works.

Love and Money: Political Messages in Recent Children's Fantasy Animation

In order to understand the unique strategies adopted in *Steven Universe*, *Korra*, and *She-Ra*, it is important to grasp the general representations of environmentalism in children's animated fantasy series. To exemplify this dominant model, this section will discuss three series—*Avatar*, *Hilda*, and *Gravity Falls*—which display attitudes that feed into the shows central to my argument. *Avatar*, which won numerous television awards and high critical acclaim, set new standards for the quality and complexity of children's cartoons in the United States. *Hilda* excelled in presenting the natural and supernatural as intertwined, full of dangers to humans, and equally full of wonder and adventure. *Gravity Falls* followed a similar strategy, but with a specific focus on challenging capitalism through its stories, in ways that relate to what Carolyn Merchant discusses as "social ecology" (2005, 139ff.).

In *Avatar*, we enter a fictional world that has been under oppressive rule for close to a century, caused by an imbalance of powers among the Fire Nation, the Earth Nation, the Air

Temples, and the Water Tribes. Each nation has a special relationship to one element and it is the role of the avatar to maintain balance and control all four elements. However, when this role is put upon an adolescent Aang, too young for the task, he runs from the responsibility and ends up encased in ice for a hundred years. The series begins with Aang being found and thawed. Working with a team of youths, Aang learns mastery over the elements and returns balance to the divisions of power among the four kingdoms. A highly successful and influential series from the early 2000s, *Avatar* set several trends that subsequent fantasy animations followed, including nuanced representations of racial and gender diversity, finding balance in nature, a fight against colonialism and imperialism, and a pacifist hero at its center. Before the final fight, for example, Aang is encouraged to let go of his love for a particular person and embrace a more universal form of love. He chooses to hold on to his feelings, even though they leave him vulnerable. Aang decides to live by his principles of not taking life, and finds a way to end the war without further bloodshed. These themes of elemental powers, love, and nonviolent ways toward peace return in later fantasy animations.

Hilda casts its heroine into a world where the natural and supernatural are inseparable. It plays on elements of horror and horror comedy. In the world of *Hilda*, humans live in walled-off towns, whereas natural spaces beyond those walls are the realms of giant trolls, miniscule elves, and other supernatural creatures. While these creatures are mostly feared by humans, Hilda has a greater sense of empathy and emotional engagement with them. She befriends dangerous creatures, trying to understand their feelings and motivations, even if they cannot speak the same language as her. In this way, even though *Hilda* employs typical tropes from horror movies, the narrative outcomes subvert traditional notions of horror: monsters are not defeated but befriended and cared for. For example, the final episode pits Hilda and her friends against a giant black dog, a symbol of depression elevated to monstrous proportions. The fearful townspeople bring in hunters to chase down and kill the dog. Hilda instead finds out from other creatures that the dog is actually a loving, overgrown puppy called Jellybean, and she brings it to safety outside the city walls.

Similar strategies of reconceptualizing monsters inform many episodes of *Gravity Falls*, a science fantasy that, like *Hilda*, emphasizes the wonder of nature by blurring the boundaries of natural and supernatural. The protagonist twins Mabel and Dipper are visiting their great uncle "Gruncle" Stan, who runs a scam tourist trap called the "Mystery Shack," full of poorly designed mythical creatures and pseudo-mystery artifacts that Stan happily sells to gullible tourists. Ironically, the shack is surrounded by genuine mysteries and natural wonders. Magical creatures like unicorns, gnomes, and fairies inhabit the local forests and scientific wonders from an interdimensional portal are hidden underneath the shack. The main antagonist is the dream demon Bill Cipher, a glowing triangle with one eye at the top, stick arms and legs coming out of its sides. A creature that brings chaos and insanity, Bill appears to be a metaphor for the dangers of money and capitalism. His name connects him to the dollar bill and his appearance matches the reverse of a dollar bill, with the eyed pyramid known as the "great seal." The show's minor antagonists include Gideon, a Trump-like child celebrity hungry for power, and Pacifica, Mabel's rival and the daughter of the richest family in town. In the episode "Northwest Mansion Mystery," Dipper discovers that Pacifica's family have been lying to the townspeople about the historic contract the townspeople signed—a contract that promised everyone equal access to the town's resources, but was used to maintain a rigid class hierarchy in Gravity Falls. In the series finale, Bill infects Stan's mind. Victory comes in the dual form of Stan purging Bill from his mind and relinquishing ownership of the exploitative business of the Mystery Shack. Both actions communicate the defeat of the chaos-creating evils of capitalism, a focus which—like the show's celebration of wild nature—aligns *Gravity Falls* with socialist approaches to ecology. As Merchant has argued, both socialism and ecology seek to challenge existing power relations, to bring about a fairer world. "The global ecological crisis is exacerbated by the globalization of capitalism," she argues (30), stressing that social ecology's commitment "to reversing the domination of nature" is also one "to removing social domination [and] class inequalities [that] have resulted in homelessness, poverty, racial oppression, and sexism" (151). In connecting economic exploitation, class hierarchy, and the destruction of nature, *Gravity Falls* is an important voice communicating resistance to the slow violence of petrocapitalist economy.

In summary, these three shows exemplify a trend in recent animated children's fantasy television for engaging with environmentalism by connecting it to such issues as colonialism (in *Avatar*), love for the seemingly-monstrous Other (in *Hilda*), and resistance to capitalism (in *Gravity Falls*). The three queer shows discussed below draw on similar approaches. Yet, they push further by connecting all three concepts and engaging with them through love and inclusion.

Queer Romances and Re-wilding: Saving the Planet in *Korra* and *She-Ra*

The challenge *Korra* and *She-Ra* pose to heterosexist and cis-sexist culture is interwoven with the call they provide to protect the planet, not through violence, but through love for the Other.[1] *Korra*, *She-Ra*, and *Steven Universe* all feature lesbian romances as major elements of their plots. They include other queer couplings, and both *She-Ra* and *Steven Universe* feature non-binary characters. Indeed, the developer of *She-Ra*, Noelle Stevenson, is non-binary; Rebecca Sugar, the creator of *Steven Universe*, is a non-binary woman. Maya Gittelman (2020) talks about *She-Ra* in terms of "inherent queernormativity" (n.p.), to examine how the world it presents is fundamentally different in its attitude to relationships from the norms of our own. The genderqueer and queering elements of *Steven Universe* have been examined by Eli Dunn (2016). Dunn's detailed and convincing analysis of the show, particularly through the character of Stevonnie, is commonly accepted in the show's fandom, with many trans YouTubers discussing *Steven Universe* as being formative from their childhoods (Dunn 2016).

Korra pushed the boundaries in Nickelodeon's representation of queer lives even further and faced a backlash from the network for doing so. Simultaneously, the show was criticized by fans of *Avatar* for losing many of the elements they had loved about that show, while gaining new fans for its differences. Fundamentally, where *Avatar* had pitted the heroes against the outright evil of imperialism—with Fire Lord Ozai cast as a straightforward villain who needed to be defeated—*Korra* places its female protagonist against morally ambiguous and nuanced political positions, emphasizing the difficulties of knowing what is "right" or "good" in particular contexts. The existing scholarly discussions of *Korra* are mainly concerned with its minority representation and ideas of child agency (Aranjuez 2015; Crawford and Chen 2018), but there have also been a number of recent insightful reviews responding to Netflix's buying the show to stream it in the United States from August 2020.

Thus, Aja Romano (2020) notes that in place of the one evil of the Fire Nation, the new show introduces a more complex set of villains for Korra to contend with, including "morally gray anarchists who can't be easily written off as evil or unsympathetic" (n.p.). Toussaint Egan (2020) likewise contrasts the two shows by their types of villain: "While Aang fought a prolific and necessary battle of good vs. evil against an unrelenting tyrant on behalf of the world, Korra's battle is more nuanced, more about fighting embedded systems of oppression, disenfranchisement, and well-intentioned totalitarianism played out via the proxy of the series' antagonists" (n.p.). In Egan's view, *Korra* ultimately asks "what role, if any, the Avatar should serve in the modern world" (n.p.).

It is in this context that I want to argue about Korra's crucial role for today's audiences. Inviting the viewers to think about the ideas of the enemies she faces, the show challenges the us-them status quo and invites consideration of how any society can accommodate its Other. The relationship between Korra and Asami is typically recognized as canon, not only because of the statement from the creators, but also because of visual parallels between their final scene holding hands and the wedding scene directly preceding it, as well as musical parallels between this final scene and the final moments of *Avatar* shared between Aang and Katara. However, in this world, we do not see any other openly queer couplings represented, and so we can only assume that their relationship is outside of the norm. Korra chooses to live her life by embracing love and resisting the given social norms where they are oppressive. This challenge to the norm is evident earlier in the series, in Korra's radical decision at the end of Season 2 to open the boundaries between the human and spirit worlds, which sees urban centers becoming overgrown with spirit vines, displacing many of their human residents. In the bizarre world of *Korra*, her work to save the world from eternal darkness is quickly forgotten. The media's measurement of her popularity rating as the Avatar drops, as Korra forces people to coexist with the supernatural plants of their world. She is exiled from Republic City, but her actions have permanently changed its landscape, creating a space for coexistence between the formerly separated worlds of humans and spirits—a cohabitation visually presented as the coexistence of industrial urban human civilization and the natural world.

Complex moral ambiguities are also central to *She-Ra*. In the first episode, the heroine Adora has to learn that she was brainwashed since her infancy into accepting an evil regime. Everything she believed was right turns out to be a lie. Later episodes show other characters experiencing and struggling with the same challenges, such as Hordak, who chooses love for Entrapta over loyalty to the cult of Horde Prime. Or Wrong Hordak, who replays Adora's and Hordak's emotional crises in a truncated, comic form, with direct references to revolutionary politics in the final season. Adora initially rejects the imperial aggression of the Horde to fight for the Princess Alliance, and trains in using her She-Ra powers under the guidance of a mysterious hologram she finds in a temple ruin. This hologram, named Light Hope, teaches Adora about the ancient civilization known as the First Ones: she tells Adora that her powers were granted by the First Ones, and must be used in service of their ideals. However, as the series progresses, Adora learns that the Horde and the First Ones were competing colonizers, and neither paid heed to the cost of lives from their war. Of these, the Horde also takes on undertones of white supremacy—especially in the fully white bodies of its "brothers," in their emphasis on purity, and casting out shadows, all of which figuratively align them with the cult of "whiteness." The rebel alliance fighting against them, conversely, is diverse in terms of race, body shape, and sexuality.

The fight to protect the planet expands in scope throughout the series, as the danger first comes from in-world colonizers, and later from interstellar aggressors. In each case, the fight is seen through what Denis Cosgrove would describe as a "whole earth" philosophy, emphasizing the "fragility and vulnerability of a corporeal earth and responsibility for its care" (263). In other words, the world is united in its challenge to aggressive colonizing and ecologically destructive forces and the rebels cooperate across national, political, and cultural borders. These are quickly merged into one connected power, when Mermista and Frosta join forces with the princesses already in the alliance. The leaders operate through a politics of care for their people, which they quickly understand is intertwined with the care for all people on the planet. In the series finale, the narrative climax of the fight against Horde Prime, the focus is not on military power or aggression, but on defense and love. Foreshadowing the climactic moment in which Adora saves the planet, Bow and Glimmer confess their love to each other for the first time. Bow then speaks to the people of the world about the need to fight Horde Prime despite the odds, "because we have each other, and we have love" (Stevenson 2020, 0:05:48–0:05:50). The focus on Adora's final acceptance of her own desire and love for Catra specifically shows that the love being presented here is not self-sacrificial. It is a love grounded in self-acceptance and self-love, one acknowledging that she too deserves to live. As Adora responds to Catra's confession, her She-Ra powers create a shield, rather than a weapon. In learning that she is loved and accepted as she is, Adora gains the power to heal the planet. Her magic frees the magic innate in their planet, Etheria, transforming Horde Prime's clones and giant drill into flora, and instantly re-wilding the planet. The finale presents a visually and emotionally powerful representation of the magic of unrepressed love, and emotional interconnection with others, as the most powerful motivation to protect the planet and the most powerful tool to defend the planet against aggressive and oppressive forces.

Steven Universe: Fusion, Chosen Family and the Politics of Nonviolence

Steven Universe shares many of the same concepts and concerns as *She-Ra*, including the focus on chosen family and love, and the preference of shield over weapon. More than the other shows, *Steven Universe* emphasizes pacificism and nonviolent responses to the climate crisis. As I demonstrate below, it fundamentally breaks down distinctions between human and non-human lives in its narrative and world-building. A common feature of many fantasy shows and games is magic crystals whose powers need to be balanced to save the world. This trope was popularized through the *Final Fantasy* game series and reemerges in *She-Ra*, with each princess gaining power from their connection to a crystal. In *Steven Universe*, the Crystal Gems and other mineral-based forms are not passive sources of power for the planet or its heroes. They are themselves the living, sentient main characters of the show. The gem-based life-forms are, culturally and historically, alien colonizers who mine planets, including their own home world, to the point of destruction. They are led by White Diamond, who like Horde Prime, aligns their colonizing with undertones of white supremacy through her emphatic whiteness and focus on purity. White Diamond not only colonizes lands: she infects people with her whiteness to control their minds and bodies, make them all speak in her voice, say her words only and move solely on her command. Figuratively, White Diamond is the ultimate white colonizer. Gems that do not fit into her world order are described as "off-color"—regardless of their color—again framing the power system in parallel with white settler colonialism.

We begin the show from the limited focalization of Steven, who does not know the history of the Crystal Gems—his family and a rebel group fighting against Home World. Our positioning alongside Steven in the narrative invites us to care for and grow to love the nonhuman: in particular, Amethyst. Amethyst is made from the minerals of Earth and so provides a face, personality, and personification of Earth's minerals for the audience to emotionally engage with. Her character engenders the moral imperative to care that Emmanuel Levinas describes as coming from the face-to-face encounter with the Other. This is made easier by the fact that the show blurs the boundaries between human and mineral, as Steven is half-Gem half-human. Gems have the ability to fuse bodies with other Gems if there is an intimate connection between them, to create a different, typically larger body, with its own name and identity. Fusion can be seen as a microcosm of conversation and intimate connection that can lead to the resolution of wider global and intergalactic problems; it is an embrace of the Other, a merging of identities. The show's climax reveals that Steven is himself a fusion of his gem and human identities. For Steven in particular, fusion breaks down the boundaries of the human and the mineral. This can be seen as a Deleuzian becoming-mineral or becoming-planet, which emotionally connects viewers to non-human, mineral, and hybrid lives, and encourages us to see the planet itself as vibrant with nonhuman life that we are connected to and should care for. In these ways, *Steven Universe* literalizes what Merchant calls "socialist ecofeminism": "Nature is an active subject, not a passive object to be dominated, and humans must develop sustainable relations with it" (2005, 208). Fusion is also remarkably similar to the theorization of self that Butler puts forward in their most recent work, *The Force of Nonviolence*:

> The thriving that is bound up with human life is connected to the thriving of non-human creatures …. If any of us are to survive, to flourish, even to attempt to lead a good life, it will be a life lived with others—a live that is no life without those others. I will not lose this "I" who I am under such conditions; rather, if I am lucky, and the world is right, whoever I am will be steadily sustained and transformed by my connections with others, the forms of contact by which I am altered and sustained.

(97)

Fusion is precisely this alteration of self through contact with others. It is an acknowledgement of the mutual interdependence of the human and the non-human. Where fusion encodes this notion, Steven's sense of "family" sets these concepts deeper into the backdrop of the show. Steven makes his family primarily not from blood relations but from three non-binary Gems who raised him. Crucially we see Steven repeatedly welcoming outsiders, Others and those not like himself, in ways that encourage the audience to see all living beings as one family. In this way, the show grows from queer culture's notion of "chosen family"—or Donna Haraway's injunction to "make kin" (2015, 161)—and expands it, as Haraway encourages, to include the nonhuman: the animal (an undead pink lion), the vegetable (specifically, watermelons and a pumpkin that Steven imbues with sentience), and the mineral. All these build up a sense of family extending beyond blood and beyond the human.

Much of the show operates in the mode of science fiction, with aliens and advanced technology. Yet, Steven's unique powers bring the show into the realm of fantasy. Steven has greater capacity for empathy than the gems around him, an ability that seemingly comes from his human side and which is transformed by his gem powers. For instance, he is able to send his consciousness into other people's bodies or dreams. He is able to leave his own body behind and hear people's inner thoughts. Throughout the show and film, Steven endeavors to talk with his "enemies" and to befriend rather than defeat them. His gem power creates a shield rather than a weapon, and even when he loses his powers completely in *Steven Universe: The Movie* (2019), he seeks to create change through conversation, understanding, and empathy. Steven's emphatic nonviolence, breaking weapons and choosing dialogue instead, resonates with Butler's reimagining of social relations in a nonviolent system:

> Nonviolence is less a failure of action than a physical assertion of the claims of life, a living assertion, a claim that is made by speech, gesture, and action, through networks, encampments, and assemblies. ... It opens up a new consideration of social freedom as defined in part by our constitutive interdependency.
>
> (2020, 19)

It is this sense of "constitutive" or "global interdependency" (18), as Butler also calls it, that Steven's nonviolence speaks to. His story embodies life not as an individual or individualist, but as always already connected with others.

Most of all, Steven wants people to let others be who they are, rather than seek to oppress and control others. The Diamonds' colonial control over the universe is also enacted in microcosm on the character Steven Universe, in ways that parallel the experiences of many trans people: until the resolution of the story, his Diamond family regularly deadname him and use the wrong pronouns for him, refusing to acknowledge or accept his identity. As the Diamonds learn to accept Steven for who he is, they also become able to acknowledge who they truly are. This is shown to be emotionally and psychologically better for the oppressor as well as the oppressed, as the Diamond elites emotionally struggle and break down under the aggressive colonizing they enact. The Diamonds learn to accept that they were not only wrong about their colonial activities. Concurrently, they were wrong about Steven's identity. The queer romances and genderqueer narratives of the story—which are present from the very beginning, in the existence of Garnet, a fusion that manifests the love of Ruby and Sapphire—are inextricable from the care for the planet that Steven's chosen family all show. In the climax of the first season, Garnet sings "I won't let you hurt my planet, and I won't let you hurt my friends" (Sugar 2015, 0:07:00–0:07:04). Again, intimate connection and engagement with the Other, learning to love those beyond our blood connections and choosing to be family with them, all make us more likely to care for the planet. From such a perspective, we are less likely to see those suffering from climate crisis as strangers, but as part of our earth's family, to whom we all share a responsibility. Ultimately, communication with and love for others are the driving force for changing the powerful oppressive minority, who limit biodiversity, racial and gender diversity in their quests for purity and perfect obedience to their law.

Conclusion

The shows discussed in this chapter represent young people striving for a better future for the planet. The protagonists try to reinstate balance between humans and nature, and to prevent colonial forces from extracting natural resources to the point of planetary destruction. While *Korra*, *She-Ra*, and *Steven Universe* imagine supernatural responses to these issues, they also suggest deep parallels between the responses to climate crisis in these shows and in our world today. Young people globally are rising up to push against climate crisis, through protest, civil disobedience, and legal action. The shows examined in this chapter are part of this larger struggle, articulating a philosophy of care for the planet that is tied up in a wider narrative of care for the Other. They advocate love for those who are different from us—including racial and species diversity—and cherish the power to be found in love of all kinds. *Steven Universe* encourages the audience to love even the nonhuman, to intimately connect with mineral, animal, and vegetable life, and to collectively engage oppressive powers in nonviolent, empathetic ways that can create freer and fairer societies for all.

Note

1   I choose not to use the words "homophobia" or "transphobia," because the suffix "phobia" implies fear, which centers the feelings of the oppressor. Alternative ways to describe these issues could include "transmisia" or "queermisia," with the suffix "misia" expressing the hatred and violence of the oppressor, as it does as the prefix in "misogyny."

References:

Aranjuez, Adolfo. 2015. "*The Legend of Korra* and Minority Representation." *Screen Education*, vol. 78: 24–7.

Attebery, Brian. 2002. *Decoding Gender in Science Fiction*. London: Routledge.

Attebery, Brian. 2014. *Stories about Stories*. Oxford: Oxford University Press.

Bould, Mark, and Sherryl Vint. 2012. "Political Readings." In *The Cambridge Companion to Fantasy Literature*, edited by Edward James and Farah Mendlesohn, 102–12. New York: Cambridge University Press.

Brown, J. P. C. 2011. "*Doctor Who*: A Very British Alien." In *The Galaxy Is Rated G: Essays on Children's Science Fiction Film and Television*, edited by R. C. Neighbors and Sandy Rankin, 161–83. London: McFarland.

Butler, Judith. 1990. *Gender Trouble: Feminism and the Subversion of Identity*. London: Routledge.

Butler, Judith. 2020. *The Force of Nonviolence: An Ethico-Political Bind*. London: Verso.

Carter, Tayler. 2016. "Monsters and Mad Scientists: *Frankenstein* and *Gravity Falls*." *Pentangle*, vol. 14: 55–60.

Chatterjee, Pratap. 2016. "Eli Lilly Raised U.S. Prices of Diabetes Drug 700 Percent over 20 Years." *Corpwatch*, November 2, 2016. https://corpwatch.org/article/eli-lilly-raised-us-prices-diabetes-drug-700-percent-over-20-years.

Cosgrove, Denis. 2003. *Apollo's Eye: A Cartographic Genealogy of the Earth in the Western Imagination*. Baltimore, MA: Johns Hopkins University Press.

Cowlishaw, Brian. 2011. "No Future Shock Here: *The Jetsons*, Happy Tech, and the Patriarchy." In *The Galaxy Is Rated G: Essays on Children's Science Fiction Film and Television*, edited by R. C. Neighbors and Sandy Rankin, 183–94. London: McFarland.

Crawford, Bonnee and Shih-Wen Sue Chen. 2018. "'Be Careful!!': Child Safety and Empowerment in *The Legend of Korra*." In *Children, Youth and American Television*, edited by Adrian Schober and Debbie Olsen, 241–59. London: Routledge.

de Beauvoir, Simone. 1949. *Le Deuxième sexe [The Second Sex]*. Paris: Gallimard.

DiMartino, Michael Dante, Bryan Konietzko and Aaron Ehasz, dir. 2005–8. *Avatar: The Last Airbender*. Nickelodeon.

DiMartino, Michael Dante and Bryan Konietzko, dir. 2012–14. *The Legend of Korra*. Nickelodeon.

DiPaolo, Marc. 2018. *Fire and Snow: Climate Fiction from the Inklings to* Game of Thrones. Albany: State University of New York Press.

Dunn, Eli. 2016. "*Steven Universe*, Fusion Magic, and the Queer Cartoon Carnivalesque." *Gender Forum: An Internet Journal of Gender Studies*, vol. 56: 44–58.

Egan, Toussaint. 2020. "Korra Is a More Important Avatar than Aang." *Polygon*, August 13, 2020. https://www.polygon.com/animation-cartoons/2020/8/13/21366631/legend-of-korra-on-netflix-avatar-the-last-airbender-aang-comparison

Gittelman, Maya. 2020. "We're Gonna Win in the End: The Subversive Queer Triumph of *She-Ra*." *Tor*, July 8, 2020. https://www.tor.com/2020/07/08/were-gonna-win-in-the-end-the-subversive-queer-triumph-of-she-ra/

Haraway, Donna. 2015. "Anthropocene, Capitalocene, Plantationocene, Chthulucene: Making Kin." *Environmental Humanities*, vol. 6: 159–65.

Hirsch, Alex, dir. 2012–16. *Gravity Falls*. Disney.

Holthaus, Eric. 2016. "The Kids Suing the Government over Climate Change Are Our Best Hope Now." *Slate*, November 14, 2016. http://www.slate.com/articles/health_and_science/science/2016/11/the_kids_lawsuit_over_climate_change_is_our_best_hope_now.html

Jackson, Rosemary. 1981. *Fantasy: The Literature of Subversion*. London: Routledge.

Lemish, Dafna. 2010. *Screening Gender on Children's Television: The Views of Producers around the World*. London: Routledge.

Lugones, Maria. 2016. "The Coloniality of Gender." In *The Palgrave Handbook of Gender and Development: Critical Engagements in Feminist Theory and Practice*, edited by Wendy Harcourt, 13–33. Basingstoke: Palgrave.

Mead, George Herbert. 1934. *Mind, Self, and Society: From the Standpoint of a Social Behaviorist*. Chicago: University of Chicago Press.

Merchant, Carolyn. 2005. *Radical Ecology: The Search for a Livable World*. London: Routledge.

Milman, Oliver. 2017. "'No Shame': How the Trump Administration Granted Big Oil's Wishlist." *The Guardian*, December 12, 2017. https://www.theguardian.com/us-news/2017/dec/12/big-oil-lobby-get-what-it-wants-epa-trump-pruitt

Moore, Mandy Elizabeth. 2019. "Future Visions: Queer Utopia in *Steven Universe*." *Research on Diversity in Youth Literature*, vol. 2, no. 1. http://sophia.stkate.edu/rdyl/vol2/iss1/5

Nash, Roderick. 1977. *Small Comforts for Hard Times*. New York: Columbia University Press.

Neighbors, R. C., and Sandy Rankin eds.. 2011. *The Galaxy Is Rated G: Essays on Children's Science Fiction Film and Television*. Jefferson, NC: McFarland.

Pearson, Luke, dir. 2018. *Hilda*. Netflix.

Piatti-Farnell, Lorna. 2014. "What's Hidden in *Gravity Falls*: Strange Creatures and the Gothic Intertext." *M/C Journal*, vol. 17, no. 4. https://doi.org/10.5204/mcj.859

Pike, Deidre. 2012. *Enviro-Toons: Green Themes in Animated Cinema and Television*. Jefferson, NC: McFarland.

Romano, Aja. 2020. "*Legend of Korra*'s Messy, Complicated Legacy." *Vox*, August 13, 2020. https://www.vox.com/culture/2020/8/13/21362113/legend-of-korra-netflix-controversy-korra-vs-aang-korrasami

Said, Edward. 1978. *Orientalism*. New York: Pantheon.

Sims, Jamie. 2018. "George R. R. Martin Answers Times Staffers' Burning Questions." *The New York Times Style Magazine*, October 16, 2018. https://www.nytimes.com/2018/10/16/t-magazine/george-rr-martin-qanda-game-of-thrones.html

Sindu, S. J. 2014. "Korrasami, Queer Representation and Saying Goodbye to the *Legend of Korra*." *Autostraddle*, December 21, 2014. https://www.autostraddle.com/korrasami-queer-representation-and-saying-goodbye-to-the-legend-of-korra-270141/

Stevenson, Noelle, dev. 2018–20. *She-Ra and the Princesses of Power*. DreamWorks.

Stevenson, Noelle, dev. 2020. "Heart (part 2)." Season 5, episode 13. *She-Ra and the Princesses of Power*. Dreamworks.

Sugar, Rebecca, created 2013–20. *Steven Universe*. Cartoon Network.

Sugar, Rebecca, created 2016. "Jail Break (part 2)." Season 1, episode 53. *Steven Universe*. Cartoon Network.

Thomas, Ebony Elizabeth. 2019. *The Dark Fantastic: Race and the Imagination from* Harry Potter *to the* Hunger Games. New York: New York University Press.

Thunberg, Greta. 2019. *No One Is Too Small to Make a Difference*. London: Penguin.

Timperley, Jocelyn. 2020. "Who Is Really to Blame for Climate Change?" *BBC Future*, June 19, 2020. https://www.bbc.com/future/article/20200618-climate-change-who-is-to-blame-and-why-does-it-matter

Weinman, Jaime. 2004. "Things That Suck: *The Smoggies.*" *Something Old, Something New*, Sep 1, 2004. http://zvbxrpl.blogspot.com/2004/09/things-that-suck-smoggies.html

CHAPTER 18
CELEBRATIONS OF RESILIENCE
Elin Kelsey

In the winter before Covid-19 I spent a month in the dark quietude of Finnish woods. I thought I was going there to write a non-fiction book. But it turns out, I wasn't. For the first time in my life, fully formed poems kept tumbling out of my head almost too fast for me to capture them on paper. Small celebrations of resilience exist within each of us, and within the greater-than-human world.

In praise of ambiguity
The wolves of Chernobyl
are radioactive,
and yet
they breed more successfully
than any other wolves in Europe

Those wolves,
like the bald head
of my dear friend Elizabeth,
are imbued
with the capacity to be
broken,
beautiful,
or both.

The upside of stress
Trees
count on the wind
to move them.

As they bend and sway,
they grow "stress wood"
strong enough
to shoulder the snow
or contort themselves toward the best light.

Trees
need stress
to hold themselves
up.

Hope blindness
I am blinded
by hope

How could I not be,
when crocuses
bloom in the winter snow
And Siberian willow warblers,
lighter than pencils,
fly 20,000 kilometers
alone
in their first year of life.

Uprooted
The palms of Ecuador
stretch out their roots
like walking sticks
Grasping, sensing, feeling their way forward.

They travel
three centimeters a day
pulling up old roots
patiently bending
toward richer soil
where they can settle.
on more solid ground.

PART III
VISIONS IN THE WATER

CHAPTER 19
ANTHROPOS AND THE OCEAN
Brian Attebery

When the world was green and new, Anthropos was out walking and came to the shore. Anthropos, whose everyday name was Child of Man, was afraid of Ocean. Ocean was so big that the other side wasn't in sight. It wouldn't stop moving and when Child walked to the edge of the water to challenge it, it sneaked past Child's feet. Out in the depths, Child could see shadows, lurking things. Child was afraid, which made Child angry.

So Child walked back to a tarry swamp near the shore. Child took a hollow stick and caught a glob of tar on the end, and then blew into the stick. The lump of tar swelled out and became a ball, then a bladder, and finally a bottle. Child made a dozen bottles, a hundred, more than Child could carry. Some of the bottles burst, and then there were sheets of tar; strings of tar, ready to be shaped into ropes and carrying bags. It took many trips but Child brought all the stretchy, squashy things Child had made to the water's edge and tossed them in, making a raft that bobbed up and down with the waves. Now Ocean didn't look so vast, so open, so much itself. Child of Man had tamed the waters. Ocean had entered the Anthropocene.

CHAPTER 20

KIM STANLEY ROBINSON'S CASE FOR HOPE IN *NEW YORK 2140*

John Rieder

Critical commentary on the fiction of Kim Stanley Robinson has been unusually preoccupied with questions about genre. This emphasis responds to the unusually rich weaving together of genres and discourses that characterizes Robinson's novels. Building a consensus that Robinson is one of the major science fiction writers of his generation, many of Robinson's most perceptive critics have found it fruitful to think about the ways his science fiction transforms the generic resources of the novel, science, and history to construct his own peculiar combinations of realism, utopia, and dystopia. Thus, Fredric Jameson's reading of Robinson's *Mars* trilogy (1992–96) argues that its commitments to realism and history galvanize a type of "speculative problem-solving" that reveals the sociopolitical, utopian potential of its "hard SF content" (2005, 394, 396). Mark Bould and Sherryl Vint (2009) emphasize the interaction of landscape, Marxist philosophy, and natural science in the generic mix of *Antarctica* (1997). Philip Wegner analyzes Robinson's "careful and extended engagement with the expectations and the possibilities of the generic form" (Wegner 2009, 99) of alternative history in *The Years of Rice and Salt* (2002). Roger Luckhurst finds that Robinson's generic strategy in his Science in the Capital trilogy (2004–7) demands a new name, "proleptic realism" (Luckhurst 2009, 171); Derrick King opts for the term "realist critical dystopia" (2015, 195) to describe the same trilogy. Gib Prettyman praises the "alternative realism" (2018, 22) of Robinson's *Aurora* (2015). Most recently, David Sergeant (2019) has analyzed Robinson's innovative approach to the historical novel in the story this chapter will turn to, *New York 2140* (2017). The argument presented here will build upon these interrogations of Robinson's generic complexity and above all his realism, but, in accordance with the theme of this volume, its point of departure is a question about myth and fantasy.

In his 2014 study *Stories about Stories*, Brian Attebery argues that the literary genre of fantasy's "main claim to cultural importance resides … in the work of redefining the relationship between contemporary readers and mythic texts" (4). Working from that premise, the editors of this volume hope to challenge the way "the stories we have been telling ourselves" about ourselves have helped create the planetary environmental crisis variously called global warming, climate change, or the sixth great extinction event by highlighting the work of narratives that "focus on anticipatory imagination of sustainable futures" and challenge "the ecocidal mythologies of techno-modernity" (Oziewicz, Introduction, 5, 6). Robinson's *New York 2140*, like the majority of his earlier work, envisions future possibilities that cut against the grain of the contemporary status quo at the ideological, economic, and political levels, and these efforts are organized around a central concern with environmental themes. But how do fantasy and myth enter into the workings of this strongly realistic sf novel? Does it aim to redefine the relationship between contemporary readers and mythic texts, and if so how?

It is important at the outset to distinguish between two very different meanings of fantasy. As a literary genre, fantasy is usually defined as a type of story where things happen that could not possibly happen in our empirical world. *New York 2140* is not this kind of story. But there is a much larger sense of fantasy that refers to stories we tell ourselves about ourselves and the world, stories that might imagine the fulfillment of our desires or the realization of our fears, a kind of storytelling that pervades everyday life and profoundly shapes social interaction at every level. When Oziewicz refers to "the ecocidal mythologies of techno-modernity" it is this type of fantasy that is at stake, and this type of fantasy is likewise at the heart of Robinson's concerns in *New York 2140*. The fantasies of techno-modernity—and especially, in Robinson's novel, of capitalist modernity—help give shape to widespread assumptions about what is possible, what is to be desired, and what is to be feared. They frame the way things are, could be, and should be. Robinson's novel challenges what Mark Fisher calls "capitalist realism: the widespread sense that not only is capitalism the only viable political and economic system, but also that it is now impossible even to *imagine* a coherent alternative to it" (Fisher 2009, 2). It does so by using a kind of realist storytelling to explore fantasies of environmental catastrophe and political revolution. Specifically, *New York 2140* engages in rewriting one of Western culture's founding myths, the myth of the Flood.

New York 2140 is an example of what has come to be called climate fiction or cli-fi, a category that qualifies as a genre only in the weak sense of a group of stories addressing themselves to a common existential situation, the contemporary environmental crisis, but in widely different narrative modes and in disparate venues lacking any common set of resources or circuits of distribution. Nonetheless the myth of the Flood clearly casts its influence over a good deal of cli-fi, sometimes quite explicitly as in Margaret Atwood's *The Year of the Flood* (2009, the second installment of her Maddaddam trilogy), and sometimes implicitly as in Paolo Bacigalupi's *Wind-Up Girl* (2009), in which the Thai seed bank could be read as an updated version of Noah's Ark. The Flood myth often imposes on cli-fi its plot of purgation and renewal, with the biblical renewal of the covenant between god and man transformed into a renewal of the social contract in various heroic cli-fi scenarios, including that of *New York 2140*. To observe that the cli-fi Flood is anthropogenic rather than the work of an angry god may not alter the basic contours of the story as much as it might seem, since in both cases global catastrophe is visited upon humanity as a kind of retributive justice in consequence of its transgressions of a pre-ordained order, whether divinely or naturally constituted. What might better distinguish the anthropogenic rise of ocean levels from the ancient Flood is that the modern catastrophe has its roots not in sin but in apparently rational planning and calculation; that is, in the Enlightenment and its technical achievements, its triumphs over the limitations of distance, the vagaries of the seasons, or the diurnal rhythms of night and day. It is precisely from this perspective that the industrial and scientific revolutions turn out to have been driven by fantasies of power that were always illusory, so that we now discover to our chagrin that "we have never been modern," as Bruno Latour argues (Latour 1993). According to Latour, the taming of nature by culture was never anything but a fantasy of purity that the real messiness and interconnectedness of worldly processes always contradicted. Cli-fi in general starts from a verdict of guilty on this set of charges, sometimes proceeding into pessimistic plots of sterility and extinction—as in Atwood's trilogy or the film *Blade Runner 2049* (2017)—but in many cases striving to find some reason for hopefulness about the future.

The plot of purgation and renewal structures recent cli-fi sf novels across a spectrum of approaches to delimiting the possible and narrating the desirable. Robinson's predominantly realist storytelling both partakes of and distinguishes itself from the modes of fantasy, satire, and utopia used in other sf narratives of climatic catastrophe and cultural or political renewal in the last few years. In Rebecca Roanhorse's fantasy novel *Trail of Lightning* (2018), for instance, the Flood opens the way for a resurgence of the Indigenous culture's ways of knowing and living. A magically constructed wall isolates Navajo tribal lands from a surrounding world inundated by the rising ocean, and within this enclosure the Sixth World of Navajo mythology has succeeded the earlier Fifth World of colonial subjugation. The young female protagonist has superhero-like clan powers, and her primary antagonist is a re-embodied Coyote figure. Nnedi Okorafor's *Lagoon* (2014) instead works out the plot of purgation and renewal in the mode of satire. Okorafor's premise is an extraterrestrial invasion that proceeds from Lagos Lagoon into the city of Lagos, where its effects expose the corruption and hypocrisy of many of the city's inhabitants, both rich and poor, powerful and precarious. Hints of a new order emerge in the process, one that not only involves a righting of political wrongs but on a broader level promises to empower nonhuman animals and cleanse the lagoon's waters of human-generated pollution. Donna Haraway takes a utopian approach to the empowerment of the nonhuman and the cleansing of the environment in "The Camille Stories," the final chapter of her 2016 book *Staying with the Trouble: Making Kin in the Chthulucene.* Her version of catastrophe and renewal draws more heavily than Roanhorse's or Okorafor's on the figure of the Ark, since a primary concern of the utopian enclaves she imagines is combating species extinction. Their project involves a wholesale cultural and technical reconfiguration of human reproductive practices—the pairing of animals on Noah's Ark of course makes reproduction always a central concern of the story—but the contours of this program are based on contemporary scientific possibility rather than on the impossibilities of Roanhorse's magic wall or Okorafor's alien invasion.

Robinson's complex web of voices, perspectives, and discourses in *New York 2140* does put satire, utopianism, and a fantasy of social transformation to work on the mythic pattern of Flood, Ark, and New Covenant, as we will see, but all of this happens under the control of its realist rhetorical stance. So while recognizing the affinity of Robinson's novel to these other works of cli-fi and the generic modes they exercise, I want to focus on the realism that holds together this piece of extrapolative science fiction set more than a century in the future in a New York city that has been radically altered by global warming. Robinson's realism operates first of all at the level of physical detail and imaginative world-building buttressed by his impressive handling of historical and scientific resources. On this stage the novel's plot then raises issues of knowledge and power that ultimately put at stake the status of competing fantasies regarding the possible and the desirable.

The basic scenario of *New York 2140* is that two massive melt-offs of polar ice caps in the twenty-first century have raised ocean levels by over fifty feet, immersing lower Manhattan all the way up to Central Park at high tide. The second of these "Pulses" is more than fifty years in the past by the opening of Robinson's novel, and New York has adapted to the new conditions by transforming the drowned portions of Manhattan into a semi-bohemian, increasingly fashionable "New Venice." The New Yorkers who stayed to navigate the post-Pulse environment have succeeded so well, in fact, that the area is attracting rampant real estate speculation by the wealthy class that earlier abandoned lower Manhattan for higher and drier ground. The struggle over ownership of a single building in the New Venice thus becomes the focal point where Robinson brings together the grand historical narratives of class struggle and global warming. The significance of Robinson's achievement unfolds from the tensions between the local and the global, the individual and the collective, and the continuous and the catastrophic that are generated at this point of coalescence between social and natural histories.

The conjuncture of social and natural histories raises both a cognitive problem for historians and a formal problem for novelists. Let me introduce a pair of essays examining the shadow cast by the Anthropocene upon the crafts of the historian and the novelist, so as to provide a framework for looking more closely at Robinson's solution in *New York 2140*.

In "The Climate of History: Four Theses," Dipesh Chakrabarty's first, and primary, thesis is that anthropogenic explanations of climate change force the collapse of the distinction between natural history and human history (2009, 201). Humans become geological rather than merely biological agents, but they can be attributed that status "only historically and collectively" (206). This means that the history of capitalism, which Robinson's novel is deeply interested in, has become entangled not only with the history of the human species but with "the general history of life"—which is to say, with humanity's dependence on the nonhuman for its survival (219). The problem facing the historian, then, is that "the task of placing, historically, the crisis of climate change thus requires us to bring together intellectual formations that are somewhat in tension with one another: the planetary and the global; deep and recorded histories; species thinking and critiques of capital" (213). Chakrabarty concludes that climate change faces us not only with what Timothy Morton would call a set of hyperobjects—"things that are [so] massively distributed in time and space relative to humans" that they are ungraspable by any form of immediate experience (Morton 2013, 1). It also transforms "us," humanity, into a kind of hypersubject: "Climate change poses for us a question of human collectivity, an us, pointing to a figure of the universal that escapes our capacity to experience the world. ... It calls for a global approach to politics without the myth of a global identity" (Chakrabarty 2009, 222).

Amitav Ghosh's *The Great Derangement* (2016) reformulates the challenge climate change poses to the narrative of history in terms of the formal limitations of the mainstream realist novel. Ghosh argues that "serious" fiction has incapacitated itself for dealing with climate change because of its conventions of probability. This incapacity rests on a formal preoccupation with the individual, the everyday, and the moral that crowds out the collective, the extraordinary, and the political. "The novel," he argues, "was midwifed into existence ... through the banishing of the improbable and the insertion of the everyday" (17). The necessary material of extraordinary events, the proven lifeblood of story traditions throughout the world, has to be formally softened or obscured by what Franco Moretti calls "filler," which Moretti explains as "very much like the good manners so important in Austen: ... mechanisms designed to keep the 'narrativity' of life under control—to give a regularity, a 'style,' to existence" (qtd. in Ghosh 2016, 17). Unlike geology, which has had to come to terms with abrupt cataclysmic change, the modern novel, Ghosh says, "has never been forced to confront the centrality of the improbable: the concealment of its scaffolding of events continues to be essential to its functioning." Hence "the irony of the 'realist' novel: the very gestures with which it conjures up reality are actually a concealment of the real" (23). Ghosh provocatively compares the habit of mind that informs the realist novel with the colonialist preference for building large cities like Mumbai and New

York on shorelines dangerously exposed to catastrophic flooding. "This is a way of thinking that deliberately excludes things and forces ('externalities') that lie beyond the horizon of the matter at hand: it is a perspective that renders the interconnections of Gaia unthinkable" (56). Ghosh contends, then, that "nothing could better expose the completeness of the literary mainstream's capitulation to the project of partitioning" than its dismissal of science fiction, the genre that has most often taken up the challenge of dealing with climate change (72). Yet, Ghosh continues, most cli-fi sf consists of disaster stories set in the future, and this is precisely what climate change is not: "By no means are the events of the era of global warming akin to the stuff of wonder tales" (73). An intellectually serious realism, his argument implies, has to be able to deal with climate change in both its catastrophic and quotidian aspects.

How well Robinson's novel handles the formal and thematic problems set forth by Chakrabarty and Ghosh depends upon its success in yoking together an sf plot of future disaster with a measure of realism that brings home the contemporaneity and urgency of the climate crisis—that is, how well it negotiates the tension between the everyday and the extraordinary, continuity, and catastrophe. These tensions can be usefully grasped first of all by looking at Robinson's handling of the novel's setting.

The setting of *New York 2140* builds upon a pair of dichotomies, between the familiar and the new and between the local and the global. Robinson's twenty-second-century New York is rich in details that make it recognizable and strangely familiar despite the premise of the fifty-foot ocean rise having submerged most of Manhattan south of Central Park. Most obvious are the place names and landmarks that punctuate the narrative—the Met Life Building and its environs, Madison Square and the Flatiron building, the streets, avenues, and neighborhoods of midtown Manhattan, the Hudson and the East River, Brooklyn Heights, and Harlem. Robinson's attention to the topography of the island of Manhattan and the surrounding boroughs is meticulous, as is his depiction of the tides, the everyday importance of which to the lives of the characters vividly brings home the way this New York has been changed by global warming. Repurposing the present infrastructure to suit the changed circumstance of the post-Flood city is rendered most fully in the worries that beset the head of maintenance of the Met Life Building, which has been transformed into a condominium. At one point, Vlade, the Met Life head of maintenance, gives his ex-wife a grand tour of the facility, which functions as a kind of thumbnail sketch of the way living arrangements in the New Venice have adapted to the new situation:

> He gave her the grand tour, starting from below the waterline, including the rooms that had been broached. Boathouse, dining hall and commons, some representative apartments occupied by people he knew well, everything from the solo closets to the big group places, occupying half a floor and accommodating a hundred people dorm-style; then up to the farm, then above that to the cupola and the blimp mast. Then back down to the animal floor, pigs chickens goats, very smelly, and right under that the farm again, to get the views of the city through the loggia's open arches.
>
> (Robinson 2017, 404)

Scenes of dining at the Met Life flesh out the rich sense of community fostered by the residents' cooperative lifestyle despite the vicissitudes of arriving at the dining hall in time to get a full serving, the careful rationing of meat, and judgments on the poor quality of the wine produced by the residents of the nearby Flatiron building.

The localized food production and repurposed environs of midtown Manhattan open out onto imaginative world-building on a broader scale. Much of this material is introduced by way of the travels of the blimp that docks on the mast atop the Met Life building, which is the property of Amelia Black, a kind of reality broadcast star. The blimp is called the *Assisted Migration* because of its mission of transporting endangered species from ruined habitats into environmental niches where they might survive and perhaps regenerate themselves—a kind of Ark helping the animal world survive the Flood. Following Amelia's travels allows Robinson to describe a North American continent transformed by the institution of habitat corridors, broad swathes of land reserved solely for nonhuman use. Also traveling in large assemblies of balloons are whole communities, called skyvillages, devoted largely to agriculture. On the water is another mobile community, the city of New Amsterdam, a floating township "directed by Holland's government to wander the Earth helping intertidal peoples in whatever way possible" (223). The retro technology of the blimp and the reversion to local agriculture in urban New York are complemented by more conventionally futuristic developments, such as the AI pilot of the *Assisted Migration*, the photovoltaic paint that coats the Met Life building, and the superskyscrapers that climb three thousand feet into the sky north of Central Park.

This mixture of familiar landmarks and place names, repurposed objects, new living arrangements, and technologies sets up an interesting dialogue between the present and the imagined future. It is this dialogue that leads David Sergeant to classify the genre of *New York 2140* as the "logical successor" of the historical novel (2019, 2). Although Sergeant seems to think that this affinity to the historical novel distinguishes *New York 2140* from other science fiction, the way that near-future extrapolative fiction of this type traces "a strange continuation of the developmental parabola of the historical novel" (6–7) as theorized by Georg Lukács was actually suggested decades ago by Fredric Jameson in "Progress versus Utopia; or, Can We Imagine the Future?" (1982). Robinson himself has consistently confirmed the close connection of his novels to historical fiction, commenting in a 2014 interview with Gerry Canavan that science fiction as a form has "a commitment to history. It's a strange version of that commitment, focusing as it does on histories we can't know; a kind of realism of the absent, made of thought experiments that use the counterfactual or the unknowable" (Canavan and Robinson 2014, 252). Sergeant describes in detail how thoroughly the perspectives of the present inhabit and inform Robinson's imagined future, particularly in the repeated references to the financial crash of 2008, thereby confirming quite forcefully Jameson's thesis that this type of sf's point is the critical exercise of seeing the present as the past of a possible future. The question Robinson's comment raises has to do with the novel's way of knowing the present through this exercise of projection. What is the cognitive status of its "realism of the absent"?

The relation of present to future in *New York 2140* resembles—but in reverse, of course—the kind of double voicing one sometimes finds in autobiographical narratives, where the story one tells about one's past combines the decisions of a past self with the perspective upon those decisions afforded the narrator by experience of their consequences. In the case of *New York 2140* the double voicing surfaces mostly in relation to issues of finance. As the plot of the novel comes to its climax with a financial crisis, it is abundantly clear that Robinson is always also talking about the crash of 2008, and that his double voicing of this future crisis has to do with what should have happened in 2008. But issues of finance and the future arise much earlier on in *New York 2140*. In the third section of part one—the novel has eight parts, each consisting of eight sections, each section told from the point of view of one of eight characters or pairs of characters—we are introduced to Franklin Garr, a Wall Street futures trader who lives in the Met Life building. Franklin's point of view is privileged within the novel as its only first person narrator. He is arguably the novel's hero, since his growth from an apparently callous and self-involved yuppie to a crucial co-conspirator in the novel's fantasy of political revolution is not paralleled by any other character's development.

On our very first encounter with Franklin, he is in the Met Life boat house "looking at the little waves lapping in the big doors and wondering if the Black-Scholes formula could frame their volatility" (16). Franklin is a hedge fund manager, so understanding market volatility is his livelihood, but also his passion. When he gets to his office, we hear this about his computer screen:

> My screen was a veritable anthology of narratives, and in many different genres. I had to shift between haiku and epics, personal essays and mathematical equations, Bildungsroman and Götterdammerung, statistics and gossip, all telling me in their different ways the tragedies and comedies of creative destruction and destructive creation, also the much more common but less remarked-upon creative creation and destructive destruction. The temporalities in these genres ranged from the nanoseconds of high-frequency trading to the geological epochs of sea level rise, chopped into intervals of seconds, hours, days, weeks, months, quarters, and years. It was awesome to dive into such a complicated screen with the actual backdrop of lower Manhattan out the window, and combined with the cappuccino and the flight down the river [in his personal hydrofoil speedboat], it felt like dropping into a big breaking wave. The economic sublime!
>
> (18)

If Franklin's enthusiasm seems egocentric at this point—only later in the novel does he turn his considerable talents away from personal profit-making toward realization of the common good—nonetheless the array of genres and temporalities on his computer screen functions as an important self-commentary on Robinson's novelistic strategies and ambitions. Like Franklin's trading calculations, the making of the novel endeavors to combine temporalities ranging from the diurnal to the geological. Its array of genres does not mirror those Franklin enumerates, but the major ones include the Abbott and Costello-like comic repartee of the computer programmers Ralph Muttchopf and Jeff Rosen (aka Mutt and Jeff); the crime investigation plot of the black female police office, Gen Octaviasdottir; the search for sunken treasure of the Huck Finn and Tom Sawyer-like pair, Stefan and Roberto; the political drama of Charlotte Armstrong, who goes from community organizer to Congressional representative; the travels and broadcasts of Amelia Black; and cementing all these together the lectures on history, geology, economics, and politics delivered in the voice of "the citizen"—Robinson's handling of the large-scale exposition of the changes that separate the early twenty-first and mid-twenty-second centuries.

This polyphonic array of voices, perspectives, and discourses in *New York 2140* tackles head-on the problems of historiography and the novel analyzed by Chakrabarty and Ghosh. The expository sections narrated by the "citizen" play a crucial role in establishing what this persona calls "the big picture" (32). They range from science writing on the glacial processes that formed Manhattan island and on the ecology of the Bight of New York, to a historical disquisition on Madison Square, to political and economic analyses of the ramifications of the First and Second Pulses in the twenty-first century and the workings of financial markets and the black economy in the twenty-second. This quasi-authorial voice mediates between the narratives of the Met Life building inhabitants and the unannounced but clear authorial presence made evident in the epigraphs that introduce each of the book's sixty four sections. All are taken from sources available at the time of the novel's composition, a grounding in the time of composition that is then heightened in the novel's repeated turning to the 2008 financial crisis as the model for the imaginary crisis in the characters' present.[1] The foundation of the novel in its time of composition is also evident in its concern with American literary tradition, particularly the New York connections of Herman Melville and Walt Whitman, and in the musical performances that take place here and there in the background, all of which are of compositions by twentieth century or earlier composers. This interplay between the varying perspectives and discursive resources of the citizen, the authorial presence, and the characters constitutes a kind of breaking of the plane of the fourth wall of a realist stage. Without violating the norms of probability in such a way as to move the story into a non-realist mode, Robinson's strategies highlight the fictionality of the imagined future in relation to a non-imaginary present, but this is a future that unfolds continuously from the present. The way from present to future is punctuated by catastrophe, but not by violation of realistic possibility. The net effect is to establish a firm communication between the disparate temporalities of climate change versus those of economics, politics, and everyday life.

Robinson's strategy encompasses the problematic hyperobjects and hypersubjects of Chakrabarty's and Ghosh's analyses most energetically by zeroing in on the problem of long-term costs. For instance, Franklin Garr, at one point, comments on the dollar valuation that the re-insurance companies have given to coastline properties worldwide. Their figure of 1.3 quadrillion dollars, says Franklin, is "far too low a valuation, if you are trying to accurately price what the coastlines of the world are truly worth. ... Because the future of humankind as a global civilization depends completely on its coastline presence" (120). The citizen, recounting the decarbonization efforts that followed upon the disastrous food shortages of the Second Pulse—amping up wind, solar, and tidal power, switching entirely to electric cars, instituting the habitat corridors, the emergence of the skyvillages and sky agriculture—adds this example of what the novel calls "expert stupidity":

But so expensive. Economists could not help but be dubious ... could we really *afford* these things? Wouldn't everything be better sorted out by the *market*?

Could we afford to survive? Well, this wasn't really the way to frame the question, the economists said. It was more a matter of trusting that economics and human spirit had solved all problems around the beginning of the modern era, or in the years of the neoliberal turn ... So hey, just continue down the chute and trust the experts on how things work!

(381)

This passage is one among many instances where this kind of polemical outburst includes an explicit reference to the present of the novel's composition as opposed to its fictional present. What the distance between those two versions of the present unfolds is the long-term costs of ignoring global warming, or in other words the contours of global warming as a hyperobject, in dire contrast to the kind of short-term thinking about what's good for the economy present to readers of this chapter in the Trump administration's roll-backs of environmental protections or in right-wing and centrist experts' head-shaking over the high dollar costs of implementing the proposals of the Green New Deal. The collective subject or hypersubject that arises in opposition to the collective choices that constitute the subject of the free market is most powerfully called "Life" in another of the citizen's disquisitions. Reflecting upon the abundance and uncontrollable proliferation of animal life in the New York harbor—salamanders, frogs, turtles, birds, whales, wolves, foxes, coyotes, skunks, porcupines, bobcats, pumas, hares, muskrats, water rats, beavers ("the mayor of the municipality"), otters, mink, fishers, weasels, raccoons, harbor seals, harbor porpoises, sperm whales, bears—the citizen launches finally into a Walt Whitman-esque warning to human pride: "Life! Life! Life! Life is going to kick your ass" (320).

At this point we are ready to return to the questions posed at the beginning of this essay about myth and fantasy. The way Robinson connects the history of capital to Chakrabarty's "general history of life" (2009, 219) opens "a global approach to politics without the myth of a global identity" (222) that can be understood as rewriting the terms of the Flood myth. The Flood itself, in *New York 2140*, is of course the rise in ocean levels due to the melting of polar ice—not a forty-day rainstorm but the slow-motion process of global warming. The figure of the Ark appears almost explicitly in Amelia Black's *Assisted Migration*, more implicitly in the cooperative living arrangements of the Met Life building and—beyond that and most crucially—in humanity's entanglement within "the general history of life," the hyperobjective, hypersubjective interdependence of the human and the nonhuman. The Covenant, then, is the work of adaptation to the conditions of the partially drowned coastal cities, the process by which, as the citizen puts it, "Lower Manhattan became a veritable hotbed of theory and practice, like it always used to say it was, but this time for real" (Robinson 2017, 209). In this vision there is no divine intervention and no return to a pre-ordained natural order. These are replaced instead with a collective effort to survive and thrive which aspires only toward participation in an unspecifiable "global identity" proper to the revised mythic pattern.

At the level of fantasy, then, the novel obviously seeks to undermine the fantasies of the market's benevolence and capitalism's inevitability. It likewise mocks the fantasies of eternal economic expansion and infinite resources that underwrite speculative finance. But its active fantasy, at the heart of the novel's plot, is one of the most familiar of everyday indulgences: the fantasy of being able to do over something that did not go well in one's past. The past event in question is the 2008 financial meltdown which Robinson replays as an opportunity for a victory of "democracy versus capitalism," as Amelia Black puts it (528). Amelia is urging her audience to participate in a general rent strike in the aftermath of a monster hurricane's damage to New York and the callous reaction of the rich in uptown Manhattan to the thousands upon thousands who are now left shelterless. The rent strike precipitates a financial crisis, but the government, instead of bailing out the banks as happened in 2008, nationalizes them. The latter part of *New York 2140* thus rehearses what Gib Prettyman, writing about Robinson's *Science in the Capital* trilogy, calls a "fortunate crisis" (2009, 192). Its function in *New York 2140* is much the same as in the earlier work; the crisis liberates people from their ordinary habits and modes of thought; it reminds people of the ecological big picture; it shows the ultimate contingency and vulnerability of the present order of things; it causes people to reassess their true needs and their relationship to "business as usual"; it frees people to be altruistic; it serves as a catalyst for experiment and for adoption of new habits.

(Prettyman 2009, 192)

The narrative vehicle for the fortunate crisis in *New York 2140* is another fantasy device familiar to anyone at all interested in popular cultural narratives over the last half century: the "hero team" (Fiske 2011, 215–17).[2] The hero team is an assembly of specialized experts who come together to perform a complex, heroic task—for example, the superheroes who league together in films like *The Avengers*, the clever crooks and conmen who band together in caper flicks like *Ocean's Eleven*, or the technical and military specialists who make up the secret task force of stories like the *Mission Impossible* series. In the case of *New York 2140* there are no super-powered individuals or action heroes. There is, however, a group of differently talented individuals fortuitously brought together in the project of protecting the Met Life building from being bought out from under them by real estate speculators. A recurring joke—the importance of which is emphasized by its being repeated three times—is that the group decides to launch a political revolution and overthrow world capitalism in order to save their building from a hostile takeover: the global is firmly rooted in the local. The team, which corresponds to the nine characters that narrate or focalize the story in addition to the citizen, is led by Charlotte Armstrong, the community organizer who successfully runs for Congress in the aftermath of the hurricane and spearheads the project of nationalizing the banks, with the somewhat reluctant help of her ex-husband who just happens to be the chair of the Federal Reserve board. Charlotte's main adviser, the mastermind behind the general strike, is Franklin Garr, who develops from casual bystander to ally to lover by the story's end. Amelia Black furnishes the skills and resources of a charismatic public figure. Gen Octaviasdottir's investigative skills and police credentials are crucial in understanding the threat posed to the building and who is behind it. The computer programmers Jeff Rosen and Ralph Muttchopf provide the initial shock to the financial system that signals its vulnerability. Vlade the maintenance manager is another steady ally of Charlotte, but perhaps most importantly Vlade is responsible for bringing the pair of homeless adolescents, Stefano and Roberto, into the protection of the Met Life building. This is crucial because Stefano and Roberto, acting on the information given them by an old map collector and expert in New York history, Gordon Hexter, uncover a sunken treasure that ends up financing the revolution—once the two chests full of antique gold coins are monetized and leveraged into billions of dollars by Franklin Garr's management. The hero team/caper flick device is what provides coherence not only to the striking diversity of ethnic identities and skills in the Met Life crew but also to such apparently disparate plot elements as the search for sunken treasure, the sabotage efforts against the Met Life building, and the abduction and subsequent rescue of Mutt and Jeff. It is Mutt who announces Robinson's plot device in a passage that parallels the self-reflective commentary provided earlier by Franklin's computer screen: "Have you ever noticed that our building is a kind of actor network that can do things? We got the cloud star [Amelia], the lawyer [Charlotte], the building expert [Vlade], the building itself, the police detective [Gen], the money man [Franklin] … add the getaway driver and it's a fucking heist movie!" (399).

Welding together natural and social history, *New York 2140* rewrites the myth of the Flood as a fantasy of successful anti-capitalist collective action. Just as certainly as this plot is a political fantasy, its main thrust is counter-fantastic, not so much in its realistic detail as in its overarching project of undermining the fantastic inevitability of the neoliberal capitalist status quo. That this inevitability is indeed fantastic is becoming more apparent than ever. I have written the first draft of this chapter while obeying stay at home orders issued by my local government during the coronavirus pandemic of spring 2020. If ever there were something that exposed the shortcomings of neoliberal ideology's unbounded faith in the free market, the Covid-19 virus is it. The pandemic calls for cooperation, not competition. It calls for shutting down the economy, not revving it up. The virus's global connectivity is both tied to and a horrifying counter-instance to the boasted efficiencies of globalization and the border-crossing regime of flexible accumulation. As such, Covid-19 presents a problem that the free market, far from being able to solve, can only make worse. Of course, global warming and the sixth great extinction have already presented themselves for decades as this kind of problem, but their time-scales are so extended, their threats so distant and dispersed, that they are much easier to ignore. One can only hope, at the time of this writing, that in the aftermath of the pandemic the short-term profit-grabbing mentality of ideologues like those who in 2020 controlled much of the world's corporate economy as well as the United States' executive branch and senate will be shaken, destabilized, and increasingly discredited by a humanity chastened by its subordination to "the general history of life."

Notes

1   Cf. Sergeant's excellent analysis of the role of the citizen in tackling what Sergeant calls the "scalar" problem of mediating between the collective and the individual levels of historical narrative.
2   My thanks to Kelsey Amos for alerting me to Fiske's essay.

References

Attebery, Brian. 2014. *Stories about Stories: Fantasy & the Remaking of Myth*. New York: Oxford University Press.

Bould, Mark and Sherryl Vint. 2009. "Dead Penguins in Immigrant Pilchard Scandal: Telling Stories about 'the Environment' in *Antarctica*." In *Kim Stanley Robinson Maps the Unimaginable: Critical Essays*, edited by William Burling, 257–73. Jefferson, NC: McFarland.

Burling, William, ed. 2009. *Kim Stanley Robinson Maps the Unimaginable: Critical Essays*. Jefferson, NC: McFarland.

Canavan, Gerry and Kim Stanley Robinson. 2014. "Afterword: Still, I'm Reluctant to Call This Pessimism." In *Green Planets: Ecology and Science Fiction*, 243–60. Middletown: Wesleyan University Press.

Chakrabarty, Dipesh. 2009. "The Climate of History: Four Theses." *Critical Inquiry*, vol. 35 (Winter): 197–222.

Fisher, Mark. 2009. *Capitalist Realism*. Winchester: Zero Books.

Fiske, John. 2011. *Television Culture*. Second edition. New York: Routledge.

Ghosh, Amitav. 2016. *The Great Derangement: Climate Change and the Unthinkable*. Chicago: University of Chicago Press.

Haraway, Donna. 2016. *Staying with the Trouble: Making Kin in the Chthulucene*. Durham, NC: Duke University Press.

Jameson, Fredric. 2005. "'If I Can Find One Good City I Will Spare the Man': Realism and Utopia in Kim Stanley Robinson's *Mars* Trilogy." In *Archaeologies of the Future: The Desire Called Utopian and Other Science Fictions*, 393–416. New York: Verso.

Jameson, Fredric. 1982. "Progress versus Utopia; or, Can We Imagine the Future?" *Science Fiction Studies*, vol. 9, no. 2: 147–58.

King, Derrick. 2015. "From Ecological Crisis to Utopian Hope: Kim Stanley Robinson's *Science in the Capital* Trilogy as Realist Critical Dystopia." *Extrapolation*, vol. 56, no. 2 (Summer): 195–214.

Latour, Bruno. 1993. *We Have Never Been Modern*. Translated by Catherine Porter. Cambridge, MA: Harvard University Press.

Luckhurst, Roger. 2009. "The Politics of the Network: Kim Stanley Robinson's *Science in the Capital* Trilogy." In *Kim Stanley Robinson Maps the Unimaginable: Critical Essays*, edited by William Burling, 170–80. Jefferson, NC: McFarland.

Morton, Timothy. 2013. *Hyperobjects: Philosophy and Ecology after the End of the World*. Minneapolis: University of Minnesota Press.

Okorafor, Nnedi. 2014. *Lagoon*. New York: Saga Press.

Oziewicz, Marek. 2022. "Introduction." In *Fantasy and Myth in the Anthropocene: Imagining Futures and Dreaming Hope in Literature and Media*, edited by Marek Oziewicz, Brian Attebery, and Tereza Dědinová, 1–11. London: Bloomsbury Academic.

Prettyman, Gib. 2009. "Living Thought: Genes, Genres and Utopia in Robinson's *Science in the Capital* Series." In *Kim Stanley Robinson Maps the Unimaginable: Critical Essays*, edited by William Burling, 181–203. Jefferson, NC: McFarland.

Prettyman, Gib. 2018. "Anthropocene Knowledge Practices in McKenzie Wark's *Molecular Red* and Kim Stanley Robinson's *Aurora*." *C21 Literature: Journal of 21st-century Writings*, vol. 6, no. 1: 1–27.

Roanhorse, Rebecca. 2018. *Trail of Lightning*. New York: Saga Press.

Robinson, Kim Stanley. 2017. *New York 2140*. London: Orbit.

Sergeant, David. 2019. "The Genre of the Near Future: Kim Stanley Robinson's *New York 2140*." *Genre*, vol. 52, no. 1 (April): 1–23.

Wegner, Phillip E. "Learning to Live in History: Alternate Historicities and the 1990s in *The Years of Rice and Salt*." In *Kim Stanley Robinson Maps the Unimaginable: Critical Essays*, edited by William Burling, 98–112. Jefferson, NC: McFarland.

CHAPTER 21
MYTH MAKES US SEE
Adam Gidwitz

Are you reading this on a screen?

Or, if you're reading this in a book, are you about to put the book down and check your phone, just in case … something?

We live with screens in our faces, and for good reason. They provide constant stimulation and instant gratification. As soon as we want to know something, the screen will tell us. As soon as we feel uncomfortable, the screen will distract us. As soon as we want something, the screen will guarantee that we have it in three days, or in less than twenty-four hours, or in twenty minutes.

Screens have become the accomplice in the ultimate crime in the history of the world: the murder of our planet.

To provide the physical materials that make up the screens (and the computers behind them), we strip the earth of trees, rocks, and fuel. We destroy the habitats of animal species that we haven't even discovered yet — and ones we have, like the northern white rhinoceros … until they are all dead.

To create and ship those screens, and all the other things we want, we pump carbon into the atmosphere, raising temperatures, killing more animals, making more of Earth uninhabitable.

But we'd be strip mining and burning down rainforests and pumping carbon into the air anyway, even without screens. What the screens do is hide our faces from what we're doing.

Myth, fantasy, and fairy tales can be the opposite of screens. Where screens stimulate instantly and distract continuously, myth and fantasy make us see.

Myth and fantasy are often rooted in nature, from the druids to Tom Bombadil to the swampy forests of Dagoba. In a fairy tale, the hero must almost always venture into the forest to find themselves. There is a reason for that. We are natural creatures and we *know* it. When we actually throw down our screens and take a hike through the woods, we *know* we belong there. We breathe and are aware of it. We hear birds, notice salamanders, freeze at the possible passing of a mammal in the underbrush just out of sight …. While we're walking, we swear we are going to do it more often. *This makes me happy*, we think.

And then we get back home and pick up our screens as fast as we can. I know we do. I do.

Because in the end, humans will do anything for comfort. Physical comfort, emotional comfort, psychic comfort. Truth? Life? We claim to love those things above all else, but we don't. We are hardwired to seek comfort.

Should we fight that?

Hell yes. Because we're also hardwired for caring. Because comfort at the price of turning Earth into a living Hell is no comfort at all. Because, really, we want to be connected: to others, to the Earth, and to everything around us. It's not always comfortable, but connection makes us so much happier. That is our choice: comfort or connection. And if we choose comfort, like the rat in the cage, we will comfort ourselves to death.

Myth, fantasy, and fairy tale, at their best, make us aware; aware of who we are and what we crave; aware of the original setting of the original story. The setting: Earth. The story: life.

We do not need parables about an Earth destroyed. We need stories that wake ourselves to ourselves. So we put down the screens, and the millions of comfort objects we have created, and go take a hike.

What awaits us is the greatest setting ever discovered. And the greatest story ever told.

CHAPTER 22
SLEEPING WITH THE FISHMEN: REIMAGINING THE ANTHROPOCENE THROUGH OCEANIC-CHTHONIC KINSHIPS
Prema Arasu and Drew Thornton

The monster is fiction's most potent symbol of the Other, a type of being who grants animation—and often animosity—to notions of alienness and fear of the unknown. Hayao Miyazaki and Guillermo del Toro are two contemporary storytellers whose work has been marked by bold interventions into the meaning of the monstrous, especially its chthonic or subterranean articulations. If the monster's estranging otherness could be imagined on a scale, oceanic-chthonic monsters constitute the opposite end of the spectrum to the human, each defining the other as its radical opposite. Can such a conceptual gap ever be breached? How could it be achieved and what advantages would it offer?

This chapter looks at two filmic narratives about monster–human kinship, Miyazaki's *Ponyo* (2008) and del Toro's *The Shape of Water* (2017), to consider how these stories reimagine the relationship between the human and the monsterized Other. The argument is that by offering visions of human–monster kinship, one that crosses yet respects irreducible differences of the human–nonhuman divide, these films are part of the contemporary search for re-entangling humans with other forms of life, including those despised or monsterized. This "kin-making," in Donna Haraway's formulation, has the potential to bring about a sense of larger togetherness and mutual precarity that many theorists have posited as crucial for reversing the most destructive tendencies of the Anthropocene.

The monstrous Other has a long tradition in literature. Some instances of the literary Other manifest hyperbolically, with forms and intents that push the limits of the imagination; these are the Chimaerae, the Leviathans, the Ungoliants, and other nightmarish conceptions, designed by storytellers to frighten with their strangeness, scale, and ferocity. But not all monsters are imagined in this vein. The realm of the monster also encompasses beings modeled in imitation of the human form: these may be semi-human, near-human or once-human entities, whose monstrosity is betrayed by nonhuman elements in their anatomy or psyche. In many stories, they result as the offspring of matings between human and animal, or human and divine. For this reason, we refer to these monsters as "hybrids."

In this chapter we identify a category of hybrid typified by combinations of human characteristics with animal or supernatural traits that we characterize collectively as "chthonic." Our examples of oceanic-chthonic hybrids defy territory and taxonomy, crossing Orphically between human and nonhuman realms. They transcend mortality, heal and plasticate the body, and offer humans immense wealth at untold moral cost—all powers that would not be out of place for agents of the realm of death. Their bodies are usually some amalgam of human with fish or other aquatic creature, signified by fins, gills, and tentacles. We thus distinguish this group of creatures using the label "oceanic-chthonic hybrids," referencing their dual-association with aquatic animality and supernaturality. "Chthonic" refers to the subterranean, and through its Greek root denotes denizens of the underworld; Christian context has layered the English meaning with connotations of the infernal. In popular culture, the tentacular aspect is perpetuated by H. P. Lovecraft's "Cthulhu Mythos," whose ongoing relevance in supernatural horror has propagated associations between chthonic forces, subaquatic realms, and cosmic evil. More recently, Donna Haraway has rehabilitated the chthonic as a politically generative space, for imagining modes of trans-species coexistence that would pivot our planetary future from the dead-ended Anthropocene into a more pluralistic, disanthropocentric era she calls the Chthulucene.

The chthonic hybrids of myth embody the unknown. Uninvited, they emerge from forbidden depths and bring with them the implicit power of those Dantean places. As a common human can no more stroll into the oceanic abyss than into Hell itself, when something from that realm walks into ours, it upends the hierarchical constructions upon which we stake our identity. Oceanic-chthonic hybrids recur in folklore across cultures, from British mermaids and Scottish selkies, to Japanese *Ningyo* (人魚, lit. "human fish") and *Sazaeoni* (栄螺鬼 lit. "horned turban snail demon"). The mythic traditions of various cultures include monsters and deities which similarly combine human and piscine traits, such as the ancient Greek primordial sea deities Phorcys, with crab claw legs and serpentine fish tail, and Ceto, whose name possibly comes from *kētŏs*, meaning "whale" or "sea-serpent." Their children, the betentacled Gorgons, in turn give their names to corals and jellyfish—*Gorgonia* and the Medusozoa.

Oceanic-chthonic hybrids figure prominently in fiction, drawing upon mythological tropes in both sympathetic and villainous representations. Newer stories are often reconfigurations of myth by authors who wish to express dissatisfaction with their antecedent's tellings: "The Little Mermaid" (Andersen 2010, orig. 1837), reimagines Friedrich de la Motte Fouqué's *Undine* (de la Motte Fouqué 2009, orig. 1811) to allow the possibility that the protagonist might attain an "immortal [human] soul" (Andersen 2010, 145). The watery followers of the cult of Dagon in Lovecraft's "The Shadow over Innsmouth" (Lovecraft 2020, orig. 1931) are more recent literary creations, contextualized within the author's overarching philosophy of Cosmicism as part of the Cthulhu Mythos. The prominence of mermaids and fishmen continues today, with roles in popular story franchises such as *Harry Potter* (1997–2018), *Star Wars* (1977–2019), *Hellboy* (1994–2019), and *Pirates of the Caribbean* (2003–17). These hybrids mark an ongoing engagement with mythological motifs within the genre of modern fantasy.

Analysis of literary oceanic-chthonic hybrids over time reveals not only that monsters are capable of becoming sympathetic protagonists, they are also increasingly viable and appealing as kin-figures and romantic leads. When framed within the context of the role of myth in the Anthropocene, these uncertain, multifarious entanglements emerge as explorations of what Haraway calls "staying with the trouble", whereby invented connections with the Other teach us to "live and die well with each other in a thick present" (Haraway 2016, 1). Haraway suggests a new era called the Chthulucene, in which we respond to the dictates of the Anthropocene by forming kinships with "chthonic ones … replete with tentacles, feelers, digits, cords, whiptails, spider legs, and very unruly hair" (2). Our examination of human-oceanic-chthonic kinships signals an ongoing negotiation of what it means to be human in the Anthropocene, in which rapid anthropogenic ecological destruction moves us to reconsider our place in the world. Faced with such a degree of change, numerous storytellers engage with the mythological hybrid monsters to explore the myriad possibilities of coexistence. In confronting the Other, uncomfortable intimacy gives way to the embrace of kinship and dialogue—sometimes clumsy, sometimes delicate—with entities who are indeed our obligate companions in the experience of life on a churning planet.

Storytelling for the Chthulucene

The hybrid ontologies and the human kinships of del Toro's Asset and Miyazaki's Ponyo hearken back to precursors in fairytale and myth, reproducing their storytelling methods and motifs. Jack Zipes identifies the modern fantasy story as the successor of the fairy tale, as both serve to propagate and reproduce cultural metanarratives (Zipes 2006, 2). Similarly, Brian Attebery suggests that the genre of modern fantasy is a place where myths can be contested, and that fantasy's cultural relevance and enduring appeal lies in its capacity for mythopoesis, providing myth with "new contexts, and thus inevitably new meanings" (2014, 3). Fantasy is a space where we redefine and rework our relationship to cultural myth; therefore it is a space where ontologies are constructed and—subsequently—deconstructed. Amongst these ontologies are the notions of the human, and of the natural, monstrous or divine Other. Human exceptionalism—the notion that humans are categorically distinct from other, "lesser" forms of life—is a cultural myth that has been continually tested and contested in fantasy texts. Over time the status of the human, in relation to the Other, has shifted: from a clearly demarcated taxonomy of human uniqueness, to a mere distinction of degrees and finally—in the Anthropocene era—a mootable distinction.

This debridement of human exceptionalism is seen in the fish hybrid bodies we discuss: metonymic explorations of the nebulous boundaries between human–nonhuman, human–animal, human–monster, natural–artificial, body–soul, sapient–dumb, and even male–female, as fish hybrids rarely conform to normative human ontologies of gender and sexual dimorphism. The hybridity of the fishman's body reveals the ways in which the ontologies of human, monster, and nature are arbitrarily constructed through signifiers such as appearance and language. One way to theorize this ontological deconstruction of the human is in terms of queer theory, which exposes the constructed-ness of supposedly naturalized categories such as gender and sexuality. Patricia McCormack positions human subjectivity in relation to nonhuman categories—including the prehuman "animal" and "monster," and variations of the posthuman—which "oppose or extend the concept of the human through the creation of hybrid desires extending in both directions of the evolutionary trajectory" (2009, 111).

A similar trend toward ontological emancipation can be seen in ecocritical theory, which approaches natural categories with the same suspicion that queer theory holds for social ones. Ecotheorists like Donna Haraway, Stacy Alaimo, and Sam Mickey recognize the process of mythologization of ecological principles and dogma that occurs in narratives, fantasy included. These scholars invest in stories—posthumanist onto-epistemologies—that "destabilize terrestrial assumptions, values, and modes of life" (Alaimo 2013, 238), including notions of the human, natural, and divine. "Coexistentialism"—Mickey's philosophy for Anthropocene coping—positions itself subsequent to "all totalizing categories that sunder the world into two clear and distinct categories of transcendence and immanence" (2016, 49–50). The human epoch must be navigated through a politic that is post-theological, post-ecological, and (ironically) post-anthropological; in such navigation the tools of queer and ecocritical theory, which perforate and distend categories, are especially useful. Viewing the oceanic-chthonic hybrids of fantasy as examples of the posthuman—not an extension but a natural implication of queer theory and ecotheory—forms the basis of our theoretical approach. In this reckoning, ecotheory and queer theory are supplicants to fantasy in the work of reconstructing the human place within ecology and natural systems. We look to fantasy to see how the posthuman may question cultural myths that prescribe categorical modes of human–animal interrelationships. Literary analysis allows us to track the reconfiguration of these frameworks of belief into newly ideated philosophies for the Anthropocene.

These new philosophies, with their origins in the fantastic, affirm the possibility of a dialogue with the nonhuman entities that creep into our lives. In fact, they are already being transcribed into practice by scholars who engage with the semiotic systems of other species: Eva Hayward's situated ethnography of cup corals, *Balanophyllia elegans,* considers the polyps' sensoria and semiotic bodiliness, finding them "sensual, sexy" (2010, 589). Marine biologist Edith Widder uses a flashing electronic jellyfish to prompt bioluminescent responses from deep-sea animals. During a submarine expedition, these blinked conversations bring a similar response from Widder—exchanging flashes with a luminous agent she suspects to be a shrimp, Widder remarks: "We don't know what we're saying. Personally, I think it's something sexy" (2011, quoted in Alaimo 2013, 246). As humans, we seem to crave linguistic connections to affirm our mutual existences, and parse deeper intimacy from the superficially alien. Communication and self-expression are sexy—and indeed vital—in the human world. Hayward and Widder are delighted to discover something that might almost be human, some language-analogue, in even the most Other of creatures. These cases of semiotic intercourse with the Other are practical demonstrations that kinship is possible because communication is possible.

Locating the Monster

The monster is a figure in fantasy whose existence suggests the possibility of other modes of being, perceiving, and communicating—ways which challenge anthropocentrism and the teleological hierarchy that places humans as the end-point of evolution. Associated with queerness, liminality, and Otherness, the monster becomes a powerful metonymy for exploring the socially constructed boundaries of normality. The monster, in Foucault's conceptualization, is understood as "a double breach, of law and nature" (Sharpe 2010, 25). Andrew Ng defines it as a transgression of what is considered natural; the concept of monstrosity, Ng argues, "calls into question the assumptions inherent to our definitions of natural law and progression," ultimately revealing the self as "a complex 'construction' of society, culture, language and ideology" (2004, 2). These and other definitions gesture at an understanding that the monster is ontologically produced through hegemonic discourses; in other words, it relies on preexisting cultural constructs—the norms of nature and humanity—against which the monster is defined.

Whereas gothic literature situated the monster as "geographically and physically other," in recent texts Ng identifies a shift of the monster from the Other to the Self—ontological relocation to "an 'elsewhere' that is intimately with(in) us" (1). Contemporary texts, he contends, "reposition the monster in the first person narrative," granting it implicit personhood (176). Indeed, the monster and the human converge in the rising figure of the hybrid. The contemporary image of the hybrid reveals that humanness—in relation to which monstrosity is constructed—is itself ultimately a construct; when it comes to human and natural, one need not be one or the other.

As a story that defies anthropocentrism and normative human categories, Guillermo del Toro's *The Shape of Water* has been the subject of much critical attention in fantasy and film studies. Alberta Adji argues that del Toro's characteristic engagement with myth, fairy tale, and monsters is indicative of a preoccupation with Otherness: of softening and humanizing the "dark mystical realm of the humanoid amphibian and the misfit" (2019, 60). Jennifer Degnan Smith frames *The Shape of Water* as a challenge to two strands of Anthropocene discourse: the myth of progress, "the heroic journey from an ignorant, primitive world to an intelligent modern world," and its compensatory myth of the fall, which "blames [progress] for the separation of humans from nature and for the exploitation of nature" (2019, 43). The Asset— the film's amphibious romantic lead—is a hybrid who is intelligent and yet physically atavistic. As such, it embodies a kind of humanity unopposed to nature. To Jilkén and Johansson, The Asset represents "the new man" of the films of the 1990s onwards—one who is "sensitive, emotionally aware, respectful" and overall more erotically appealing to women (Gill 2003, quoted in Jilkén and Johansson 2019, 138).

Likewise, the works of Hayao Miyazaki demonstrate a generative engagement with myth. Miyazaki's films often draw on myths, fairy tales, and fables of both Japanese and global provenance, with sensibilities that demonstrate both a grounding in Japanese culture and a keen worldly awareness. *Ponyo*'s titular protagonist assumes her amphibious hybrid form in a quest for self-determination. That quest, in turn, becomes a quest for kinship which, according to Dani Cavallaro, "defies the very ideology which anthropocentrism has striven to assert" (2014, 86). Themes of non-anthropocentric living, coping, and coexisting recur among creator Miyazaki's works—recognized by Haraway in her identification of *Nausicaa of the Valley of the Wind* (Miyazaki 1984) as a creative inspiration for "The Camille Stories" (Haraway 2016, 151–2).

Monstrous Bodily Ontologies

The protagonists and romantic leads in *The Shape of Water* and *Ponyo*—as with their predecessors in *Creature from the Black Lagoon* (Arnold 1954) and "The Little Mermaid"— are oceanic-chthonic beings who challenge humanity and monstrosity by their mismatched signifiers. Though they exhibit monstrous traits, they are characters for whom the label "monster" is of contested adequacy.

Hybrids—as with all monsters of myth and fairy tale—signify monstrousness through the imagery of visual, behavioral, and facultative otherness. In the case of hybrids, though they may possess near-human form, their status among the Other is betrayed by an imperfect affectation of human nature—be it physical aberration, sub-human intelligence, or the inability to speak. Language in particular, given that it requires both physical and mental faculties to perform, is a signifier of humanity which marks the monster or hybrid being in question as deserving of our sympathy.

The Asset in *The Shape of Water* serves as our major example of an oceanic-chthonic hybrid who eludes conventional modes of signification. The Asset displays many physical signifiers of monstrosity. He is greenish in color, has gills and scales, wide-set pupil-less eyes, and webbed hands. He lacks verbal communication, and in his captive state bites fingers off his persecutor, Strickland. However, treated with kindness and offered alternative methods of communication, he is shown to be every bit as human as Elisa. He also appears to be more human/humane than Strickland, who fails to display compassion and ultimately is cast as the monster himself.

Hybrids like The Asset unsettle binary of divisions of human–monster by presenting bodily and behavioral traits with unreliable or conflicting significations. Strickland resolves this ontological uncertainty with an appeal to divinity: "You may think that thing looks human. It stands on two legs, right? But we're created in the Lord's image. You don't think that's what the Lord looks like, do you?" (del Toro 2017). For Strickland, the physical signifiers of humanity are rigidly prescribed within the religious mythos. As he hunts his subject, however, Strickland's deteriorating health and sanity lead him to an outward visage that matches his inner monstrosity.

Elisa recognizes The Asset's inner markers of humanity. She aids the creature to escape torture at Strickland's hand. Asked why she would help a being that's "not even human," Elisa replies via sign language: "If we do nothing, then neither are we" (del Toro 2017). The shaky parameters with which we measure humanity are brought into question: upon first encountering The Asset, Giles sees his fins and scaly skin and determines that these qualify the being as not human, implicitly undeserving of their sympathy. For Elisa, by contrast, humanity is equated with empathy—a quality for which The Asset shows a capacity in their shared touch across the glass. This leads Elisa to teach The Asset the rudiments of sign language and allows her to confirm that he possesses all of the qualities she requires in a sexual/romantic partner— including a phallus—regardless of the absence of spoken language and other conventional signifiers of sentience. Mitchell and Snyder identify the significance of alternative (sign) language as a signifier of non-normativity and observe how the relationship between Elisa and The Asset "results from a material recognition" that informs the structure of their "alternative navigations" in communication (2019, 155). The predominance of nonverbal language in *The Shape of Water* challenges the narrative that the human is distinguished from the monstrous by language. A trope seen in its fairy tale and mythic precursors—most notably, Hans Christian Andersen's "The Little Mermaid"—is shown here as no longer sufficient to demarcate between the human and the Other.

Subaquatic, Subhuman

"The Little Mermaid" is now ubiquitous in popular culture, with changes to the tale reflecting incremental reconfigurations of the nonhuman and hybrid over time. In the original version, the unnamed mermaid falls in love with the prince she rescues from a shipwreck; as she ventures closer to the shore, she grows increasingly unhappy with her fish tail, the most overt signifer of her transversal hybridity. She is known for her beautiful voice, but sacrifices this in return for legs and a chance to earn an immortal soul. In Andersen's version, the little mermaid may only gain a soul if she can win the Prince completely, so that he loves her with his "whole soul" (Andersen 2010, 151). Without her voice, however, she is unable to win his love. The internal paradox of "The Little Mermaid"—and the source of its tragedy—is that the mermaid's human ascendancy is contingent on the prince's true love, but that self-same love seems to require the fact of her humanity. Thus the predicate for the hybrid's incipient humanity is its already-human-ness, an ontological bootstrap that fixes beings in immutable, non-porous categories: those with an immortal soul, and those without. This intransgressible delineation between humans and animal—i.e., those with souls and those without—is typical of Western storytelling and reflects what Matthew Chrulew describes as a "fundamental gulf" within Greek and Christian thought (2018, 19). In this original version of "The Little Mermaid"—as in *Undine*, its inspiration—the hybrid figure seems to be doomed from the beginning, implying that monsters should not attempt to cross the gulf that separates human from animal. Andersen, admittedly, grants his mermaid a possible path across the gulf; at the moment she dissolves into seafoam he has her metamorphose, into a "daughter … of the air," who by enough "good deeds" may become human in the distant future (Andersen 2010, 167). However, the 300-year duration of this limbo serves to reinforce the mermaid's subhuman status; it communicates the stygian vastness of the chasm that separates her from her desire.

In fantasy we witness how writers and storytellers have grappled with the imposed conceptual gap between human and nonhuman; tales of hybrids—and their engagement with humans through kinships and sensual couplings—show the queering of the boundary between human, animal, and monster, through exploration of their shared temporality and mattering. Hybrids like the little mermaid and The Asset remind us that things which appear monstrous contain the potential to become human; in turn, we all have the disquieting potential to become monstrous. Hybrids manifest all the possibilities of humanity and monstrosity. By intermingling these possibilities within a single body or identity, they embody both horrifying and revelatory modes of being. Narrative parallels between newer texts and their precursors demonstrate the legacy of mythic influence, and often direct creative inspiration, that contemporary texts carry. Contemporary readings of authors such as Andersen and Lovecraft interpolate some sense of the authors' critical awareness, even skepticism, of the punitive boundaries that Christian storytelling exhorts. Both authors struggle with theological prescriptions in the face of the human-as-animal and animal-as-human; their hybrid protagonists challenge absolutes with their efforts at transcendence. The changes made to the ending of *Undine* / "The Little Mermaid" across retellings represent a disruption of the hierarchy that places humans above monsters and animals, indicated by wider changes in cultural attitudes toward monsters, and an assault upon the sanctity of the human. For instance, in Disney's *The Little Mermaid* (Clements and Musker 1989), the mermaid is presented as less alien and closer to a human from the start. Now named Ariel, she is ultimately granted a human form at the film's end, without Andersen's original requirement for a period of diffuse purgatory. The price—because there is always a price—is now "merely" Ariel's complete submission to the patriarchal order (Hastings 1993). That said, these disparate endings indicate a reconsideration of the hybrid's ability to transcend their sub-human ontology and an acceptance of the human as much less rigid category than it was for Andersen's contemporaries.

The Myth of Human Exceptionalism

The conceptual narrowing of the human–animal boundary we see in the changes made to the story of The Little Mermaid represents a categorical desanctification of the human in light of evolutionary theory in the nineteenth century (Darwin 2010, 919–20). However, evolutionary biology itself is a heavily narrativized science, and scholarly thought then and since remained broadly embedded in a teleological hierarchy; one in which humans—some races more than others—are positioned as the "natural" apex of the evolutionary endeavor. When viewed in light of the succession of human evolution from the sea to the land, the mermaid or fishman's transcendence becomes more tangible, but at the same time, so does the reverse: the human's descent into the sea.

Miyazaki's *Ponyo* embraces the narrative of evolutionary relationality, lathering scientific dogma into a refractive bubble of fantasy. The film plays this relationship out in both directions, with protagonists Ponyo and Sōsuke tracing a journey that weaves in and out of the life-giving ocean. Ponyo's father, the wizard Fujimoto, concocts elixirs with mysterious genetic effects—these brews variously accelerate and reverse evolution, cause alchemical abiogenesis, animate water with autonomous life, and transform living beings back into the seawater from which all life first originated. Wishing to eliminate "disgusting" humans and the ecological degradation they cause, Fujimoto plots to amass sufficient magic to reset the planet's evolutionary trajectory with a Cambrian-era "explosion" of life (Miyazaki 2008). When the goldfish Ponyo gains access to this magic, she is able to transfigure herself into human form, incidentally flooding the nearby coastal town and filling it with prehistoric sealife. Reuniting with her human friend Sōsuke and his mother, Lisa, human-Ponyo begins to acquire spoken language, joyfully embracing her place in an unconventional family.

Ponyo is a reimagining of "The Little Mermaid" that weaves into its fold the mythic strains of ecological and evolutionary narratives, reaching all the way back to our shared conception in Earth's primordial ocean. The film's penultimate scene sees Sōsuke meet Ponyo's parents—Fujimoto and the sea goddess Granmamare—in an idyllic undersea bubble surrounded by schools of Devonian fish. Here his declaration of love for Ponyo, regardless of her form, restores the balance of nature upset by Ponyo's unleashed magic. A story that for Andersen was a moralizing tale about the metaphysics of the Christian soul, in Miyazaki's hands becomes a cautioning story about humanity's moral duty to maintain balance with nature. It also becomes a story that imbues non-humans with the potentiality and impetus to become human while simultaneously collapsing the ontological ceiling that holds humans aloft and distinct from nature.

When Andersen's version of the tale finally acceded to grant the mermaid a soul, that soul was airborne and ethereal. The young Miyazaki, reading this story for the first time, could not accept the premise that a creature such as the mermaid "didn't have a soul" (Miyazaki 2008, quoted in Cavallaro 2014, 91). Thus his retelling imbues Ponyo with a spirit and existence that is more earthy and entangled with earthly goings-on—chthonic in Haraway's sense of the word.

More than a facile notion of bodily conformity, Ponyo's humanity is founded in relationships and connections, feelings and compassion. It is driven by a desire to coexist and relate with humans. The dialogues in Miyazaki's film extend beyond the mode of mere spoken language: Sōsuke and Lisa use a signal lamp to speak with Sōsuke's father Captain Koichi, who is stuck at sea. Koichi tries to woo Lisa into forgiveness of his absence by a display of colored lights that ought to impress any bioluminescent sea-critter. Nonverbal communication appears to be on Miyazaki's mind when imagining hybrid relationships. Referring to a scene where Ponyo communes wordlessly with an infant, the filmmaker states that "they're communicating as living creatures, not just human beings" (Miyazaki 2008, quoted in Cavallaro 2014, 86). This idea, contends Cavallaro, points to a wider worldview in which "what matters most about

157

a creature is not its humanness, but rather its livingness," whereby ecological entanglement unites living things "beyond their species-specific and genus-specific attributes" (Cavallaro 2014, 86).

In *Ponyo* the notion of transcendence is done away with completely. The barriers between fish and human, land, and sea become physically and ontologically blurred. The tale provokes a reversal of the burden of policing the boundaries of humanity. Whereas Andersen required the little mermaid to prove her worth to the prince, in Miyazaki's film it is the human Sōsuke who has to prove himself worthy to Ponyo. It is the human who must declare his devotion to Ponyo, in both her fish and human forms.

Watery End

Hybrid beings in fantasy and myth represent the fragile ontology of the human and the porousness of our bodily boundaries. It is not surprising that they are often drawn on as a source of horror: they are uncanny, abject, liminal, and thus unsettling. But by virtue of their human aspect they are also spirited, joyous, caring, and loving, in unapologetic and genuine fashion. Reimagining oceanic-chthonic hybrids as romantic leads articulates an epistemological shift in favor of a complicated bodily ontology for the human monster.

The fantasy genre demonstrates that story and myth are infinitely contestable, being constantly reworked by fantasy in the collective imagination. In the imaginations of del Toro and Miyazaki, this process of contesting is demonstrated by first placing the human in relation to the monster—that is to say, the inscrutable chthonic Other—and then exploring their possible hybrid forms. These hybrids often accompany syncretic modes of fantasy, wherein multiple contentions of reality interpenetrate in a tentacular fashion. Our arrival at a point where we acknowledge the expressiveness of chthonic entities, such as fish, shrimp, and corals, demonstrates a profound shift in the ontology of the human—to the extent where these Others can be deemed persons and even "sexy."

Ponyo and *The Shape of Water* affirm that semiotic intercourse with the Other is possible, and indeed fruitful—not just with fictional near-humans, but with strange chthonic ones in the real world: Hayward's un-blind, tentacular cup corals and Widder's alien, flashing shrimp. Dialogues with these creatures point toward Haraway's strategy of "making kin" as an Anthropocene coping mechanism. On a more conceptual level, hybrids herald the death of categories. They tell us that—as necessitated within Mickey's coexistentialism—time is up on notions of human, animal, nature, and the divine. With ancestry, anatomy, and language no longer functional delineators of the human and Other, we see fishmen play the role of chthonic psychopomps, ushering the ghosts of these concepts beyond the veil of the realm of thought.

The Anthropocene represents a great relocating force, as we bear witness to the weirding of geographies, geologies, and ecologies, the estrangement of cultures, symbioses, and species. As the earth contorts, it dredges up long-settled strata, perturbs ancient interrelationships, and grasps tentacularly for new connections, systems, and stabilizations. Perhaps this is within Haraway's intent for the term "Chthulucene"—to evoke a sense of the planet's collective writhing, and the need to reach out, make contact, stabilize, and hold firm to the earth to manage its troubled irruptions. Stories of ancient, semi-human figures pulled from the deep— figures who breach the surface and make sensual contact with the human realm—form one way in which we are challenging deeply engrained notions of human uniqueness. As these oceanic-chthonic hybrids and their human kin learn to communicate, as they learn to make peace with the forced proximities and uncomfortable intimacies brought about by Chthulucene upheaval, we see an upwelling of humanity from the alien depths of monstrosity. Hybrids invite us to "unmoor ourselves from terrestrial and humanist presumptions" (Alaimo 2013, 235). Like Sōsuke's immersion into the Devonian sea, contrasting the little mermaid's diffusion into airy limbo, they invite us to "descend, rather than transcend" (Alaimo 2013, 235) in our reimagining of the human relationship with the other.

References

Adji, Alberta Natasia. 2019. "Falling for the Amphibian Man: Fantasy, Otherness, and Auteurism in del Toro's *The Shape of Water*." *IAFOR Journal of Media, Communication & Film*, vol. 6 no. 1 (Summer): 51–64. Doi:10.22492/ijmcf.6.1.03.

Alaimo, Stacy. 2013. "Violet-Black." In *Prismatic Ecology: Ecotheory beyond Green*, edited by Jeffrey Jerome Cohen, 233–51. Minneapolis: University of Minnesota Press.

Andersen, Hans Christian. (1867) 2010. "The Little Mermaid." In *Hans Andersen's Fairy Tales: Second Series*, edited by J.H. Stickney. Project Gutenberg eBook no. 32572: 2010, https://www.gutenberg.org/ebooks/32572.

Arnold, Jack, dir. 1954. *Creature from the Black Lagoon*. Universal, CA: Universal Pictures.

Attebery, Brian. 2014. *Stories about Stories*. Oxford: Oxford University Press.

Cavallaro, Dani. 2014. *The Late Works of Hayao Miyazaki: A Critical Study, 2004–2013*. Jefferson, NC: McFarland & Company.

Chrulew, Matthew. 2017. "The Philosophical Ethology of Dominique Lestel." In *The Philosophical Ethology of Dominique Lestel*, edited by Matthew Chrulew, Jeffrey Bussolini, and Brett Buchanan, 17–44. Abingdon: Routledge.

Clements, Ron, and John Musker, dir. 1989. *The Little Mermaid*. Burbank, CA: Walt Disney Pictures, 1998. VHS.

Darwin, Charles. 2010. *Evolutionary Writings*, edited by James Secord. New York: Oxford University Press.

de la Motte Fouqué, Friedrich. 2009. *Undine*. Project Gutenberg eBook no. 2825: 2009, http://www.gutenberg.org/ebooks/2825

del Toro, Guillermo, dir. 2017. *The Shape of Water*. New York: TSG Entertainment.

Gill, Rosalind. 2003. "Power and the Production of Subjects: A Genealogy of the New Man and the New Lad." *Sociological Review*, vol. 51, no. 1 (February): 34–56.

Haraway, Donna J. 2016. *Staying with the Trouble: Making Kin in the Chthulucene*. Durham, NC: Duke University Press.

Hastings, A. Waller. 1993. "Moral Simplification in Disney's *Little Mermaid*." *Lion and the Unicorn*, vol. 17, no. 1 (June): 83–92.

Hayward, Eva. 2010. "FINGERYEYES: Impressions of Cup Corals." *Cultural Anthropology*, vol. 25, no. 4 (November): 577–99, www.jstor.org/stable/40930490

Jilkén, Olle, and Lina Johansson. 2019. "Aquatic Heterosexual Love and Wondrous Cliché Stereotypes: Amphibian Masculinity, the Beast Bridegroom Motif and 'the Other' in *The Shape of Water*." *Coolabah*, vol. 27: 136–49, https://revistes.ub.edu/index.php/coolabah/article/viewFile/30522/30673

Lovecraft, Howard Phillips. 2020. The Complete Works of H.P. Lovecraft. https://arkhamarchivist.com/ebook/The%20Complete%20Works%20of%20H.P.%20Lovecraft.pdf

MacCormack, Patricia. 2009. "Queer Posthumanism: Cyborgs, Animals, Monsters, Perverts." In *The Ashgate Research Companion to Queer Theory*, edited by Noreen Giffney, and Michael O'Rourke, 111–26. Abingdon: Taylor & Francis.

Mickey, Sam. 2016. *Coexistentialism and the Unbearable Intimacy of Ecological Emergency*. Lanham, MD: Rowman & Littlefield.

Mitchell, David T. and Sharon L. Snyder. 2019. "Room for (Materiality's) Maneuver: Reading the Oppositional in Guillermo del Toro's *The Shape of Water*." *Journal of Cinema and Media Studies*, vol. 58 no. 4 (Summer): 150–6, Doi:10.1353/cj.2019.0045

Miyazaki, Hayao, dir. 1984. *Nausicaä of the Valley of the Wind*. Tokyo: Topcraft. Netflix.

Miyazaki, Hayao, dir. 2008. *Ponyo*. Burbank, CA: Walt Disney Pictures; Santa Monica, CA: Kennedy/Marshall, 2009. Netflix.

Ng, Andrew Hock-soon. 2004. *Dimensions of Monstrosity in Contemporary Narratives: Theory, Psychoanalysis, Postmodernism*. London: Palgrave Macmillan.

Sharpe, Andrew N. 2010. *Foucault's Monsters and the Challenge of Law*. Abingdon: Routledge.

Smith, Jennifer Degnan. 2019. "*The Shape of Water*: An Ecopsychological Fairy Tale." *Ecopsychology*, vol. 11, no. 1 (March): 43–8. Doi:10.1089/eco.2018.0064

Widder, Edith. "The Weird, Wonderful World of Bioluminescence." TED Talk. March, 2011. http://www.ted.com/talks/edith_widder_the_weird_and_wonderful_world_of_bioluminescence.html

Zipes, Jack. 2006. *Why Fairy Tales Stick: The Evolution and Relevance of a Genre*. Abingdon: Taylor & Francis.

CHAPTER 23
FISH GIRL'S DILEMMA
Donna Jo Napoli

Any world—any time and place—has its challenges, and while those challenges vary, rising to meet them requires the same personal qualities: resourcefulness, intelligence, diligence, commitment, courage. The list includes whatever is necessary to do the hard work for success—where success today means survival on a personal, societal, and global level. Myths and traditional stories—the ones that are passed from generation to generation—have stood the test of time; they speak to us, even when they are about battling witches or living in castles although we may not believe in witchcraft and might have never set foot in a castle. Their relevance to us is at a gut level; they draw us into the dilemma and make us understand how much a character is willing to struggle and sacrifice in order to achieve their goals.

My thoughts these days often go to Fish Girl. The mermaid in this story struggles to know the truth of her own history and situation and to gain her freedom, intellectually, emotionally, physically. Yet I wonder what happens to her in this human world that she has chosen to inhabit by the end of the book. When she lived in the huge fish tank that Neptune had built for her, she had a pristine, if every limited, environment. The inhabitants of the tank were all fed. The water was filtered. There wasn't much to worry about. Entering the human world had to be a shock. Though we can trust that a human family would care for her, she would now encounter the stresses of modern life outside the tank.

One thing that might well interest her more than others is how human behavior has been destroying the health of the oceans. Heavy industrialization as well as widespread deforestation led to high contaminant levels across the world's oceans extending down to full ocean depth. This pollution affects all levels of marine communities—from plants to predators—and disrupts ecosystem functioning. Dumping of refuse leads to floating litter and debris, particularly plastic debris. When marine animals ingest enough microplastics, they die. The oceans are putrefying and their biodiversity is shrinking. And human behavior is the culprit.

Fish Girl grew up in the caring arms of Octopus. She grew up swimming with Turtle and the herrings, listening to the munching of the sea urchins as they eat. She loves her marine friends. Will she accept her human identity once she realizes that humans are threatening those very creatures? Will she feel defiled by having human skin? Will she want to jump out of that skin? A sequel swirls around in my head—one in which Fish Girl, in the form of the human girl Mira, tries to speak for the oceans. But humans find her silly. They call her idealistic. They say that the economy of the world will collapse if anyone should take her recommendations seriously. Fish Girl loses all hope of prevailing. She looks at all she has gained by escaping from Neptune's tank and taking on human form. And she gives it up; she returns to the ocean. Better a mermaid in a dying ocean than a human killing that ocean.

I doubt I'll ever write that sequel. I don't know, but I doubt that David Wiesner would be interested in collaborating on such a sequel. I write for young readers—and, though I often deal with heavy topics, I always end on a note of hope. I couldn't write a book that did otherwise; it would go against my philosophy of what nourishes a child's soul.

But the message of today's world is clear—maybe for Fish Girl, and definitely for the rest of us. We need to ask what we are willing to give up and how hard we are willing to work in order to achieve basic goals. Goals like living decently, morally. Recognizing the right of all creatures to live decently puts a huge responsibility on us, if we are only willing to accept it. What gives us that will? The same things we see in our myths and traditional stories: the faith that we know what is right and we can do it.

CHAPTER 24

FROM CULTURE HERO TO EMISSIONS ZERO: CRITIQUING MAUI'S EXTRACTIVIST MINDSET IN DISNEY'S *MOANA*

Christopher D. Foley

Despite Disney's widely publicized research into Polynesian cultures prior to the making of *Moana* (2016), the film was not without its vocal critics. Of particular concern to many Pacific Islanders has been the film's critical treatment of Maui, the great "culture hero" and trickster of pan-Polynesian mythologies. As Ida Yoshinaga has demonstrated, Maui's transformation over the course of the film's numerous stages of revision was both visual and characterological in nature. In addition to the troubling expansion of Maui's body type from "classically lean to comically large," which drew criticism for trafficking in "racist tropes of obese Polynesian bodies," Maui's character also "grew cruder as [he] became secularized" (Yoshinaga 2019, 190). He thus "devolved," in the words of dissatisfied critics, from "the cunning[,] justice-driven [, and] resourceful trickster of various Oceanic folklores" to an "insecure, fearful, narcissistic anti-hero[,] whom many Pacific Islanders labeled a 'buffoon'" (Yoshinaga 2019, 190; see also Ka'ili 2016a, "Goddess Hina").

From the perspective of comparative mythology, Maui might be the greatest culture hero the world has ever known (Westervelt 1910, vi–viii). Insofar as he is credited with stealing fire for the benefit of humans, he might be viewed as a Polynesian analogue to Prometheus from ancient Greek mythology. However, Maui is also celebrated for many other heroic feats and major discoveries beyond the theft-gift of fire. He is praised for harnessing natural elements such as the wind, sky, and sun; for introducing the production of staple crops such as yams, taros, and breadfruit; and for the invention of critical maritime technologies such as sails, fishing baskets, and fish hooks. He is also acclaimed for the discovery of new islands (McLeish 1996; Ka'ili 2016b, "Demigod Maui"). This broader and deeper heroic legacy highlights that Maui's geographic and cultural scope of significance to Polynesian peoples, stretching from New Zealand to Hawaii to Easter Island, greatly exceeds that of Prometheus. Furthermore, unlike any of the Greek or Roman gods, Maui is a living mythological figure who continues to play a central role in ways of life practiced by indigenous peoples throughout the Pacific Islands (Ka'ili 2016a, "Goddess Hina"). All of these considerations make Maui's imaginative transformation in Disney's 2016 fantasy film both profound and deeply problematic, especially from the perspective of Polynesian peoples who feel marginalized and exploited by *Moana* in its final form.

In this chapter, I propose that one way to contextualize the problematic changes that Maui's character underwent during the film's numerous stages of revision is to recognize the ideological connections between these changes and the film's evident ecological anxieties. Insofar as Moana's quest to restore Te Fiti's stolen heart is a race against impending environmental destruction, for Motunui and the entire world, the fantasy film's narrative resolution clearly reflects a wish-fulfillment of ecological restoration. Furthermore, despite the fact that the film ostensibly represents a preindustrial society, the long-term ecological consequences of Maui's theft arguably represent some of the most dire threats humans face in an era of climate change and ocean acidification: the gradual blight of staple crops on which both traditional and modern societies rely for continued survival and the widespread extinction of fish and other forms of oceanic life. Building on Brian Attebery's claim that fantasy narratives in literature and film enable modern audiences to reconnect to the cognitive structures transmitted by myths and the "worlds they generate" (2014, 9), I argue that the re-visionary critique of Maui's cultural and environmental legacy in *Moana* functions as an imaginative interrogation of both the anthropocentric benefits and the Anthropocenic consequences of combustion technologies developed since the dawn of the Industrial Revolution. Such an interrogation raises important considerations regarding the central, if also uneven, role that fire and technologies of combustion have played in the historical and geological onset of the so-called "Anthropocene." In probing the film's critical and, at times, contradictory treatment of Maui's mythically inspired cultural legacy, I also draw upon Patricia Yaeger's critical concept of an "energy unconscious" (2011) in order to demonstrate that the film's ecofeminist critique of Maui's "heroic" legacy doubles as a critique of the extractivist mindset fundamental to both carbon-based capitalism and colonialism as global systems originating in Western Europe. Perhaps most importantly in the context of this volume, attending closely to the film's contradictory and ultimately problematic treatment of Maui's mythic legacy also (re) orients us to questions that continue to confront contemporary audiences, artists, and scholars as we attempt to collectively imagine and enact a transition to sustainable energy infrastructures in an era of accelerating climate change, sea-level rise, and ocean acidification.

Maui, Myth, Fantasy

In the downtime following their adventurous escape from the Kakamora, Moana and Maui resume their frequent topic of debate: the trickster demigod's ambivalent cultural and environmental legacy within the imaginative world of the film. Despite Maui's androcentric assumption of self-importance—as in "Little girl, I am a hero"—Moana interprets his legacy quite differently from an ecological perspective: "Maybe you were a hero," she suggests, "but now … you're just the guy who stole Te Fiti's heart [and] cursed the world" (Musker and Clements 2016, 50:06–50:16). While the film clearly shares Moana's ecofeminist perspective on the destructive legacy of Maui's larcenous mineral extraction, it also credits Maui with two thefts, not just one. In addition to stealing Te Fiti's heart, of course, Maui has also stolen "fire from down below" (39:20–39:23).

Like the many other accomplishments catalogued in Lin-Manuel Miranda's contagiously catchy song, "You're Welcome," Maui's theft of fire from the underworld clearly *has* improved the lives of humans. It is also a transgressive act for which Maui escapes divine vengeance, a notable departure from the origin myth(s) upon which this element of the film's backstory is based. The film's double-vision regarding Maui's two thefts cues examination of the film's engagement with Maui's mythic record, especially as it concerns the origins of anthropogenic fire. If fantasy narratives in literature and film offer contemporary audiences "a way of re-connecting to traditional myths and the worlds they generate" (Attebery 2014, 9), *Moana*'s reworking of Maui's mythic legacy highlights Anthropocenic anxieties central to the film, including a growing uneasiness about our dependence on fossil fuel extraction and related combustion technologies.

The prospect of analyzing salient connections between Disney's filmic representation of Maui and the oral tradition of Maui's mythological feats in Polynesian cultures is a fraught one, given the uneven economic and creative control mediating the "collaboration" between the Disney Story Trust and the Oceanic Story Trust that Yoshinaga has critiqued (2019, 201–4). Substantial evidence does suggest, however, that *Moana*'s creators drew particular inspiration from the Maori myth concerning Maui's descent into the underworld and his interactions with the "guardian of fire," Mahuika. Here is a textual version of the myth, as recorded by W.D. Westervelt:

> Maui's mother decided that he should go to the under-world and see his ancestress, Mahuika, the guardian of fire … [As he departed, Maui's mother] warned him against attempting to play tricks upon the inhabitants of the lower regions.

> Maui gladly hastened down the cave-path to the house of Mahuika, and asked for fire for the upper-world. In some way he pleased her so that she pulled off a finger nail in which fire was burning and gave it to him. As soon as he had gone back to a place where there was water, he put the fire out and returned to Mahuika, asking another gift, which he destroyed. This he did for both hands and feet until only one nail remained. Maui wanted this. Then Mahuika became angry and threw the last finger nail on the ground. Fire poured out and laid hold of everything. Maui ran up the path to the upper-world, but the fire was swifter-footed. Then Maui changed himself into an eagle and flew high up into the air, but the fire and smoke still followed him. Then he saw water and dashed into it, but it was too hot. Around him the forests were blazing, the earth burning and the sea boiling. Maui, about to perish, called on the gods for rain. Then floods of water fell and the fire was checked. The great rain fell on Mahuika and she fled, almost drowned. Her stores of fire were destroyed, quenched by the storm. But in order to save fire for the use of men, as she fled she threw sparks into different kinds of trees where the rain could not reach them, so that when fire was needed it might be brought into the world again by rubbing together the fire sticks.

> (1910, 74–5)

That *Moana*'s creators drew inspiration from this myth in particular is evident in a number of key moments in the film. First, the visual representation of Maui's theft of "fire from down below," which is tattooed on his stomach during the "You're Welcome" episode, portrays the trickster demigod in the underworld with a female deity who clearly resembles Mahuika. At the moment Maui makes off with fire from the altar over which she presides, this female deity's flaming fingernails are extinguished (Musker and Clements 2016, 39:18–39:24).

The myth of Maui and Mahuika also apparently informs the film's visual representation of Maui's attempt to escape with Te Fiti's stolen heart. In Gramma Tala's opening tale, Maui attempts to escape from the "Mother Island" by transforming himself into a hawk. As in the myth of Maui and Mahuika, despite his transformation into a bird of prey, Maui is vengefully pursued by "smoke and fire." In *Moana*, this pursuit assumes the shape of Te Kā, a so-called "demon of earth and fire" (02:20–03:18). If we read the film's double-vision concerning Maui's two thefts against this contextual myth of Maui and Mahuika, *Moana* evidently displaces both Mahuika's attempted retribution against Maui and the environmental apocalypse threatened by her divine vengeance from Maui's first theft of "fire from down below" onto his second theft of Te Fiti's luminous green "heart." In so doing, the film's "energy unconscious" posits anthropocentric extraction and combustion of fossil biomass as the principal ecological threat haunting the imaginative world of the film and its contemporary audiences.

Patricia Yaeger first introduced the concept of an "energy unconscious" in her 2011 *PMLA* editor's column, which helped to frame the emergence of the energy humanities as a field of scholarly inquiry. Drawing inspiration from both Pierre Macherey and Fredric Jameson, Yaeger suggested that literary texts such as Kerouac's *On the Road* (1957) might reveal historically and culturally situated resource anxieties through their representations of crucial textual absences "'around which a real complexity is knit'" (Macherey 1978, 101, cited in Yaeger 2011, 306). Following Yaeger's brief but provocative line of inquiry, how might we read *Moana* as a narrative field in which contradictions and conflicts between energy-driven modes of production play out? In the context of this diachronic comparison between Maui's mythic record and its appropriative adaptation in Disney's fantasy film, the latter's attempted evasion of geopolitical responsibilities and erasure of geopolitical class-conflicts attending the extraction and expenditure of fossil fuels worldwide are particularly relevant.

Despite the fact that *Moana* purports to represent a preindustrial indigenous society, its "energy unconscious" reflects the film's contemporary petrocultural origins in the Global North. This energy unconscious operates on multiple levels: visual, metaphorical, and structural. First and foremost, Maui's ecologically destabilizing theft of Te Fiti's "heart" is represented as an act of mining. Using his ability to shapeshift, Maui transforms himself into a series of increasingly smaller animals in order to make his way into the cavernous interior of the "Mother Island." Once he has entered the cavernous interior, he digs into the side of the mountain with assistance from his phallic fishhook in order to extract the luminous green mineral (Musker and Clements 2016, 01:30–02:20). Second, the "life draining away from island after island," which Gramma Tala identifies as an environmental consequence of Maui's mineral extraction, is viscous and black. Environmental "life"-blood in the film thus bears a remarkable resemblance to crude oil, both visually and behaviorally, as it skims the surface of the ocean. This outgoing flow of oily liquid, which clearly saps Motunui of its ecological vitality, is directly linked to the blight of the island's coconut groves and to its dramatically declining fish population (26:14–26:54). These twin threats posed to human societies in the film are strongly suggestive of climate change and ocean acidification, both of which are fueled by the extraction and burning of fossil biomass worldwide—especially by, and in the economic interests of, transnational corporations headquartered in the Global North.

Traumatic traces of the film's energy unconscious are also implied in Moana's nightmarish vision, which imaginatively enacts the threat of ecological destruction facing Motunui if Te Fiti's heart is not restored. After making unexpected landfall on her home island, Moana places her hand on a palm tree as she gazes out upon Motunui. The palm tree immediately begins to disintegrate into a gray-and-black substance, which first resembles charcoal and then coal ash as it continues to crumble. Moana then hears the voices of her parents, who rush toward her pursued by an apocalyptic tidal wave, which also appears to be composed of coal ash. Just before the tidal wave engulfs her parents completely, Moana awakens from her nightmare (53:26–54:10). As these examples illustrate, at nearly every moment that environmental devastation is visually and narratively represented in *Moana*, it assumes the haunting shape of exhumed, exhausted, and environmentally degradative fossil fuels.

Furthermore, although the film leaves no doubt that Maui's larcenous resource extraction has brought the world to the brink of environmental catastrophe, Gramma Tala's opening tale also suggests that Maui is not the only male character who views Te Fiti's heart through this ecologically catastrophic lens (01:20–1:40). The film's monstrous male characters—i.e., the Kakamora and Tamatoa—likewise seek to "possess" the luminous green heart through acts of piracy or conspicuous consumption. Even Hei Hei's remarkable devolution from a cunning trickster figure to the least intelligent animal sidekick in the Disney catalogue can be read from this interpretive angle (Yoshinaga 2019, 189–90). The "silly" rooster's mechanical bobbing for food, especially in his repeated attempts to consume an inedible rock, bears an uncanny resemblance to the mechanical bobbing of an oilfield pumpjack (Musker and Clements 2016, 12:45–13:15).

In addition to critiquing the ecological consequences of male attitudes toward the natural world, *Moana* also suggests how self-destructive this mindset is to men themselves. This is particularly evident in the film's climactic recognition scene. Convinced he must distract Te Kā so Moana will have time to restore Te Fiti's heart, Maui is evidently willing to engage in one final, suicidal act of warfare against his perceived nemesis, the so-called "lava monster." Only Moana's climactic epiphany that Te Kā and Te Fiti are the same female deity—and that the film's perceived villain, therefore, is no villain at all—saves Maui from his courageous but tragically wrong-headed intentions at this moment (1:26:54–1:28:14).

Once Moana recognizes that Te Kā is actually Te Fiti, she instructs the ocean to "let her come to me." As the ocean literally parts before her, Moana's song "Know Who You Are" communicates a sense of gendered interpersonal identification and empathy between the film's two most important female characters, an element that underscores the film's thematic ecofeminist framework (Kongwattana 2018; Ambarwati, Setiyawan, and Ihsan 2018). Prior to restoring the heart, Moana and Te Kā share a hongi, the traditional Maori greeting in which two people touch their noses together. While the hongi is not represented as an exclusively female act in the film, it does feature prominently in Moana's dramatic exchanges with her mother and grandmother as they voice support for her journey toward self-actualization. The film thus suggests that the harmony between humans and the natural world may be restored by recognizing and literally embracing the interdependence of all beings on earth, as Moana and Te Kā/Te Fiti do when they share a hongi (Musker and Clements 2016, 1:28:14–1:29:58). Through its explicitly gendered contrast between Moana and Maui at this epiphanic moment of recognition, the film intimates that Maui's "heroic" determination to solve the environmental problems his theft has created would not work. Even more pointedly, the film suggests that any proposed solutions to our current ecological crisis which double down on the androcentric logic of (capitalist) possession, (imperialist) conquest, and (militaristic) destruction could only prove suicidal.

One of the film's producers, Osnat Shurer, revealed in a 2016 interview with Buzzfeed News that despite the countless variations of the narrative that *Moana*'s creators workshopped, one of the guiding visions for the storyline was always that "what we [the audience] perceive as the villain of the film is actually 'nature wronged'" (Flaherty 2016). Shurer further communicated that this foundational vision for the narrative was inspired by the Disney Story Trust's on-site research in Polynesia: "It ties back to everything we learned when we spent time in the [Pacific]

Islands ... that our relationship with nature is the key, honestly, to our lives" (Flaherty 2016). While the film's creators thus appear genuine in their environmental and cultural sympathies, the imaginative and narrative encoding of these inspirational ideas for consumption by Western audiences proves particularly problematic at the intersection of environmental ideals and gendered indigeneity. In its representation of admirable female characters such as Gramma Tala and Moana, who share close bonds with the non-human world and the ocean in particular, the film celebrates and also reinscribes entrenched Western associations between indigenous women and "Nature." As a number of ecofeminist scholars have demonstrated, however, Western patriarchal associations between women, especially indigenous women, and "Nature" have long inspired the mutual subjection and exploitation of (indigenous) female bodies and the nonhuman world (Garrard 2012, 26–30). Furthermore, insofar as the film critiques white Western andro-extractivist systems through its representation of indigenous and mythological Polynesian masculinity, its critique is not only blunted but problematically displaced. It has not been indigenous Polynesian men but those from Western Europe and the Global North more broadly whose andro-extractivist logic and its resultant systems of social and environmental exploitation, from colonialism to industrial capitalism to globalization, have brought the world to the brink of ecological catastrophe in the twenty-first century. In *Moana*'s explicitly gendered critique of Maui, therefore, the film skirts the unevenly shared geopolitical responsibilities and burdens of living in an era of era of accelerating climate change, sea-level rise, and ocean acidification. Highlighting these inequalities has been a key driver in scholarly debates concerning the efficacy and fairness of the "Anthropocene" as an everyone-is-equally-guilty signifier for our current geological era.

Debating the "Anthropocene"

As suggested above, the film's imaginative bifurcation of the mythic origins of anthropogenic fire—of the benefits it has bestowed on humans on the one hand, and of the combustion technologies developed since the dawn of the Industrial Revolution on the other—raises important considerations regarding the central, if also uneven, role that fire and combustion technologies have played in the onset of the Anthropocene. Highlighting the fact that anthropogenic emissions of carbon dioxide and methane from the Industrial Revolution onward are recorded geologically in ice core samples taken from Greenland and Antarctica, Paul Crutzen and Eugene Stoermer first proposed the designation of the "Anthropocene" in 2000. Since their seminal proposition, scholars have debated two key aspects of their thesis: (1) the temporal origins of the newly proposed geological period under consideration and (2) the linguistic appropriateness of the term itself, which suggests that humans as a species have ushered in a new geological era en masse.

Concerning the temporal origins of human beings as geological agents, several scholars have called attention to the fact that anthropogenic changes to the environment—including greenhouse gas emissions—have occurred for as long as humans have been able to cultivate fire on demand. Andrew Glikson, for example, has postulated three stages of the Anthropocene: (1) the "Early Anthropocene," which began approximately two million years ago, from which time the earliest possible evidence of fire usage by *H. Ergaster* dates; (2) the "Middle Anthropocene," marked by the development of extensive domestic agricultural endeavors, enabled by the large-scale burning of surface biomass; and (3) the "Late Anthropocene," which commenced with the onset of the Industrial Revolution and combustion of fossil, rather than surface, biomass. In Glikson's estimation, neither the "Middle" nor "Late" stages of the Anthropocene are likely to have occurred without the advent of anthropogenic fire (2013, 91). Environmental historian Stephen J. Pyne has gone so far as to suggest that the "Pyrocene" might be the most appropriate signifier for this geologically revolutionary era, which in his estimation stretches back not only to the "pyric transition" of the Industrial Revolution but all the way back to "that Promethean moment" when humans first acquired the power to cultivate fire at will. As the collective owners of a "species monopoly" over fire on a fire-prone planet, Pyne argues, humans have transitioned with relatively little resistance from "cook[ing] meat" to "cook[ing] landscapes" to "cook[ing] the planet" in an astoundingly brief period of geologic history (2015).

Uncannily, many anthropogenic fire myths register an awareness of the revolutionary and even potentially apocalyptic shift in the balance of power relations between humans, the gods, and the natural world that ensues with the advent of anthropogenic fire. Prometheus' theft-gift of fire, for example, upset the balance of power between gods and humans as well as between humans and the natural world. It resulted, on the one hand, in the human consumption of choicest animal meats and, on the other, in the divine retribution of Pandora's box for human beings, in addition to the punitive binding and torture of Prometheus himself (Hamilton 1942, 85–93). In the Maori myth of Maui and Mahuika, Maui's mischievous attempt to obtain fire from his ancestress in the underworld nearly results in the pyro-apocalyptic destruction of the Earth by the vengeful Mahuika. The description of that near-environmental apocalypse—"the forests were blazing, the earth burning, and the sea boiling"—resonates with contemporary dystopian visions of our own Anthropocenic future (Westervelt 1910, 75).

Despite the temptation to universalize anthropogenic fire and its environmental consequences, however, it is also crucial to recognize that fire itself—like so many mythic pyro-genitors—is a "shapeshifter" (Pyne 2015). Not all fuel sources burn equally, nor are the environmental consequences of divergent anthropogenic fire practices equal in magnitude or severity. Consider the fact that it took roughly 6,000 years for anthropogenic concentrations of atmospheric CO_2 to increase from ~260 ppm to ~280 ppm by the mid-eighteenth century. Since the Industrial Revolution, however, in a span of less than 300 years, concentrations of atmospheric CO_2 have increased from ~280 ppm to more than ~400 ppm (Glikson 2013, 91). Energy use is "uneven," in other words, in the context of human history and world geography (Yaeger 2011, 307). Indeed, as Pyne has acknowledged elsewhere, there are actually "two grand realms of combustion" throughout the globalized world today: one in which the burning of fossil biomass predominates and the other in which the burning of surface biomass still prevails (2009, 445). The "crude" geographic division between these two realms of combustion roughly approximates the Brandt line dividing the Global North from the Global South. In other words, not all "anthropoi" have contributed equally to the "genesis" of this new geologic epoch. Ongoing scholarly debates about the linguistic appropriateness of the signifier "Anthropocene" highlight this important fact. Alternative signifiers that have been proposed by Donna Haraway and others, such as the "Plantationocene" and "Capitalocene," seek to highlight the fact that the anthropogenic changes driving the rapid acceleration of both greenhouse gas emissions and biodiversity loss across the globe have been caused by exploitative social systems, namely, Western capitalism and colonialism (Haraway 2015, 159–60). These systems have privileged a select few, predominantly white human beings through the immiseration and exploitation of the nonhuman world and of the vast majority of other, predominantly non-white human beings.

Reckoning with Climate Justice

If we eschew the "Anthropocene" signifier for our current geologic epoch in favor of the "Capitalocene" or the "Plantationocene," the unfairness—and general inefficacy—of *Moana*'s imaginatively laying the sins of our current ecological and geological state-of-existence at Maui's feet becomes self-evident. Not only have indigenous Polynesian peoples contributed far less climate-changing carbon dioxide and methane to the earth's atmosphere during the past 300 years than those in the Global North, but Kiribati, Tuvalu, and Vanuatu are among the island nations most vulnerable to the threat of sea-level rise in the coming decades (Spears 2014; Mellino 2016). The creators of *Moana* do appear to have grappled with the threat of sea-level rise in Polynesia insofar as the "island itself had to be pulled back up" from beneath the ocean's surface in a number of workshopped resolutions to the film's quest narrative (Flaherty 2016). However, the film in its final form has also been critiqued for evading and even deflecting from contemporary indigenous climate- and environmental-justice concerns, such as the ongoing opposition of indigenous groups to the further development of techno-scientific and petro-industrial infrastructures in contested territories like Hawaii, the Dakotas, and South Texas (Yoshinaga 2019, 192; Collier 2019).

Additionally, as both Yoshinaga and Tēvita O. Ka'ili have argued, the corporate film-making process that Disney deployed for *Moana* arguably reimposed the extractivist logic the film ostensibly critiques. Given the uneven creative control and economic power dynamics operating between the Disney Story Trust and the Oceanic Story Trust, Yoshinaga's eviscerating critique concerning the corporatized mechanisms of "symbolic expropriation" at work via Disney's neocolonial capitalist machinery is certainly valid (2019, 188–9). Ka'ili has argued along similar lines that Disney's omission of the companion goddess Hina from the film contributes to the loss of gendered symmetry and harmonious gender balance so characteristic of Polynesian myths and other arts forms. Such a loss is particularly significant in light of the film's overriding binaristic framework for articulating its contemporary ecological anxieties. For Ka'ili, this loss is not merely aesthetic. It is also cultural and spiritual—so much so that Ka'ili frames the film's omission of Hina as a "form a colonial erasure[,]" which places Disney's "mining of Polynesian stories" on a par with other neocolonial extractivist industries (2016a, "Goddess Hina"). For these reasons, despite its imaginative interrogation of Maui's mythic record as a pyro-genitor and its evident Anthropocenic anxieties, *this* particular Disney film is in no position to subvert the extractivist logic that continues to drive the worldwide development of oil and gas projects in the interest of transnational corporations headquartered in the Global North.

The silver lining is that such vocal criticism has not been in vain. While the creative partnership between the Disney Story Trust and the Oceanic Story Trust was clearly not as socially or environmentally just as Yoshinaga, Ka'ili, and many other Pacific Islanders would have liked, Disney does seem to have responded to their criticism by improving the balance of creative power between the company's chief creative team and representatives of the Sámi people during the making of *Frozen 2* (2019). Although the collaborative dynamics operating behind the scenes remain obscured by the enforcement of non-disclosure agreements in consulting contracts, representatives of the Sámi people appear in published media accounts to be substantially more satisfied with the collaborative dynamics of *Frozen 2* than Pacific Islanders were with the collaborative dynamics of *Moana* (Last 2019; Fouche 2019). In light of the comparatively more egalitarian creative partnership between Sámi representatives and the Disney creative team in the making of *Frozen 2*, it is noteworthy that the origins of environmental disruption and dislocation in this latter Disney film are revealed to be the Kingdom of Arendelle's implementation of an extractivist, resource-grabbing development project—the dam—alongside King Runeard's act of genocidal aggression toward the indigenous Northuldra tribe, who had been living in harmony with the natural world as well as the residents of Arendelle up to that point. Compared to *Moana*'s problematic displacement of colonial guilt onto the figure of Maui, *Frozen 2* offers a more environmentally just narrative framework for audiences in the Global North to internalize. It intimates that true change with respect to our ecologically precarious state-of-existence will not be possible until those who have benefited—and continue to benefit—from historically implemented systems of social, racial, and environmental exploitation acknowledge that history of systemic exploitation. Only after making that acknowledgment can we begin to consider what "the next right thing" to do might be—for ourselves and for the planet.

References

Ambarwati, Susi, Radius Setiyawan, and Pramudana Ihsan. 2018. "Ecological Feminism Issues Depicted in *Moana*'s Screenplay by Jared Bush." *Tell Journal*, vol. 6, no. 2: 97–105.

Attebery, Brian. 2014. *Stories about Stories*. New York: Oxford University Press.

Bourne Jr., Joel K. 2019. "Coal's Other Dark Side: Toxic Ash that Can Poison Water and People." *National Geographic*. February 19, 2019. https://www.nationalgeographic.com/environment/2019/02/coal-other-dark-side-toxic-ash/

Buck, Chris and Jennifer Lee, dir. 2020. *Frozen 2*. Burbank, CA: Walt Disney Home Entertainment.

Collier, Kiah. 2019. "In Key Vote, Federal Regulators OK Controversial South Texas Gas Export Facilities." *Texas Tribune*. November 21, 2019. https://www.texastribune.org/2019/11/21/federal-regulators-ok-controversial-south-texas-lng-export-facilities/

Crutzen, Paul J. 2002. "Geology of Mankind." *Nature*, vol. 415: 23.

Crutzen, Paul J. and Eugene F. Stoermer. 2000. "The 'Anthropocene'." *Global Change Newsletter*, vol. 41: 17–18.

Dalby, Simon. 2018. "Firepower: Geopolitical Cultures in the Anthropocene." *Geopolitics*, vol. 23, no. 3: 718–24.

Flaherty, Keely. 2016. "'Moana' Almost Had a Very Different Ending." *Buzzfeed*. November 25, 2016. https://www.buzzfeed.com/keelyflaherty/moana-is-the-disney-princess-we-all-need-right-now

Foa'i, Opetaia and Lin-Manuel Miranda. 2016. "Know Who You Are." In *Moana: Original Motion Picture Soundtrack*. Burbank, CA: Walt Disney Records.

Foley, Stephen F. et al. 2013. "The Palaeoanthropocene – The Beginnings of Anthropogenic Environmental Change." *Anthropocene*, vol. 3: 83–8.

Fouche, Gwladys. 2019. "Disney's 'Frozen 2' Thrills Sámi People in Northern Europe." *Reuters*. November 29, 2019. https://www.reuters.com/article/us-film-frozen-2-norway-sami/disneys-frozen-2-thrills-smi-people-in-northern-europe-idUSKBN1Y318H

Garrard, Greg. 2012. *Ecocriticism* (2nd Edition). London: Routledge.

Glikson, Andrew. 2013. "Fire and Human Evolution: The Deep-Time Blueprints of the Anthropocene." *Anthropocene*, vol. 3: 89–92.

Hamilton, Edith. 1942. *Mythology*. New York: Little, Brown, and Company.

Haraway, Donna. 2015. "Anthropocene, Capitalocene, Plantationocene, Chthulucene: Making Kin." *Environmental Humanities*, vol. 6, no. 1: 159–65.

Hatmaker, Susie. 2017. "Coal Ash." In *Fueling Culture: 101 Words for Energy and Environment*, edited by Imre Szeman, Jennifer Wenzel, and Patricia Yaeger, 87–90. New York: Fordham University Press.

Ka'ili, Tēvita O. 2016a. "Goddess Hina: The Missing Heroine from Disney's *Moana*." *Huffington Post*. Last modified December 6, 2016. https://www.huffpost.com/entry/goddess-hina-the-missing-heroine-from-disney's-moana_b_5839f343e4b0a79f7433b6e5.

Ka'ili, Tēvita O. 2016b. "The Demigod Maui: Modern Day Lessons from Ancient Tales of Oceania." *Huffington Post*. Last modified December 3, 2016. https://www.huffpost.com/entry/the-demigod-maui-modern-day-lessons-from-ancient-tales_b_5788c6e7e4b0cbf01e9f8508.

Kongwattana, Pattarapong. 2018. "*Moana* (2016): Negotiating Patriarchy from the Ecofeminist Perspective." *Veridean E-Journal*, vol. 11, no. 4: 1076–90.

Last, John. 2019. "Hollywood Gets Indigenous Consultation Right in *Frozen 2*, Sámi Experts Say." *CBC News*. Last modified November 23, 2019. https://www.cbc.ca/news/canada/north/frozen-2-consultation-sami-1.5370801

Macherey, Pierre. 1978. *A Theory of Literary Production*. Translated by Geoffrey Wall. London: Routledge.

McCormick, Kristen and Michael R. Schilling. 2014. "Animation Cels: Preserving a Portion of Cinematic History." *Conservation Perspectives: The Getty Conservation Institute Newsletter,* vol. 29, no. 1. Accessed January 2, 2020. https://www.getty.edu/conservation/publications_resources/newsletters/29_1/animation.html

McLeish, Kenneth. 1996. "Maui." In *Bloomsbury Dictionary of Myth*. Accessed January 7, 2020. https://search.credoreference.com/content/entry/bloommyth/maui/0

McMahon, Xandra. 2019. "This CU Boulder Teacher Consulted on 'Frozen'—And Was Sworn to Secrecy." *CPR News*. Accessed April 22, 2020. https://www.cpr.org/2019/12/22/this-cu-boulder-teacher-consulted-on-frozen-and-was-sworn-to-secrecy/

Mellino, Cole. 2016. "Meet the World's First Climate Refugees." *Ecowatch*. January 5, 2016. https://www.ecowatch.com/meet-the-worlds-first-climate-refugees-1882143026.html

Miranda, Lin-Manuel. 2016. "You're Welcome." In *Moana: Original Motion Picture Soundtrack*. Burbank, CA: Walt Disney Records.

Musker, John and Ron Clements, dir. 2016. *Moana*. Burbank, CA: Walt Disney Home Entertainment.

Pyne, Stephen J. 2009. "The Human Geography of Fire: A Research Agenda." *Progress in Human Geography*, vol. 33, no. 4: 443–6.

Pyne, Stephen J. 2015. "The Fire Age." *Aeon Magazine*. May 5, 2015. https://aeon.co/essays/how-humans-made-fire-and-fire-made-us-human

Spears, Stefanie. 2014. "Disappearing Islands: How Sea Level Rise Impacts Communities." *Ecowatch*. November 13, 2014. https://www.ecowatch.com/disappearing-islands-how-sea-level-rise-impacts-communities-1881969930.html

Topel, Fred. 2016. "*Moana* Directors Talk the Film's Influences and Fun References." *Den of Geek*. November 21, 2016. https://www.denofgeek.com/movies/moana-directors-talk-the-films-influences-and-fun-references/

Vaughan, Hunter. 2019. *Hollywood's Dirtiest Secret: The Hidden Environmental Costs of the Movies*. New York: Columbia University Press.

Westervelt, W. D. 1910. *Legends of Maui: A Demigod of Polynesia, and of His Mother Hina*. Honolulu: The Hawaiian Gazette Co., Ltd.

Yaeger, Patricia, Laurie Shannon, Vin Nardizzi, Ken Hiltner, Saree Makdisi, Michael Ziser, and Imre Szeman. 2011. "Editor's Column: Literature in the Ages of Wood, Tallow, Coal, Whale Oil, Gasoline, Atomic Power, and Other Energy Sources." *PMLA*, vol. 126, no. 2: 305–10.

Yoshinaga, Ida. 2019. "Disney's *Moana*, the Colonial Screenplay, and Indigenous Labor Extraction in Hollywood Fantasy Films." *Narrative Culture*, vol. 6, no. 2: 188–215.

CHAPTER 25
FINDING BALANCE AND HOPE IN THE INDIGENOUS PAST
David Bowles

When the Spaniards first looked down at Tenochtitlan, that gleaming city on an island in the Valley of Mexico, they were dumbfounded. Hundreds of thousands of people lived in that metropolis, crisscrossed with canals, burgeoning with chinampa gardens that seemed to float on the water, cleaner and more efficient than any European city. A careful system of dual dikes kept brackish water out. Human waste was efficiently recycled.

Such careful integration of humans and environment isn't surprising in hindsight. At the heart of Aztec (and more broadly, Nahua) thought was the importance of balance between chaos and order, creation and destruction. That duality was personified in the two brother gods of creation: the trickster Tezcatlipoca and the savior Quetzalcoatl.

It took the gods five tries, the Aztecs believed, to get the world right, to find an equilibrium between the needs of hungry, greedy humans and the biosphere. Four times the experiment had been a disaster. The world had ended in darkness, in floods, ravaged by winds, scoured by flame. Even this fifth attempt, they suspected, would one day fall as well, wracked by earthquakes as humanity digs deeper and deeper into the bedrock.

That perspective and all its attendant trappings—the stories and rituals and sacred songs—were systematically destroyed by the Spanish, replaced with the arrogant sense of ownership of the world so typical of Christian Europe.

But bits and pieces of the Nahua worldview survived. The children and grandchildren of the conquered discovered they could use the alphabet of their conquerors to record the old ways, the old words.

And, as a distant inheritor of that tradition, diffused by time and the genetic blending we call mestizaje, I seek to take that desperate final cry, scrawled in alien letters but in the clear tongue of the ancestors, and transmit it to modern audiences. In translations. In retellings. In original stories and books rooted in that powerful indigenous tradition.

Because sometimes hope can only be found looking backwards.

Sometimes, to reimagine our future, we must remember our past.

Sometimes the problem lies not with the technology, but with the cultural and philosophical underpinnings of the ways in which we use it.

Sometimes, the ancestors whisper, to build something better, you must tear down what presently exists.

No creation can happen without raw materials.

Raw materials only come from destruction.

I want adults and children alike to immerse themselves in fictional worlds shaped by ancient Mesoamerica. I want them to be inspired to dig deeper and read English translations and adaptations of the voices that, against all possible odds, have survived to speak to us today.

Let my work be a conduit.
If that is all I ever do, I will be content.
I'm convinced there's no other way we survive.
The way of the conquerors? It has clearly failed us.

CHAPTER 26

REIMAGINING YOUTH RELATIONS WITH MOANANUIĀKEA (THE LARGE, EXPANSIVE OCEAN): CONTEMPORARY NIUHI MOʻOLELO (MAN-EATING SHARK STORIES) AND ENVIRONMENTAL ACTIVISM

Caryn Lesuma

Hanauma Bay Nature Preserve is a marine conservation district on the island of Oʻahu in Hawaiʻi, home to dozens of species of native fish and coral. It is also the most popular tourist snorkeling destination in the state, and its 3,000 visitors per day has resulted in significant coral trampling, water pollution, and damage to fish populations despite state efforts at preservation (Severino et al. 2020, 8–9). After closing in mid-March of 2020 as a result of public health efforts to limit transmission of the novel coronavirus, Hanauma Bay became part of a study by the Hawaiʻi Institute of Marine Biology to measure the effects of human presence at the site. The results are revealing: by August, researchers' preliminary data found that the water in the Bay is 42 percent clearer than before the closure (Serota 2020). That such significant environmental damage is occurring even in a conservation district underscores a need—long overdue—for increased protections for Hawaiʻi's beleaguered shores and marine areas. Unfortunately, decades of government bureaucracy and unbridled tourism, the state's primary economic driver, have resulted in ignored warnings from the scientific community and, more importantly, the Indigenous Kānaka Maoli, or Native Hawaiian community.

Unfortunately for Hawaiʻi, the voices of Kānaka Maoli urging the return of sustainable practices and environmental protections that were in place prior to the overthrow of the Hawaiian Kingdom in 1893 have largely been ignored by the American settler state; as a result, overfishing, pollution, coral bleaching, shoreline erosion, and sea-level rise continue to intensify in the region, even as the number of tourists each year rises.[1] This state of affairs is the result of what Kyle Powys Whyte calls "industrial settler campaigns" that continuously disrupt and destroy Indigenous lands and erase traditional relationships among humans, animals, and the environment (2017, 207).

In Hawaiʻi, industrial settler campaigns have contributed to Anthropocenic environmental damage that has disrupted Kānaka Maoli relationships to land, ocean, and ever-dwindling native species. For Kānaka youth, these same campaigns have prevented access to ancestral knowledges, practices, and moʻolelo—a Hawaiian ancestral narrative form that articulates cultural values and operates across the range of functions which in Western narrative categories include, but are not limited to those of "story, tale, myth, history, tradition, literature, legend, journal, log, yarn, fable, essay, chronicle, record, article, minutes, as of a meeting" (Pukui and Elbert 1986, 254).[2] As a result, Brandy Nālani McDougall has called for the enactment of "ola

(i) na moʻolelo," or "living moʻolelo," as a method to "decolonize by reconnecting with ancestral moʻolelo and continuing to create our own moʻolelo" in order to imagine new realities into being (2016, 4). Using McDougall's framework, I examine two Indigenous moʻolelo written by Kānaka authors that imagine relationships between mythical figures and contemporary humans in order to address environmental damage to the ocean caused by settler colonialism. Both Bryan Kamaoli Kuwada's short story "All My Relations" and Lehua Parker's YA trilogy The Niuhi Shark Saga portray contemporary Indigenous youth and their interactions with niuhi, beings feared in ancestral moʻolelo as sentient, shape-shifting sharks that often hunt and eat humans. Through an analysis of how Kuwada and Parker's "new" moʻolelo adapt and transform early written versions of niuhi moʻolelo, I argue that the human–niuhi relationships in the stories imagine possibilities for a future where Kānaka youth learn to decolonize both themselves and others in order to be in good relations with the ocean and its inhabitants. These contemporary moʻolelo thus function as both promise and warning that caring for Moananuiākea—a Hawaiian term meaning large, expansive ocean—and restoring relationships among species and ecosystems cannot be achieved without also disrupting ongoing environmental depredations caused by settler colonialism.

Indigeneity and the Anthropocene

In order to analyze how contemporary Kānaka Maoli writers are imagining possibilities for environmental rehabilitation, it is important to understand Indigenous conceptions of the Anthropocene. For Indigenous peoples, the Anthropocene is more than an impending environmental collapse as a result of human activity. It is a current reality that has been going on since the arrival of settlers hundreds of years ago:

> The environmental impacts of settler colonialism mean that quite a few indigenous peoples in North America are no longer able to relate locally to many of the plants and animals that are significant to them. In the Anthropocene, then, some indigenous peoples already inhabit what our ancestors would have likely characterized as a dystopian future.
>
> (Whyte 2017, 207)

Rather than imagining bleak dystopic futures as a way to explore or warn about current environmental practices, many indigenous peoples are already living in what they consider to be an environmentally devastated post-apocalyptic world. As Grace Dillon asserts, "The Native Apocalypse, if contemplated seriously, has already taken place" (2012, 8). Cultural practitioner Hiʻilani Kawelo explains that for Kānaka Maoli:

> The ʻāina [land] allows us to maintain a reciprocal connection. For some people, that connection has been severed completely … people don't have opportunities to connect with the ocean and fisheries because they don't have a place to practice. Second, I'm also talking about cultural disconnection … Some people don't even know what it is that we still have.
>
> (2014, 168)

This dissolution of traditional relationships between humans and the environment is a key marker of Indigenous dystopia, attributed by Whyte to generations of forced relocation, habitat destruction, species extinction, and settler educational campaigns that have historically erased Indigenous languages and cultural knowledges (Whyte 2017, 208).

Whyte argues that the current dystopian realities of Indigenous lives is a result of what he terms "industrial settler campaigns," defined as actions by settler states that

> *both* dramatically changed ecosystems … *and* obstructed indigenous peoples' capacities to adapt to the changes … Indeed, settler industrial campaigns paved the way for industrial and capitalist collective actions whose ecological footprint contributes significantly to today's climate destabilization ordeal.
>
> (209)

In Hawai'i and the Pacific, settler industrial campaigns began as missionary agendas, lucrative trading, and plantation industries—including whaling, sugar, and pineapple—with "all of these old and oppressive exploitations, now transformed into tourist destinations and military bases … We know that all of this consumption produces dire effects on the land, air, and even this great sea" (Osorio 2015, 214). In other words, considering the Anthropocene without explicitly acknowledging the effects of settler colonialism on the environment erases the ongoing dystopic realities of many Indigenous peoples, most notably "the particular systems of interdependent relationships of humans, nonhumans, and ecosystems that matter to many indigenous peoples" (Whyte 2017, 213).

For Indigenous peoples, then, environmental activism cannot be successful without also reckoning with the legacy and impact of industrial settler campaigns. Kwaymullina and colleagues explain that hopes for "science" or "technological innovation" to solve issues surrounding environmental collapse are ultimately hollow: "Rather, it will be human beings embracing a different way of relating to the environment than the current dominant paradigm that sees people take too much, too often" (2012, 7). Dillon emphasizes the importance of rejecting the "accelerating effect of techno-driven western scientific method" in favor of "Indigenous scientific literacies," or "practices used by Indigenous peoples over thousands of years to reenergize the natural environment while improving the interconnected relationships among all persons (animal, human, spirit, and even machine)" (7). In the Pacific, Tongan scholar 'Epeli Hau'ofa declared of Indigenous Pacific Islanders that "there are no people on earth more suited to be guardians of the world's largest ocean than those for whom it has been home for generations" (2008, 38). According to Kanaka Maoli scholar-activist Jonathan Kay Kamakawiwo'ole Osorio, this can only be accomplished by restoring reciprocal relationships among ancestors, descendants, 'aumākua—meaning family/personal gods—land, sea, and the rest of the world: "We cannot make a future for ourselves that does not provide for all of those relations" (2015, 215). These arguments indicate that, despite an ongoing Anthropocenic dystopia, Indigenous scholars and practitioners believe that environmental intervention and rehabilitation are possible through restoring relationships and replacing settler industrial campaigns with Indigenous practices.

I will be analyzing contemporary moʻolelo through this Indigenous framework of the Anthropocene; in addition to exploring possibilities for conservation and marine rehabilitation, the stories must also be understood as written from within an existing dystopia where relationships between humans, animals, and ecosystems have been lost as a result of settler colonialism.

Indigenous Storytelling as Rehabilitation

The ways that Indigenous peoples view the Anthropocene reflects their conceptions of time, which have a direct effect on contemporary storytelling. Grace Dillon asserts that "viewing time as pasts, presents, and futures that flow together like currents in a navigable stream is central to Native epistemologies" (Dillon 2016, 345). Because of this, Indigenous oral histories and ancestral stories contain invaluable information about conservation practices in specific locales as well as histories of relations between humans and the environment. It also means that these stories are as relevant today as they were prior to the arrival of settlers. Dillon underscores the importance of the forms of knowledge in these stories: "Indigenous scientific literacies represent practices used by Indigenous peoples over thousands of years to reenergize the natural environment while improving the interconnected relationships among all persons" (2012, 7).

In Whyte's Anishinaabe community, repairing relationships between humans and the environment is accomplished through the sharing of ancestral stories that explain the history of those relationships (2017). Understanding how species are related and interact within a specific ecosystem allows contemporary Indigenous peoples to reject the erasure caused by industrial settler campaigns in order to "learn from, adapt, and put into practice ancient stories and relationships involving humans, nonhuman species, and ecosystems to address today's conservation challenges in the Anthropocene" (Whyte 2017, 213).

In Hawai'i, Kānaka Maoli storytellers also see a connection between ancestral narratives and contemporary responsibility. Brandy Nālani McDougall explains the layered meaning of her composite term "ola (i) nā moʻolelo" as "'ola nā moʻoleloʻ (the moʻolelo live) and ʻola i nā moʻoleloʻ (Live the moʻolelo, or live because of the moʻolelo), intended to recognize how we live moʻolelo and how moʻolelo live through us" (McDougall 2016, 3). McDougall's framework for telling and retelling ancestral moʻolelo emphasizes the responsibility of Hawaiian storytellers to "decolonize by reconnecting with ancestral moʻolelo and continuing to create our own moʻolelo, for when they are repeated over and over, allowed to live on our tongues and in our bodies, they will grow in mana, and become true by the power of belief" (4). For Kuwada, creating and sharing contemporary moʻolelo allows writers to "breathe not only our mana, but our possibilities into these moʻolelo, and give the readers and listeners a chance to see not only what has been, but also what could be" (Kuwada 2010, 116–17). For Kānaka Maoli storytellers, retelling ancestral moʻolelo and creating new, "living" moʻolelo are as much about conveying culture and ideas as they are about personal action and responsibility to act on that knowledge.

Throughout contemporary Oceania, Indigenous writers have developed living moʻolelo by mixing oral literatures with Western forms such as novels, poetry, plays, and short stories. Michelle Keown states that this practice allows writers to "[explore] the relevance of Pacific oral traditions to contemporary sociopolitical realities" (2007, 179) in an effort to "combine these traditions with contemporary motifs and energies in order to free ancestral spirits and invite them into the modern world" (175). This meeting of ancestral and contemporary stories has been called "remythologizing." As Selina Tusitala Marsh explains it, remythologizing is a method in which

> writers draw upon the cultural weight embodied by a mythic figure and reimagine it within a contemporary environment; they both revitalize the myth and culturally invigorate it in the present day … Additionally, through reimagining, writers activate the space of cultural memory, creating contemporary parallels with archaic initiatory elements, demonstrating that culture is dynamic and open, rather than closed and static … When writers remythologise cultural figures they individually enact a collective remembering—and … remembering is key to identity.
>
> (2016, 263)

This is particularly prevalent in Young Adult fiction in Oceania, where remythologizing often occurs literally in narratives rather than metaphorically. In other words, writers for youth frequently place mythic figures within the mundane space of our contemporary world in order to rehabilitate the spaces that teens inhabit with Indigenous histories erased by colonial agendas.

The practice of creating living moʻolelo through remythologizing is apparent in both Parker's trilogy and Kuwada's story. In both, the past affects the present and implicates the future simultaneously, with opportunities for its teen characters to restore broken relationships between human and niuhi that in turn rehabilitate marine environments destroyed by industrial settler campaigns.

Niuhi Moʻolelo: Nanaue and Kaʻahupāhau

A niuhi is defined as a "man-eating shark … any Hawaiian shark longer than 3.5 m" (Pukui and Elbert 1986, 267). As feared inhabitants of the ocean, niuhi are described in a Hawaiian proverb as "He niuhi ʻai holopapa o ka moku. *The niuhi shark that devours all on the island*" (Pukui 1983). Mary Kawena Pukui's interpretation of this proverb defines niuhi as "a powerful warrior. The niuhi shark was dreaded because of its ferociousness. It was believed that a chief or warrior who captured this vicious denizen of the deep would acquire something of its nature" (Pukui 1983). In ancestral moʻolelo, niuhi are often portrayed as akua or kupua—gods or demigods—able to shapeshift between human and shark form.

In this section, I will briefly summarize the two niuhi moʻolelo that are remythologized by Parker and Kuwada in order to better establish points of convergence and departure. It is important to note that in antiquity, moʻolelo were told orally, and the same story usually has multiple versions depending on the context of its telling, including place, politics, and storyteller. Kānaka Maoli call this practice of multiple narratives makawalu—literally, "eight eyes"—and place high cultural value on this multiplicity because it "allows for multiple levels and new insights of understanding" (hoʻomanawanui 2014, xl). Because of this, I have chosen well-known versions that, based on their story details, are most likely the versions that Parker and Kuwada build upon in their moʻolelo.

In her English-language version of the moʻolelo "The Shark-Man, Nanaue," Emma Nakuina conveys the story of Nanaue, a half-human, half-niuhi child conceived of a human mother and the shark-god Kamohoaliʻi. Because Nanaue would be raised on land with his human family,

[Kamohoaliʻi] particularly cautioned the mother never to let him be fed on animal flesh of any kind, as he would be born with a dual nature, and with a body that he could change at will. In time Kalei was delivered of a fine healthy boy, apparently the same as any other child, but he had, besides the normal mouth of a human being, a shark's mouth on his back between the shoulder blades.

(Nakuina 1907, 257)

After being given meat by a doting grandfather during his childhood, Nanaue develops an insatiable appetite that culminates in an obsession with human flesh. He indulges his craving by luring villagers into the water, changing into his shark form, and devouring them.

After being caught and spared punishment through the intervention of his father, Nanaue is banished from the island. Unable to resist his desire to eat humans, Nanaue resumes his murdering on another island, where he is relatively unknown. Ultimately, however, he is captured in his shark form and killed by the people of Molokaʻi.

The second moʻolelo tells a story of the shark-goddess Kaʻahupāhau. Pukui translates and interprets a well-known proverb about Kaʻahupāhau as follows: "Hoʻahewa na niuhi ia Kaʻahupāhau. *The man-eating sharks blamed Kaʻahupāhau.* Evil-doers blame the person who safeguards the rights of others. Kaʻahupāhau was the guardian shark goddess of Puʻuloa (Pearl Harbor) who drove out or destroyed all the man-eating sharks" (Pukui). Samuel Kamakau identifies Kaʻahupāhau as a sister of Nanaue's father Kamohoaliʻi, who in this version establishes a kanawai, or law, "that no shark must bite or attempt to eat a person in Oahu waters" (1964, 73). She and another brother, Kahiʻukā, enforced the kanawai when visited in Puʻuloa by niuhi who desired to eat humans. A battle ensued in which Kaʻahupāhau and Kahiʻukā were victorious, ensuring the safety of humans on the island from niuhi.

The moʻolelo of both Nanaue and Kaʻahupāhau underscore the fraught relationships between humans and niuhi even in antiquity, and the laws created to protect them from each other. The niuhi played an important role in imbuing humans with a healthy respect for the ocean. In the section that follows, I examine contemporary remythologizations of these Nanaue and Kaʻahupāhau moʻolelo that explore possibilities for rehabilitating human–niuhi relations after several hundred years of estrangement. Parker's story is built on the moʻolelo of Nanaue, while Kuwada bases his on Kaʻahupāhau and the niuhi of Puʻuloa.

Contemporary Remythologizations of Nanaue and Kaʻahupāhau

The Niuhi Shark Saga

Lehua Parker's young adult trilogy The Niuhi Shark Saga (2016a, 2016b, 2019) is a remythologization of the story of Nanaue. While Nanaue is no less dead in Parker's narrative than he is at the end of Nakuina's moʻolelo, the fallout from his human-devouring indiscretion creates the primary conflict in the story: readers learn midway through the series that Nanaue's actions resulted in the severing of all human–niuhi relations and prompted a decree from Kanaloa, the primary akua of the ocean, that "no male Niuhi-human is allowed to live. After Nanaʻue we all accepted the kapu [taboo or prohibition]" (Parker 2016b, 22). Accordingly, Parker's trilogy centers around Nanaue's contemporary male cousin, a teenager named Zader Westin who is the illicit child of a niuhi mother and a human father. To prevent his detection by Kanaloa and the other niuhi, Zader is raised on land and taught that he is allergic to water and raw meat in order to keep him from reinforcing Nanaue's legacy. Of course, by the second book Zader learns the truth of his heritage and is given a chance to prove that he will not repeat the cycle, but only if he willingly chooses exile from his human family.

During his exile from Hawaiʻi, Zader learns about his niuhi nature and refines his ability to transform into a shark. As part of his niuhi education, he is taken to various ocean locales throughout the world. Visiting water off the coast of Thailand that is subject to extensive dynamite fishing, Zader describes the experience from a shark's point of view:

> Falling into this water was like falling into a grave. Bitterness and death flooded my gills. I could taste gunpowder and spark as I tried to clear my throat ... Frantic, I started to swim as fast as I could, darting in every direction, looking for good water in an ocean of bad. Exhausted, I surfaced near the buoy and changed back to my human shape, floating on my back and sucking warm, wet air into my lungs in relief.
>
> (Parker 2016b, 169)

Experiencing the degradation of the world's oceans as a niuhi gives Zader purpose and motivation for ocean-based activism. Using his talent as an artist, he begins to create art that draws attention to the environmental degradation caused by settler industrial campaigns throughout the world. The art is installed inconveniently and guerrilla-style, often overnight, and provides humans with a niuhi's view of what is happening beneath the water, reflecting Zader's conviction that "people have to decide for themselves that the ocean is worth preserving. They have to understand the damage they're doing" (170). Zader's activism targets a broad range of developments, including "a drilling platform off the coast of Texas; an ocean-front seawall near a Mexican resort; a retaining wall in a new California development—each image detailed the costs to marine life and to the planet of the waste, pollution, run-off, and devastation happening in the ocean right in front of them" (201).

Importantly, Zader's activism is only possible because, through his actions and heritage, he is able to repair the relationship between humans and niuhi that had been severed by Nanaue generations before. He admits to himself after completing his exile and returning to his human family, "I'd figured out how to bridge the Niuhi and human world" (251). For Zader, the reestablishment of good relations between niuhi and humans is a prerequisite to both his familial reconciliation and his environmental activism. As an individual able to exist as both human and niuhi, Zader's newfound dual identity gives him the power to resist industrial settler campaigns affecting the ocean. As he tells his niuhi birth mother, "We Niuhi understand how important our oceans are ... We know because we see ... Humans live on land—they can't know what we know unless we tell them" (253). Parker's moʻolelo believes that the determination and talents of Kānaka Maoli youth are great enough to meet the contemporary challenges facing our oceans. Zader's story illustrates the importance of restoring relationships and heritage in order to combat industrial settler campaigns that are a major cause of environmental damage.

"All My Relations"

Unlike Parker's optimistic portrayal of repaired relationships and effective activism, Kuwada's short story "All My Relations" functions more pessimistically as a warning that underscores the consequences of choosing to perpetuate industrial settler campaigns. The story is narrated by an unnamed niuhi, whom we discover midway through the story was one of the sharks defeated by the shark-goddess Ka'ahupāhau and her brother Kahi'ukā at the battle of Pu'uloa and forced to abide by the law against eating humans. Kuwada remythologizes the story by ironically pointing out how Ka'ahupāhau and Kahi'ukā were ultimately betrayed by an industrial settler campaign brought on by the humans they had fought so hard to protect:

> After their victory, they declared that no shark shall eat human flesh in the seas around O'ahu ever again. And do you know how your chimp forebears repaid that boon? Your leaders built a military base on their home ... no one has seen Ka'ahupāhau or Kahi'ukā since the base was constructed.
>
> (Kuwada 2017, 106)

While the niuhi narrator continues to abide by the ancient mandate despite the disappearance of the divine pair, he has only been able to do so by maintaining his human form and satisfying his desire for flesh with the fish that he hunts via spearfishing.

The centuries-long broken relationship between niuhi and humans is apparent when the niuhi meets a human child after one of his dives. When the boy addresses him as "uncle," a term of respect and good relations for all adult males in local culture, the niuhi is both offended and disgusted, thinking, "As if we could be related. I am a glorious kupua, a niuhi even. A ravening killing machine, sending your ape-descended ancestors into the never-ending night. Leaving their entrails to twist in the salty currents of the sea. I am the tax your people pay for living by the shores of the great Moananuiākea" (104). He softens, however, when he senses a fearlessness in the boy, whose "eyes glitter as he eyes my spear, maybe even a spark of hunger. Once more, I look him over, with an appraising eye, not as meat, but as something else ... perhaps this boy is a hunter too" (107). In a reversal of honorifics, the niuhi ironically nicknames the boy "Uncle," and the interaction generates a delicate alliance that surprises even the niuhi, who offers to teach the boy spearfishing and continues to mentor him in sustainable fishing practices over the course of several months.

As the boy grows and his skill improves, the niuhi struggles with the relationship on several levels. He initially questions his judgment when Uncle acts too much like a human child, thinking, "Regret surges for my lapse yesterday. What was I thinking? This wet paper bag a *hunter?*" (107). As time progresses, however, the niuhi admits that "Uncle's a quick study" (109) and, later, "I watch him appraisingly ... maybe he is more of a hunter than I thought" (111). Despite his appreciation of Uncle's potential as a hunter, the niuhi feels an additional strain on their relationship as a result of human destruction of the marine environment. Speaking directly to the reader, the niuhi's tone is accusatory:

You idiot bone-sacks have killed so much reef and habitat with your sunscreen and your dumping and messed up the food chain with your long-liners and overfishing. You know what pisses me off even more though? You don't even eat the fish yourself. You send it off for other people far from here to eat. There is no justice in that.

(Kuwada 2017, 109)

Here, the niuhi directly links industrial settler campaigns to environmental degradation, clearly struggling to separate Uncle from the rest of the humans who have perpetuated the damage. This struggle is exacerbated by Uncle himself, who, against the wishes of the niuhi, consistently catches more fish than he needs for his family so that he can sell them to purchase fancy diving gear and an expensive underwater camera. The niuhi becomes more and more frustrated with Uncle over time, admitting that "I sometimes think he doesn't understand why we do this. Why we hunt for our food ... I mean that there is a responsibility to being in the ocean, swimming in the salt blood of this planet. There is a weight to being predator or prey, and it is something you gut-bags have forgotten" (112). Despite the time he has invested in teaching Uncle, the niuhi fails to see any meaningful attitudes or actions from Uncle that indicate he understands the responsibilities that come with the knowledge he has been gifted.

Ultimately, Uncle's desire for money and fame unravels the tenuous relationship that he has developed with the niuhi. The final straw comes when Uncle chooses to hunt and kill another shark for sport, with the sole purpose of recording footage for his successful monetized YouTube channel, where he "posts dive footage set to local reggae music and gives dramatic recounting of how he speared his fish" (112). When Uncle ignores the niuhi's directives and chooses to kill the shark, he effectively severs their relationship. Enraged, the niuhi thinks, "It was a mistake to think one of you could be anything more than meat ... *Uncle*. As if we could be related. I say the ritual words. Then I feast" (114–15). With his refusal to observe sustainable fishing practices, Uncle commits a crime that the niuhi views as serious enough to justify violating the centuries-long law against eating humans.

Unlike Parker, in "All My Relations" Kuwada questions the ability of today's youth to rise to the challenge of learning sustainable practices that will protect the marine environment. The moʻolelo likewise questions whether youth who have been immersed in contemporary consumer and social media culture are capable of decolonizing and assuming responsibility for resisting industrial settler campaigns. According to this view, Uncle's demise is an inevitable outcome that functions as a warning for both adults and youth that without significant individual decolonization, even Indigenous peoples can perpetuate the Anthropocenic apocalypse by participating in settler industrial campaigns.

Conclusion

While "All My Relations" is not explicitly a young adult narrative like The Niuhi Shark Saga, both stories benefit from being read through what Petrone and colleagues call a Youth Lens, which "provides a way for readers to examine representations of youth within texts and a way to explore how these representations function as a part of cultural discourses of adolescence/ts that carry larger ideological messages" (Petrone et al. 2015, 511). Both stories portray their adolescent characters as "symbolic placeholders," which Petrone and colleagues explain occur frequently in literature written by adults about youth: "Adolescence often functions as a discourse surrogate for broader social, political, and/or nationalistic agendas and concerns. For example, common discourses of youth as 'the hope for the future,' or, alternately, as problems to worry over, exemplify how adolescence takes on symbolic meanings" (510). In the context of Indigenous youth in the Anthropocene, the young age of both Zader and Uncle represents the key role that the rising generation will have to play in restoring ancestral relationships and dismantling settler industrial campaigns. For Parker, Zader and his youth compatriots undoubtedly symbolize hope that they will be up to the task, while for Kuwada, Uncle's capitalistic tendencies reveal a concern that contemporary youth are unequipped to intervene in the Anthropocenic apocalypse.

I assert that both perspectives are valid and should be interrogated closely by all adults working to involve Indigenous youth in environmental and decolonial activism. As Kwaymullina and colleagues explain:

> In the context of children's literature and ecology the idea of sustaining environmental and cultural awareness is shared via the written word—how it is used, presented, and read, particularly with ideas of the child reader in mind. Our children will be the ones who struggle with the ripples we leave in our wake and they will be the ones who count the cost of our decisions as they in turn make decisions for the generations that will follow them. If we teach the right values then the behaviour of our children will reflect those ideas. In the Aboriginal way it's about getting the story right, so that they can learn the right ways to be.
>
> (2012, 7)

Through their contemporary moʻolelo, Parker and Kuwada set expectations for Indigenous youth intervention in the midst of an ongoing Anthropocenic apocalypse. Both narratives remythologize ancestral moʻolelo in order to emphasize the dual importance of restoring reciprocal relationships with local ecosystems and replacing settler industrial campaigns with sustainable Indigenous practices. While Parker's narrative expresses confidence that our youth can successfully rise to the challenge of decolonization in order to restore relations with the plants and animals in their environments, Kuwada leaves us with a sobering warning against becoming too entrenched and/or complicit in settler colonial systems of thought and action. Living moʻolelo like these offered by Parker and Kuwada can thus help both youth and adult readers to interrogate their own relationships to the Anthropocene in order to imagine and then create a just environmental future for our beloved Moananuiākea.

Notes

1 In January 2020, the last month before visitor counts dropped due to the Covid-19 pandemic, 862,574 visitors arrived in Hawaiʻi, a 5.1 percent increase from the previous year. The number of total tourists in the islands at any one time was estimated at around 269,421 (Yamane and Chun 2020, 1).

2 The ability of moʻolelo to serve so many purposes makes it a valuable tool for conveying information and cultural knowledge. Kuwada explains that "a common understanding of 'moʻolelo' is as a succession of talk, which often gets read as a reference to the way stories and knowledge were passed

down through the Hawaiian oral tradition" (2010, 109). In addition to carrying culture through story, as noted by Kaiwipunikauikawēkiu Lipe, moʻolelo can also be used "to learn, teach, connect, and make sense of the world" when applied as an "engaged practice and methodology for teaching and learning" (54).

References

Dillon, Grace. 2012. "Imagining Indigenous Futurisms." In *Walking the Clouds: An Anthology of Indigenous Science Fiction*, edited by Grace Dillon, 1–12. Tucson: University of Arizona Press.

Dillon, Grace. 2016. "Native Slipstream: Blackfeet Physics in *The Fast Red Road*." In *The Fictions of Stephen Graham: A Critical Companion*, edited by Billy J. Stratton, 343–56. Albuquerque: University of New Mexico Press.

Hauʻofa, Epeli. 2008. *We Are the Ocean*. Honolulu: University of Hawaiʻi Press.

Hoʻomanawanui, kuʻualoha. 2014. *Voices of Fire: Reweaving the Literary Lei of Pele and Hiʻiaka*. Minneapolis: University of Minnesota Press.

Kamakau, Samuel Manaiakalani. 1964. *Ka Poʻe Kahiko: The People of Old*, edited by Dorothy B. Barrere, translated by Mary Kawena Pukui. Honolulu: Bishop Museum Press, 1964.

Kawelo, Hiʻilei. 2014. "Fishponds, Food, and the Future in Our Past." In *The Value of Hawaiʻi 2: Ancestral Roots, Oceanic Visions*, edited by Aiko Yamashiro and Noelani Goodyear-Kāʻopua, 163–70. Honolulu: University of Hawaiʻi Press.

Keown, Michelle. 2007. *Pacific Islands Writing: The Postcolonial Literatures of Aotearoa/New Zealand and Oceania*. Oxford: Oxford University Press.

Kuwada, Brian Kamaoli. 2010. "Finding Mana in the Mundane: Telling Hawaiian Moʻolelo in Comics." *Anglistica*, vol. 14, no. 2: 107–17.

Kuwada, Brian Kamaoli. 2017. "All My Relations." In *Pacific Monsters*, edited by Margrét Helgadóttir, 104–15. San Bernadino, CA: Fox Spirit Books.

Kwaymullina, Blaze, Brooke Collins-Gearing, Ambelin Kwaymullina, and Tracie Pushman. 2012. "Growing up the Future: Children's Stories and Aboriginal Ecology." *M/C Journal*, vol. 15, no. 3: 7.

Lipe, Kaiwipunikauikawēkiu. 2016. "Moʻolelo for Transformative Leadership: Lessons from Engaged Practice." In *Kanaka ʻOiwi Methodologies: Moʻolelo and Metaphor*, edited by Katrina-Ann R. Kapāʻanaokalāokeola Nākoa Oliveira and Erin Kahukawaikaʻala Wright, 53–71. Honolulu: University of Hawaiʻi Press.

Marsh, Selina Tusitala. 2016. "'Nafanua and the New World': Pasifika's Writing of Niu Zealand." In *A History of New Zealand Literature*, edited by Mark Williams, 359–73. Cambridge: Cambridge University Press.

McDougall, Brandi Nālani. 2016. *Finding Meaning: Kaona and Contemporary Hawaiian Literature*. Tucson: University of Arizona Press.

Nakuina, Emma. 1907. "The Shark-Man, Nanaue." In *Hawaiian Folk Tales*, edited by Thomas G. Thrum, 255–68. Honolulu: A. C. McClurg & co.

Osorio, Jonathan Kay Kamakawiwoʻole. 2015. "All Things Depending: Renewing Interdependence in Oceania." In *Huihui: Navigating Art and Literature in the Pacific*, edited by Jeffrey Carrol, Brandy Nālani McDougall, and Georganne Nordstrom, 210–16. Honolulu: University of Hawaiʻi Press.

Parker, Lehua. 2016a. *One Shark, No Swim*. 2nd ed., United States: Makena Press.

Parker, Lehua. 2016b. *One Truth, No Lie*. United States: Makena Press.

Parker, Lehua. 2019. *One Boy, No Water*. 5th ed., United States: Makena Press.

Petrone, Robert, Sophia Sarigianides, and Mark A. Lewis. 2015. "The Youth Lens: Analyzing Adolescence/ts in Literary Texts." *Journal of Literacy Research*, vol. 46, no. 4: 506–33.

Pukui, Mary Kawena. 1983. *ʻŌlelo Noʻeau: Hawaiian Proverbs and Poetical Sayings*. Kindle. Honolulu: Bishop Museum Press.

Pukui, Mary Kawena and Samuel H. Elbert. 1986. *Hawaiian Dictionary*. Honolulu: University of Hawaiʻi Press.

Serota, Nathan. 2020. "Research Chronicles Improved Conditions at Hanauma Bay during Closure." Honolulu: City and County of Honolulu.

Severino, Sarah J. L., Kuʻulei S. Rogers, Yuko Stender, and Mathew Stefanik. 2020. *Hanauma Bay Biological Carrying Capacity Survey: 2019–20 2nd Annual Report*. Honolulu: University of Hawaiʻi Institute of Marine Biology.

Whyte, Kyle Powys. 2017. "Our Ancestors' Dystopia Now: Indigenous Conservation and the Anthropocene." In *The Routledge Companion to the Environmental Humanities*, edited by Ursula K. Heise, Jon Christensen, and Michelle Niemann, 206–15. New York: Routledge.

Whyte, Kyle Powys. 2018. "Indigenous Science (Fiction) for the Anthropocene: Ancestral Dystopias and Fantasies of Climate Change Crises." *Environment and Planning E: Nature and Space*, vol. 1, no. 1–2: 224–42.

Yamane, Marisa and Jennifer Chun. 2020. "Hawaiʻi Visitor Statistics Released for January 2020." Honolulu: Hawaii Tourism Authority.

CHAPTER 27
THE FUTURE THAT HAS YET TO BE IMAGINED
Shaun Tan

I recently completed a collection of short illustrated stories, *Tales from the Inner City*, about animals living in alternative urban realities: bears with lawyers, rhinos on freeways, crocodiles inhabiting the upper floors of skyscrapers—images that have been haunting my imagination for many years, finally driven into ink and paint, somewhere between artistic obsession and critical inquiry. I suppose that on reflection the book has a number of environmental messages, but they are somewhat indirect and unconscious, as I think is necessary in any good story or painting. That is, I've never been very good at producing creative work which tackles a theme or agenda from the outset (I've tried often and failed often!) I realize that the best thing is to write and paint first, ask questions later. So rather than any grand meditation on the Anthropocene and its anxieties, I typically begin with very small and specific objects with unclear meaning, often just odd or amusing. That said, it doesn't take long for deeper anxieties to shine through.

For example, an orca floating in the sky over an urban sprawl. I had no idea what this fairly spontaneous mental image was about until I sat down to write, draw, and paint, as if struggling to recall a dream and wrangle some meaning out of it:

> We took the orca from the sea and put it in the sky. It was just so beautiful up there, so inspiring. But the calls of the mother never stopped. From a cold and foreign sea, her subsonic wavelength penetrated all concrete, steel and urban clamour, reverberated through pipes and sewers, kept us awake all night and broke our hearts. We knew we had done something unforgivable. We promised to set things right. But so many years have passed, and the mother is still calling out. So many years have passed and the orca is still in the sky. We just don't know how to get it down.

It was only later when reviewing the documentary *Blackfish*, about the sad circumstances of an orca named Tilikum at Seaworld, taken from its mother as a calf, psychologically damaged and unable to be returned to its natural habitat, that I realized the connection with my own story, or at least a common anxiety borne of that reality: one where humans routinely interfere with the natural world and then have great trouble restoring it to an original state. We do have a bad habit of embarking on ambitious projects without an exit strategy, in war as much as environmental conquest. Living in Australia, a country with the world's highest rate of extinction, largely due to a plethora of introduced species that seemed like a good idea at the time (again, without any exit strategy), I'm particularly mindful of this. Obviously a documentary like *Blackfish*, which in itself might be called a work of art braced by critical imagination and insight, has great power to effect change. And indeed, the film resulted in a profound shift in popular opinion and legislative action relating to orcas in captivity and other activities of theme parks.

But what can works of fiction do? Particularly the kind of work that I pursue, surrealist fantasy, usually seeded by dreamlike images. Can they enact change in a world that desperately needs it? Or do they just float above, like a lost fictitious orca, a light entertainment? The honest answer is that I'm not sure. But I do know that all things begin in the imagination: every action, innovation, and transformation that has occurred in the world first began in someone's imagination. And long before that, in a deeper realization that such imagination is even possible. That we are living in one of many alternative universes, that nothing is inherently "normal," and that history is replete with fantastic twists and turns, dramatic changes in conception, revolutionary understandings.

When I think about the future that I can so far imagine for my two young children, a world of unsustainable obsessions fueled by appalling leadership and public ignorance, I feel quite fearful and pessimistic. But what gives me hope is *the future that has yet to be imagined*. When I write and paint, I feel optimistic. I feel doors opening up, opening to things not yet known or thought about, I feel oxygen flowing in. I feel more intelligent, empathetic, and inventive. I hope that my young readers—and for some reason my books, perhaps because of their accessibly illustrations, find those readers first—take that point to heart before all other considerations of theme, meaning, or authorial intention: that it is possible to imagine previously unimaginable things, and that this world is, indeed, just one of many possible realities, and changeable. But in the first instance we need to understand the strange ways in which it has been so deeply transformed by human action and misguided desire, at an emotional as well as cognitive or scientific level, and perhaps dreams and fantastical stories have some place here, as they have for the many troubled generations before us.

Plate 27.1 Orca in the sky, *Shaun Tan*

Plate 27.2 Eating local, *David Wiesner*

Plate 27.3 Hope and curiosity, *Kate Samworth*

Plate 27.4 Hope sails far, *Pavel Čech*

PART IV
PLAYING WITH FIRE

CHAPTER 28
ANTHROPOS AND THE FIRE
Brian Attebery

Fire was Anthropos's friend because Child of Man had Fire inside. Child knew this because Fire danced like Child. Fire sang to itself as Child did when Child was happy. Fire was always hungry. And Fire, like Child, was a source of heat. When Child made a mistake and sat down in the snow one time, the snow melted to water underneath.

Before Child found Fire, Child often went without food because roots could not be eaten raw. Child was cold in the night, especially after Child sat in the snow and got all wet on the bottom. The night was full of beasts that Child was afraid of. But with Fire burning, there was plenty to eat, it was warm, and the beasts stayed outside the circle of light, their eyes glittering with frustration.

If Child had Fire inside, maybe other things did too. Water was so cold and shapeless. If Child could find Fire inside it, maybe Water would be friendlier. A little Fire would give Air more substance. Earth was dull and heavy, but maybe it hid a fiery heart. So Child went on a quest.

The first hidden Fire Child found was in Air. One wild, windy, stormy day, the clouds towered high and bumped up against each other. Where they rubbed, panels of cloud lit up from behind. The sky growled. Child thought clouds might be like rocks: when you strike them together, you get a spark that can remake a dead Fire.

There came a sudden flash and crash, so close together that it was hard to tell what was sight and what was sound. Child dropped to the ground and buried head in arms, ready to die. But once Child could hear again, Child heard crackling and roaring and overhead saw a tree in flames. The Fire in Air had set it ablaze. Child wanted to keep some of that fire though Child had nothing to put it in. But Child could watch for another storm and be ready next time.

Child wandered for many days looking for Fire in Earth. Far away Child spied a strange mountain with a plume of smoke near the top. Child walked to that mountain, and in a deep cleft in the rocks Child saw a red glow. Child found a way down into the cleft, where Child's feet started to burn and the air was rank with smoke and steam. Child could see Earth boiling red in its rocky basin. Child was carrying an earthen pot to catch Earth's Fire but the boiling Earth was too far down and the rocks all around were too hot to touch. So Child broke a branch from a dead tree to use as a firebrand. It didn't matter if Child couldn't get a potful of melted Earth; all Child needed was the Fire. The brand started to smoke and then caught Fire. Child ran all the way home and used the still-smoldering branch to light the hearth fire. So there was Earth's Fire safe.

Child couldn't find any Fire in Water. When Child tried to burn Water, the Fire just went out. Child was unhappy, so Child brought out wine Child had made from last year's grapes. It was cold, so Child warmed it up in a covered pot. Steam rattled the lid. Child uncovered it and saw water collected on the lid's underside. Child licked the water and it tasted strange and strong. Maybe this was Water's Fire. Child created a special pot where Child could boil and collect the Fiery parts of wine and soon had a small flask of it. Child poured a few drops on the coals and they burst into flame.

So there was Earth Fire in the hearth and Water Fire in a flask. Child waited for the next stormy day and went looking for trees that might have collected some of Air's Fire. A white streak split the Air overhead and struck a dry branch, which began burning fiercely. Child used another stick to knock the burning one down, and soon Child's stick was on fire as well, so Child left the branch on the tree and hurried back home with the torch held overhead.

It was time to bring them all together: Earth's Fire, Air's Fire, Water's Fire, and the Fire inside Child. Child stuck the torch into the already smoldering logs and then poured the whole flask of Water's Fire over it. "Here I am," Child said to the Fire. "I am like you, Friend Fire."

But the three Fires together were bigger than Child expected. Fire jumped from the hearth to the nearby brush and lit it. Child's home Fire spilled out and met the storm-caused Fire that was still burning in the forest.

The great Fire consumed everything in its path. As it ate up the fallen Child, Fire said to itself, "That was some strange-tasting tree." But Fire wasn't particular.

CHAPTER 29

CONVERT OR KILL: DISANTHROPOCENTRIC SYSTEMS AND RELIGIOUS MYTH IN JEMISIN'S BROKEN EARTH

Derek J. Thiess

Better known for his scientifically informed fiction such as *Jurassic Park*, Michael Crichton was also a well-known climate change denialist. Instead of adopting the Kyoto protocol, he argued, we should "establish twenty-first century policy mechanisms … [and] deal correctly with [the] complexity of non-linear systems" (Crichton 2005). His message was that "we can't predict the future, but we can know the present," meaning that we ought to focus our efforts on such pressing issues as AIDS or starvation. One of the more overlooked dimensions of such denialism is the misdirection from the environment as a global biological concern *to* social systems. This is an apologetic strategy. It divides the social system, with its history of colonial and racial violence, from the biological systems in which these histories exist. The end effect of the apologetic strategy is to delay action. For this very reason, it is important to pay attention to apologetics, especially apologetics that apply dominant Christian belief and symbology to environmental science. The very notion of the "system" has given way in some work to "speaking religiously" and in an overtly Christian manner about the sciences (see Latour, *Modern Cult*).[1] This chapter looks at a similar conflation of the social system and the biological in N. K. Jemisin's Broken Earth trilogy—one that leaves the reader within a recognizably Christian framework. This series has won praise from theorists of both social justice and the Anthropocene for its compelling story of a woman navigating exclusionary politics amidst a global disaster. Its main characters are powerful magicians who topple the political system that enslaves them, but then replace that system with their own magically transcendent one. These novels indeed create a disanthropocentric world and offer a powerful challenge to systemic racism. But they do so by privileging our society's dominant religious myths. In the process, ironically, they subvert their own disanthropocentrism and reinforce a Christian exclusionary religio-politics of seeing otherness—human and nonhuman—as monstrous.

The emphasis on systems, particularly in historical and social scientific work, has come to mean an inherently anti-individual, collectivist approach to situations in which multiple factors play a role in determining results. Hence, systemic racism involves complex interactions between historical, political, economic, and interpersonal factors that result in oppression. Systems are vital, dynamic processes of relational interactions that subsume the individual human or the scientific product within a web of influences that transcends humanity. Thus, the meaning of this inflationary term has been stretched taut, becoming nearly vacuous. In their introduction to *Posthuman Ecologies*, Braidotti and Bignall (2019) define systems as "emergent knowledge formations … whose processes are complex, relational, nonlinear, heterogeneous and heterogenetic, [which enable] a clearer vision of the 'three ecologies'—environmental, socioeconomic and subjective—of the posthuman condition" (14). The key to defining systems appears to lie in attaching modifiers, which no one seems to challenge critics to define. For the sake of clarity here, I will focus on "disanthropocentric" systems to reflect the demand for expanding perspective beyond the human in discussions of climate. And I will reference "complexity," because it has been used most openly in fields such as STS as a means to maintain the importance of religion in scientific, secular discussions (again, see Latour). The core of my argument is that decentering the human, dissolving it in transcendent systems both social and biological, has long been an apologetic strategy to maintain the centrality of religious myth within a wide array of discourses.[2]

Such systems both rely on inherited mythologies and themselves travel in myth creation, in the sense that their use may authorize belief. Crichton anticipates the mythic; his denialism and fiction demonstrate that the moment of hesitation created by the fantasist might also be used to create disbelief in climate change. As Brian Attebery (2014) puts it in the context of cultural appropriation, "Stripped of context and cultural valuation, the myth becomes a sort of paper currency that the writer is free to spend any way she chooses: to buy a few shivers, a little ready-made awe, or some deeply discounted spirituality" (131). However, it is easy to dismiss Crichton's false dichotomy between systems and individual suffering as overly conservative and perhaps regressive. Hence the focus, here, on Jemisin's work. In her popular trilogy, a hero journeys through an apocalyptic landscape in search of her daughter, taken by the father after he killed her son. This landscape, in which humanity had abused the Earth's resources enough that Earth gained sentience and now threatens humanity with seismic destruction, has led some to suggest the novels are about climate change. But as Jemisin herself explains in a series of tweets, climate is mere backdrop: "The characters face disaster, sure, but it's people. The disaster is people … Climate change is also a people disaster! But we don't generally think of it in those terms. We focus on the symptoms … not the system" (@nkjemisin, June 29, 2019). This authorial intervention ought to give us pause, particularly considering Crichton's statement above—the misdirection from climate to the suffering of people. But is Jemisin likewise instructing us to focus on the complex social systems that surround us to the neglect of the physical manifestations of something as mundane as climate destruction? And if so, is this an equally mythic authorization of (dis)belief?

There is of course a wide gulf between Crichton's statement and Jemisin's, as there is between their fictional portrayals of complex systems. As works of science fantasy, Jemisin's Broken Earth novels place scientific questions and myth within the same thought experiment. The protagonist Essun is an orogene who is able to magically control the stones and earth. On this fantastic continent named the Stillness, being an orogene—or the more derogatory rogga—immediately marks one as an outsider, a dangerous and inhuman entity to be feared and, when possible, controlled. It is the discovery that she passed her abilities to her son, for example, that prompted her husband to kill him. But the key is control. Orogenes are enslaved by The Fulcrum, an organization of orogenes overseen by the Guardians, those trained to control and direct the powers of the orogenes. The continuity of the Stillness, in fact, on a continent in which cities are regularly destroyed by the "evil Earth," has been accomplished by enslaving these people for millennia and using their powers to quell the virulent ground. The plot of the novels centers on Essun's escaping from these oppressive powers, finding her daughter, and ultimately ending the Seasons—the story's term for the regular seismic/climatic events that all but destroy civilization. The novels have rightly won a great deal of critical acclaim for "ask[ing] us to imagine the legacies of White American exploitation of peoples of color" and have taken the Hugo Award for best novel an unprecedented three times (Murphey 2018, 114).[5]

On their surface, then, these novels appear to effect the same misdirection that Crichton did—to shift our focus from climate and environment to the suffering of marginalized peoples. But of course, the situation is more complex than that. Kathryn Yusoff (2018) has praised Jemisin's trilogy as a poetic expression of what she terms a "Black Anthropocene." This is a powerful responsorial position, countering what she calls "white geology" and is necessary because

> The human and its subcategory, the inhuman, are historically relational to a discourse of settler-colonial rights and the material practices of extraction, which is to say that the categorization of matter is a spatial execution, of place, land, and person cut from relation through geographic displacement (and relocation through forced settlement and transatlantic slavery). That is, racialization belongs to a material categorization of the division of matter … into active and inert.
>
> (Yusoff 2018, 2)

The geological, as a product of the colonial endeavor, is not to be trusted as its taxonomies bear all the marks of colonialism, including its inherent dehumanization. To counter this mistrust, Yusoff calls for an "insurgent geology" in which the "inhuman can be claimed as a different kind of resource than in its propertied colonial form—a gravitational force so extravagant, it defies gravity" (100). Broken Earth, with its orogenes, its attention to the racialized divisions that accompany the colonial project of taxonomy, and the African American authorial hand that guides it would seem to grant the Black Anthropocene a fantastic mythopoesis.

Yet I want to offer a note of caution, not to the project of decolonizing our geologic perspectives, but rather, to the unguarded optimism for complex systems. Terms such as "complex" and "system," whose meanings are stretched taut at the outskirts of their application within the humanities and social sciences, seem to pervade criticism of the Anthropocene. The anthropological approach, which played its own role in the history of colonization, has good reason to eschew the biological (for instance, the legacy of "scientific racism") and traces of this avoidance may be found across the works of critics of the Anthropocene and fantasy writers who invoke it. Among the former, Jeffery Jerome Cohen (2015), for example, suggests that "by refusing our unnuanced taxonomies, by bluntly insisting upon a world in which its materiality is not mere substance awaiting human use, stone invites a more ethically generous mode of worldly inhabitance, a more capacious, disanthropocentric redefinition of a word that we have allowed to become impoverished, *alive*" (250). Even as it forges a concrete connection to Jemisin's stone-working orogenes, this statement also sounds remarkably similar to Yusoff's: give life to stone, because to categorize the inhuman has a racial, colonial history. In both Cohen and Yusoff, then, the prime mover of history must exist outside of human reckoning. In Yusoff's words, "The God's-eye view is inverted into a lithic-eye view to produce a geologic commons from below" (4). If we build our tower of history from stone, we may collectively, via the social system, find God in the great machine of time.

This postlapsarian analogy to disanthropocentrism, I would argue, is vital to tying these disparate strands of thought together. The tower built of stone represents the force greater than the reckoning of the human. This is a fitting image of the social (and perhaps even the discursive) system, but the postlapsarian also places the specifically disanthropocentric systemic approach within a Christian framework. This framework may be the ultimate point, because as stonelore from Jemisin's 2015 *The Fifth Season* tells us, "at the height of human hubris and might, it was the orogenes who did something that even Earth could not forgive: They destroyed his only child" (380). Orogenes are not merely slaves stifled by the oppressive forces of colonization and the geologic erasure of history. They are the "gods in chains," expressions of disanthropocentrism, especially as Essun returns the Earth's son, the moon, raising the proverbial rock for its resurrection and the salvation of the Earth itself. She may do this because she has access to the transcendent system, which in the case of these novels is the magical force of orogeny that subsumes all living things, including stone. Essun herself, however, is also a type (in the theological sense of the term, a figure in early scripture who anticipates a later figure, in this case, her more powerful self as a stone eater) as she sacrifices herself and another unborn child for her daughter, becoming an immortal. This similarity to Christian theology is a final reminder within these novels that "human beings, too, are ephemeral things in the planetary scale" (150). To seek the systems that surround and engulf us is to seek a transcendence that, in this context, resonates with dominant Christian mythologies.

My point here is that while Jemisin's fiction accomplishes a powerful disanthropocentric challenge to certain power structures, it essentially recreates a Christian passion narrative and a puritanical fear of the non-Christian countryside. The books thus grant Christian power structures a continuity that does not challenge the ruptures such institutions have created via apologetics for colonialism. The role of an overtly Christian perspective in the mythmaking process of fantasy, one which is tied historically to the colonial projects that a critic such as Yusoff indicates, is one that ought to be interrogated. Farah Mendlesohn (2008) offers a distinction between fantasy and sf in that "Fantasy, unlike science fiction, relies on a moral universe: it is less an argument with the universe than a sermon on the way things should be, a belief that the universe should yield to moral precepts" (5). To extend this analogy further, perhaps, than Mendlesohn meant it, while Crichton may be arguing with the order of things, Broken Earth is sermonizing. This sermon is very nearly a perfect example of the counter-Reformational credo, ne plus ultra, a reminder that the proper, moral focus of humanity should lie within the Earth and that the great magical systems that tie together all living things belong to God. The emphasis on these systems, even as it recapitulates a disanthropocentric perspective, leaves the reader with a story of transcendence that continues rather than ruptures Christian-centered religio-politics. If "people are the disaster," either in these novels or within the context of climate and the Anthropocene, then transcendent systems that resolve into exclusionary religious myths will do nothing to mitigate that disaster.

The Gods in Chains, the Ghosts in the Machines

At the center of the very deserving praise of the Broken Earth novels is their giving representation to identities largely overlooked by the fantastic. This includes considerations of race and ethnicity as well as sexualities, complex gender expressions, and national and cultural loyalties. These last especially occupy much of the exposition of the novel, as the characters encounter several comms, or communities, and explore the inclusions and exclusions that occur in each. But there is a nearly universal fear throughout of the orogene and their supposed alignment with the "evil Earth." Thus, religious divisions also feature in the story. Religion itself has a metonymic place as well—serving as Mendelsohn's sermon, in other words. Attebery, too, offers a kind of warning that "fantasy can serve as a neutral meeting point for differing worldviews and different understandings of religious myth—but only if we agree that what we are reading is fantasy, an agreement that breaks down at exactly the same points where consensus reality fails to hold" (141). As fantasy, this trilogy clearly offers a meeting point for several worldviews, and it would not be right to hold the religious apart from these other explorations. However, even as religion in these novels is part of their internal social system, not all constituent nodes within the systemic play the same role. In other words, a look at the religious myths of the Stillness world, before recontextualizing them with the kind of community enclave politics for which the novels are celebrated, offers a potentially different appraisal of those religious elements.

The setting of the novels is immediately recognizable as dystopic, though more specifically one might recognize it as a postlapsarian society. The very source of the fall is left ambiguous. A lorist recitation from *Fifth Season* (2015), for example, offers a picture of a time when "life and Earth, its father thrived alike" and in which "The people became what Father Earth needed, and then more than He needed. Then we turned on Him, and He has burned with hatred ever since" (115). A climatic disaster is mentioned in which humanity "poisoned waters beyond even his ability to cleanse, and killed much of the other life that lived on his surface" (379). In all these suggestions, the stepping outside the bounds of the natural systems of the world and dominating these systems are essentially a succinct description of the Anthropocene. However, this description quickly directs us back to a recognizably religious language: it was "at the height of human hubris" that the Earth's child was killed (380). This is only one version of an evolving origin mythology, but it sets the tone for an alignment of systemic and climatic catastrophe with what is clearly a Christian mythology.

I am not suggesting that these novels present an obvious transposition of Christian myths into a simplistic fictional world. Jemisin's complex world-building is a far cry from texts in which, as Attebery phrases it, "at moments where one would like to see [some]character depth or an ambiguous and ambivalent symbol, one gets, instead, a Sunday-school lesson" (166). The novels are intensely focused on character development, particularly that of their protagonist, who bears a different name at different stages of her life: Damaya/Syenite/Essun. In fact, *The Fifth Season* presents a kind of awakening for her, as three narratives coalesce: the young Damaya taken by the Guardians to train and serve as a Fulcrum Orogene, Syenite sent on a mission with the powerful Alabaster as a cover for forced breeding and who runs afoul of the powerful and violent Guardians; and Essun, living in secret until she must start a quest to find her kidnapped daughter amid the chaos of a new Season—a climatic/tectonic disaster. But this complex character development also comes with a kind of apotheosis. In a climactic moment in this first novel, Syenite and Alabaster are attacked by a Guardian assassin, and when Alabaster is incapacitated, Syenite accidentally destroys an entire city. Time slows as the Guardian's knife comes toward her heart and she has the realization: "*We are the gods in chains and this is not. Rusting. Right*" (Jemisin 2015, 263, original emphasis). Mistrusted for their power to manipulate the magic that runs through all things, the orogenes become a universal symbol of the fear behind societal exclusions as well as the violence of those exclusions.

It is not accidental that the orogenes are the mythical focus of the novel, that they embody the magical elements. When they become too powerful, through a magical transubstantiation that involves getting eaten a piece at a time by stone eaters, they become immortal stone eaters themselves. While they represent a people oppressed for their magical abilities, in the proximity of this magic to a hegemonic Christian mythology, they become even more complex characters. In this particular expression of myth, the Broken Earth novels seem to vacillate between a "way of laying claim to a more cultural position" and a "way of renouncing that privilege, of relinquishing the role of supposedly neutral observer and arbiter" (Attebery 2014, 192–3). Unfortunately, while the texts would seem to indicate that these mythic elements operate by the latter method, in the manner in which this mythology mingles with community politics, it nonetheless recreates the privileged cultural position of religious dominance. Before returning to this connection in the next section, it is worth highlighting moments in the second and third novels that both complicate and solidify the connection between their internal mythic system and Christian myth.

Once again the second novel, *The Stone Sky*, involves several story-lines moving around the continent of the Stillness and through millennia. The main parallel is between Essun, who joins a comm in which orogenes and "stills" coexist and must navigate local politics, and her daughter Nassun. Nassun travels with her father to Found Moon, befriending both Schaffa—Essun/Syenite's old Guardian who has lost much of his memory—and a stone eater intent on destroying the Earth. Of particular interest is that the origin myth of the Seasons is narrated by Essun's companion stone eater, Hoa/Houwha. This narrative explains how the Seasons originated from the "hubris" of a city named Syl Anagist, a massive civilization that has built a magical engine in order to solve their energy problems forever by exploiting the magic that the Earth itself produces. The important detail here is that while the subject of the experiment is energy, the manner of the narrative's critique is a mixture of a kind of anti-Enlightenment philosophy with a recognizable Babellian narrative. In an oft-quoted scene, Hoa explains that the colonial power of this civilization was such that:

> Syl Anagist's assimilation of the world had been over for a century before I was ever made; all cities were Syl Anagist. All languages had become Sylanagistine. But there are none so frightened, or so strange in their fear, as conquerors. They conjure phantoms endlessly, terrified that their victims will someday do back what was done to them—even if, in truth, their victims couldn't care less about such pettiness and have moved on.
> (Jemisin 2017, 210)

The length of that quotation is necessary, because so often critics shorten it to discuss only the fear of the conquerors. In the preceding narration, one finds the fall. All languages were one, until the fall.

The connection then is between the act of discursive (de)construction and the larger colonial project, and in the narrative's own diction one finds ready-made mythic tropes. As Hoa's team connects to the powerful obelisks ready to start the giant magical engine, already prepared to sabotage the experiment for what was done to their ancestors and themselves, they discover part of their system has been hijacked. As Hoa puts it, they "perceive the disruption first as a *ghost in the machine*" (336, emphasis mine). What has happened is that the Earth, which is sentient, has taken control of a section of the machine intent on redirecting it toward humanity. In response, Hoa and his team redirect the energy to an obelisk on the moon, the blast from which sends the moon out of orbit. In the wake of the "loss of his son" the Earth seeks a "cleansing fire" and brings the obelisks it controls crashing down in the first Season, known as the Shattering. There is a convergence, then, between the materialistic search for more energy—itself a driving engine of the Anthropocene—and the colonial endeavor that offers a powerful critique of both in our near destruction. This convergence also likely explains Jemisin's statement that the disaster in these novels "is people." Yet what lies outside of this critique is that very feedback loop, the ghost in the machine, or the books' magical system.

It is in the second novel that this system is most fully examined. Alabaster has used an obelisk and begun the process of transformation, his companion stone eater Antimony carefully taking communion with each piece of his body that becomes stone in order to grant him eternal life. Alabaster himself completes the process as he teaches Essun to use the magic present around them, so that she can bring the moon back to orbit. But it is the description of that magic itself that is of note, as Alabaster asks her to sess (perceive) the magic within his changing body. He tells her to sess for "something else, neither flesh nor stone. Something immaterial, and yet it is there for you to perceive. It glimmers in threads strung between the bits of him, crossing itself in lattices, shifting constantly" (2016, 101). This magic, which issues directly from the earth, is transcendent, beyond the realms of stone or of flesh. Orogenes are its priests. As Alabaster phrases it, "To make the earth move we put something of ourselves into the system and make *completely unrelated things* come out" (101). The system, that which transcends flesh and stone and makes mere nodes of them within its latticework, is the magically transcendent and Father Earth is its wellspring. Here the connection between disanthropocentrism and religiosity is most clear.

The connection between the mythical transcendent magic of this trilogy and Christianity is underscored in one final moment of irony. In *The Obelisk Gate* Alabaster offers a history lesson, reiterating the mythic origins of the Seasons in what was done to the Earth's son, but more specifically to the orogenes: "The stories say we're agents of Father Earth, but it's the opposite: We're his enemies. He hates us more than he hates the stills, because of what we did" (165). Although eventually convinced of this history, Essun initially dismisses it, "Like those weird cults that crop up from time to time. I heard of one that asks an old man in the sky to keep them alive every time they go to sleep. People need to believe there's more to the world than there is" (166). The humor in this passing reference makes the connection between the magical system and Christianity more tangible. It is possible to make more connections—Alabaster and John the Baptist, perhaps—but the examples quoted so far should suffice to suggest that the magical system of these novels resonates with Christian mythology. In other words, these texts reflect what Attebery suggests in the context of C.S. Lewis, that "fantasy can work as a sort of theological thought experiment" (70). And as the comparison to Lewis likely demonstrates, there is a long tradition of such engagement with Christian mythology. While Attebery also points out potential pitfalls to this engagement, namely, "being accused of trivializing religion" or of "getting it wrong," on its surface there is nothing problematic about drawing on Christianity in the creation of a fantastic magical system.

But herein lies this chapter's primary contention with much criticism of the fantastic: while Attebery, for example, rightly indicates the ways that fantasy may become a kind of contact zone for the meeting of fictional representations of myths, such criticism rarely places the myths of the colonizer at the center of its analysis. That is, it is absolutely vital to note the erasures and appropriations that occur when outsiders use myths rightly belonging to other cultures, particularly when those cultures have been the targets of colonialism and globalization. It is another thing altogether when fantasists become apologists for real-world religions. Adopting and incorporating the mythology of a religious system complicit in colonialism is fraught with dangers, not just of continued proselytizing, but also of re-entrenching the very divisions drawn in the colonial project. Thus, one more narrative operating in the background of these novels deserves analysis, particularly in the context of their candid exploration of racialized community politics.

"There Is a City"

The power of Jemisin's novels, as many have noted, issues from their direct engagement with Otherness and community politics. It is these politics, coupled with the earthly apocalypse of the seasons, that produce Yusoff's "God's eye view" from below. The characters in the Broken Earth trilogy transgress physical, social, and spiritual boundaries; they develop what Kinitra Brooks (2017) has referred to as the "larger societal anxieties through certain themes of disquieting interstitialities often referred to as monsters" (5). Particularly given the colonial background of the Niess—beings bioengineered to become tuners and ultimately the distant ancestors of the contemporary orogenes—themes of monstrosity play a central role in the larger societal exclusion of the orogenes. The texts tell us as much as they attempt to upend historically exclusionary monstrosity. Essun tells herself early on that "you may be a monster, but you are also great" (Jemisin 2015, 232). Later she reiterates this monstrosity in her identification with the Other, accusing herself: "The pity of a disguised stone eater has galvanized you as the screams of a fellow human being haven't. Such a monster you are" (Jemisin 2016, 57). Later, as her daughter Nassun accidentally kills someone and accuses herself of being a monster, Schaffa, Essun's old Guardian who traumatized her as a child, now reassures her daughter, "perhaps ... But you are my monster" (198). This last example in particular highlights the interstitiality of the monster and its ability to undermine simplistic good–evil binaries.

Such direct expressions of monstrosity are often fraught with their own kind of historical erasures and in the ironic engagement with Christian mythology the Broken Earth books are no exception. As I have outlined elsewhere, the concept of monstrosity is linguistically and culturally intertwined with a history of exclusionary religio-politics and with Christian apologetics itself (Thiess 2019). The category of monstrosity highlights the fact that much of exclusionary politics *is* religio-politics: "The monster is more than simply a large body to fear ... It also exists on a certain trajectory, at one end of which lies the Roman Christian polis and its attendant power and privilege, while on the other lies the wilderness" (15). While this chapter cannot engage all the linguistic aspects of monstrosity, there is one component that is applicable throughout these novels: the association of the monster with the wilderness as opposed to those in power at "the center of the circle," or within cities. The explorations of monstrosity at an interpersonal level within these novels may be remarkably complex, but it is notable that the characters show a rather consistent disdain for the rural areas to which they are forced, a contemptuousness that resonates with the religio-political nature of monstrosity. A closer look at this disdain reveals the general conceptual trajectory of these novels as a kind of return to the city as the center of the circle of religio-political power.

The novels begin by pointing out the clear connection of the powerful city of Yumenes to its history of colonization. While Yumenes is the "oldest, largest, and most magnificent living city in the world," it is also the "heart of an Empire" with all that comes with Empire (Jemisin 2015, 2). Thus, when the setting changes to focus on Essun it also connects her small village of Tirimo—"the sophisticated people of Yumenes laugh (laughed) at such primitive digs"—to her physical description: "Her skin is unpleasantly ocher-brown by some standards and unpleasantly olive-pale by others. Mongrel midlatters, Yumenescenes call (called) people like her" (10). Thousands of years of colonialism are marked at the physical and the societal levels. In this way the novels begin with a clear connection to the mechanisms of exclusionary politics. In fact, the narrative frequently reiterates that "everyone is measured by their standard deviations from the Sanzed mean" (112). What unites all people, regardless of their proximity to this racial mean, is their mutual exclusion of monsters, or orogenes. The distance of the people of the small town of Tirimo from the center of political power does not save them. They too are a community and thus operate within the logic of the colonial system.

When Essun destroys Tirimo, distraught from the murder of her son Uche at the hands of Jija, her act is more than revenge. It is divine retribution from a "God in chains" against the backwards folk of a small town who, through the inflationary logic of the system, caused her son's death. So even as the comm's leader tries to help her out the gates, she passes judgment: "*You cowards. You animals, who look at a child and see prey.* Jija's the one to blame for Uche, some part of you knows that—but Jija grew up here in Tirimo. The kind of hate that can make a man murder his own son? It came from everyone around you" (57). In this judgment, just before she nearly destroys the town, Essun employs the same kind of dehumanization of which she accuses its inhabitants. But the narrative also explains in Hoa's voice: "You aren't just inflicting death on your fellow villagers, of course. A bird perched on a nearby fence falls over frozen, too" (58). The destruction of Tirimo is not merely a violent feedback loop within the systemic logic of colonialism—there is *special providence* in it as in the proverbial fall of the sparrow, a movement away from the petty and mundane of the pastoral life and toward the transcendent.

Though Essun repents of this destruction immediately, the narrative itself betrays a consistent tendency to align the small town and the pastoral with the deserving victims of her divine justice. There are repeated references to Essun's origins in the "little backwater" town of Palela, where Schaffa comes to take her from parents who had locked her in a barn (94). The tutor takes her to the Fulcrum where she is fascinated by the running water of a shower, but "tries not to be obvious about it, because some of the other grits are Equatorials and would laugh at her, the bumpkin" (192). Later, in the Syenite storyline that involves her traveling to the smaller coastal city of Allia to clear coral from its harbor, she and Alabaster meet a bureaucrat who treats them in an exclusionary, dehumanizing manner consistent with the novels' portrayal of orogenes as monstrous. Her response to the leadership caste of a midsize city she will ultimately destroy is most telling. As she replies "if you were in my position, you'd be the representative of an independent and powerful organization, not some two-quarts backwater flunky" (215). It is a well-earned response from a frustrated person facing discrimination and without the larger context might go unnoticed. But the many statements criticizing such backwater places and the longer arc of the story speak to underlying issues with monstrosity.

The latter two novels confront colonialism and migration/refugeeism directly as the characters become part of a comm. While *The Stone Sky* begins with a rather frank examination of how the ancient civilization of Syl Anigist was built on the colonial, racist exploitation of the Niess, it also depicts Essun killing the entire population of the city of Rennanis, whose inhabitants tried to take over her comm. Again, this is divine, retributive justice, a redemptive violence invited by would-be colonization. But it is also an act of colonization as Essun's comm is forced to move into the vanquished city. Moreover, this moment signals a return of the kind of derision of the pastoral and obsession with the city noted in the first novel:

> Its buildings aren't nearly as beautiful or impressive as those of Yumenes, but then Yumenes was the greatest of the Equatorial cities, and Rennanis barely merited the title. 'Only half a million people,' you remember someone sneering, a lifetime ago. But two lives ago, you were born in a humble Nomidlats village, and to what remains of Damaya, Rennanis is still a sight to behold.
>
> (2017, 276)

This could be the internalized logic of colonialism turned upon itself, the self-loathing of the rural, and thus represent self-reflective criticism. But the final novel reverses the narrative of colonial destruction. It is Alabaster who laments the pitiful nature of the people of the Stillness, these "pathetic creatures we are now, huddling behind our walls and putting all our wits, all our learning, toward the singular task of staying alive … Once we were so much more" (2016, 163). And it is this trajectory that the rest of the narrative will follow—back to the city on the other side of the world where the stone eaters dwell.

Essun and Nassun reunite at this city, one having come to save the world and the other to destroy it. Interestingly, Nassun's reaction to the city mirrors her mother's reaction to so many other places: On traveling to it, she feels she "may never understand why, if Mama had the whole of the world open to her after somehow escaping the Fulcrum, she chose to live in such a placid, backwater place" (307). The narrative arc of these novels, therefore, consistently affirms that the return to great cities will signal the redemption of humankind. Likewise, the very end of the novels signals that this arc will continue. Nassun saves the world, but her mother will join the stone eaters in their city, traveling to the placid backwaters to convert or kill their bumpkin residents. It seems clear that it is this great city of gods from which the earth's next great crusades will be launched.

The narrative of monstrosity—a religio-political, exclusionary model implicated in the weight that apologetics offers to colonialism—coalesces here with Broken Earth's use of Christian mythology, and with surprising results. As fantasy, the trilogy may well be a sermon, a push toward the moral precept that exclusionary politics require a radical, and even violent, revision in the name of justice. It reflects the disanthropocentric "need to rethink the empirics of this social geology—that is, to pay attention to the material composition of these geologic moments—and epistemically not to reproduce those arrangements of power in the telling" (Yusoff 2018, 105). Yet the books also insist on the "language of inhuman proximities" (101), traveling in the transcendent and in myth. Not just any myth, though, but rather the founding mythology of the country in which Jemisin writes. Richard Slotkin (1973) once wrote that it was in the context of a "genre of colonial Puritan writing that the first American mythology took shape—a mythology in which the hero was the captive or victim of devilish American savages and in which his (or her) heroic quest was for religious conversion and salvation" (21). Even while expanding perspective beyond the human lifetime, Jemisin's works have not really changed the colonial impulse; Alabaster and Essun plan to use their magical, lithic powers to make a "better world" in the savage backwaters. In other words, even as these novels suggest that a transcendent system may be the key to overcoming oppression, they also recreate mythic structures indistinguishable from the missionary Christian beliefs that have informed colonialism for centuries.

Critics such as Attebery have argued, and rightly so, that the fantastic is a kind of contact zone, in which culturally specific myths can meet. What I am suggesting here is that we must also consider the myths themselves, their origins in addition to their uses. Much criticism of the Anthropocene has, whether intentionally or not, reasserted a spiritual or mythical belief system in line with the dominant religious structures—structures that have for millennia cooperated with and fueled colonial endeavors. We must be more mindful of these histories, even when—as in Jemisin's case—the aspiration is to envision a disanthropocentric future. I offer, by way of conclusion, a final convergence of events. Less than a year after *The Obelisk Gate* won Jemisin her third Hugo, another immensely popular fantasy was concluding to considerably less critical acclaim. Critics of the television show *Game of Thrones* attacked its hastily and shoddily produced final season. They denounced its portrayal of violence toward women and people of color or mocked the seemingly trite symbolism of the dragon, Drogon, melting the eponymous throne. However, no one criticized the fact that the show resolved into an apparent theocracy. This lack of criticism should give us pause. Even as the fantastic throne burned, the world was reacting to a real-world fire in the Cathédrale Notre-Dame de Paris. The outpouring of support to repair the building was immense and rapid. Raising more than 750 million euros in ten days, the amount was more than most private efforts at wildfire relief, including relief collected for the concurrent Australian wildfires. What does this say about our attachment to religious symbols or our appreciation of biological systems that constitute our world? Religious institutions, symbols, and the myths they embody continue to enjoy an unchallenged place, including within fantastic fictions and the criticism that engages them. The imperial, magical city from which Essun, Hoa, and Alabaster will launch their crusade is, from one perspective, strikingly similar to the majestic Notre-Dame cathedral and many like it that have presided over centuries of colonial conquest. What I suggest is that perhaps, in a way, it was Drogon who set fire to Notre-Dame and maybe—purely figuratively speaking—we should too.

Notes

1 Known for popularizing systemic thinking in History of Science and STS with his emphasis on "networks" and "assemblages," Bruno Latour has recently been significantly more that his critique of science is based in religion, either his own Catholicism or "natural religions" associated with Gaia. For more on the relationship of his thought to Jemisin's works, see my "Prepping for the Latourian Apocalypse, from Doomsday Preppers to Broken Earth," *Fantastika Journal*, vol. 5, no. 1, pp. 61–75."
2 In addition to Latour, another germane example is the employment of complex systems in the History of Science in order to contradict the so-called "conflict thesis" of the historical antagonism between science and religion. It is inherently apologetic and exculpatory of religious systems to claim, as some have, that there was no antagonism because the Pope once wrote Galileo a poem, or because Newton was a secret alchemist. For more, see my *Relativism, Alternate History, and the Forgetful Reader* (Lexington 2015).

References

Attebery, Brian. 2014. *Stories about Stories*. Oxford: Oxford University Press.

Braidotti, Rosi and Simone Bignall. 2019. *Posthuman Ecologies: Complexity and Process after Deleuze*. London: Rowman & Littlefield Publishers.

Brooks, Kinitra. 2017. *Searching for Sycorax: Black Women's Hauntings of Contemporary Horror*. New Brunswick, NJ: Rutgers University Press.

Cohen, Jeffrey Jerome. 2015. *Stone: An Ecology of the Inhuman*. Minneapolis: University of Minnesota Press.

Crichton, Michael. 2005. "The Case for Skepticism on Global Warming." Speech. National Press Club, Washington, D.C., August 25, 2005.

Hall, Melinda. 2019. "What Future People Will There Be? Neurodiverse Heroes for a Changing Planet." *MOSF Journal of Science Fiction*, vol. 3, no. 2:15–17.

Jemisin, N.K. 2015. *The Fifth Season*. London: Orbit.

Jemisin, N.K. 2016. *The Obelisk Gate*. London: Orbit.

Jemisin, N.K. 2017. *The Stone Sky*. London: Orbit.

Jemisin, N.K. 2019. "Twitter/@nkjemisin. I'm often at a loss for what to say … " June 29, 2019, 6:48 p.m. https://twitter.com/nkjemisin/status/1145011159751438337

Mendlesohn, Farah. 2008. *Rhetorics of Fantasy*. Middletown, CT: Wesleyan University Press.

Murphey, Kathleen. 2018. "Science Fiction/Fantasy Takes on Slavery: N.K. Jemisin and Tomi Adeyemi." *Pennsylvania Literary Journal*, vol. 10, no. 3: 106–15.

Slotkin, Richard. 1973. *Regeneration through Violence: The Mythology of the American Frontier 1600–1860*. Norman: University of Oklahoma Press.

Thiess, Derek J. 2019. *Sport and Monstrosity in Science Fiction*. Liverpool: Liverpool University Press.

Yusoff, Kathryn. 2018. *A Billion Black Anthropocenes or None*. Minneapolis: University of Minnesota Press.

CHAPTER 30
REIMAGING THE UPRIGHT APE
Jane Yolen

If he only stood on his hind legs,
missing the long ache of tail,
the swing between trees,
that distinguished him from angels.
If he only missed the invented club,
the sharp spike of spear and fear
that brought down rare meats
to his (as yet) uninvented table.
If he had only used his fingers
for fight and flight,
not totaling up the kill, the days of sun,
the numbers of his children.
If he had not invented language
which led to story, which taught purpose,
and history both ahead and behind.
If he had not dreamed, both big and small.
The world would still be an Eden
of green and growing,
of eat and eaten, where the pieces
of death were small enough
to fit in a pocket, had he imagined one,
or invented one, or needed one,
though now he spends most of his days
filling one, and losing a world as he goes.

CHAPTER 31
MYTHS OF (UN)CREATION: NARRATIVE STRATEGIES FOR CONFRONTING THE ANTHROPOCENE

Jacob Burg

Fantasy is a genre rooted in mythic world building, or world creation. What happens then when it concerns itself with world destruction? Amongst contemporary fantasy novels, a subgenre has emerged that confronts the Anthropocene's deranging scale and inescapable telos by evoking myths of (un)creation. These narratives do not nostalgically restore an idyllic past or wistfully envision a utopian future, preferring instead to imagine a way through our current bind by mapping its disorienting complexity in clearer terms. Nor do they fetishize spectacular endings and "the experiences of living under conditions of crisis," because to do so would only ignore "the causes of [those] conditions" (Leong 2016, 10–11) or suggest that a clear ending exist. To describe these myths' narrative operations, I use the open-ended and nonlinear term "(un)creation" in place of the definitive and linear concept of destruction. Given our current planetary precarity, I argue that we must adopt a salvaging spirit by articulating possibilities of life outside of the Anthropocene's linear progress narratives and teleological thought. Myths of (un)creation do precisely that, striving to fulfill Donna Haraway's contention that it is "our job to make the Anthropocene as short/thin as possible and to cultivate with each other in every way imaginable epochs to come that can replenish refuge" (2015, 160). New myths of (un)creation—of capitalism, ecocide, and progress—serve as one such refuge because they see our crisis for what it is: a toxic amalgamation of human and nonhuman actants spurred on by ideologies that are more legibly identified through labels such as the Plantationocene (Haraway 2015), Capitalocene (Moore 2016), and White Supremacy Scene (Mirzoeff 2018).

While I have no interest in relitigating terminological issues, it is important to briefly identify ecocriticism's nominal fault lines because they form the foundation of the fantasy stories discussed in this chapter: Rebecca Roanhorse's *Trail of Lightning* (2018), N.K. Jemisin's *The Fifth Season* (2015), Jeanette Winterson's *The Stone Gods* (2009), and Victor LaValle's *The Changeling* (2018). Indeed, all four novels dive straight into those symbolic fissures, nestling into the crevice of (un)creation at our planet's core. Once there, they disassemble words and worlds. Once there, they occupy the ethical position that Stacy Alaimo describes as "dwelling in the dissolve" of material boundaries now "unraveled by unknown futures" by recognizing "the networks of harm and responsibility that entangle even the most modest of actions" (2016, 2). Once there, they replenish refuge by assembling a repository of symbols that allow readers to think in scalar terms just as readily as they trace plot developments, identify thematic resonances, and invest in characters. These are narratives that invite us to reflexively experience "derangements of scale" (Clark 2012, 150). They ask to be read across vast registers of space and time—from a regional climate to an entire ecosystem; from one day to one millennium—pressuring us to rethink our position within the biosphere, one that abandons deranged notions of human agency. In identifying this subgenre's most salient narrative features, my goal is to establish an investigative framework that readers can use to reassess the stories they consume and produce. While this chapter is not intended as an ethical checklist, it does have the makings of an ideological resistance starter kit—a collection of a few narrative tools that have been used in contemporary fantasy, and upon which we can continue to build as we push beyond the impasses we so often find ourselves caught in when attempting to conceptualize and, more importantly, act upon the Anthropocene.

There are two main features that distinguish myths of (un)creation and the worlding work they perform: first, the use of temporal estrangement, which is largely achieved through dilation and fragmentation of linear, Anthropocentric temporality; and second, the reimagining of kin work, i.e., the labor a family undertakes to survive. Both of these strategies place pressure upon the enduring distinctions between human and nonhuman forms of matter, as well as the subsequent socioeconomic relations founded upon those distinctions. Fantasy serves as a particularly useful generic substrate for these narrative strategies because it strays from a stultifying mimesis and is "fundamentally playful"; as Brian Attebery puts it, fantasy's "way of playing with symbols encourages the reader to see meaning as something unstable and elusive, rather than single and self-evident" (2014, 2). Despite our efforts to fix the Anthropocene in place, it is fundamentally fluid. Fantasy helps us move with it.

Fantasy Matters: Time, Family, and Mythic Stories

If fantasy is escapist, perhaps it will let us escape what Mel Chen (2012) describes as the oppressive animacy hierarchies—e.g., human > animal > plant > stone—governing our world. Perhaps it will help us unearth a world buried beneath the surface, where marginalized matter might finally matter. After all, "the conceptual and formal ties between fantasy and ecological crisis are [more] intimate" than we might realize given that "ecological crisis demands the adaptation (and sometimes abandonment) of ... ideas like 'the natural,' the picturesque, the local or the straightforwardly mimetic" (Buse 2013, 265). Fantasy is useful in environmental crises because its imagined matter veers away from those categories often used within activists' rhetoric, which simplifies human agency in order to situate that agency within a clear, but ultimately illusory cause-and-effect relationship—e.g., "Buy an electric car and save the planet!" Conversely, fantasy is so powerful as a genre because, as Attebery explains, "it uses symbols to tell the truths that the conscious mind cannot grasp or fears to face" (2014, 21). And what describes the Anthropocene better than that which we cannot grasp and/or are too afraid to face? Of course, fantasy is not a magical balm for all of our planetary woes, but its ability to combat crisis comes just as much, paradoxically, from its ethical and imaginative failures as from its rich store of environmental symbols. Chief amongst those ethical and imaginative failures are fantasy's habits of whiteness. Defined by Helen Young, these habits manifest most directly when the genre "constructs the Self through Whiteness and Otherness through an array of racist stereotypes, particularly but not exclusively those associated with Blackness" (2016, 11). By confronting the genre's systemic racial issues and the distinctions between human and nonhuman matter that racial thinking establishes, fantasy writers are able to critique the same underlying forces that allow the Anthropocene to reproduce the socioeconomic and race-making technologies which extend the life of the crisis. These writers can dive into the ruins of fantasy, excavating a truth the genre otherwise helps society to hide: "the Anthropocene is presented teleologically, as the end of the late liberal modalities of life," yet "other worlds have long since been surviving their enforced apocalypses of subjective deformations and ecological deaths raised in the context of colonialism and slavery and in the ongoing presents of settler colonialism and anti-blackness" (Yusoff 2019, 1–2). Myths of (un)creation make these worlds visible. They reckon with what survival can and should mean. More specifically, they deconstruct—if not outright displace—Western Man. Following Syvlia Wynter and Alexander G. Weheliye, when I use the term "Man," rather than human or people, I do so in order "to designate the modern, secular, and Western version of the human that differentiates full humans from not-quite humans and nonhumans on the basis of biology and economics" (Weheliye 2014, 139). Myths of (un)creation deconstruct this figure, who has been the face of the Anthropos and the dominant figure in commercial fantasy, by reexamining his relationship to time and family.

In many respects, fantasy worlds are built through time and family because these two interrelated narrative axes help establish the created world's existential and social rules. For example, a broadly medieval setting and an emphasis on the right of primogeniture create the worldly boundaries of many high-fantasy stories. Likewise, we regularly conceptualize our world through time and family. They are, in fact, the two relations that most extensively cloud our ability to grasp the Anthropocene. While narratives come easily enough when structured by embodied and/or historical time, each of those temporal registers is intertwined with climatological time, which conveys "the sense of a natural world of wind and oceans that marks the limits of narrative" (Markley 2012, 44). Expanded to accommodate geological scales, time becomes incomprehensible. How then can we think across scales? Myths of (un) creation reflect each temporal mode against the others like funhouse mirrors, estranging the categories in order to make them more intelligible. In a similar fashion to time, when family is reordered to include matter lower on the animacy hierarchy—like plants or stone—it begins to lose its shape, if not its socioeconomic and political force. How then can we preserve some model of agency without oppressing others? For that, myths of (un)creation focus on kin work. In general, they leverage the isomorphic relationship between the creative acts undergirding our world and the creation of fantasy worlds in order to disassemble the Anthropocene.

Finally, although our world is made up of all forms of matter, some beyond our ken, it is also infused with stories that carry material force. I argue that these stories can be rewritten, providing us with "ways of experiencing, engaging, reading, and interpreting any world that is to be worth living in" (Buse 2013, 266). Even more specifically, "mythopoeic fantasy" offers us the narrative means to reexamine "our perceptions of the environment" through "engaging with the non-human," such that we "view nature as a part of a community, not a commodity" (Brawley 2007, 292–4). By casting off entrenched frameworks of possession and excavation, we can transform our biosphere. Consequently, we can recognize that sustainability efforts are built upon "an idealized homeostasis between humankind and environment that never existed" (Markley 2012, 60). Sustainability preserves hierarchies of matter, creating stable conditions for some, but upheaval for many others. Rather than hastily cobble together a new status quo that remains haunted by exploitative conditions, we need something more radical, something more fantastical. If so, survival—that is, the survival of a planet habitable for humans, whatever forms we may take—comes through (un)creation.

Temporal Estrangement: Dilation, Fragmentation, and Reiterative Cycles

Climate catastrophe has already occurred in Rebecca Roanhorse's *Trail of Lightning* and N.K. Jemisin's *The Fifth Season*. The future is past, and the past returns to rewrite the future. Roanhorse's Sixth World, which refers to the current iteration in a sequence of worlds created by giant floods, and Jemisin's fifth season, which refers to a recurrent climate event that reshapes the planet, both dilate normative temporality and collapse it back in on itself through perpetual crises, thereby reframing time as a mythic after-image of an historical before. For example, when reflecting on the sequence of ecological disasters that led to the current state of the world, Roanhorse's protagonist Maggie Hoskie, a Navajo (Diné) woman who hunts mythic monsters that have returned post-crisis, reminds herself that "the Diné had already suffered their apocalypse over a century before. This wasn't our end. This was our rebirth" (Roanhorse 2018, 23). In contrast to Man's linear progress narratives, Roanhorse's world spirals through an ever-present history. She writes a situated fantasy such that the Anthropocene's otherwise hidden truths emerge between empiricist and constructivist perspectives, between the narrated effects of climate change and the Diné reality of living with and against crisis (Attebery 2014, 188).

The gods and heroes that roam Dinétah—formerly the Navajo reservation—after another great flood represent the forms of matter that exist on a greater durational scale than the likes of Maggie. They "have lived many lives in many worlds," sometimes existing in people's dreams and legends, and other times returning in person (Roanhorse 2018, 101). As a form of matter, these gods and heroes adapt and survive. Through this adaptation they influence the world's temporality and the novel's plot, often directing Maggie like a pawn on a cosmic chessboard. In fact, their affective dispositions to human matters estrange embodied and historical time, inviting readers to connect the immediate action occurring in the Sixth World—i.e., Maggie's attempts to uncover the origins of monsters made from a collage of organic matter—to the distant machinations of the five worlds that sit beneath the Sixth like so many layers of cultural and geological trauma. In this fashion, the novel represents stratigraphic time as "a layering of past events in ways that do not simply entail invariant linear succession but allow for the potentialities of past times to resurface or be excavated" (Clark 2017, 169). Stratigraphic moments occur when Maggie interacts with mythic figures, discusses the interrelated histories of her kin and the planet, and tracks the changes in her environment's ontological boundaries. These are also the moments when the novel most resolutely adopts Alaimo's ethical position of dwelling in the dissolve. Maggie performs exposure by acknowledging her vulnerability to the gods and assuming culpability for her violence in order "to inhabit a fraught sense of political agency that emerges from the perceived loss of boundaries and sovereignty" (Alaimo 2016, 5). Across the novel, embodied matter and climatological matter sustain one another, suggesting a collective relation to time that is not absorbed by endings, or indebted to crisis-laden capitalist chronologies that motivate desperate extraction and hording. Maggie defeats the monsters by novel's end, but this new, personal state of affairs persists in its precarity. It carries in its promise that the sixth world will inevitably lead to the seventh.

The Fifth Season similarly oscillates between the personal and the planetary in order to imagine available modes of survival. From the outset, readers are emplaced in a here and now by the prologue's cartographic title "you are here" (Jemisin 2015, 1). The "here" is the Stillness, a world constantly beset by catastrophic earthquakes that set off new geological eras. The "now" is layered; rather than being thrown into the novel *in media res*, we are thrown in at the end of the world, twice over: first, through a personal ending in which a woman discovers the body of her dead child, and then in a repeated ending that is "writ continentally," such that the child's death suggestively leads to the world's death (1). Indeed, the connection between individuals and planets is constantly interrogated through the tweaking of temporal and material boundaries. On occasion, the present and past tenses even coexist: "The sophisticated people of Yumenes laugh (laughed) at such primitive digs, when they deign (deigned) to speak of such things at all" (10). The narrator here offers a sly temporal inversion inflected by crisis. The present tense is a vestige of the past, when the people of Yumenes were still alive to laugh, which means that the past tense is now a marker of the new present. Relatedly, the narrator uses conditional sentences to reimagine matter's animacy hierarchy: "If [the scouts] had touched it, they might have been fascinated by the density of the object's surface" (12). This fossil-like matter, later revealed to be the narrator, exists in a normative world only in the conditional, as an object of fantasy. And its animacy only becomes apparent through indeterminate jumps into a future—"the object grows still for a long while"; "After a time" (12)—that is already past.

After describing the mysterious obelisks created by a dead civilization in a failed attempt to save its world from catastrophe, the fossil-as-narrator shifts from a planetary perspective to a personal one. Such a quick scalar transition is a hallmark of myths of (un)creation. So, too, is the salvaging mentality adopted by the narrator, who motivates the sudden transition by suggesting there is a "need to keep things grounded, ha ha" (Jemisin 2015, 9), as if it had sensed readers withdrawing from the obelisks' climatological time. The self-conscious laughter at the geological pun also belies the novel's trans-corporeal ethics, which Alaimo describes as a state of being "in which bodies extend into places and places deeply affect bodies" (2016, 5). Crucially, the fossil-as-narrator helps the reader understand how to think trans-corporeally by parsing a subtle distinction that has become increasingly important in the Anthropocene: the world is constituted through words, so whenever someone says "'the world has ended,' it's usually a lie, because *the planet* is just fine" (Jemisin 2015, 14). In describing the ontological stakes in this fashion, *The Fifth Season* clarifies that the matter which creates our world and the matter that creates our planet are coextensive but not coterminous. In the last instance, their material fates diverge. What then does it mean for the world to end, but for the planet to persist?

The Fifth Season begins to answer that question just as soon as it raises it. The prologue's imagined reader ("you") is reimagined in the first chapter. Indeed, as befits a novel focused on the making and unmaking of worlds, *The Fifth Season* writes an imagined reader into its story, only to write them out in short order. In chapter one, fittingly titled "You, at the End," it becomes clear that the prologue's second person pronoun actually references one of the novel's three protagonists, a woman named Essun. The novel is full of these divergences and convergences. For example, even though the chapters are divided between the perspectives of Essun, a young girl named Damaya, and a woman named Syenite, it is eventually revealed that they are in fact the same person, just at different points in time. Linear causality is therefore replaced by a fragmented assemblage of geological selves implicated within a complex stratigraphy. Beyond disrupting the chapters' chronology in order to convey the porosity of her characters' being and the elasticity of time, Jemisin also ends almost every chapter with textual fragments, often of scripture-like aphorisms written on stone tablets. These tablets have suggestive names like "On Survival" and "The Incomplete Truth," implying epochs of time and types of matter unaccounted for by history. While *The Fifth Season* is an encyclopedic novel, complete with a map of the world, an appendix of the Fifth Seasons, and a glossary of terms, it takes great pains to point to its own gaps. Through its non-chronological structure, fossilized narrator, and use of textual fragments, the novel gestures toward the hidden matter that cannot be conveyed in maps (space), histories (time), or dictionaries (language). It "demonstrates an awareness of the incompleteness of any one source of vision" (Attebery 2014, 192); consequently, its narrative strategies demonstrate how we might persist in a fragmented world as a planetary whole.

Myths of (un)creation also interrogate the Anthropocene through reiterative cycles. For example, over the course of three distinct yet connected narratives, Jeanette Winterson's *The Stone Gods* (2009) imagines the rise and fall of a series of worlds. In essence, the novel narrativizes an epistemological effect known as anthropogenesis. As defined by Kathryn Yusoff, this term refers to the "two things [that] explicitly happen in the nomination of the Anthropocene: 1) the production of a mythic Anthropos as geologic world-maker/destroyer of worlds, and 2) a material, evolutionary narrative that re-imagines human origins and endings within a geologic rather than an exclusively biological context" (2016, 5). The Anthropocene merely creates "a new origin story and ontics for man" that does little to actually reckon with the problem it is intended to name (3). Winterson's novel disrupts anthropogenesis by counterintuitively embracing origins and endings. *The Stone Gods* imagines planetary life cycles, creating a series of stories that, when read individually, are driven by an unyielding cause-and-effect relationship between human activity and environmental disaster, but when read together, are driven by the resilience of potential. Told in four parts, the novel begins with the story of a futuristic society that seems like the descendent of our own: facing environmental catastrophe, governed by inept leaders, and engrossed by a variety of consumer technologies, people have put all of their hopes in colonizing a new world. The temporal twist is that we are not witnessing the future collapse of Earth, but the collapse of another planet known as Orbus, which led to Planet Blue's (i.e., Earth's) colonization. This is the first in a series of entropic moments that depict Man as the great destroyer and nature as the great recycler. In essence, Winterson satirizes humanity and its foibles through narrating the entirety of the Anthropocene not just once, but twice over: Orbus gives way to the bounteous Planet Blue, which is then drawn to the edge of environmental collapse by the same catastrophic decisions made millennia before. In fact, the pilot leading the colonizing mission to Planet Blue theorizes "that life on Orbus began as escaping life from the white planet—and the white planet began as escaping life from … who knows where?" (Winterson 2009, 56). Man's ravaging effect on matter is a universal constant; seeking origins or endings in this infinite system is pointless.

The relationship between Billie Crusoe and Spike, a robot–human hybrid, comes into focus against that recursive backdrop. Neither abides by the corrosive utilitarianism that drives other characters to believe "that everything on earth—and beyond—might be scalable, and thus exchangeable at market values" (Tsing 2015, 40). They do not see matter's inherent potential as an extractable resource best used to reaffirm or further the current structures of life. Instead, Spike helps Billie understand potential on a cosmic scale, as the main state of a universe that is "neither random nor determined": "It is potential at every second. All you can do is intervene" (Winterson 2009, 62). For Spike and Billie, intervention comes through love. When Spike kisses Billie for the first time, it challenges her human-centric assumptions about Spike—e.g., robots do not experience desire. From then on, their repeated relationships serve as destruction's cosmic twin; each time, their love evolves through a precarious world. Notably, "[a] precarious world is a world without teleology," and therefore it can be unbound from the Anthropocene (Tsing 2015, 20). The potential of the universe embodied by the multiple Spikes and Billies disrupts a strictly determinist chronology and reveals an essential truth that can help us resist our penchant for anthropogenesis: "Indeterminacy, the unplanned nature of time, is frightening, but thinking through precarity makes it evident that indeterminacy also makes life possible" (Tsing 2015, 20).

The Stone Gods ultimately roots life in the transition of states of matter. As Spike assures Billie while dying for the first time, "This is one state—there will be another" (Winterson 2009, 89). Indeed, Spike's existence as nonhuman matter is essential to the novel's representation of (un)creation. She is, as Billie notes, "a living thing that did not breathe," and she is by extension constantly "reinterpreting the meaning of what life is, which is, [Billie] suppose[s], what [they] have done since life began" (82). The novel traces the fits and starts of this reinterpretation, construing persistent life as that which exceeds linear time and teleological thinking. As a myth of (un)creation, the valuable lesson *The Stone Gods* has to teach us is one focused on repetition, and the potential for reevaluation imbued in reiterative cycles. Rather than focusing on how we can start anew (on Planet Blue) or reach some glorious ending (somewhere new), the novels asks us to consider, "What if this new world isn't new at all but a memory of a new world?" (87). In response it provides us with a metafictional moment at the start of the third story in which Billie finds a text entitled *The Stone Gods*. She proceeds to flip through it without regard for its order: "No point starting at the beginning—nobody ever does. Reading at random is better" (119). Billie then reads the moment from the first section of the novel when she lays alongside Spike, amazed by her matter. In opening herself to randomness, this version of Billie recognizes the imprint left on her by an alternate self. Randomness begets repetition, and repetition begets recognition. In the end, the novel suggests that we should learn to live time materially through the relationship between here and not here, rather than chronologically through the relationship between past, present, and future. It is estranging to think of time in that manner, but as the novel notes with its final sentence, "Everything is imprinted for ever with what it once was" (207). To confront the Anthropocene, we must render time immaterial by better imagining its material.

Embracing Kin Work: Disturbance, Dissolution, and Reconstitution

A new model of kin work arises within the fluctuations of temporal estrangement that are used by myths of (un)creation to rescale our perspectives and rearrange our definitions of matter. This model of kin work takes its cue, in part, from Haraway's contention that "kin are unfamiliar … uncanny, haunting, active" (2015, 162). Building from that premise, I argue that uncanny kin do not exist in direct opposition to Man's family unit. Rather, myths of (un)creation imagine how the models coexist in a disturbance-based ecology "without either harmony or conquest" (Tsing 2015, 5). Living in disturbance reorients survival from a strategy predicated on conquest—i.e., a group's survival implies the destruction or depletion of "antagonistic" matter—to one focused on cultivating livable collaboration. Not unlike Alaimo's ethical recommendations to dwell in the dissolve of unknown futures and embrace trans-corporeality, Tsing reminds us that "the evolution of our 'selves' is already polluted by histories of encounter" (29). Myths of (un)creation redirect dread and disgust—affects that prompt us to revert to survival-as-conquest—in order to explore the (non-extractive) value of new coalitions of matter. Consequently, these myths demonstrate how the priorities of kin work can shift from antagonistic containment and capitalist extraction to contaminated collaboration and adaptive awareness. Only after this shift occurs can we see our true caretaking obligations.

Relatedly, Victor LaValle's *The Changeling* (2018) ties its interrogation of our caretaking obligations to a reexamination of our relationship to fairy tales. In doing so, it views making kin as "a creative process of fashioning care and reciprocity," and kinship as "an effect of social struggle," rather than an inherently biological precursor to struggle (Benjamin 2018, 64–5). Indeed, making kin must involve reimagining normative family stories and storytellers. LaValle's novel does that through its focus on the traumatic relationship between Apollo Kagwa, his wife Emma, and their infant son Brian: shortly after Brian is born on the subway, Emma says he has been replaced by a doppelganger; Apollo tries to persuade her otherwise, but she chains him to a radiator, kills the child, and runs away. Hoping to find and kill her, Apollo goes on a mythically inflected journey to a hidden island near Manhattan and then to an enchanted Forest Park in Queens. Along the way, he discovers that his wife was telling the truth: a man broke into their apartment and stole Brian, replacing him with the changeling descendent of a troll. The troll, first brought over to America by the abductor's great Norwegian ancestor, has been trying and failing to raise a child for generations. Apollo kills the troll and reunites with his family only after he disassembles his reality. He does not restore his family to what it used to be; he rethinks it as it ought to be: kin.

Apollo first crosses into a new, more perceptive world when Brian is born. In an instance of temporal estrangement, Apollo discusses the birth in terms of "slow time" and fixates on the moment "when their child had existed in two worlds at once—reality and eternity … The entire family had been Here and There. Together. A fairy tale moment" (LaValle 2018, 161). Although framed by revisionist language that tries to replace a biological understanding of kin with an expression of cosmic, otherworldly unity, the scene still reifies a normative family. In part, this is because the novel has no interest in rejecting biological reproduction as such, particularly given the history of genocide and enforced sterility haunting its black protagonists; it has no interest in reimagining matter without reckoning with how blackness has been categorized as inanimate or less-than-animate matter as a way to justify systemic oppression. However, the novel does have an interest in using mythic encounters to resituate biological relations within a liberating cultural vocabulary of kinship and kin work.

This interest starts to become clearer in Apollo's second interaction with Brian, when he visits the child's grave. At first, he looks at the body and realizes with horror that, contrary to what he had started to believe, his son is actually dead. Fantasy is provisionally cast aside as a way to understand it better. Only by acknowledging his son's death, which symbolizes the death of a normative mode of futurity rooted exclusively in biology, is Apollo able to see the world as it actually is. Once he breaks the spell, he realizes that he is holding a bundle of thorns and organic matter that is strangely animate: "Not really alive, but impossible to think of it as truly dead. An automaton. Fueled by blood and belief" (LaValle 2018, 316). In this pivotal scene, the novel expressly fights against abjection and pure horror. Apollo soon begins to relate to the changeling not as a stand-in for his son, but as another form of matter still worthy of compassion. The changeling's glamor disappears; it is (un)created through Apollo's empathy: "You deserved better than you got. … I'm sorry if you felt any pain" (317).

The trilogy of kin encounters between Apollo and Brian concludes when Apollo and Emma find their son in the troll's cave. Rather than return to his parents, Brian at first returns to the troll. Like the brief connection between Apollo and the changeling, a provisional interspecies bond has formed. It is only broken by Apollo and Emma's invasion, which prompts the troll to swallow Brian. Apollo then kills the troll and manages to pull Brian from its stomach, such that he is "the only child ever born twice" (LaValle 2018, 427). Through this rebirth, and in conjunction with the previous two Apollo–Brian encounters, LaValle offers a new vision for the sort of kin work needed to combat our planetary crisis. From the realization of Brian's desire to be with the troll, to the violence of killing the poor caretaker, to the hope of rediscovering Brian, the novel represents the complexly affective and material connections bound up in our biosphere. Making kin is not just a singular act—e.g., Brian's first birth. It is comprised of "daily actions that transform partial relations into deeper ones" in order to sustain kin networks (Clarke 2018, 33). As a tool against the Anthropocene, *The Changeling* disrupts the affirmation of Man's normative family through the collaborative kin work performed by Apollo, Emma, Brian, and even the troll. Together, they see the unseen and feel the unfelt in their haunted, disturbance-based ecology. Together, "they lived happily today" (LaValle 2018, 431).

Kin work also invests in depleted resources: it traces supply lines, unmasks exploitation, and disrupts those who seek to control the biosphere. In *The Fifth Season*, as in *The Changeling*, this work begins with the dissolution of the family: Damaya, the youngest version of Essun, is given away by her parents because she is an orogene, meaning she has the ability to control the planet's energy; Syenite, the name taken by Damaya as a student in the authoritarian academy that trains orogenes, is forced to mate with another powerful orogene in order to reproduce the slave labor the Stillness's empire relies on to keep itself economically and geologically stable; finally, Essun's partner kills her son and runs away with her daughter once her son's orogene powers are uncovered. In all three timelines the normative family unit self-destructs. Each time, Essun, who is a woman of color, has her world torn asunder to preserve a patriarchal status quo that sees difference only as a resource to be harvested and discarded. While Essun's position as a woman of color does not signify in quite the same way as it would in our own world because different phenotypical features are valued in the Stillness, it nonetheless intersects with her orogene identity and together these two aspects symbolically position Essun in a state of abjection and oppression. Consequently, *The Fifth Season* imagines new modes of relating to other humans and forms of matter (e.g., the fossil-as-narrator named Hoa) in response to the failures of the "consumption-oriented settler-colonial family" (TallBear 2019, 167). In addition to disassembling the family unit to reveal the rot at its core, the novel resituates humanity in relation to the planet in order to cultivate new patterns of kinship, ones previously unnoticed or outright rejected: "There are things that you should be noticing, here. Things that are missing, and conspicuous by their absence," Hoa warns readers before reminding them that "human beings, too, are ephemeral things in the planetary scale. The number of things that they do not notice are literally astronomical" (Jemisin 2015, 150). Through its repeated invocation, absence becomes a pedagogical tool that shines a light not so much on what is actually absent, but rather on the smooth, naturalized processes by which we have learned to make things absent. What and how we notice is informed by the stories we tell, and the domineering lore of Essun's world, not unlike our own, tells only of Man's conquest. Kin work tries to unmake that legacy.

In addition to using absence as a pedagogical tool, the novel also asks readers to consider "that there are more people in this world than just humankind" (Jemisin 2015, 151). The term "people" is divorced from the toxic categorizations of Man and reimagined as beings constituted through kin work. For example, Essun becomes a person in this revised sense by cultivating relationships with other orogenes, Hoa, and even the obelisks which "bond, sort of, to certain orogenes" (393). Altogether, each of these connecting threads weaves together to form a kinful fabric that is disruptive because it bands together oppressed peoples (orogenes), because it acknowledges intimate relations to other forms of explicitly nonhuman matter (Hoa), and because it remains open to the transformative force of vast geological histories, which we helped create and which helped create us (obelisks). Crucially, the kin work undertaken by Essun is not one rooted in procreative population expansion. Unlike the empire's leaders, who enslave orogenes to ensure environmental stability and manage the population, Essun becomes invested in breaking that population- and sustainability-focused system through redefining life. Indeed, Essun's desire to (un)create her world maps onto Michelle Murphy's concept of afterlife, which she defines as "the struggle to exist again *but differently* when already in conflicted, damaging, and deadly conditions, a state of already having been altered, of already being in the aftermath, and yet persisting" (2018, 113). Essun makes an afterlife for herself and her planetary kin by embracing a wide world of matter. She does not hope to restart her old family life in this new fifth season, despite her desire to find her lost daughter. Biological connection is respected and incorporated into her kin making project, but it is not the determinant force. In the end, *The Fifth Season* confronts the reader's sense of the possible, pries open the category of kin to include non-familial and non-amorous relations. It imagines a planetary afterlife in which Essun disentangles matter from Man.

Conclusion: Materializing (Un)creation

Myths of (un)creation enact their trans-corporeal ethics by dilating and fragmenting time, striating space, and restructuring our understanding of matter. Their aim is to pull us into a more fluid world, one divorced from the Anthropocene's totalizing system. These myths do not always withhold narrative closure, but they do ask us to understand closure differently, such that we do not continue to invest in the teleological thinking and linear progress narratives undergirding the oppressive powers of Man and his vision of the material world. After all, "as long as we imagine that humans are made through progress, nonhumans are stuck within this imaginative framework too" (Tsing 2015, 21). In some of the novels I have discussed, that framework is disrupted by estranged time that is "shaped by myth and ritual into recurring cycles of death and renewal," with the pedagogical power coming in particular from those narratives' respective emphases on who and what is renewed (Attebery 2014, 199). In other novels, Man's framework is disturbed by the eruption of relations of matter formed across ontological scales and without regard to animacy hierarchies. Collectively, if we are going to be able to materialize (un)creation, we must live amongst the strangeness that the Anthropocene does not allow us to narrate or experience. We must transform refuse into refuge, not by altering refuse's material nature per se, but by changing our perspectives on the world by listening to unheard narratives and by working with that refuse as the kin that it is and always has been. (Un)creation is a fraught narrative and material process, but it begins by shifting fantastically from this world to another one already all around us.

References

Alaimo, Stacy. 2016. *Exposed: Environmental Politics and Pleasures in Posthuman Times*. Minneapolis: University of Minnesota Press.

Attebery, Brian. 2014. *Stories about Stories: Fantasy and the Remaking of Myth*. Oxford: Oxford University Press.

Benjamin, Ruha. 2018. "Black AfterLives Matter: Cultivating Kinfulness as Reproductive Justice." In *Making Kin Not Population*, edited by Adele E. Clarke and Donna Haraway, 41–66. Chicago, IL: Prickly Paradigm Press.

Brawley, Chris. 2007. "The Fading of the World: Tolkien's Ecology and Loss in *The Lord of the Rings*." *Journal of the Fantastic in the Arts*, vol. 18, no. 3: 292–307.

Buse, Katherine. 2013. "Genre, Utopia, and Ecological Crisis: World-Multiplication in Le Guin's Fantasy." *Green Letters*, vol. 17, no. 3: 264–80.

Chen, Mel. 2012. *Animacies: Biopolitics, Racial Mattering, and Queer Affect*. Durham, NC: Duke University Press.

Clark, Nigel. 2017. "Anthropocene Bodies, Geological Time and the Crisis of Natality." *Body & Society*, vol. 23, no. 3: 156–80.

Clark, Timothy. 2012. "Scale." In *Telemorphosis*, edited by Tom Cohen, 148–66. Ann Arbor, MI: Open Humanities Press.

Clarke, Adele E. 2018. "Introduction." In *Making Kin Not Population*, edited by Adele E. Clarke and Donna Haraway, 1–40. Chicago, IL: Prickly Paradigm Press.

Haraway, Donna. 2015. "Anthropocene, Capitalocene, Planationocene, Chthulucene: Making Kin." *Environmental Humanities*, vol. 6, no. 1: 159–65.

Jemisin, N.K. 2015. *The Fifth Season*. New York: Orbit.

LaValle, Victor. 2018. *The Changeling*. New York: Spiegel & Grau.

Leong, Diana. 2016. "The Mattering of Black Lives: Octavia Butler's Hyperempathy and the Promise of New Materialisms." *Catalyst: Feminism, Theory, Technoscience*, vol. 2, no. 2: 1–35.

Markley, Robert. 2012. "Time." In *Telemorphosis*, edited by Tom Cohen, 43–64. Ann Arbor, MI: Open Humanities Press.

Mirzoeff, Nicholas. 2018. "It's Not the Anthropocene, It's the White Supremacy Scene, Or, the Geological Color Line." In *After Extinction*, edited by Richard Grusin, 123–50. St. Paul: University of Minnesota Press.

Moore, Jason, ed. 2016. *Anthropocene or Capitalocene? Nature, History, and the Crisis of Capitalism*. Oakland, CA: PM Press.

Murphy, Michelle. 2018. "Against Population, Towards Afterlife." In *Making Kin Not Population*, edited by Adele E. Clarke and Donna Haraway, 101–24. Chicago, IL: Prickly Paradigm Press.

Roanhorse, Rebecca. 2018. *Trail of Lightning*. New York: Saga Press.

TallBear, Kim. 2019. "Forum on Making Kin Not Population: Reconceiving Generations." *Feminist Studies*, vol. 45, no. 1: 159–72.

Tsing, Anna. 2015. *Mushroom at the End of the World: On the Possibility of Life in Capitalist Ruins*. Princeton, NJ: Princeton University Press.

Weheliye, Alexander. 2014. *Habeas Viscus: Racializing Assemblages, Biopolitics, and Black Feminist Theories of the Human*. Durham, NC: Duke University Press.

Winterson, Jeanette. 2009. *The Stone Gods*. New York: Mariner Books.

Young, Helen. 2016. *Race and Popular Fantasy Literature: Habits of Whiteness*. New York: Routledge.

Yusoff, Kathryn. 2016. "Anthropogenesis: Origins and Endings in the Anthropocene." *Theory, Culture & Society*, vol. 33, no. 2: 3–28.

Yusoff, Kathryn. 2019. "Geologic Realism: On the Beach of Geologic Time." *Social Text*, vol. 37, no. 1: 1–26.

CHAPTER 32

THE STEPPING STONE, THE *BOULDER*, AND THE *STAR*: A FABLE FOR THE ANTHROPOCENE

Grace L. Dillon

One moonlit night the stepping stone felt itself gripping and aligning and smoothing itself into the granite-lined walls, underwater caves, and sure underpinnings of the nearby *Boulder*. The Boulder's rockiness was unmoved by blustering winds, thrashing tree-limbs, floodings of waters, or scrapings of any who dared to climb its fortress-like limbs.

The eye of the stepping stone—for it did have an eye so small it was unseen by most who gazed upon it—this eye swiveled and gazed up towards the sky, caught by the light of one particular *Star* that shone with great steadiness upon the waters. It seemed to this stepping stone that the *Star*'s light, if not the *Star* itself, was streaming closer and closer to its own planet-by-day, star-by-night. It might even collide with the *Boulder* if the *Star*'s steady progression was not stopped somehow.

The *Boulder* seemed to be aware of this imminent collision but its reaction when timidly questioned by the stepping stone was to stiffen, adjust itself even further into the night sky, and grimly resolve not to be moved. The *Star* flitting here and there as clouds covered and recovered its light seemed to be even more reluctant to re-direct its path. Instead, this *Being-of-another-planet* journeyed only faster and kept to its course.

Desperate to be better heard by both the *Boulder* and the *Star,* the stepping stone called upon others who would suffer the impact of the *Boulder-Star* collision.

"What say you?" it asked *Makwah* the black bear, sliding into sleep and rumbling with wrath at its interrupted nap. "How feel you?" it asked the ever-dancing white jack rabbit *Naanabozboh*, as that trickster slid in and out of its shapes as little star, jack rabbit, manitoh, boy-person, and runner all in the twinkling of the stepping stone's eye. "What think you?" it urged the cooing, murmuring, and meowing stuffed animal gliding in and out of its complicated animal-person, human-person, plant-person, mineral-person, and spirit-person guises. "What say you?" repeated the stepping stone, flinching at the lack of responses. "What say you?" faltered out the stone as the *Boulder* loomed towards the descending light of the *Star*.

The stuffed animal tumbled to the edge of the waters, the *Makwah* ambled out of his cave to the edge of the soaking cattail ferns, and the dancing jackrabbit trembled and shivered on the bramble-tangled, thin-soiled cliff above the waters. All three animals, fake fur dissolving into animated, real being devolving back into simulated, remained quiet about their true sayings, feelings, and thinkings. One was stoic, the others fretful as they awaiting the clash. The light-dappled waters stilled in tense anticipation of the impending collision.

If an eye can see and an ear can hear, can a body shift? So thought the stepping stone in its last minutes as a stone. Then a small but dense *bridge* appeared to the calmly sensible makwah, the indecisive stuffed animal, and the jittery jackrabbit. This *bridge* appeared to trail through the torrent of waters as the light of the *Star* descended onto this planet where it had visited only once before.

The light, once so strikingly focused in the eye of the stepping stone, now appeared splayed and disoriented in the revolving gaze of the *bridge*. The light was cast abroad even as it gathered more closely, a paradox that tickled the fancy of the *Boulder*. The Boulder's imploding "geh-faws" shook the land but also re-settled its earth and soil and foundations under the descending-light-pressuring-*Star*-heat.

Can the *Star*, then, touch lightly the shoulder of the *Boulder*; can it shine and glisten less maniacally in sky-on-waters-on-land? Can it bow down some of its burden of the descending light and tether it to the shoulder of the *Boulder*? Can it shed some of its glow, get away from its own consuming shadow, and murmur in consonance with the *Bridge*, the *Makwah*, the *Jack-rabbit* and the *Stuffed Animal*? Will its other-planet voice join this chorus that heralds and surrounds, the *Boulder*? Can the vanished stepping stone, now temporary *bridge* mediate this *Star*'s tumble into the *Sea*? Will the *Ocean* waves smooth out the ridges of the *Boulder* in time for the *Star* to settle down without too much hurt? Can the *Star* remain for awhile, exchanging glances with all who gaze upon her, mirrored and bounced off the gleaming edges of the *Boulder*?

One might as well ask: "Can the *Creator* harness both the manitoh and human, enwrap mineral dust with star dust, balance together while distancing the remnants of the common pot?" "Can the Greater Bird, then, move more assuredly upon the waters?" ... And, as the moonlit nights gather more fiercely and abundantly as one, "may a mere daughter of human-persons bring about and share such a story?"

CHAPTER 33

ON MONSTERS AND OTHER MATTERS OF HOUSEKEEPING: READING JEFF VANDERMEER WITH DONNA HARAWAY AND URSULA K. LE GUIN

Kim Hendrickx

In "Some Thoughts on Narrative" Ursula K. Le Guin says that stories are typically told in the past tense, because this allows for forward movement: and then this happened, and then that happened (1989a, 38). Like stories, cells and organisms move forward and develop, as Le Guin reminds us in the same essay. They do not stay put and constantly organize themselves in relation to their surroundings. The word "organism" is rooted in "organization." There is, in other words, a close kinship between the matter of stories and the matter of living: both move forward, develop, evolve, and sometimes mutate into strange twists of plot. How things will organize is not always predictable in good stories, nor in complex ecologies. To explore that kinship—to see how it works on levels deeper than a mere analogy— this chapter proposes a reading of Jeff VanderMeer's Southern Reach Trilogy (2015). Its strange ecosystem, I argue, offers a different storyline than that of "nature" to be preserved, dominated, or controlled—an ecocentric storyline whose closest analogue is Rachel Carson's *Under the Sea-Wind* (1941). I will not discuss the latter in detail as it is a work of biology rather than fiction. The focus, instead, is on the exercise of building a connection between VanderMeer's weird and invented ecology on the one hand, and the real-world ecology carefully described by Carson on the other. How does fiction help us appreciate and think about ecosystems? And how might ecosystems themselves invite us to turn to fiction? In considering these questions, this chapter is less a systematic analysis than coming to grips with a gut reaction I get when I read about the Anthropocene in terms of monsters, shock, and horror. I become obstinately contrarian when I am expected to display a sense of awe in the face of environmental crisis, when certain texts tell me that bedazzlement is the appropriate reaction when faced with a world we are no longer in control of. I just don't think that is news. First, what is it that we thought we controlled? And second, I believe that it is important to actively *refuse* such a state of bewilderment. The refusal matters in a way that relates to the work of Ursula K. Le Guin, who never used the fantastic to divert attention away from everyday matters like housekeeping. The *eco* in ecology and economy derives from the Greek oîkos, meaning "house" or "household." Our age, however, is one of wide-ranging domestic violence. Monsters and spectacularism are not going to help us. The question "what I am going to tell my kids," however, is something I can, and must, work with. It requires imagination, listening, and responding. The Southern Reach Trilogy helps us imagine what it might be like to start listening and responding to that larger household we call ecology. That the trilogy is weird fiction, rife with monsters and horror, is all the more interesting if we can turn them into matters of housekeeping rather than spectacular metaphors for our troubled times. Accordingly, I start with the monsters and the horror, make a brief stopover at Haraway's Chthulucene, and then explore how a storied ecology may help us better relate to ecology in the real world.

Area X and the Biologist

> The tower, which wasn't supposed to be there, plunges into the earth in a place just before the black pine forest begins to give way to swamp and then reeds and wind-gnarled trees of the marsh flats. Beyond the marsh flats and the natural canals lies the ocean and, a little farther down the coast, a derelict lighthouse. All of this part of the country had been abandoned for decades, for reasons that are not easy to relate. Our expedition was the first to enter Area X for more than two years, and much of our predecessors' equipment had rusted, their tents and sheds little more than husks. Looking out over that untroubled landscape, I do not believe any one of us could yet see the threat.
>
> (VanderMeer 2015a, 3)

So reads the opening of *Annihilation*, the first book of The Southern Reach Trilogy by Jeff VanderMeer.[1] *Annihilation* is told by "the biologist" in the first person. It is an account written by the protagonist while on expedition in the mysterious Area X. It has been left for readers to find beneath a trapdoor in a lighthouse. The lighthouse is the only stable reference point that appears both in Area X and on the maps of that territory. The official explanation for Area X—a swathe of forest, marshland, and coastline in the now-abandoned southern coastal area of the United States—is an "event" thirty years previous. No description of the event is available, other than a vague reference to an ecological disaster. Area X sealed itself off by some kind of border and started transforming, mutating, and developing an ecology of its own. A government agency, The Southern Reach, has been set up to survey, control, and—in all likelihood—*contain* Area X within its current border. At irregular intervals, the agency has sent eleven expeditions into Area X, the members of which returned, if they did, with severe memory loss; some of them with fatal cancer; and some did not return at all. One expedition ended in mass suicide; another with its members shooting each other. Little material evidence comes back across the border. Evidence such as samples, video footage, or testimony from expedition members do not seem to add up to any kind of knowledge. Instead, the evidence induces profound disorientation within the agency, in a sense that is both psychological and awkwardly architectural. The biologist is part of the twelfth expedition into Area X, together with three other women: the psychologist, the anthropologist, and the surveyor. "All of us were women this time, chosen as part of the complex set of variables that governed sending the expeditions" (VanderMeer 2015a, 3). Not exchanging personal names is another strategy to try and make expeditions successful, even though there is no standard by which to measure any degree of success.

The Southern Reach Trilogy has been praised for its suspenseful and distinctively textured world with elements of Lovecraftian horror, but reminiscent also of Thoreau's ecstatic writings about nature and Rachel Carson's lyrical and factual engagement with ecology. The trilogy never fully reveals whether Area X is still part of our world, even though it is dotted with remnants of human civilization: an overgrown hamlet; a lighthouse; rusty equipment strewn about. The origins and nature of the "border" remain unclear too: neither the characters in the novel nor the reader know for sure whether it is organic, a local fissure in time and space, or something else entirely. It is suggested at many points that its border is expanding. Area X is an unsettling and horrific place, with its share of Lovecraftian presences unbearable for human minds to accommodate. Yet, Area X is not indescribable either and the books are full of close descriptions of plants and wildlife, mosses, lichen, and algae. Told from the perspective of the biologist, *Annihilation* is the book where these descriptions are at their sharpest. At several points in the novel, biological detail and sensory experience coalesce into lyrical homages to biodiversity, describing a buzzing richness of life so vast that it almost tips over into the monstrous. The longer she stays in Area X, the more the biologist's perception alters, revealing an "ongoing horror show of such beauty and biodiversity that I couldn't fully take it all in" (43). As days go by, she does start to take in the landscape while the landscape seems to be taking in part of her. On the way to the lighthouse, for example, the biologist describes entering into a different mode of awareness, a silent ego dissolution, exposing a landscape of emotion and intensified biological diversity:

> Now a strange mood took hold of me, as I walked silent and alone through the last of the pines and the cypress knees that seemed to float in the black water, the gray moss that coated everything. It was as if I travelled through the landscape with the sound of an expressive and intense aria playing in my ears. Everything was imbued with emotion, awash in it, and I was no longer a biologist but somehow the crest of a wave building and building but never crashing to shore. I saw with such new eyes the subtleties of the transition to the marsh, the salt flats. … The strange quality of the light upon this habitat, the stillness of it all, the sense of *waiting*, brought me halfway to a kind of ecstasy.
>
> (89–90, original emphasis)

Rather than "becoming one" with the landscape, the biologist experiences a multitude of intensified subtleties that, it seems, she *must* relate to and tell about, as if the landscape wanted to be told, and as if the monstrous were a mere perceptual distortion for eyes and minds unable to accommodate the prodigious and intense richness of life's fizzy insanity. The important difference from cosmic horror is that VanderMeer's work does not emphasize or radicalize the distinction between the human and the monstrous. Rather, it leaves the door slightly ajar for humans to know Area X in some way, even if that kind of "knowing" may come at an unthinkable price.

Whose Horror?

Area X offers a different storyline than that of "nature" to be preserved, dominated, and controlled. While in our world we keep referring to "nature" and "the environment," Area X cannot be understood in those terms. Ecology and ecosystem, however, make sense, because these terms point to a diversity of relations that may change, mutate, create, destroy, and evolve. In contrast to "nature," ecology is not a stable object of either patronizing admiration or economic exploitation. It is historical and ongoing, reconfiguring itself with new elements.

It does not care about what is wild or natural or human or alien. Area X is an interesting figure that intensifies the technical meaning of the term "ecology" and what it might imply to start thinking in ecological terms. In that sense, it has a lot in common with Donna Haraway's concept of the *Chthulucene* (Haraway 2016). But what is the Chthulucene? Is it another geological epoch, like the Anthropocene, or something else?

While the Chthulucene is often taken to be an alternative name for the geological–cultural concept of the Anthropocene, my sense is that Haraway does not so much propose it as a label to describe reality—which reality? whose reality?—but as a speculative figuration to think with. The affordance of speculative figurations is that they do not represent something else that we might be familiar with (as a metaphor would do) nor do they refer back to the reality we pretend to know. Reality must always be turned into a question for Haraway because claims to reality and realism are easy ways to impose authority, along with a master narrative that would matter for everyone. Speculative figurations acknowledge the narrative character of our ways to understand and relate to the world. While the Anthropocene is on the brink of becoming the official name for our present geological epoch, Haraway replies with the Chthulucene because, for her, *anthropos* takes us back to the usual narrative where Man controls the fate of all living beings. "Unlike the dominant dramas of Anthropocene and Capitalocene discourse," Haraway writes, "human beings are not the only important actors in the Chthulucene, with all other beings able simply to react. The order is reknitted: human beings are with and of the earth, and the biotic and abiotic powers of this earth are the main story" (2016, 55). It is a bit unfortunate that Haraway refers to the biotic and abiotic powers of the earth as "the main story," because I understand her Chthulucene as, first and foremost, a place of many stories. In this perspective, the Chthulucene is not an actual story in itself. Rather it is a different mode of attention, another way of noticing, that may give birth to new stories.

The reference to Cthulu in the Chthulucene would seem to imply that Haraway invites her readers to think in terms of Lovecraftian cosmic horror. A good deal of scholarship about the Anthropocene has used cosmic horror tropes and references to H. P. Lovecraft, "weird" literature, and the "new weird" (Ulstein 2017). The knot of cosmic horror, Anthropocene, and Chthulucene is interesting to untie, and helpful to allow a better appreciation of the difference between monsters in cosmic horror and those in The Southern Reach Trilogy.

Haraway's Chthulucene refers to the Greek *chthonios*, meaning "of, in, or under the earth and the seas" (Haraway 2016, 53). Haraway twists this term into *chthulu*, rendering homage to a particular spider in the Californian redwoods (*Pimoa cthulhu*) that was named after Lovecraft's *Cthulhu*. In a short endnote, Haraway says that she is determined to "rescue" the spider from the Lovecraftian version of horror: "Lovecraft's dreadful underworld chthonic serpents were terrible only in the patriarchal mode. The Chthulucene has other terrors—more dangerous and generative in worlds where such gender does not reign" (Haraway 2016, 174, note 4). But what has gender got to do with horror? Was not Lovecraft trying to touch an old, ancestral string, irrespective of gender and hardwired into our very being as a species? Was he not clear that cosmic horror arises when all rationality, and reality itself, are overpowered by the intrusion of an unthinkable and unbearable monstrous presence? How can such horror be anything but *universal*?

Haraway does not elaborate on this but I think the key to understanding cosmic horror as *gendered* lies in the question of what we are afraid of losing. This begs at least two other questions: What do we think we *have*? And who do we think we *are*? For cosmic horror to work, we need ourselves to be the kind of humanity that can only conceive of its relation to other beings in terms of control: e.g., rationality, urban planning, public order, and the control over means of production. All these forms of control are patriarchal in the sense that they have been historically and systematically reserved for a particular type of man—a self-assured white and Western male—and definitely denied to all women. It is within this specific historical context of power that universality is assumed where only one particular *kind* of horror is at play: Man masters nature and other humans; and losing that power is a horror he cannot bear. The legendary last words of the ill-famed character Kurtz, a colonial ivory trader in Joseph Conrad's *Heart of Darkness*, epitomize the type of dread the white colonial male faces when control falters in a bewildering ecology: "the horror, the horror." Horror it may be, but it is the horror of a specific kind. It is intimately tied to historical and political patterns of control with colonialism in its wake. Cosmic horror can be seen as the ultimate failure of control, and of rationality itself. The impossible geometries in the world of Lovecraft's Old Ones mock man's orderly planning of public space. In this type of horror narrative, all possible storylines sooner or later end in paralysis. Once it is saturated with madness in the face of the unthinkable, the story can be taken no further.

That is, as long as madness and horror signal the loss of control. But what if we have never been in control in the first place? If not, it makes sense, as Haraway does, to question both the Anthropocene and cosmic horror as, at once, very impressive and very one-dimensional. Their heroes are Anthropos and His spectacular negation. The story must end in shock and awe. This is a resolution of sorts, but why seek resolution rather than ongoing process and transformation? This is Le Guin's question in her essay "The Carrier Bag Theory of Fiction" (Le Guin 1989b). Stories need forward movement, she says, but that does not mean they have to be linear. Why do we liken time to an *arrow* anyway? Le Guin notes the prominence of sharp and pointy objects in the way we tell about the Ascent of Man. The patriarchal evolutionary story takes on the same form as the objects we tell it with: straight and pointy. But, Le Guin asks, what about receptacles to carry the wild oats and berries early humans picked to feed themselves, for example? What if we conceived of the evolutionary story, and stories more generally, as carrier bags instead of objects that smash, thud, stab, and kill? Weapons call for heroes, but narrative does not work that way with carrier bags: "It's clear that the Hero doesn't look well in this bag, he needs a stage or a pedestal or a pinnacle. You put him in a bag and he looks like a rabbit, like a potato. That is why I like novels, instead of heroes they have people in them" (Le Guin 1989b, 169). Things jumble in a bag and there is no straight heroic path to salvation or Progress.

Nor does it lead to the logical opposite: collapse, doom, or cosmic horror. Things jumble, and most of all, they go on. Le Guin notes that there is combat and aggression in the bag too. And I take it that there is horror in the carrier bag. But it is a horror of a different kind and quite possibly *worse* than cosmic horror because there is no easy way out—by instantly going insane, for example. In Le Guin's novella *The Word for World Is Forest* (Le Guin 2015 [1972]), the colonial horror is not like Conrad's Kurtz losing his wits. The horror lies in the fact that the local population, in defeating their oppressor, have learned how to kill. That is the horror they will have to live with. It is a kind of horror that they must face up to and ask: *how* will we cope with this; what arrangements will we make now that our society, our living together, has changed irreversibly? Facing such questions requires imagination and intelligence. It requires stories to think with.

In The Southern Reach Trilogy the government agency in charge of surveilling Area X undermines precisely those requirements in its attempts at being clever and in control of things. The agency sets up strategies to control the flow of information: expedition members are stripped of their personal names, given incomplete information about the mission, and trained to fall under hypnotic suggestion. These strategies aim at achieving "scientific objectivity" but in practice they create disastrous situations because the expedition members cannot properly converse with one another. Since they cannot properly think, no collective knowing emerges out of any of the expeditions. In this sense, the trilogy can be read as a colonial story about a strange ecosystem, populated with unknown critters instead of an indigenous human population. Numerous expedition members die horrible deaths; some go mad; some commit suicide; some kill each other. The question is whether all this horror and madness are actually caused by an alien and hostile environment. What if they originate in organized ignorance, in designed mis-capacity and unwillingness of expedition members to adapt? And in a lack of imagination on the part of the authorities? In all these ways, Area X challenges human colonial fantasies about venturing into a new world without adapting—without willing to become transformed in one way or another. In Conrad's *Heart of Darkness*, Kurtz wanted only control but was not willing to adapt. In the second book of The Southern Reach Trilogy, the director of the government agency is nicknamed Control. Not surprisingly, he also fails to adapt and imagine a different relation to Area X than in terms of authority. The individual titles of the trilogy—*Annihilation*, *Authority*, and *Acceptance*—suggest different dispositions with respect to Area X. In *Annihilation*, the biologist reflects that they might not be pursuing the right strategy. As she and another expedition member descend underground into a spiraling structure, they both feel that they are approaching some kind of living presence and they impulsively draw their guns: "Holding the gun made me feel clumsy and odd, as if it were the wrong reaction to what might confront us" (VanderMeer 2015a, 52).

While Lovecraftian monsters signal the end of human understanding and any possibility for humans to interact with the nonhuman, Area X is more akin to Haraway's Chthulucene, where monsters usher in an urgent question of *address*: how to confront and address them? Horror is real in Area X, but what if it reflects, more than anything else, an organized bereavement of the imagination? A violent lack of politeness? An obstinate inability to rethink one's place with respect to other sentient beings?

Ecology and Responsibility

Asking how to address a person, an animal, an entity or a situation implies taking a position. An address is always directed at someone and this means that the speaker speaks from somewhere, just as our postal and email addresses locate us. The question of address is also an ecological question, because the position or location of humans, animals, plants, and trees with respect to one another *matters vitally*. This is true when we address other forms of existence too, like friends and kin who have passed away: we tend to ask *where* they are now, and we create places where we can connect to them, where we can address them and they can address us (Despret 2019). If locations and positions matter, then the term "responsibility" takes on a different tone. Liberated from the restricted and weighty meaning of "carrying blame," the term gains a new kind of importance which is precisely about becoming "response-able" or able to respond (Haraway 2016, 34). Becoming response-able/responsible involves searching, or even inventing the terms of a conversation that is sensitive to where things and beings are located with respect to each other. And how things might shift and change as a consequence of our actions.

Through the characters and institutions portrayed, the Southern Reach Trilogy plays out different responses to Area X, and it sets up a very interesting contrast between The Southern Reach agency on the one hand and the biologist on the other. "The shadowy Southern Reach is in many ways a window into the ideological and imaginative inheritances that have shaped western attitudes towards the environment" (Margeson 2018, 40). The idea of "the environment" and of "nature," I would add, bears the traces of those same inheritances. External to humans, nature in this framework is a foreign land to discover, admire, protect, exploit, destroy, (eco-)manage, and rebuild. It is another word for a realm that is *available* for human intervention and control. Availability, of course, is the default assumption for imperialism and colonialism.

In contrast, the character of the biologist steers the reader away from "nature" and offers an entry point into ecology as a mode of attention, a form of thinking, and a way of being and evolving with other species. As suggested throughout the novels, ecology comprises a variety of relations: symbiosis, parasitism, predator-prey, and speculative forms of emulation and mimicry. Ecology is not *nice*. It may turn extremely violent depending on where and when you are situated. But such violence can be acknowledged and its nature questioned. In human history, much violence has gone either unrecognized or considered as a price to pay for imperialist projects defended in the name of progress and civilization. Today's market economists speak in terms of "negative externalities" when they turn the costs and realities of environmental degradation into a column on the balance sheet. In ecological thinking, however, violence cannot be hidden in rows and columns. One is obliged to face it and become response-able. And opting for less violence in the future is a real possibility. The violence and horror in Area X can, I believe, be read as consequences rooted in ill-adjusted acts of intrusion on the part of humans. This view takes on a particular edge when you take into account that the biology of Area X tends to emulate and mimic humans. It is not a passive reflection—a "mirror of society"—but an ecosystem that actively learns, incorporates, reinvents, and responds.

Taken together in all its aspects, Area X provides a human–nonhuman relatedness that is more complex and challenging than that implied in the concept of the Anthropocene. Though referred to in a variety of contexts, the Anthropocene is originally a geological concept acknowledging the traces of human activity in the Earth's sedimentary layers. Naming the Anthropocene as the epoch following the Holocene turns humans into a geological force and the Earth's crust into a registry or archive of that force. That acknowledgment is important, as it certifies the impact of humans on the planet: a truth set in stone. But we need other figures and stories to think with if we want to address living ecosystems. Some ecologies are more fragile than others; some people and nations pollute more than others; some economies wreak more environmental havoc than others; and there are weird and inventive forms of life—both human and nonhuman—that we might learn from. Cosmic horror, a vengeful Earth, or "hyperobjects" are of little help if what we need is more intelligibility, more imagination, and more sensitivity to the richness of these ecosystems. Stories can turn very complex matters into something intelligible, into something we recognize and can relate to. Stories and characters convey *importance* to things, persons, and places.

Importance

While Area X and its monsters get most of the attention in book reviews and analyses, it is worth noting that Area X is but one among a series of places that are important to the biologist character. In the early twentieth century, the philosopher Alfred North Whitehead asked an enigmatic question: "What is it that gives the sense of importance?" (Debaise 2018, 25). If we think or feel something is important, where does that sense come from? What does importance really mean and imply? Different passages in *Annihilation* convey a sense of importance that arises when you start paying attention to a particular place and ecosystem. In *Annihilation*, the biologist recounts: "My lodestone, the place I always thought of when people asked me why I became a biologist, was the overgrown swimming pool in the backyard of the rented house where I grew up" (VanderMeer 2015a, 43). The biologist's parents did not take care of the pool, and so the pool took care of itself. Weeds around it started to grow, algae formed, and all kinds of critters moved in. As a child, the biologist sat around the pool pretending to be a biologist documenting all the life in that little ecosystem. At some point, her parents could no longer afford the rent and they had to move out of the house and into a tiny apartment. "One of the great traumas of my life," the biologist recalls "was worrying about the pool. Would the new owners see the beauty and the importance of leaving it as is, or would they destroy it, create unthinking slaughter in honor of the pool's real function?" (46).

Importance *grows* in the biologist's account. It initially grows out of neglect—not acting has consequences too—but then branches out into different lifeforms gathering in and around the new ecosystem, including the biologist. The chain of consequences with respect to the place has been transformed along with the situation: there is no longer a choice between keeping the pool clean or leaving it be. The fate of the pool has now become a matter of life and death: the destruction of an ecosystem versus "honoring the pool's real function." The pool is a small and bounded ecosystem and the biologist is bound to it. Importance emerges in the way things become bound together.

Annihilation develops the biologist's personal story around such specific places and bounded ecologies: the swimming pool; tide pools at a place called Rock Bay; an empty parking lot overgrown with weeds; and Area X itself. Though the nature and actual stretch of its border are undetermined and at some point perhaps gone, Area X is still defined by that border, like a giant tide pool of horrific strangeness, beauty, and "pristine wilderness."

In the biologist's account, importance arises out of encounters between herself and specific places. For Whitehead, importance *is the property of a situation*—you plus the place—and not a "subjective" appreciation that you may have with respect to it. Etymologically, something that is important is something that bears consequences; it *brings in*, or imports, consequences. When you enter a particular ecosystem, you bring in your presence and the place is not indifferent to it. Dragonflies may alter the course of their flight; ants may choose to crawl over your feet or not.

In that sense, importance cannot be detached from a specific situation, in contrast to its common use where we seem more or less free to decide whether we think something is important or unimportant. Importance, in its older and stronger sense, is not about personal or collective appreciation, but about the type of consequences you have to proceed with, never being fully in charge of the full equation. It is literally an ecological concept. You cannot fully decide, but you can make a bet on the kind of consequences you want to avoid or bring about. Fictional characters are one means to convey importance in this sense.

Importance is at odds with the concept of "the environment." The biologist does not put it in those terms, but VanderMeer offers a hint by having his character paraphrase a sentence from a manifesto in our real world—not the world of the Southern Reach—called *The Coming Insurrection* (The Invisible Committee 2009, 75): "Never has a setting been so able to do without the souls traversing it."[2] In the original text, this phrase refers to capitalism and control policies which have, over time, severed the vital bonds of importance between humans and their lifeworlds. For the writers of the manifesto, the concept of "the 'environment" is the result of this violent separation: "There is no 'environmental catastrophe'. The catastrophe is the *environment itself*. The environment is what's left to man after he has lost everything" (74, original emphasis). For the authors of the manifesto, what we are in danger of losing are the strings that weave people, places, and other forms of life into relations of importance. There are still people and trees, for sure, but capitalism does not need them: it needs human resources and timber. In *Annihilation*, the biologist reflects on the world outside of Area X as "what it had always been during the modern era: dirty, tired, imperfect, winding down, at war with itself. Back there, I had always felt as if my work amounted to a futile attempt to save us from who we are" (VanderMeer 2015a, 30). Deceived by many things, she seems to long for a world that does not care about humans who have stopped caring themselves. At the same time, she knows that we are always already inhabiting an ecology and inhabited by it. Area X intensifies what she has always known into something she can feel and become part of. There is no room for the environment in Area X.

Speculative Ecologies

Science fiction writer William Gibson claims that he does not write about the future but about the present (Rothman 2019). That writing is trying to catch up with the ever-evolving and mutating present. Turn the process of time into a succession of moments and you will see that time itself, even life, becomes impossible. The arrow of time, as Zeno has argued, will remain stuck between the archer and the target. In fact, the arrow could not have gotten there in the first place. Nor the archer. It appears that we cannot cut up the flow of things without getting our minds into trouble. Would a "fact" be to ecology what the "present" is to time?

This is the sort of question that engaged Rachel Carson, a biologist who sought to describe ecological relations between species, oceans, landscapes, people, pesticides, bacteria, and chromosomes. Carson needed narrative and elements of fiction to write about those relations. Her book *Under the Sea-Wind* is written from the perspectives of, respectively, a sanderling called Silverbar, a mackerel called Scomber, and an eel called Anguilla. This was not a matter of style, a way to bring lightness in what would otherwise be a dry descriptive account. Rather she needed narration and characters in order to be accurate about the facts. I imagine that for Carson those facts were, in the first place, relations. Rather than bare facts, the smallest possible units of reality are, perhaps, tiny little stories. It is interesting to think of the kinship between the matter of stories and the matter of living in that sense: that it is perhaps more than an analogy. And that fiction may take us closer to truth. "Truth," as anthropologist Genly Ai puts it, "is a matter of the imagination" (Le Guin 1969, 1). This is a crazy thing to think in times of relentless fact-checking, post-truth discourse, and fake news accusations, but it is perhaps even crazier to mistake fiction for lies, and to limit truth to facts only (Le Guin 2019,

108–9). Fiction tells about things that did not happen and it does not claim to be factual. The reader knows the things described did not happen. Fiction is not deception but artifice. If the art is well mastered, it allows opening up a register of truth different to that available to fact. In some cases, artifice helps telling about facts too. Carson wanted to describe the ecology she had observed in a particular part of our existing world. But Carson's commitment to "make the sea and its life as vivid a reality for those who may read the book as it became for me" (Carson 2007 [1941], 3), required artifice and imagination. Carson had to move elsewhere, inside her characters, in order to write better about what was happening in her here and now. But she was clear throughout about her "art" and never claimed that she had actually encountered a mackerel called Scomber. She used the character to approach the real, and she wrote a book of fact in the past tense.

VanderMeer's Area X does not exist in the real world. And yet it is alive for its readers, troubling our habits of thought. It brings more imagination and, quite possibly, more elements of truth in discussions about our curious present called the Anthropocene. As this chapter suggests, the ecology and story of the Southern Reach make a case against the Anthropocene as a concept to think with beyond its geological designation. What we get in return is a strange ecology which reminds us that real-world ecology is often "weird" and capable of innovation too. I am not inclined to insist so much upon the weird aspects in these novels. Area X is not radically beyond all comprehension: there are enough elements to sustain the possibility of relating to its ecosystem. The ambivalent relationships to Area X that work well for the story work equally well to speculate beyond the story, and that is perhaps no coincidence. Both stories and real ecologies are speculative. Both are replete with possibilities that depend upon the imaginative resources of humans and other species in knitting mutual ties of importance.

The speculative character of ecologies becomes very clear when compared to what the term "nature" implies. With nature, the imagination does not do a very good job, proposing stories where only people have real agency. What the concept of nature has done best in the West is to provide a moral and political vantage point for those in positions of authority and power (Daston and Vidal 2004). Many acts of discrimination and violence have been committed in the name of what is deemed "natural" as opposed to "unnatural": racism and the supposed natural superiority of some races over others; eugenics as a way to sift out errors and the unnatural; colonialism, homophobia, genocide; and the list goes on. The concept of nature works like a mirror: it is separate from us yet we see only ourselves in it. The reflected image makes us want to aestheticize and manage it, while the physical separation from that reflection makes it easy for us to consider it a mere resource. Either way, nature has always encouraged irresponsible behavior. The concept of nature is infused with the will to control and comes, as I discussed, with its own horror: a spectacular loss of all means of control: human order, rationality, and morality. The concept of nature leaves humans ill-prepared for a world without mirrors, and cosmic horror arises in the face of unthinkable, radical Others. Within the scheme of nature, full control or madness are the only alternatives. Humans either rule or take the easy way out by going insane.

But ecology does not provide that escape route. There is no mirror standing between different beings or different ecosystems. Things relate to each other and *how* they relate changes with what happens amongst them. Ecology requires intelligence from all of its participants. With no "natural" moral and political order to fall back on, the question of how to relate to other lifeforms and fellow humans must be asked anew. Likewise, violence cannot be taken out of the equation or set aside as a "negative externality" because nothing is external. Bad housekeeping will sooner or later affect the entire household. So, "what are we going to tell our children" is a good question to start from. And while I have no answer to what we parents should say, I believe that the worst parent, and the worst housekeeper, is the one who does not listen or notice, lacking the imagination for both.

Speculative fiction enlarges the imagination. It renders readers and writers more sensitive to the world and it empowers them to notice it better. That way it enlarges reality. It is perhaps the closest we can get to wizardly shapeshifting and becoming someone or something else—for a while at least. The art of writing and thinking is to make some of that magic last.

Notes

1 The two other books of the trilogy are *Authority* (2015b) and *Acceptance* (2015c). I am grateful to Rob Geukens, a Belgian writer of fiction, fantasy and children's books, for passing *Annihilation* to me on a cold November night, the dark wind tugging fiercely at our party hats.
2 The citation, slightly modified with respect to the original text, appears in *Acceptance*, the third book of the Southern Reach, on page 241 and reads "never has a setting been so able to live without the souls traversing it." VanderMeer says in the acknowledgments that this manifesto had "tremendous influence" on the biologist's/Ghostbird's thinking. The manifesto is cited or paraphrased three times in *Acceptance*.

References

Carson, Rachel. 2007 [1941]. *Under the Sea-Wind*. New York: Penguin Books.

Conrad, Joseph. 1994 [1902]. *Heart of Darkness*. London: Penguin Books.

Daston, Lorraine and Vidal, Fernando, eds. 2004. *The Moral Authority of Nature*. Chicago, IL and London: The University of Chicago Press.

Debaise, D. 2018. "The Minoritarian Powers of Thought: Thinking beyond Stupidity with Isabelle Stengers." *SubStance*, vol. 47, no. 1: 17–28.

Despret, Vinciane. 2019. "Inquiries Raised by the Dead." *HAU: Journal of Ethnographic Theory*, vol. 9, no. 2: 236–48.

Haraway, Donna J. 2016. *Staying with the Trouble. Making Kin in the Chthulucene*. Durham, NC: Duke University Press.

Le Guin, Ursula K. 1969. *The Left Hand of Darkness*. New York: Ace Books.

Le Guin, Ursula K. 1989a. "Some Thoughts on Narrative". In *Dancing at the Edge of the World*, 37–45. New York: Grove Press.

Le Guin, Ursula K. 1989b. "The Carrier Bag Theory of Fiction". In *Dancing at the Edge of the World*, 37–45. New York: Grove Press.

Le Guin, Ursula K. 2015 [1972]. *The Word for World Is Forest*. London: Gollancz.

Le Guin, Ursula K. 2019. "Making Up Stories". In *Words Are My Matter. Writings on Life and Books*, Boston, MA and New York: Mariner Books.

Margeson, Christopher. 2018. "Imagining the Anthropocene: The Weird Ecology of Jeff VanderMeer's *Southern Reach Trilogy*." Utrecht University: MA Thesis English and Comparative Literature, August 10, 2018. http://dspace.library.uu.nl/handle/1874/368557

Rothman, Joshua. 2019. "How William Gibson Keeps His Science Fiction Real." *The New Yorker*, December 9, 2019. https://www.newyorker.com/magazine/2019/12/16/how-william-gibson-keeps-his-science-fiction-real.

The Invisible Committee. 2009. *The Coming Insurrection*. Los Angeles: Semiotext(e).

Ulstein, Gry. 2017. "Brave New Weird: Anthropocene Monsters in Jeff VanderMeer's *The Southern Reach*." *Conentric: Literary and Cultural Studies*, vol. 43, no. 1: 71–96.

VanderMeer, Jeff. 2015a. *Annihilation*. London: Fourth Estate.

VanderMeer, Jeff. 2015b. *Authority*. London: Fourth Estate.

VanderMeer, Jeff. 2015c. *Acceptance*. London: Fourth Estate.

CHAPTER 34
THE SERIOUSNESS OF WRITING FUNNY
Molly B. Burnham

The ability for children to believe in the possible and the impossible at the same time is not surprising to anyone who spends anytime with them at all. When I taught elementary school, this was a daily occurrence. They could believe that they would never learn to paint a picture and at the same time that they would become a famous painter. They would believe with certainty that math skills were pointless while being just as certain that they would become an astronaut. They would know that although they were not a dog, they could speak "dog." This balancing act is one of the most important qualities in children. It allows them to approach the world with awe and wonder, with creativity and imagination. It is their superpower.

Now, I'm not naïve and I'm not saying children are either. Children are smart and savvy and can smell a fake from a mile away. They also get into bad moods. They hurt, get mad, and seem close to giving up, but because of their creative superpower, they don't. Without a doubt, it's one of the reasons I love writing for children. They don't give up. Even if they say they are. They don't.

The art of holding these seemingly contradictory positions lies at the heart of optimism. Many people poo-poo optimism, but I would argue that optimism is one of the most powerful forces of nature. It is a key component for creating change. And it is not for the weak of heart. The profound issues and struggles in today's world are serious, heartbreaking, and, to many, quite overwhelming. Faced with the enormous challenges of the Anthropocene, with cynics, deniers, and entrenched power that keeps destroying the planet for short-term profit, young people need all the optimism they can get. Optimism—a belief you *can* change things—leads to action. This is why optimism is always under attack, both by external and internal forces. Today, in a world of climate change and pandemics, it needs to be cared for and nourished. More than anything else, optimism requires humor. It relies on healthy and regular doses of laughs.

All of us who work with children know that humor is their lifeblood. Laughter flows out of them like bees from a hive. When humor is handled well, it creates something fantastic, mind-expanding, that nourishes the child's inner optimism. Humor has the power to be emotionally restorative. It replaces negativity with joy and returns us to a weirdly optimistic trust that change is possible even in the face of unimaginably rotten odds. Without humor, imagination and creativity cannot flow. And without imagination and creativity flowing, well … we're stuck.

My job as a writer dedicated to humor is to take it incredibly seriously. Because, when handled poorly, humor is destructive, painful, and crippling. First and foremost, like many things in this world, humor is about power. To land the restorative laugh, the author must understand power structures within the story. Power is a dynamic experience that can change quickly. When we are powerless, things are not as funny as when we hold power. And when we hold power, we are ripe for something funny to happen to us. A lot of my humor occurs when someone who holds power experiences something surprising that knocks them for a loop.

Humor also comes into play when someone powerless is suddenly elevated to power. Humor reminds everyone that we need to be able to laugh at ourselves, at our clinging to power and its illusions: including the illusion of being the masters of this planet.

When a child reads a funny book, they are not only releasing tension and reinvigorating themselves, they are also learning how to be optimists. They are learning the ability to carry on in the face of impossible odds. Most importantly for our world caught in the trap of dependence and destructiveness of fossil fuels, humor communicates the hope for change. It deflates the cynic, the pompous, the self-important, and the self-centered. Instead, it elevates the optimist, the humble, the problem-solving, and the creative. Humor makes it possible to imagine and fight for the world to be different from the destructive past and the exploitative present. Humor is the lifeblood of staying involved, engaged, and creating change. And kiddos are leading the way.

CHAPTER 35

LITERALIZING HYPEROBJECTS:
ON (MIS)REPRESENTING GLOBAL WARMING
IN A SONG OF ICE AND FIRE
AND *GAME OF THRONES*

Markus Laukkanen

HBO's *Game of Thrones* (2011–19), one of the most popular and influential pieces of audiovisual fiction of the past few decades, ended in 2019: its finale was viewed live by 19.3 million people in the United States alone. The series, a juggernaut of the so-called golden age of television (see Poniewozik 2015; Waldfogel 2017), was adapted from a critically and commercially successful book series (see Sheenan 2011) that has been instrumental in reimagining what contemporary fantasy can be: George R. R. Martin's A Song of Ice and Fire (1996-Present) that has been instrumental in reimagining what contemporary fantasy can be. However, as the television series came to close in 2019, after eight seasons of continuously growing audience, it left a large portion of its viewers disappointed. Almost two million signatures were collected for a change.org petition to "Remake Game of Thrones Season 8 with competent writers." Why were the fans of the series so unhappy? This chapter suggests one possible answer, which is that the books and the TV series have been perceived as offering different confrontations with the Anthropocene and global warming. For all the differences between the books and their filmic adaptation, A Song of Ice and Fire lends itself to a reading in which Martin moves from a simple analogy into a reconstruction of the logic of global warming as a means of rendering it representable. This chapter argues that while the television series largely fails to adapt the core of what makes the books resonate as climate fiction, enough of climate change and global warming concerns were carried over into earlier seasons to create audience expectations that the last season appears to have abandoned.

A Song of Ice and Fire as Climate Fiction

Climate Fiction, or cli-fi, is defined as a subgenre of speculative fiction whose "pivotal themes are all about Earth, examining the impact of pollution, rising sea levels and global warming on human civilization" (Ullrich 2015; Di Paolo 2018, 2). That global warming is a central theme of A Song of Ice and Fire and *Game of Thrones* has been proposed often by both fans and critics (Miller 2018). This thematic interpretation of the series is not an obscure one. The climate of Westeros, the primary setting in Martin's tale, is one of the great world-building mysteries of the series. In this fantasy world winters and summers are irregular and last for years. The nature of these strange seasons has been a recurring subject of discussion by the series' fans: speculations have ranged from magical explanations to planetological theories (Reddit; A Forum of Ice and Fire). What remains, regardless of which explanation is correct, is the unfathomable nature of the climate of this world, and the imminent danger it poses to all humanity.

Fantasy and Myth in the Anthropocene

This chapter takes as its starting point a contention that a story about the sinister, magical winter that is threatening to engulf all of Westeros resonates so strongly with contemporary audiences largely because of its eerie parallels with the creeping effects and consequences of global warming in our real world. Both are existential threats that seem too complex and too distant to grasp. Both are perceived as problems for the future, and not everyone even believes in them. Winters, while irregular, do happen in Martin's fictional world. It is difficult for the characters located far away from the icy Northern frontier to believe that this winter will be different, that it will be an apocalyptic event, a second mythic long night. Meanwhile, in our reality, some argue that since climate has always been changing and since weather is just weather, there is no need to worry, no need to act yet. Alternatively, even if changes brought about by global warming are real, another denialist argument holds that they are not caused by humans—and anyway there is nothing we can do to stop them.

The rulers of Westeros are too preoccupied, constantly bickering with and plotting against each other, to make plans for what is coming, just as in our real world the sphere of global politics seems to lack the capability for appropriate action. To effectively tackle global warming, one would have to rise above the immediacy of tangible economic demands and conflicting interests of the various nation states that inhabit our planet. In both Westeros and our world, token action is the norm. More troops might be sent to the wall of ice that guards the realms of men as members of the night's watch—an organization tasked but woefully unequipped to deal with the threat of the long night from beyond the wall. Meanwhile, in another world, commitments to reduce carbon emissions are regularly made and triumphally announced even as those very same emissions keep rising higher year after year.

The parallels are hard to miss. In one analysis, Marc Di Paolo goes into detail about the allegorical interpretation of the wall and those who man it as a commentary on climate change (in)action in our world (Di Paolo 2018, 243). He puts forth the idea that the extensive descriptions of food in A Song of Ice and Fire—depictions that have often puzzled readers— serve a thematic rather than merely an aesthetic function. As the series goes on, Di Paolo notes, the list of foods shrinks, communicating to the reader the threat of food-insecurity that is one of the more immediate effects of both climate change and the apocalypse approaching Westeros (255). The big-picture message drawn from this type of allegorical reading can be powerful. As Charli Carpenter states: "The argument seems clear: if existing governance structures cannot manage emerging global threats, expect them to evolve or fall by the wayside" (Carpenter 2012).

But are we really looking at a clean and simple allegory where the parallels are difficult to miss? While the apocalyptic winter that seems to always be just around the corner does lend itself to a reading in which it stands in for global warming and the chaos it brings, the claim that A Song of Ice and Fire series concerns global warming must be qualified. After all, the first installment of the book series was published in the mid-1990s. The 1990s was a time when the greenhouse effect and global warming were already known, a time when they entered the larger discourse and when the first tentative steps were taken to reduce the potential damage they might cause. That said, these concerns were not yet a centerpiece of the wider cultural conversation (see Uekötter 2014, 129–30), and global zeitgeist was preoccupied with the cultural anxieties surrounding the fall of the Berlin wall (Di Paolo 2018, 251). While I am not entirely convinced that Martin was unaware of global warming when he began plotting his series, the environmentalist of the 1990s generally rallied around other things, such as pollution, the health of the ozone-layer, the protection of rainforests and of the oceans. Given this context, Di

Paolo speculates that A Song of Ice and Fire is an example of unintentional cli-fi. According to this argument, Martin pivoted the focus of the story toward issues of global warming when he realized that, increasingly, readers were interpreting it that way (Di Paolo 2018, 10).

Hyperobjects

I approach global warming via Timothy Morton's concept of hyperobjects—extremely large and complex objects that are massively distributed in time and space relative to humans (Morton 2013(a), 1). One of the defining characteristics of hyperobjects is their viscosity. Hyperobjects like global warming are sticky. Once they are recognized, it appears that they have been everywhere all along. For Morton, humans exist within hyperobjects. They are all around us and cast their terrifying shadows on all aspects of human life: a stranger at a car park makes a comment to Morton about the weather, and Morton feels the oppressive presence of global warming take over the conversation, whether it is acknowledged or not (Morton 2013(a), 99). By Morton's logic, everything in our world is, of near deterministic necessity, about global warming. This includes art, which in the time of hyperobjects must automatically and directly include them (109). This argument finds purchase when discussing a work of fiction like A Song of Ice and Fire which, I argue, is deeply concerned with the logic of hyperobjects. The series' HBO adaptation is significantly newer than the books and is a product of the age of climate consciousness: an age, as Morton puts it, after the end of the world (24).

If the magical winter of Martin's world is read as a direct analogy for global warming, the winter should be a viable candidate to be analyzed as a hyperobject within the fictional world of the series. I will, however, approach the question from a different angle: I propose that the whole series is about hyperobjects. While Morton's coinage is significantly newer than the beginning of Martin's series, I see compelling reasons to interpret the books as an attempt to grapple with two enormous elemental forces—or objects—that frame Martin's invented world, namely Ice and Fire. The name of the series has been an object of fan theories for a long time. The mystery is pointed out explicitly in the second volume of the series: "What is the song of ice and fire?" "It's no song I've ever heard" (Martin 1999, 876). A queen in exile, Daenerys Targaryen, asks the question of a disgraced knight, Ser Jorah Mormont, and it is unsurprising that the knight has no answer either: after all, how could he know about the hyperobjects that threaten to end his world, not only in Morton's sense of making the concept of the world obsolete (Morton 2013(a), 6), but also in a more literal sense.

Morton has enumerated five characteristics of hyperobjects, many of which overlap with each other. These characteristics are viscosity, nonlocality, temporal undulation, phasing, and interobjectivity (1–2). Viscosity, which I explained earlier, stands apart from the other characteristics since it has to do with how hyperobjects are noticed, unlike the four others which all have to do with how they are perceived. Nonlocality means that no single local manifestation of a hyperobject is that hyperobject itself (48). Phasing refers to hyperobjects occupying a high dimensional phase space and being invisible to three-dimensional humans most of the time. Interobjectivity means that hyperobjects exist not as singular entities but as meshes, constituted by many different objects (83). From the point of view of my analysis these three characteristics collapse into nonlocality. It is not the hyperobject itself that we perceive, but an interobjective mesh of different objects; the hyperobject is phased and as such not ever wholly present nor is it ever completely localized into one focal point: one character or object cannot represent the whole of the hyperobject. Lastly, temporal undulation refers to the unimaginably large timescales of hyperobjects. Hyperobjects distort temporal–spatial relationships, creating the feeling that we are already lost within them (55).

Robert Frost's poem "Fire and Ice" explicitly concerns the apocalypse and ponders how the world will end. The poem's answer is that the likelier culprit is fire, but if the world were to end twice, then ice would be just as effective. In a literal sense, the world ending by fire might refer to either warfare or to the sun expanding and consuming the Earth; ice, in this scenario, could then refer to a new Ice Age or the inevitable heat-death of the universe. Frost associates these elemental forces with human emotions: fire with desire, ice with hatred. Whether or not this poem is referenced in the name of the series—as I think it may be—Martin, like Frost, clearly casts Ice and Fire as two massive forces, either of which might lead to the ending of the world. They are the dangerous hyperobjects casting their shadows on all things in the story.

The determining roles of Ice and Fire are highlighted in the series' belief systems. Both A Song of Ice and Fire and Game of Thrones depict a religion in the world of Westeros based around these two forces, that of the red god R'hllor and of the Unnamed Lord of Ice. As Melisandre, a fire-worshipping priestess, explains the two forces to the skeptical smuggler Davos Seaworth: "On one side is R'hllor, the Lord of Light, the Heart of Fire, the God of Flame and Shadow. Against him stands the Great Other whose name may not be spoken, the Lord of Darkness, the Soul of Ice, the God of Night and Terror" (Martin 2000, 348). Melisandre sees the Heart of Fire and the Soul of Ice as opposites engaged in a mythic battle. If we follow this interpretation, as Di Paolo does by conceptualizing the magical winter as a direct analogy of global warming, Melisandre may be seen as a fiery environmentalist. For Di Paolo, the character of Melisandre offers the lesson that radical environmentalist convictions alienate potential allies, something that can be ill afforded in the current fight against global warming (Di Paolo 2018, 248). This is a valid interpretation, although if we look at Ice and Fire as separate but connected hyperobjects, one of which—Ice—is aligned with environmental catastrophe whereas the other—Fire—signifies warfare, this simplistic dualism falls apart. Both Ice and Fire are destructive forces. They do not battle each other. Instead, they compound each other's effects, accelerating the story toward Frost's vision of an end of the world that happens twice over.

Westeros is brimming with conspiracy and mystery. "Dragons and darker things. … Old powers waken. Shadows stir" (Martin 2005, 14). There are always deeper currents at play. The world the story takes place in becomes strange, difficult to explain. What is told in the books can rarely be taken at face value, and often falls apart on closer inspection. A Song of Ice and Fire is long and expansive, nearing 1.8 million words and counting. There is an endless list of details that support a staggering variety of readings. This, in addition to the hyperobjective nature of Ice and Fire, creates a sense of being trapped within the story as if it too were a hyperobject. It seems there must be vast and unfamiliar things lurking underneath the surface, that teasing out those hidden forces might explain everything. The series' fandom is notorious for creating labyrinthine theories aimed at making sense of the true nature of Martin's imagined world.[1] The books call for a paranoid style of reading, and it is no coincidence that the cli-fi interpretation of the epic is often also referred to as a fan-theory (Segall 2018).

Compared to the books, the Game of Thrones TV series largely lacks the ever-present sense of the coming winter. Its threat is localized and limited to the northern storyline of Jon Snow, rather than existing at the periphery of the larger, multi-plot story. In the books, much is made of the summer's last harvest being ravaged by war, leaving Westeros woefully ill-prepared for the coming winter. There are mentions of a lack of resources in the television adaptation as well, but awareness always stays at the level of off-hand remarks, as if relic-dialogues carried over from the books. The sense of being trapped within a hyperobject is utterly absent.

When it comes to representing the nonlocal and interobjective nature of hyperobjects, *Game of Thrones* fumbles. In the books, the Others act as harbingers of the hyperobject of Ice that threatens to consume Westeros. In the TV series, these beings, renamed as white Walkers, are no longer personified manifestations of the nonlocal danger of winter but rather represent the primary danger themselves. Morton's definition of nonlocality is that "any 'local manifestation' of a hyperobject is not directly the hyperobject" (Morton 2013(a), 1). *Game of Thrones*, unlike its source material, fails to portray winter as a nonlocal issue; instead, it reduces it to a handful of magical beings led by the Night King—a character added by the show's scriptwriters but assigned such a central villain role that even the most devoted fans of Martin's work tend to forget that no such character exists in the series. Making the Night King the locus and endpoint of the magical climate catastrophe is a move that fundamentally weakens the show's thematic confrontation of the Anthropocene.

In the books both Ice and Fire manifest in multiple hyperobjective forms that are viscous and interobjective, at once local and nonlocal. Ice not only drives the undead army of the Others, but also powers the telepathic magic of the greenseer Bloodraven. It is the way in which the lavish descriptions of food are replaced by references to cannibalism; it is represented in the cold lips of Euron Greyjoy, a deranged prophet of an icy apocalypse; it lives in the endless labyrinthine systems of limestone caverns filled with darkness; it is remembered in the legend of the rat cook who feeds an unknowing king his own son baked into a pie, and much more. Likewise, Fire in the books is not only dragons and wildfire—a napalm-like alchemical concoction that burns hot enough to melt sand. It is also Lady Stoneheart, the vengeful reincarnation of Catelyn Stark; it is represented in the image of a magician who climbs a ladder of fire; it is announced in the arrival of a comet that foretells doom; it lives in the obsidian candles burning in the cellars of the order of maesters' secretive stronghold, the Citadel, and much more.

This representational complexity from the books is also abandoned in the television show's conclusion. In the third episode of the show's last season Arya Stark destroys the Night King. That act alone ends the threat of winter altogether. If the winter in *Game of Thrones* represents global warming in any meaningful way—as has been argued in the discourse of the series' online fandom, in ad-monetized online entertainment-media and in the academy (see Di Paolo 2018; Segall 2018)—what are we to make of this ending? Does the series, inadvertently, suggest that the way to prevent a catastrophic climate future is to kill the villain responsible for global warming? Or that global warming is an insidious assault on humanity that originates from the outside and is orchestrated by a singular evil character? Does it communicate that others are literally responsible for the climate catastrophe, and we are merely its victims?

Metaphor and Myth: On Representing Global Warming

In a posthumously published collection of theological essays, C. S. Lewis, one of the founding fathers of modern fantasy, wrote, "in the enjoyment of a great myth we come nearest to experiencing as a concrete what can otherwise be understood only as an abstraction" (Lewis

2014, 57). Literalization of metaphors as a tool is not exclusive to speculative fiction, but it is often considered its defining feature (see Stockwell 2000; McHale 2018; Chu 2010). Many studies on the subject concern science fiction (SF) rather than fantasy, or the wider category of speculative fiction, yet most of this scholarship acknowledges that literalization of metaphors is a device common to all genres of speculative fiction, fantasy included. In Peter Stockwell's view, "[a] literal reading of a possibly metaphorical deviant sentence cues up a science fictional (or surrealist, or magical, or other alternate) world," and therefore "science fiction can be seen to treat metaphorical expressions and metaphorical worlds differently from other genres" (Stockwell 2000, 179)—this claim applies to fantasy equally well.

The genre-defining literalization of metaphors, Stockwell continues, "invites readers to exercise their isomorphic cognitive capacities" in a way that can create new, systematically arranged understanding and allows for new perspectives on familiar things (Stockwell 2000, 201–2). The notion of seeing global warming anew through fiction, of creating its novel, systematically arranged understanding, certainly resonates with what A Song of Ice and Fire seeks to achieve. If hyperobjects were to be interpreted as metaphors, then the erratic cadence of seasons could be seen as their literalization. Morton describes phasing, one of the characteristics of hyperobjects, with a metaphor: to three-dimensional humans phased hyperobjects seem to "come and go, like seasons" (Morton 2013(b), 40). In Martin's world the seasons are broken, they are concrete manifestations of the hyperobjects that envelope Westeros. Echoing Morton's metaphor, they do come and go like seasons, because they are literal seasons.

There is, however, an inherent problem in attempting to analyze the depiction of global warming in Martin's work as an instance of metaphor literalization. Hyperobjects are literal, concrete objects that humans collide with (Morton 2013(a), 2). The literalization of what is already literal would constitute a tautology. That said, something very similar to fantasy's literalization of metaphors does seem to be taking place when Martin's series meshes with, or cues, the readers' conceptual frames for thinking about global warming. This something is not metaphorical but is complex enough to be difficult to perceive as a concrete object unless translated into a structure through which we may perceive that very complexity. If this be so, Martin's saga about, metaphorically, confronting global warming would be an example of Brian McHale's idea of reading SF as literalized narratology (McHale 2018, 319) rather than of literalization of metaphors. Global warming is obviously not a narratological phenomenon or a narrative. However, in literalizing the concepts and categories of narrative theory, speculative fiction, according to McHale, "estranges [narratological concepts], giving us glimpses into their internal workings" (319). Literalizing narratology conveys to the reader a systematically arranged understanding of the workings of an enormously complex system. The ways in which global warming is represented in A Song of Ice and Fire bear a clear similarity to this process.

Katheryn Hume argues that fantasy, rather than representing its subject-matter in a specific way—such as literalizing metaphors—would be better understood through the things it chooses to represent: "some of the experiences that move us most derive from more alien realms of experience, which we have represented in literature through the use of fantasy" (Hume 1984, 43). Fantasy, Seo-Young Chu suggests, is at its best when it is "cognitively estranging" (Chu 2010, 7). Chu's theory is an elegant reversal of Darko Suvin's classic conception of SF as a genre that cognitively estranges familiar things (Suvin 1979, 4). In Chu's articulation SF—and fantasy, by extension—represents things that are cognitively difficult to grasp. Indeed, it is successful representation of cognitively estranging referents that makes fiction qualify as SF for her.

The significance of Chu's proposal to my reading of A Song of Ice and Fire is this: Chu sees science fiction's and fantasy's tendency to literalize metaphors as a tool for representing cognitively estranging referents: objects of representation that are neither known nor unknowable but exist somewhere between those endpoints of a spectrum. This space evokes what is called wonder. And it is the measure of wonder that characterizes any successful narrative representation of cognitively estranging referents, for example, I suggest, hyperobjects like global warming. According to Chu, "SF is distinguished by its capacity to perform the massively complex representational and epistemological work necessary to render cognitively estranging referents available both for representation and understanding" (2010, 7). In other words, if global warming is included as one of those cognitively estranging referents—difficult or even impossible to represent as itself, as all hyperobjects are—the affordance of fantasy and SF is that it can literalize metaphors that help us grasp it in ways that would otherwise be impossible.

Martin's approach to confronting global warming takes the discourse beyond the literalization of metaphors and toward the representation of Chu's cognitively estranging referents. A Song of Ice and Fire does not offer a vision of a planet literally on fire or any such direct literalization of language-based metaphors, even if that might be "[a] literal reading of a possibly metaphorical deviant sentence" in the vein of Stockwell's analysis (Stockwell 2000, 179). Instead, it recounts a mythical conflict between universal forces that, through having the characteristics of hyperobjects, maps onto real-world issues like global warming.

According to Attebery, fantasy, in creating myth, draws on the sense of mystery and meaning common to myths. It plays with symbols, providing them with new context and new meanings (Attebery 2014, 2–3). Suspended between wonder and anxiety, Martin plays with the signifiers of hyperobjects of Ice and Fire, and with symbols associated with them, thus encouraging the reader to see things like global warming anew. This operation takes the logic of hyperobjects and translates it into the language of myth. In this way the books can represent something that is very difficult to represent, and enable the reader to even learn something. That learning is certainly not scientific: reading A Song of Ice and Fire will not grant one the ability to understand climatological and mathematical models of global warming. Rather, the learning comes in the form of a new perspective, one that can make hyperobjects like global warming visible, make them thinkable as dangerous objects, and make them emotionally meaningful in human terms, like Frost's desire and hatred embedded in his end of the world scenarios. Attebery suggests that deep, private understanding cannot be shared as such, but the mythic pattern that creates a space for such understanding can be communicated (54). I argue that the creation of those mythic patterns is at the heart of fantasy's way of playing with metaphors and abstract concepts.

A Song of Ice and Fire might not have originally been intended as cli-fi, as Di Paolo claims (see Di Paolo 2018, 10). And it might not be about hyperobjects as such, considering its creation predates Morton's coinage and definition of the term. Nonetheless, Martin's work concerns living in a world threatened by unimaginably vast mythic forces that are almost beyond human control and to a large extent unknowable. It attempts to represent these cognitively estranging referents by forging a mythic pattern that creates space for understanding these forces. In this sense, the books incorporate the logic of hyperobjects and thus render global warming available for representation and understanding.

Lost (and Found) in Adaptation

As mentioned earlier, the finale of *Game of Thrones* left a large and vocal part of its viewership with a strong but vague unease about the ending of the series. Google's video-sharing platform YouTube is filled with lengthy video-essays about the ways in which the last season betrayed the legacy of the series. Some of the most popular of these essays have been viewed more than 7 million times at the time of this writing (see Think Story 2019). The fandom still has high hopes for the books to fix the story, for there is still hope that Martin will complete the saga. But there does not seem to be an equally strong consensus about how and why the television adaptation failed. Many of the video-essays and lengthy forum posts focus on detailed explorations of just that question: What did the series fail to live up to? My suggestion is that one significant failure of the HBO adaptation is its gradual abandonment the books' commitment to depicting human entanglement with hyperobjects.

I briefly explored the meaning of the book series' title earlier. A Song of Ice and Fire is a cryptic name for a fantasy epic: instead of focusing on the characters or the plot, it evokes the vast, alien, and threatening objects that the series is haunted by. These objects lie at the core of its many themes. They are what imbues everything else in the novels with meaning and with a sense of applicability to issues beyond the fictional world of Westeros. The title refers to the hyperobjects that loom underneath the surface of the series' world-building, their presence tinging the whole series with an anxiety and an uncanny sense of doom. Repeatedly, Ice and Fire are suggested to hold the keys to the mysteries of the story: if only we knew the answer when Daenerys asks: "What is the song of ice and fire?" Yet those same objects also threaten to destroy the fabric of the series' story by consuming everything else in it. After all, what is the significance of politics and backstabbing in a world that is being consumed by hyperobjects? As Di Paolo puts it, "Who cares [about who will rule]? What about the zombies?" (Di Paolo 2018, 253). This larger question reverberating throughout the series parallels the ways in which hyperobjects intrude on our world and change what is seen as meaningful in it. Considering the hyperobject of global warming, Morton declares that the world has already ended; part of Martin's series appeal may be that it is set in a world that has already ended too.

It is telling that HBO used a different name for the adaptation. *A Game of Thrones* is the title of the first book of the series but was chosen for the entire television series. The game that the first book refers to, as well as the name of the adaptation, gestures at all at the political plots and conspiracies that take place in Westeros. The aim of that game is to claim the Iron Throne, to become the ruler of the Seven Kingdoms. Since this politics is part of the world of Ice and Fire, some hyperobjective manifestations are still preserved in the adaptation. Even though they are never really explored, the remnants of the abandoned thematic through-line are detectable in lines of dialogue like: "People's minds aren't made for problems that large. White walkers, the Night King, an army of the dead—it's almost a relief to confront a comfortable and familiar monster like my sister" (Mylod 2017, 0:32:50–00:33:03).

The renaming of A Song of Ice and Fire into *Game of Thrones* is an apt metonymy for the differences between Martin's novels and their television adaptation. As the show develops and moves further away from its source material, the underlying sense of unease is lost. Where much of the lasting appeal of A Song of Ice and Fire comes from that sense of depth—a depth with krakens lurking in it—*Game of Thrones* gradually becomes a shallow pool masquerading as an ocean. This thematic shallowness seems to be intentional. In a 2013 interview, David Benioff, one of the HBO show's two creators and main writers was asked a question about the themes of the series. His reply has been widely circulated among the series' disgruntled fandom "Themes," he disparagingly said, "are for eight-grade book reports" (Greenwald 2013).

It becomes unfortunately clear, after the fact, that *Game of Thrones* was never going to tackle large issues that drove the popularity of the books. A Song of Ice and Fire is a multifaceted exploration of the hyperobjects of ice and fire—a mythic parallel to our current predicament as a species caught up in global warming—whereas *Game of Thrones* is a marketable product. The contrast between these two works of fiction says something about the difficult challenge of representing cognitively estranging referents like global warming. It also illustrates some of the consequences of failing to do so. The realities of television production—and perhaps of neoliberal capitalism as such—seem like plausible culprits for this failure to depict the monsters created by our modern economic systems. It is no coincidence that the Capitalocene is one of the strongest alternative terms for the Anthropocene.

Making hyperobjects representable is a process that necessarily makes them less like hyperobjects. For cognitively estranging referents to be rendered understandable and representable, they must be transformed into something that can be grasped. This is a necessary trade-off, since representing global warming—like other hard-to-grasp phenomena—is an important affordance of speculative fiction. However, a measure of structural similarity must be maintained. Otherwise, if the qualities of hyperobjects are lost, the whole effort of attempting to represent them in the first place is jeopardized. This is exactly what happens in *Game of Thrones*. A lack of thematic clarity in the show results in the disquieting message of the series being abandoned in favor of something else, something predictable and familiar, like the story of human greed and thirst for power.

Regardless of the dangers of failing to represent something that is fundamentally difficult to represent, it remains clear that what Martin does in the books, and even what *Game of Thrones* managed after a fashion, is important. After all, even the dis-hyperobjectified *Game of Thrones* sparked the imaginations of viewers to speculate about the connections between the show and the themes of global warming. The endless essays by fans, dissecting the problems of the later seasons of the adaptation, display an emerging understanding about the logic of global warming through the analysis of the specific ways in which the series failed to consistently portray it. For example, a video-essay by vlogbrothers (Hank and John Green) argues that a key difference between the invasion of the undead in *Game of Thrones* and our real-world struggle against global warming is that in our world "there is no boss-man we get to stab and be done with it" and that "our Night King is, maybe unsurprisingly, ourselves" (vlogbrothers 2019).

Conclusion

What else but speculative fiction can begin to issue the moral call to wake us up to the myriad dangers of global warming? What other art form offers better narrative tools to help us imagine hopeful visions of a new way of life in which we learn to navigate the many difficulties of the Anthropocene? What other form of storytelling can better assist us in representing global warming itself in all its uncanny vastness? Indeed, as Chu insists, speculative fiction is the best tool we have, since any fiction becomes speculative precisely when it begins focusing on representing those cognitively estranging referents (Chu 2010, 7). This sentiment has a long tradition in fantasy criticism too: as Kathryn Hume once put it, "To answer questions about the nature of the universe without using fantasy is practically impossible" (1984, 121). A more nuanced version of this argument holds that fantasy is especially capable of portraying cognitively estranging referents such as global warming because its genre-specific structures of meaning-making lend themselves exceptionally well to confronting complex issues that are difficult, if not impossible to grasp through realistic representation. In representing these cognitively-estranging referents through a variety of literalizing practices, fantasy creates mythic patterns that give us a better grasp on the reality of hyperobjects those metaphors gesture at.

A Song of Ice and Fire is not complete yet nor is it likely to be finished any time soon. It is possible that Martin's series will fall into the same trap its HBO adaptation did: that of collapsing the complex mesh of hyperobject representations into a single anthropomorphized villain, a poor man's Sauron who just happens to be ice-blue. So long as the series is unfinished, however, it continues to signify the cognitively estranging referent of global warming in one additional way. Global warming is not finished in our real world either: we do not know how it will turn out in the future. What we are waking up to is an uneasy premonition of impending disaster, a knowledge that the worst may still lie ahead, raising questions about mitigating action in the present.

In this chapter I have argued for a cli-fi interpretation of A Song of Ice and Fire according to which the books confront the Anthropocene through the representation of hyperobjects. Most of the mysterious undercurrents of Martin's work that have captured an ever-growing audience arise from that representation. The applicability of hyperobjects to thinking through issues like global warming makes the series relevant. While the television adaptation of the books largely abandons the thematic core of the story, its remnants seem to hold enough substance that it can help parts of its audience along a path toward greater climate consciousness.

Note

1   For example, some argue that there is an elaborate conspiracy to end dragons and drain the world of magic, others maintain that the moon is not a moon but a secret satellite that enhances telepathy through technological means (Reddit).

References

Attebery, Brian. 2014. *Stories about Stories: Fantasy and the Remaking of Myth.* Oxford: Oxford University Press.

Carpenter, Charli. 2012. "Game of Thrones as Theory: It's Not as Realist as It Seems—And That's Good." *Foreign Affairs*, March 29, 2012. https://www.foreignaffairs.com/articles/2012-03-29/game-thrones-theory

Chu, Seo-Young. 2010. *Do Metaphors Dream of Literal Sleep?: A Science-Fictional Theory of Representation*. Cambridge, MA: Harvard University Press.

Di Paolo, Marc. 2018. *Fire and Snow: Climate Fiction from the Inklings to Game of Thrones*. Albany: SUNY Press.

Greenwald, Andy. 2013. "Winter Is Here: How Game of Thrones Became the Most Important Show on Television." *Grantland*, March 27, 2013. https://grantland.com/features/the-return-hbo-game-thrones/

Hume, Kathryn. 1984. *Fantasy and Mimesis: Responses to Reality in Western Literature*. New York: Methuen.

Lewis, C. S. 2014. "Myth Became Fact." In *God in the Dock: Essays on Theology and Ethics*, edited by Walter Hooper, 54–60. Grand Rapids, MI: William B. Eerdmans Publishing Company.

Martin George, R. R. 1999. *A Clash of Kings*. New York: Bantam Books.

Martin George, R. R. 2000. *A Storm of Swords*. New York: Bantam Books.

Martin George, R. R. 2005. *A Feast for Crows*. New York: Bantam Books.

McHale, Brian. 2018. "Speculative Fiction, or, Literal Narratology." In *The Edinburgh Companion to Contemporary Narrative Theories*, edited by Zara Dinnen and Robyn Warhol, 317–31. Edinburgh: Edinburgh University Press.

Miller, Matt. 2018. "George R. R. Martin Explains the Real Political Message of *Game of Thrones*: And Republicans Might Not Like It." *Esquire*, October 17, 2018. https://www.esquire.com/entertainment/tv/a23863674/george-rr-martin-game-of-thrones-politics-trump-climate-change/

Morton, Timothy. 2013(a). *Hyperobjects: Philosophy and Ecology after the End of the World*. Minneapolis: University of Minnesota Press.

Morton, Timothy. 2013(b). "Poisoned Ground: Art and Philosophy in the Time of Hyperobjects." *Symploke*, vol. 21, nos. 1–2: 37–50.

Mylod, Mark, dir. 2017. *Game of Thrones*, season 7, episode 3. "The Queen's Justice" written by David Benioff and D. B. Weiss. Aired July 30, 2017. HBO.

Poniewozik, James. 2015. "Emmy Awards 2016: A Show for a 'Peak TV,' Blockbuster Era" *New York Times*, September 21, 2015. https://www.nytimes.com/2015/09/21/arts/television/emmys-2015-andy-samberg-review.html

Segall, Mason. 2018. "George RR Martin Confirms Popular Fan Theory about *Game of Thrones*'s White Walkers" *Mental Floss*, October 23, 2018. https://www.mentalfloss.com/article/561583/george-rr-martin-confirms-game-of-thrones-fan-theory-white-walkers

Sheehan, Bill. 2011. "Book Review: George R. R. Martin's 'A Dance with Dragons.'" *The Washington Post*, July 12, 2011. https://www.washingtonpost.com/entertainment/books/book-review-george-rr-martins-a-dance-with-dragons/2011/06/20/gIQAuJ1z9H_story.html.

Stockwell, Peter. 2000. *The Poetics of Science Fiction*. Harlow: Pearson Education.

Suvin, Darko. 1979. *Metamorphoses of Science Fiction: On the Poetics and History of a Literary Genre*. New Haven, CT: Yale University Press.

Think Story. 2019. "How *Game of Thrones* Should Have Ended." *YouTube* video, 16:32, May 22, 2019. https://www.youtube.com/watch?v=G0mncEl4nVU

Uekötter, Frank. 2014. *The Greenest Nation? A New History of German Environmentalism*. Cambridge, MA: MIT Press.

Ullrich, J. K. "Climate Fiction: Can Books Save the Planet?" *The Atlantic*, August 14, 2015. https://www.theatlantic.com/entertainment/archive/2015/08/climate-fiction-margaret-atwood-literature/400112/

vlogbrothers. 2019. "What *Game of Thrones* Is Really About." *YouTube* video, 10:37, May 3, 2019. https://www.youtube.com/watch?v=ibg1-0gfwjI

Waldfogel, Joel. 2017. "How Digitalization Has Created a Golden Age of Music, Movies, Books and Television." *The Journal of Economic Perspectives*, vol. 31, no. 3 (Summer): 195–214.

INDEX

Index

geology 139, 197, 204
Ghosh, Amitav, *The Great Derangement* 1, 4, 61, 139–40
Gilgamesh, the epic of 16–18, 21, 23–4
Glikson, Andrew 168–9
global warming, representation of 138–46, 235–44
Gravity Falls 120–2
greenhouse gases 168–9, 236

Hall, Matthew 92, 95
Haraway, Donna. *See also* Cthulhucene
    "Make Kin, Not Babies" 29, 37–8
    Staying with the Trouble 20, 28–9, 37, 138, 151
Harry Potter series. *See* Rowling, J. K. 103–12
Harry Potter World, Universal Studios. See Rowling, J. K. 104, 110
Hayward, Eva 153, 158
Heckert, Jamie Vishwam 78
Henderson, Barbara, *Wilderness Wars* 67–8
Henfrey, Thomas 78
Hesiod, *Theogony* 21
heterotopia 103–4
    heterotopic landscape 105–8
Hilda 120–2
Hiltner, Ken 105
Hodgson, William Hope 19
Holmgren, David 77–84
hope 4–5, 8, 21, 23, 30, 64, 66–7, 70, 101, 131, 136, 162, 174, 185, 189, 234
    hopescape 103–12
horror 94, 119, 121, 158, 215, 221, 222. *See also* cosmic horror
Howe, Cymene, and Anand Pandian, "Lexicon for an Anthropocene Yet Unseen" 20
human expansionism and exceptionalism 3, 67, 88, 152, 156–8
Humbaba 16, 23, 24
hybrids, oceanic-chthonic monsters 150–9
hyperobjects 48, 66, 139, 235–44

icebergs 114–15
importance (Whitehead) 228–9
indigenous
    and the Anthropocene 119, 170–1, 174–5, 177–9
    dystopia 178
    storytelling 6, 44, 57, 60–1, 168, 175, 179–80
    youth 119, 177, 185
industrial revolution 17, 108, 164, 168–9
industrial settler campaigns 176–80, 182–4
Irigaray, Luce 97–8
Irvine, Alexander C. 105

Jaques, Zoe 94, 104
Jeffers, Oliver, *The Fate of Fausto* 66–8
Jemisin, N. K. *See* Broken Earth trilogy 199–205
Jilkén, Olle and Lina Johansson 154
Johns-Putra, Adeline, *Climate Change and the Contemporary Novel* 4, 28, 30, 64

Kaʻili, Tēvita O. 163, 170
Kane, Sean 6, 59
Keen, Suzanne 74
Kelsey, Elin 5
Kimmerer, Robin Wall 4
kin and kin-making 89–91, 125, 150, 158, 214–17, 226. *See also* Harraway, Donna
kinship 96–8, 150–4, 215, 216, 221, 229
Kipling, Rudyard, *Puck of Pook's Hill* 19
Kohn, Eduardo 41–4
Kroeber, Karl 103

landscape 103–8 *See also* heterotopia
Latour, Bruno, *We Have Never Been Modern* 137
LaValle, Victor, *The Changeling* 208, 215–6
Le Guin, Ursula K. 16, 28, 61, 64, 74, 221, 225, 229
    carrier bag theory 44
    "National Book Award Acceptance Speech" 5
    "Woman, Wilderness" 17
Legend of Korra, The 116–17, 122–4
Leong, Diana 208
Lewis, C. S., Narnia series 19
    That Hideous Strength 19
liminality 29–30, 32–3
literalization of metaphors. *See* fantasy 239–41
Lovecraft, Howard Phillips 20–1, 22, 151, 156, 224–5

Mackintosh, Craig 83–4
Mahy, Margaret
    Alchemy 95–6
    Heriot 97–8
    Maddigan's Fantasia 96–7
    The Changeover 93–5
manitoh 219–20
Marder, Michael 91–2
Markley, Robert 210
McDougall, Brandi Nālani 176–7, 179
Meeker, Joseph W. 60–2
Mendlesohn, Farah 198
Merchant, Carolyn 103, 105, 120, 122, 125
Metamorphoses, Ovid 51, 93, 94
Mickey, Sam 152, 158
Miéville, China, *Un Lun Dun* 58, 62, 63
Milner, Andrew, and J. R. Burgmann, *Science Fiction and Climate Change: A Sociological Approach* 4
mindscape 103–11
Miyazaki, Hayao, *Ponyo* 154, 157–8
Moʻolelo 176, 177–81
Moana
    cultural controversy 163, 164
    ecofeminist elements 164
    ecological anxieties 166–7
    responses of Pacific Islanders to 170–1
    revisions to Maui's character 164–5
Moananuiākea 177, 183
Mollison, Bill, and David Holmgren, *Permaculture One* 78

248

Index